D1784084

Christmas 2004

Dear John,

Thanks for your friendship
and great conversations
over the years. I appreciate
you! Love,

Kay

STIRRING AUSTRALIAN SPEECHES

STIRRING AUSTRALIAN SPEECHES

The definitive collection, from Botany to Bali

EDITED BY

Michael Cathcart AND **Kate Darian-Smith**

MELBOURNE UNIVERSITY PRESS

MELBOURNE UNIVERSITY PRESS
An imprint of Melbourne University Publishing Ltd (MUP Ltd)
PO Box 1167, Carlton, Victoria 3053, Australia
mup-info@unimelb.edu.au
www.mup.com.au

First published 2004
Text © Michael Cathcart and Kate Darian-Smith 2004
Design and typography © Melbourne University Publishing Ltd 2004

This book is copyright. Apart from any use permitted under the *Copyright Act 1968*
and subsequent amendments, no part may be reproduced, stored in a retrieval
system or transmitted by any means or process whatsoever without the prior
written permission of the publishers.

Every effort has been made by the editors and the publisher to contact copyright
holders of materials quoted extensively. Unacknowledged copyright holders may
contact the publisher.

Designed by Luke Flood, Clear Design
Typeset in Malaysia by Syarikat Seng Teik Sdn. Bhd.
Printed in Australia by McPherson's Printing Group

National Library of Australia Cataloguing-in-Publication entry

Stirring Australian speeches.

  Bibliography.
  Includes index.
  ISBN 0 522 84681 5.

  1. Speeches, addresses, etc., Australian. I. Cathcart, Michael, 1956– .
  II. Darian-Smith, Kate.

808.85

For our fathers

John Dunlop Cathcart (1925–2004)
Ian Darian-Smith (1927–)

Contents

ACKNOWLEDGEMENTS

Thank you to all the speech makers, their families or copyright holders who have given permission for the reproduction of speeches in this collection.

At Melbourne University Publishing, we thank Louise Adler who persuaded us to bring this collection to fruition. Sybil Nolan was an exemplary editor: perceptive, encouraging and patient. Kirsty Manning-Wilcox oversaw the smooth production of the book and Lexey Odgers also helped. Diana O'Neil provided the initial suggestion for the collection many years ago.

We are very grateful to Kim Torney for her research assistance in the location of sources, her companionship in archives and her engagement with this project; and to Elizabeth Hartrick who tracked down images and archival material. Thank you to Graeme Powell and staff at the National Library of Australia; and to staff at the Mitchell Library, State Library of New South Wales; the LaTrobe Library, State Library of Victoria: Australian National Archives, in Melbourne and Sydney; and the Public Record Office, Victoria. Our selection of speeches for inclusion in the collection has benefited from the generous suggestions and advice of many colleagues over a long period, including Fay Anderson, the late Jan Bassett, Tony Birch, Andrew Brown-May, Verity Burgmann, David Carter, Michael Crozier, David Day, Paul Fox, Peter Gahan, David Goodman, Tom Griffiths, Jenny Gregory, Caroline Jordan, Julia Horne, Rosemary Hunter, David Lowe, Lee Kersten, Ross Jones, Stuart Macintyre, Tim Rowse, Connal Parsley, Sarah Scott, Glenda Sluga, Nick Vlahogianis, Paul Strangio, Richard Trembath, Chris Wallace-Crabbe, Mark Weblin and Sara Wills. The Australian Centre and the Faculty of Arts at the University of Melbourne continue to provide a collegial research environment. We also thank our fellow participants at the Life Writing seminar, where our discussions have helped us to think more critically about biography, action and language. Support in other ways has always been there from Hannie Rayson, Jack Grant, and Nick, Zoë and Eirene Vlahogiannis.

A Note on Editing

In compiling this collection, we have, wherever possible, located original primary sources of accounts of the delivery of speeches, and transcripts of speeches. It is not unusual for there to be some discrepancy between a written transcript and the actual words that were spoken, and, if possible, we have checked across sources and opted for the spoken version. The reporting of speeches in the colonial period was often in indirect speech, and we have transposed this into direct speech. Many of the speeches here have been abridged, and we have endeavoured to maintain the arc of the argument and the meaning of the original speech. Other speeches have been reproduced here in full. At the end of each speech in this book we have indicated our editorial intervention and the source of the speech, with full bibliographical details being given in the Select Bibliography and page references given in the Notes.

FOREWORD

A Spark from God Knows Where

The centenary of Federation, the new millennium and great changes in the world have made Australians suddenly more reflective about their history. We are now collecting, reading and interpreting important speeches made during our nation's story in the hope of understanding who we really are. It is as if we realise that we have reached a watershed. The way ahead is uncertain; but knowledge of where we have come from may illuminate our path.

Countless things, beyond words, combine to make up the history of a continental nation such as Australia. There is action, music, cheering on the sporting field, the smell of the wattle and the sound of the cicadas at Christmas-time. The unique fauna and flora of Australia amazed Joseph Banks and James Cook on their fateful journey. But human beings exchange thoughts by language. From the start, the newcomers to Australia recorded the important moments in this communication. In effect, this is a book that tells some of the history of Australia through the words of important chroniclers. By compiling their speeches and presenting them in order of utterance, not only are we helped to remember critical events; the words take us into the moods and values, the passions and fears, the hopes and doubts of earlier times. If we think long and hard enough about this work, perhaps we will come closer to an appreciation of the Australian experience.

The editors, Michael Cathcart and Kate Darian-Smith, have included many contributions that remind us of familiar events. From Governor Phillip's address to convicts through the years of emerging colonial independence to Federation and beyond. From the period between the sacrifices of two world wars, through the Great Depression to the struggles between Chifley and Menzies. From the still more familiar times of present memory to the efforts to banish the small-mindedness of past thinking about Aboriginals, women, gays, protesters, White Australia and other subjects of prejudice. The general course of these events is well known. But the merit of history through speeches is that it presents a series of time capsules: capturing the contemporary attitudes and debates so that we see events in the context of feelings. In part, this helps us to understand why things happened as they did and what Australians felt about them at the time. Recording events and undertaking scholarship about them are not enough. With due acknowledgment of the dangers of selectivity, this collection helps us enter the spirit of the times. It adds a dimension often missing from the history books.

Of course, we can debate endlessly the selection, the notable omissions and the speakers and themes overlooked. Long before Arthur Phillip's arrival, the Aboriginal inhabitants of Australia had orators and story-tellers. They did not write their history on paper but passed it from one generation to the next in song lines, doubtless embroidered by those with special gifts of poetry and spiritualism. Some will complain about the comparative lack of women's voices. Yet the history of public events in the colonial and federal eras was largely that of a patriarchy. It will be different, we hope, in the new enlightenment. The dominance of voices from Sydney and Melbourne is also a reflection of the forces of population and economics. The voice of conservative values is relatively muted. As the editors explain, passion and stirring speeches are not the stuff of those who are satisfied with their lot.

So this is a sampling. Yet its range of topics and record of the changes we have accomplished illustrate the way progress can be made through the exchange of ideas by people fortunate enough to live in a land with strong institutions and many blessings. It is no coincidence that one of the few constitutional implications, unanimously upheld by the High Court of Australia as inherent in the representative democracy of the century-old Constitution of the Commonwealth, involves a broad right of communication on matters of government and politics. In a land that has fought no revolution or civil war and boasts no Bill of Rights, Australia has long enjoyed vigorous public debate. This book is a record of the exercise of that privilege.

Yet it also illustrates the changing character of public speaking. The communication of ideas today largely occurs through the radio, television and the Internet. This puts a premium on brevity, packaging and over-simplification of complex ideas. Speech writers are now in vogue. On great occasions, we can never be sure whether we are listening to the authentic voice of the speaker or the verbal manipulations of a team of script writers, in tune with opinion polls, popular spin and 'dog whistles' rather than deep feelings sincerely held. In future, books like this will probably come in electronic form. We will want more than to read words on the printed page. Future generations will demand the images of body language and the immediacy of questions and answers so as to reduce (even if they cannot eliminate) the insincerities of speech-by-committee.

Contemporary Australians should therefore savour this book because it captures an art in its heyday that is now undergoing greater change than ever before. That is not to say that change is new to rhetoric. Some of the techniques, and many of the ideas, in these pages now seem hopelessly old-fashioned. Even many of the heroes of our youth, as we read, hear and see them today, appear out of date and wooden. So, doubtless, it will be in the future. In the world of sms messages and nanotechnology, we can hardly expect that the techniques of public communication will remain unchanged.

And yet, as this book shows, there can be occasions when great ideas, reduced to words, can move human beings to strive for a fairer nation and a better world. The immediacy of physical contact between speaker and audience may decline. The tolerance of wordiness and illogicality may be reduced. The insincerities and attempted distortions may be spotted more quickly. But there are still worlds to conquer and injustices to be corrected.

So long as that is so, there will be people who seek to persuade other human beings—the only species capable of wholly altruistic action—to rise above themselves and to think new and bolder thoughts. When this happens, it will still be a kind of magic. However briefly, the speaker by the poetry of voice and mind will stir hearts and quicken action. Churchill declared that 'the soul of man, frozen in a long night, can be awakened by a spark coming from God knows where'. At the darkest moment, he proclaimed with assurance: 'people in bondage need never despair'.

The place is different. The times are different. The bonds have changed. But his message remains. Humans can make a better world. They need people to describe that place and to persuade them of the path that leads there. This book records attempts to awaken the soul of Australia. Graphically, it shows how we have changed. But it also shows how we must change further. In two centuries, we have made a generally successful nation. In the next, we must create a juster Commonwealth, surer of its geography and of its special role as a microcosm of humanity's variety. And for that, we will need more sparks to awaken our soul.

Michael Kirby
Justice of the High Court of Australia
August 2004

Introduction

The speakers who are represented in this book are people who have had the courage and the conviction to speak out, over two centuries, on issues that matter. Their ideas have stirred the nation, just as their words have drawn upon forms of language that are—in many different stylistic and linguistic ways—vibrant and powerful.

According to popular stereotype, Australians have always been an inarticulate lot. In the nationalist tradition promoted by the *Bulletin* in the 1880s and 1890s, the archetypal Australian, the male rural worker or bushman, was strong on mateship and inventiveness, but economical with words. Educational authorities once bemoaned Australians' lack of sophistication and want of eloquence and denigrated the 'colonial' inflections of their speech. It was as though those with an Australian accent were less capable of expressing a lofty emotion or propounding a sophisticated idea. In time of war, the legendary Aussie digger—despite his delight in cheeky anti-authoritarianism—was reputedly a laconic and plain-speaking man. This collection exposes the inadequacy of such stereotypes and prejudices. It shows that at the heart of Australia's development is an energetic national conversation—a history of passionate and democratic debate which draws directly on the vigorous liberal–humanist traditions of the nineteenth century. It celebrates the long history of Australians speaking out in public about issues of deep-felt concern—about ideas that have stirred the nation to argument, reflection and action.

This collection is about 'speech-making as history'.[1] Across our selection, it is possible to track many—although certainly not all—of the key issues that have preoccupied Australian political, cultural and social thought over the past two centuries. During the nineteenth century, Australian settlers spoke out against the transportation of convicts and debated the form a representative government should take. They spoke about relations with the British Empire and their immediate geographical region. They argued about taxes and the equitable distribution of land; about education, the rights of workers and women's suffrage. From the late 1880s, they made speeches about Federation and the associated issues of immigration and defence. During the twentieth century, many of these concerns continued to be central to public debate. But, in a break with the past, some speakers posed alternative and radical solutions to, for example, questions about immigration or citizenship or Australian culture. New voices—including those of women and Indigenous Australians—were more frequently heard. And new ideological forces, such as communism and anti-communism, along with the broader changes wrought by internationalization and globalism, were influencing political culture and hence speech-making.

In compiling this collection, we have located fine speeches advocating changes or developments calculated to lead to a 'better' Australia. That is not to say that the preservers of privilege and the agents of intolerance and violence were not a powerful presence in Australian society; but the person who wants no change has little reason to speak out with passion—unless it is to resist a change that is already afoot. Certainly the resolute defences of the status quo are here: see, for example, Major-General 'Curly' Hutton's splendid address to the boys of Sydney Grammar School on their responsibilities as the leaders of the British Empire. But it is the desire for social progress that has most often moved Australians to mount the podium or soapbox. Most of our speech-makers are calling for more freedom, not less; greater social justice, not less; and an expansion, rather than a retraction, of equalities and opportunities. As we put this collection together, we became fascinated by the way so many arguments about social questions in the past have contemporary resonances. In the 1890s, Western Australia's first premier, John Forrest, advocated a partnership of state enterprise and private capital that sounds radical today because it presents a contrary view of public ownership to the one that has dominated Australian public policy since the 1980s. In 1872, Victorian parliamentarian Thomas Fellows opposed state aid to government schools because he favoured the range and independence offered by a private school system. His arguments are still run by the advocates of 'choice' in education today.

The majority of speech-makers in this collection have had an impact on Australian life as political leaders, social activists or cultural commentators. Indeed, some of their speeches are landmark moments in Australian domestic or foreign policy: examples include Al Grassby's 1973 speech, which launched a policy of multiculturalism; and Percy Spender's post-war recipe for Australian international relations, which stressed Australia's geographical position in the Asia–Pacific region. Other speeches mark times of intense national crisis: think of Prime Minister John Curtin's World War II addresses to the 'men and women' of the United States and Great Britain.

This collection of speeches documents important court decisions, key social reforms and a few lost causes. It brings us the voices of Australians debating the issues that have inspired or inflamed them. It also gives us insights into the forms of debate, persuasion and dissent that have been available in Australia—from the rousing public meeting or measured public lecture to the parliamentary speech and the radio talk. In addition, it encapsulates the diverse genres of Australian speeches, illustrating how the language of speech-making and the practices of oratory have evolved.

The first public speech in this collection is an authoritative proclamation—indeed a threat—delivered shortly after the First Fleet landed in 1788, at the place now known as Sydney. The governor of this new British penal colony, Arthur Phillip, warned the convicts that they would be punished if they misbehaved. But the new citizens of Sydney soon began to challenge such autocratic authority. The British settlement of Australia occurred precisely at the time when the revolutionary ideas of the Enlightenment were sweeping Europe and the United States of America. Philosophers and radicals argued that the natural rights of 'man' were, in the words of the US Constitution, self-evident truths. And several authorities in convict Australia, including Governor Phillip himself, had deep sympathies for such a notion. In the 'new' land of Australia, the common person might dream of a better, happier life—of a fairer and more democratic society.

And these ideas took root. Early in the nineteenth century, we hear the powerful and articulate voices of colonists who were motivated by a strong sense of their 'rights' and of 'the public good'. The common venue for these debates was the public meeting—a social phenomenon sweeping Britain, the United States, Canada and New Zealand. By mid-century, Australia had reached what historian David Goodman has referred to as the public meeting's 'golden age'.[2] Sometimes these were formal debates, chaired by a citizen of standing. Sometimes they were outright protests. Thus in 1848 the liberal journalist (and future English chancellor of the exchequer) Robert Lowe spoke against the evils of the convict system to a 'Great Protest Meeting' of five thousand colonists at Circular Quay. In Melbourne in the 1850s, protest meetings of several thousand citizens gathered to agitate against bills that appeared to be keeping land in the hands of the squatters. In 1853, Daniel Deniehy addressed a public meeting in a Sydney theatre called to debate a new parliamentary system—and delighted the crowd with his ridicule of William Wentworth's plans for a colonial aristocracy. Such meetings were serious and engaging occasions: the speeches were reported, often verbatim, in the newspapers in the days afterwards. The advocates who could move such vast crowds, in an era before the microphone, were speakers of immense power and skill. Indeed, their performances could be almost sacramental—as was the occasion when Peter Lalor spoke of democracy and justice beneath the Southern Cross to an open-air meeting of 12,000 angry miners at Bakery Hill near Ballarat in November 1854.

The high point of formal oratory in Australia coincided with a period of intense political and cultural activity as the colonies moved towards Federation. Perhaps more than ever, a politician's success was largely dependent on being a persuasive speech-maker. William Holman, for example, entered the New South Wales Parliament with a reputation as an outstanding speaker. As the son of professional actors, with a father who taught elocution classes in Sydney to many aspiring politicians, Holman had been unusually well instructed in logic and rhetoric.[3] There was great anticipation in the press about his parliamentary debut—not just about what he might say but about how he would say it. In the event, his fifty-minute address on the colony's resolution on federalism was deemed a stylistic triumph. According to the *Sydney Daily Telegraph*, 'the maiden speaker was literally overwhelmed with congratulations from both his own and the Opposition sides of the House ... A feature of Mr Holman's speech was the extreme rapidity with which he spoke without destroying in any way the excellence of his diction'.[4]

In the second half of the nineteenth century, those who sought a public career often turned to debating societies for assistance in public speaking. Mechanics' Institutes and workingmen's clubs played an important role in providing instruction on, and critical engagement with, new ideas about topics as diverse as science, engineering and the arts. The Mechanics' Institute movement was strong in Australia, with the first such institute founded in Hobart in 1827. By the 1860s all colonial capital cities and major towns had one; and hundreds more were established in the two decades before Federation.[5] In 1861 John Woolley, in a speech included in this volume delivered at the opening of the Wollongong School of Arts, spoke of the central role of such popular education organizations in fostering both patriotism and public responsibility within the colonies. This emphasis on self-improvement meant that, alongside libraries, classes, billiard rooms and dance-halls, the Institutes hosted debating societies. One of the most influential was the debating group at the Sydney Mechanics' School of Arts, which boasted membership of many who were later to be active across the political spectrum.[6]

Debating, with its formal rules of argument and reply, was an increasingly popular educational and leisure activity towards the end of the nineteenth century, with societies also established at universities, schools and churches. In 1906, the most famous public debate in Australia, billed as a gladiatorial contest between the ageing George Reid and the upcoming William Holman, addressed the topic of socialism. For two consecutive April nights, an audience consisting of university professors, professional and commercial men, and 'almost every government official in every political organization in Sydney' squeezed into Sydney's Centenary Hall, blocking all entrances and spilling into the aisles.[7] The last word was given by Holman, who claimed state socialism would 'initiate a genuine republic in Australia, where all men shall be free, all men shall be equal, and no man shall make them afraid'.[8] One result of this grand public event, reflected H. V. Evatt, was that 'Debating societies sprang up in school after school. At the slightest provocation, obscure politicians began to challenge one another to public debate.'[9] The Reid–Holman debate was likened[10] to the series of public debates about democracy and slavery held between Abraham Lincoln and Stephen A. Douglas on the Illinois prairies in 1858: 'one of the truly great incidents in American political life'.[11] But unlike the Lincoln–Douglas debates, it remains a little-known encounter in Australian history.

In the United States and Britain, involvement in anti-slavery activities in the 1830s and 1840s had drawn some women into public meetings and into speaking before an audience. In Australia, women appear on the public platform later, with the notable exception of Caroline Chisholm. Her speech in this collection to a gathering of hundreds of male miners at Castlemaine begins with several comments stressing the respectability of her character. When Louisa Lawson and Frances Gillam Holden founded the Dawn Club in May 1889, it was not only to provide a forum for discussion of topics connected with 'woman's and therefore humanity's well-being'[12] but a place where women could engage in debate and be informally instructed in the art of public speaking. Lawson persuaded the debating club at the Sydney Mechanics' School of Arts to admit her, and she became the first woman to join its board of management. She urged other women to develop public speaking skills as a means of influencing opinion. Women emerged as prominent public speakers for temperance or suffrage causes, although many accomplished speakers — such as Vida Goldstein — often attracted as much press coverage for their appearance as for their words. But by the early twentieth century, as this collection demonstrates, Australian women were some of the most assured speakers in the public sphere. Included here are the views of Jean Devanny on fascism, Miles Franklin, Nettie Palmer and Katharine Susannah Prichard on Australian writing and culture, and Jessie Street on the United Nations. We hear the diverse opinions, spanning several decades, of Enid Lyons, Germaine Greer, Anne Summers and Pru Goward on women's reproduction, work and family responsibilities.

In many Australian cities by the end of the nineteenth century, public spaces were set aside where speakers could advocate and argue about unorthodox or dissenting ideas. These open-air forums attracted trade unionists, communists, loyalists, socialists, Irish patriots, people with theories about eugenics and tax reform, pacifists, imperialists, people spouting religious heresies and a score of others. In Sydney, the forum for such speakers was in the Domain. In Adelaide it was in the Botanic Park. In Melbourne, various locations on the banks of the Yarra were officially designated for speakers after the 1890s. Indeed some city councils specially landscaped these places with mounds or circles to make the speakers more visible. So vibrant were these forums that Prime Minister John Curtin, his voice raspy not only from chain-smoking but from years of open air oratory, used to claim that Melbourne's Yarra Bank had been his 'university'.

These venues had all the vibrancy of a popular market. But the wares on offer were ideas. Such gatherings gave people, who would otherwise be voiceless, an opportunity to be heard. And they gave their audiences new ideas to ponder or to ridicule. The Aboriginal activist Pearl Gibbs recalled delivering her first public speech in the Sydney Domain in 1937. She was accompanied by her colleagues William Ferguson and Michael Sawtell, who came equipped with a three-foot ladder. Ferguson and Sawtell climbed the ladder in turn to speak to an audience of no more than six or seven people, shouting against the competition of a nearby communist spruiker surrounded by a large crowd. Then, as Gibbs recalled, it was her turn to climb the little ladder:

> I got up there and I shook and I shivered and the ladder was rocking and the reason was because of all this hate and resentment I'd had … I was so fighting mad, I didn't know what to say first because there were so many things … and all this hatred. I couldn't talk. They had to get me down on the ground and then I started! You think my voice is loud now but it is nothing to what it was. And the people came—a woman was a sort of novelty speaker then and so the crowds came. And that was my first experience of public speaking.[13]

This collection includes a collage of speeches given on Melbourne's Yarra Bank during the hard Depression year of 1936. The irony is that the words so hotly spoken have not evaporated into the air but have survived because this right to free speech was not uncontested. Many public speakers who opposed the government, or presented 'dangerous' views, were under police surveillance—and many of their speeches were dutifully recorded by police stenographers. Indeed, the secret police file of Yarra Bank transcripts for that one year covers some thousand pages.[14] As we now know, throughout the twentieth century there was considerable surveillance of dissenters and non-conformists in Australia. Police and security files contain thousands of transcripts of Australians who addressed public meetings speaking against war, conscription, capitalism, censorship and so on. Of course this tradition of protest and dissent continues to the present day, as demonstrated by a number of vibrant public speeches included in this volume that fly in the face of official government policies and opinions.

In this celebration of an Australian liberal tradition of open debate, we should not forget that freedom of thought and speech has always had its opponents. Colonial governors used censorship laws to suppress seditious talk and undesirable publications. In the 1920s and 1930s the federal government stopped communist and fascist literature, and many classic books, from entering Australia. During the Cold War, the Menzies Government attempted to suppress left-wing speech and introduced a secret form of self-censorship under which newspaper editors refrained from publishing stories on subjects banned by a so-called D-notice.[15] The task of dismantling this demeaning—and distinctly unliberal—regime began in the 1980s. Nevertheless, the censorship of some public speakers still continues—the controversial ongoing refusal to grant a visa to Holocaust denier, historian David Irving, being the best known case. One of the themes that runs through this collection is the importance of free speech, as articulated in the philosophical position of John Anderson or the robust questioning of propaganda during wartime by the journalist and self-proclaimed 'stirrer' Brian Penton.

Public lectures on all manner of topics—Aborigines, irrigation, socialism, faith-healing, poetry ... (the range was endless)—have been major public events in both colonial and modern Australia. In the age before television, they were a popular form of entertainment and information, attracting crowds to church halls, town halls, theatres, scientific and artistic societies, mechanics' institutes, clubs and universities. Lecturers might sometimes entertain their audience with a magic lantern show, slides, films and even music. Public lectures have maintained their strong popularity throughout the twentieth century, and, against all the odds, continue to pull crowds. Writers' festivals have become major forums for speech-making; universities, societies and interest groups continue to present lectures on topics designated as important to the general public. In 2001, for example, the Melbourne International Arts Festival staged a rich program of Deakin Lectures. The heavy-duty program included lectures on the politics of water, Australia's relations with Asia and a conversation (via video) with the Arab intellectual Edward Said. The venues, including the vast Melbourne Town Hall, were packed. This collection includes highlights from several public lectures presented throughout Australian history, a number of which were considered significant enough to be published, often in pamphlet form. These include William Spence's utopian vision on 'New Unionism' in 1892; Frederic Wood Jones on universities and the 'spirit of adventure' in 1937; A. R. Downer in defence of the 'White Australia' policy in 1960; Bernard Smith on Australian painting and the myth of isolation in 1961; and—much more recently—public figures such as Peter Doherty on the significance of Australian science or David Malouf on the meanings of heritage within Australian culture.

Before the decline of church-going in the 1960s, the most common form of public speech in Australia was the sermon. In fact, if we discount various land-claiming ceremonies performed by Captain James Cook, the very first English speech on Australian soil was a sermon, delivered by the Reverend Richard Johnson in January 1788, commemorating the safe arrival of the First Fleet. By the 1880s church-goers in Melbourne could choose, according to listings in the *Argus* newspaper, from over one hundred Christian services every week. Every Sunday morning in cities, towns and tiny settlements, preachers climbed into the pulpits of their churches, looked down on their congregations and regaled them with moral, spiritual and political lessons—and sometimes fanned the fires of sectarian conflict between Catholic and Protestant. Sermons tend to lose their impact with the passing of time—and we have included only one in this collection—though other clergymen, including John Dunmore Lang and Daniel Mannix, appear with speeches on secular questions.

The courts, of course, are dramatic forums for argument and speech-making. The pronouncements of judges determine the destinies of people in profound ways and may affect the way we live for decades afterwards. We have selected several. Redmond Barry's sentencing of the bushranger Ned Kelly is an Australian classic. In 1886 William Windeyer defended the rights of young women to walk safely in city streets. Justice Henry Bournes Higgins handed down one of the sacred texts of Australian liberalism in 1907 when he established the principles by which the state would set and enforce the basic wage. The strict legalism of Chief Justice Owen Dixon and the maverick judgments of Justice Lionel Murphy are both represented. So too is the 1992 decision of the High Court in the *Mabo* case, probably the most widely celebrated and the most widely loathed decision of any Australian Court. This decision acknowledged that traditional Aborigines had long held their lands under a system of native law. It reflects not just the arguments put to the court during the hearing but two centuries of debate about this very issue by both Aborigines and Europeans. Indeed, as this collection shows, the matter of Aboriginal rights was debated in a Sydney public meeting in 1838, at a time when several prominent whites believed that the Aborigines had been robbed of their possessions. And as our selection makes clear, the devastating effects of colonialism on Indigenous rights have proven to be one of the most complex and troubling matters of public debate, crucial to discussions of human rights, land ownership and national identity.

A stirring speech is one that seamlessly melds thought and expression, and uses language—and the skills of rhetoric, performance, logic and memory—to persuade, seduce or cajole an audience. The national conversation we allude to is an exchange between speaker and listener. Often the impact of a speech can be gauged from the audience's response: they might call out, cheer, applaud, boo, fall asleep or leave the room. It was customary in colonial newspapers, in a practice that lingered into the twentieth century, to insert audience responses into the transcripts of public speeches. Where possible, we have retained such indicators, as well as including other information on the occasion of the speech and its immediate impact on listeners.

Robert Menzies, a virtuoso speaker himself, understood that an effective speech was not simply a statement of views or a reasoned argument. A great speech was an act of communion between speaker and the members of the audience. It should reach their 'hearts and minds', he said. It should be 'made *to* them and not merely in their presence'. It should stir 'noble and humane emotions'.[16] In 1948, Menzies complained that the rise of new technology had damaged public speaking. Speakers were losing the art of performance. There was a 'growing disposition' to read speeches in a dull way 'with head poured over the typescript, without point or emphasis, or point or climax'. Menzies believed that this decline in speechmaking was partly due to the introduction of the microphone, which placed itself between the speaker and the audience and severed the 'old intimate contact' created by the power of the unaided human voice. But it was, he believed, also the result of media pressures. Speeches were 'reported' before they were delivered, press releases were inevitably read (and increasingly written by professional speechwriters), and the imprint of the speaker's personality—not to mention the stimulus of a live audience —drained them of language that was both flexible and persuasive.

Menzies, of course, became a skilled user of the microphone. He discovered its great secret: it actually grants the speaker the power to whisper in the audience's ear and then to thrill them with the grandest acts of declaration. He was especially adept as a performer in front on the wireless microphone: some of his most memorable speeches were given on the radio—most notably his agenda-setting 'The Forgotten People', reproduced in this collection. Indeed, the advent of the radio in the 1920s (the ABC was formed in 1932), meant an intimate kind of public talk was added to the national conversation. This required the speaker to imagine a connection with an audience that was now, at least theoretically, unbounded by temporal or spatial constraints—and to structure and deliver a speech accordingly. Commentators such as William Macmahon Ball and Vance Palmer, present in this collection, presented regular programs of radio talks for years. During the Second World War, the ABC broadcast radio speeches by Australians from an astonishing range of political perspectives. A number of radio speeches are included here as representative of the ideas that were thus disseminated into public debate. Today, ABC Radio National is the only major radio station that still broadcasts talks and lectures. We have not, however, included selections from radio lectures if these are widely available in printed form, as are the annual Boyer lectures.

The introduction of television in Australia in 1956 further revolutionized the relationship between the public speaker and what were now termed 'viewers'. While election speeches and debates have sometimes been televised, on the whole television coverage of speeches has generally extended to their newsworthy aspect or to brief highlights of what was said. On television, speeches in an extended form are almost non-existent. Indeed it is extremely difficult to develop a complex argument about a social or economic issue on commercial TV. An argument becomes 'a message' delivered in the five-, ten- or thirty-second grab. For this reason, there are no speeches selected here that were first aired on television.

Not surprisingly, a goodly proportion of the speech-makers in this collection are politicians. Parliament, as the name literally says, is the institution where the act of speech (or parley) takes place. The process of federation, by which the national parliament was set up, was itself the product of a massive exercise in speech-making and debate, at a series of meetings of colonial representatives held during the 1890s to thrash out the terms of the Constitution. Any list of the most outstanding orators to hold the position of Prime Minister would certainly include Alfred Deakin, Billy Hughes, Robert Menzies and Gough Whitlam. Each was a cunning master of the brutal cut and thrust of politics. And each was a master of debate—all four were as effective in the public meeting as they were on the floor of the house. In the cases of Robert Menzies and Gough

Whitlam, we have deviated from our general rule of selecting only one speech from an individual, because of the importance of several of their public speeches—which in Menzies' case stretched over the decades in which he was a leading political figure.

Today, the liberal tradition that has shaped two centuries of public debate in Australia is undergoing change. Speechwriter (most notably for Paul Keating) and historian Don Watson argues that the powerful pro-liferation of a corporate language of the global management class has 'van-dalized' the words that lie at the foundation of Australian culture. For Watson, a public language laden with platitudes and dot points is in-filtrating the public sphere, purging it of a robust capacity for debate, dissent, diversity and argument.[17]

James Curran's illuminating book *The Power of Speech* contains some hints about the reasons why this pressure to conform meets so little resistance from middle Australia. Since Federation, successive Australian Prime Ministers were able to speak comfortingly of Australian national-ism as if we were a single (white) people, speaking one language—and were British.[18] But in the 1970s Australian nationalism took on a new form. It emphasized diversity over unity. Alarmingly for many Anglo-philes, this move to pluralism occurred at a time when trade and cultural links to Britain were declining and Asia was gaining prominence as a trading partner and a source of migrants to Australia. In addition, the audacious claims of globalization were making old national certainties seem obsolete. A number of recent speeches selected for this collection allude to these very anxieties.

In transposing spoken language into written text for this collection, we have endeavoured to retain its immediacy and impact. In our intro-duction to each speech, we have sketched in the historical context, and the forum, where these speeches were originally delivered and in many cases we have indicated the individual style of the speaker. These speech-makers, from the most famous to the little-known, are Australians who, at a key moment in our national conversation, have attempted to imagine and invent Australia's future.

PART ONE

Part One: 1788–1899

In the year 1787 five hundred prisoners and their keepers sailed from England to the opposite end of the world—to a place as distant as legend. When these ragged prisoners were unloaded onto the hillsides of Sydney Cove, there was every danger that their jailers might rape, scourge, torture or hang them. Such torments were not unknown in the gut-rotting prisons of England. But, on these new shores, these outcasts also had a chance to seize redemption—not from the hands of priests but from the hands of the Enlightenment. For the convicts had crossed the seas in an age when the power of magistrates, factories and profit was being challenged by liberal notions of individual rights and freedoms. The radical spirit which, in Britain, would inspire opposition to the slave trade might yet touch the lives of the prisoners of the First Fleet.

Governor Arthur Phillip's new settlement of Sydney trespassed on the lands and waters of the indigenous Eora people. Like the convicts, these Aborigines were now in a moral lottery. In the years that followed, some found themselves in deadly combat with greedy or debauched white men. Others encountered new settlers who honoured Whitehall's policy that the natives were to be treated with 'amity and kindness'. These Australians, whether indigenous or recent arrivals, were now engaged in a great struggle between brute force and civil society. And two of the key attributes for a civil society—a free press and the freedom of public speech—soon began to shape the future of the Australian colonies.

At first it seemed that British settlement would be little more than a series of convict colonies in New South Wales, Van Diemen's Land and Moreton Bay, far removed from each other on a vast continent inhabited by the Aborigines. But free settlers were attracted by cheap labour and land, and by the 1820s, sheep farmers or 'squatters' were earning ample profits by commandeering vast tracts of Aboriginal territory and turning them to pasture. For the remainder of the century, explorers and settlers pushed further into the fertile coast-hugging regions and then into the dry inland country, seeking fodder and water and marking out stock routes to the markets in the rapidly expanding towns.

This frontier Australia called to ambitious men and women in the British Isles whose chances for fortune or happiness were cramped by the old world. By the 1830s and 1840s emigrants were unloading their possessions and hopes on the docks of the antipodean colonies. It had become clear that talk of 'Botany Bay' had lost its power to terrify criminals at home. In any case, an increasingly respectable population was calling for an end to transportation. Where, they asked, was the virtue in creating a nation of thieves?

Many weighty issues exercised the consciences of the emerging colonial societies. Citizens of good will debated whether or not the Aborigines actually owned their traditional lands. If they did, some said, then certainly Aborigines were entitled to compensation for their losses. Others demanded the right of British citizens to be tried by a jury of their peers. And when radical colonists campaigned for the right to vote, there were varied opinions about the forms and powers that a colonial parliament should adopt.

The popular appetite for representative government, for an independent identity and for personal wealth were intensified by the discovery of gold in Victoria and New South Wales in the 1850s. From across the globe, adventurers and fortune-seekers flooded to the Australian colonies. Thousands came from England, Scotland and Wales. The Irish came— with their passionate Catholic faith, their love of a lark and their hostility to Britain. There were Americans, with their talk of democracy and their determination to resist unelected tax collectors. And there were the Chinese, who worked hard and tried to avoid the antagonism of European diggers. In this great hubbub of newcomers, the voices of egalitarianism, nationalism and racial hostility rang out. White Australians were embracing a culture of mateship and learning to mistrust Asia.

The gold rushes brought social upheaval. Women with children were 'left behind' in the towns as their menfolk searched for gold. At Ballarat in Victoria a bloody conflict between miners and British officials hastened the adoption of self-government in the eastern colonies. But democracy was still a wild, perhaps dangerous, idea. In the 1850s, radicals in the eastern colonies succeeded in establishing manhood suffrage as the system of voting for their lower houses of parliaments. But these assemblies were kept in check by legislative councils representing the holders of property. In Sydney, William Charles Wentworth may have gone too far when he advocated that a new hereditary aristocracy should sit in the upper house. But only just: in New South Wales the legislative council was nominated by the governor.

Gold also brought wealth and labour to the colonies, and a sharp hunger for land. Indeed, the reform of land distribution was to be a central issue from the late 1850s to the 1870s. As selectors took up their runs in the bush, agricultural societies discussed how European farming methods could be best adapted to the Australian environment. Meanwhile, the growth of urban centres was astounding. New educational and cultural institutions—mechanics institutes, universities, libraries, galleries and museums—were swiftly established to meet the needs of a swelling middle class. Suburbs spread, trams and railways were built, and factories proliferated. By the 1880s Melbourne was a truly marvellous, modern metropolis, the leading British city in the southern hemisphere. But not all Australians shared in this prosperity. Young working-class men expressed their disaffection at the inequity of opportunity, often violently, by turning to bushranging or by joining the pushes that roamed the inner cities. While colonial law and order attempted to deal with these offenders, on the increasingly remote frontiers, some settlers meted out their own justice to the Aboriginal people they had dispossessed.

Unlike their counterparts in Britain and the United States of America, most liberals in the colonies saw the state not primarily as a threat to individual liberty but as a civilising agent offering individuals a chance of social improvement. It was the state that built roads. It was the state that, for the most part, sponsored exploration. It was the state that, in 1872, built the Overland Telegraph, which enabled news, business and government to pass between Britain and the colonies in a matter of hours. And it was the state that began to take responsibility for educating the children who were unable to attend schools run by churches or for profit.

The 1880s saw the emergence of a new colonial nationalism, epitomized by the writing in the *Bulletin*. By the 1890s radical democratic ideas had also taken on new vigour. A cruel depression exposed the brutality of a society in which wealthy employers could starve and sweat their workers—or refuse them work altogether. Trade unions began to organize workers into strikes and lockouts. Radical women were campaigning for the right to vote (a right they won in South Australia in 1894). At the same time, the new Labor Party was bringing the workers' interests into the halls of government and challenging the traditional power of the great grazing, agricultural, shipping, banking and mining interests.

It was also in the 1890s that politicians from the various colonies began to confer seriously about an ambitious new project: the creation of a federal system of government. At large federal conventions, and in the drafting of a national constitution, politicians hotly debated the various powers of the states and of the new Commonwealth parliament. Amid wondrous celebrations in 1901, the colonies accepted the federal compact and a united Australia looked forward into the new century.

Arthur Phillip

Address to Convicts, 1788

At the height of the antipodean summer of 1788, eleven ships filled with British people and their supplies ploughed into the blue waters of the Eora people on the eastern coast of a vast 'new' continent. The ships lowered their sails, then dropped anchor in a sheltered cove near the mouth of a little river. The newcomers rowed ashore and cut a clearing in the forest, where they established a camp of tents and crude huts. Captain Arthur Phillip did not know the name of the place. He called it after his patron—Lord Sydney. The foreigners numbered roughly one thousand. Around half were convicts. The rest were soldiers, government officials, military officers and their wives. Their first speech-maker was the chaplain, Richard Johnson. On Sunday 3 February 1788 he preached on the text 'What shall I render unto the Lord for all his benefits toward me?'

The first speeches on more worldly matters were delivered on 7 February. That morning, the convicts assembled in a freshly cut clearing. Next, the soldiers and officers marched into the little arena with music playing and flags flying. When all were gathered, the new magistrate, David Collins, read them a series of documents, declaring that British authority now ran in this corner of the globe. A wind stirred the trees, and the waves splashed against the rocky shoreline.

Then it was the turn of Governor Arthur Phillip. Arthur Phillip (1738–1814) is known to most Australians as the commander of the First Fleet and the first Governor of New South Wales. He oversaw the initial establishment of the penal colony, where his challenges included ensuring that the convicts did not starve and negotiating with the Aboriginal owners of the land. According to David Collins, the Governor—

adressing himself to the convicts, assured them, among other things, that 'he should ever be ready to shew approbation and encouragement and people of the m. abandon'd principles. To punish these shall be my constant care, and in this duty I ever will be indefatigable, however distress'g it may be to my feelings. Not to do so would be a piece of the m't crual injustice to those who, as being the m't worthy, I have first nam'd; for should I continue to pass by y'r enormity with an ill-judged and ill-bestowed lenity, the consequence would be, to preserve the peace and safety of the settl't, some the more deserving of you must suffer with the rest, who might otherways have shewn thems's orderly and useful members of our community. Therefore you have my sacred word of honour that whenever ye commit a fault you shall be punish;d, and m't severely. Lenity has been tried, to give it further trial would be vain. I am no stranger to the use you make of every indulgence. I speak of what comes under my particular observation: and again I add that a vigorous ex'n of the law (whatever it may cost my feeling) shall follow closely upon the heels of every offender.'

When the talking was done, Phillip inspected the troops. Then he joined his senior officers for 'a cold repast' in his tent. Watkin Tench, an officer of the British Marines, recorded in his diary that 'many loyal and public toasts were drank in commemoration of the day'.

Extract.
Sources: David Collins, *An Account of the English Colony in New South Wales*, London, 1789, vol. 1, p. 8; Watkin Tench, *A Narrative of the Expedition to Botany Bay*, 1789.[19]

Aborigines Protection Society Debate
The Land Belongs to the Native Inhabitants, 1838

Among the features of colonial Australia were the large public meetings at which settlers debated key issues of the day, under the chairmanship of a prominent and respected colonist. Such meetings were especially influential before democratic forms of government were introduced in eastern Australia. So it was that, in October 1838, citizens of Sydney attended the inaugural meeting of the Aborigines Protection Society. The London branch of the Society had produced a report that condemned the way Europeans had defrauded Aborigines of their lands. In fact, since the 1820s some prominent colonists believed that Aborigines should receive compensation for the land and property which had been taken from them. According to the *South Australia Gazette & Colonial Register*, the issue had 'begun to excite considerable interest in Sydney'.[20] The Sydney press were divided: the *Sydney Morning Herald* was scornful of the suggestion, while the *Sydney Gazette* editorialized that 'the claims of the Aborigines on our attention have been powerfully, and, we are happy to say, successfully advocated'.[21] The legitimacy of Aboriginal title was a question on which two prominent lawyers, Richard Windeyer (1806–1847) and Sydney Stephen (1821–1875), took opposing sides as they debated the proposition 'that the land belongs to the native inhabitants'.

R. Windeyer, Esq.:

I entirely disagree with the sentiments expressed in the Address or Report of the Society in London, that the lands of the natives have been usurped by *fraud and violence* by the Europeans, without paying any regard to the just rights of the natives. I cannot look upon the natives as the *exclusive* proprietors of the soil; nor can I entertain the ridiculous notion that we have no right to be here. I view colonization on the basis of the broad principle laid down by the first and great Legislator in the command He issued to man 'to multiply and replenish the earth.'

The hunting propensities of the natives cause them to occupy a much larger portion of land than would be necessary to their support if it were under cultivation. And the only way to make them cultivate it is to deprive them of a considerable portion of it. The natives have no right to the land. The land, in fact, belongs to him who cultivates it first.

Captain [Charles] Sturt states that he has travelled 300 miles, and only met one family. Now, I wish to know whether these 300 miles belong to this one family? No. He only has a title to the lands who first bestows labour upon it. I am myself a large landholder, and I certainly consider myself to have good title to that land. If we have no right to be here, we have nothing to do but to take ship and go home. But we do have a right, and by recognising this principle I carry with me nineteen-twentieths of the country gentlemen.

I admit that the government has a duty to protect the natives, because they are unable to protect themselves; and I hope the formation of this society will induce the present local government to protect them, not only by the appointment of three or four protectors, but by making every magistrate a protector. Let it not be supposed that, in making that remark, I begrudge the salaries of the gentlemen who have been appointed protectors. Mr [George] Robinson has well earned his salary, and if it were only as a pension he ought to have it. He deserves all that we can give him. I hope Mr Robinson will be able to suggest some plan to the government for the protection and civilization of the blacks; but, I confess, I am not very sanguine of success. It is, however, our duty to make the attempt.

At this point, 'Dr. [Rev. John Dunmore] Lang rose to explain the difference between himself and the last speaker. In stating the principles recognized by this Society he did not mean to say *that the natives were entitled to be paid out of the Treasury the five or ten shillings per acre that had been paid for the land but that they were entitled to an equivalent to as much value of some kind as the land is worth to them. This was all that the British legislature meant by assuming the principle that the land belonged to the blacks.'*[22]

Sydney Stephen, Esq.:

As to the opinion expressed by my friend Mr Windeyer that he who first cultivates the land has the exclusive right to it, I can not help remarking that, if correct, this denies to the Aborigines any right whatever to live upon the soil; for the uncivilised savage is sometimes here and sometimes there, passing over a vast tract without knowing how to bring the capabilities of the ground into operation.

The great question is, whether we are to give them no equivalent for that which we have taken from them. Have we deprived them of nothing? Is it nothing that they are driven from the lands where their fathers lived, where they were born and which are endeared to them by associations equally strong with the associations of more civilised people? (Hear!) I believe that their affections are as warm as the Europeans—and it is a worse affliction to them to be driven from the small spot where their affections are centred, to rove though a country in which they are strangers.

We Europeans may travel from country to country and from our superior intellect, and the resources we have from an enlightened mind, we can always make ourselves at home among people of our own standing. Not so the poor black, who has no resources for happiness beyond the occupation of sufficient hunting ground to maintain himself and satisfy nature. Perhaps he obtains his subsistence by fishing, and occupies a slip of land on the banks of a river, or the margin of a lake. Is he to be turned off as soon as the land is required, without any consideration whatever? (Hear, hear.)

I rejoice that persons have been appointed by the government whose particular duty it will be to watch over and protect the interests of the blacks; for what is everybody's business is nobody's business. (Cheers.) I have heard a good deal of the murders committed by the blacks, but I would ask if they have not been more sinned against than sinning. And if they multiply the number of atrocities committed by them four-fold, this only proves the more imperative necessity that protectors be appointed.

How is an end to be put to these atrocities? By extermination? What man will deliberately sign his hand to such a proposition? Some may assert that there is no other way to subdue them, and call them 'brutes' and 'animals'. But what are they who have given them these appellations? Will any man come forward and attempt to prove that they have no souls? (Hear.) Have any proper attempts been made for their civilization? They have not yet had fair play—they have been courted by the missionaries with the Bible on the one hand, and have, at the same time, been driven away and destroyed by the stock-keepers on the other. I think that they may be reclaimed if the proper course is adopted. Gain their confidence —let them see that the Europeans really take an interest in them—teach them to cultivate the soil and to enjoy the comforts of civilised life—and they may be made useful members of the community.

I think it is right then to give them land. The acquisition of property will of itself have a beneficial effect upon them. Even the lower animals are influenced by a regard to what belongs to them. The next thing to be done is to secure to them the property so given: but who is there to see that their land is not trespassed on—that their cattle are not destroyed— and that they are not oppressed—unless protectors are appointed? That they can be reclaimed there can be no question. You have only to look to Flinders Island, where Mr Robinson has, much to his credit, brought them to a state of civilization, and rendered them useful to society and contented in themselves. If this does not show the necessity of protectors being appointed here, I do not know what does. (Hear, and applause).

Reproduced in full.
Transposed from indirect speech; original italics.
Sources: Speeches in *South Australian Gazette & Colonial Register*, 17 November 1838, p. 4; additional sources in *Sydney Gazette*, 20, 23 October 1838; *Australian*, 18 October 1838; *Sydney Morning Herald*, 22 October 1838.[23]

Robert Lowe

No Convicts for New South Wales, 1849

Robert Lowe (1811–1892) was a politician, a poet and an orator of great eloquence who during the 1840s was to oppose the British government and lead the call for democratic self-government. Born in Nottinghamshire, Lowe was an albino with impaired vision, and his boyhood was a sheltered one. But he was to emerge as a brilliant scholar and debater, graduating from University College, Oxford, before training as a lawyer. In 1842, as his eyesight deteriorated further, he emigrated to Sydney with the intention of establishing himself financially. He was soon appointed to the Legislative Council, where he was to oppose Governor George Gipps by supporting the separation of Port Phillip—soon the colony of Victoria—from New South Wales. Lowe then took on the squattocracy over the issue of the monopoly of land ownership. By 1848 he was prominent in the anti-transportation movement. The transportation of convicts to New South Wales had ceased in 1840, but eight years later it was briefly resumed despite firm opposition within the colony. On 11 June 1849, after the convict ship *Hashemy* arrived in Sydney, a Great Protest Meeting of five thousand people gathered at Circular Quay. The crowd stood in the pouring rain, waiting for Lowe, who was scheduled to chair the meeting. The speeches began, interrupted by enthusiastic cheering at Lowe's late arrival. He bounded on to the platform, and immediately launched into a rousing speech on the evils of the convict system. Lowe returned to England one year later, where he had a long and brilliant political career in the House of Commons, serving as chancellor of the exchequer in liberal governments. But in contrast to his agitation for the expansion of democracy in Australia, Lowe's radicalism was considerably tempered in the old country.

It is with great pleasure that I undertake the task of seconding the adoption of the protest of the people of the colony of New South Wales, against the outrage which has been so insultingly and offensively perpetrated upon us by the resumption of transportation. The time for discussion on the principle of the convict question is past. We were not meeting to exclaim against the proposals of the English Government. The threat of degradation has been fulfilled. The stately presence of our city, the beautiful waters of our harbour, are this day again polluted with the presence of that floating hell—a convict ship. (Immense cheers.)

We have lived again to behold the cargo of crime borne across the waves to us. In our port we behold a ship freighted, not with the comforts of life, not with luxuries of civilised nations, not with the commodities of commerce, in exchange for our produce; but with the moral degradation of a community—the picked and selected criminals of Great Britain. These are the people that Great Britain sent here—educated in her crowded streets amongst her starving masses. New South Wales must be the university at which these scholars in vice and iniquity must finish their course of instruction. New South Wales must alone supply the college where these doctors in crime can take their last degree. (Cheers.) Here it is where the rubbish—the moral filth of Great Britain—must be shot; but the colonists at least have done their duty, and I congratulate you upon it. Out of the Legislative Council, and in the Council, you have refused to become parties to this oppression, and now that it is forced upon you, you have met indignantly to protest against it. It is true that in the Council the opinion of the representatives of the people has been silently asserted, but it has been unanimously asserted, for I could not call the miserable minority in the Council that differed from the people on this great question worthy of the title of 'an opposition'. (Cheers.) Those who are really opposed to the renewal of transportation have done their duty—they have not given up one point. Day after day they have been called upon to yield up something. Overture after overture has been made to Mr. Cowper and myself, by my honorable and learned colleague Mr. Wentworth for some compromise. (Groans for Mr. Wentworth.) But we have taken our stand—we have felt that the people are with us; and thanks to the noble declaration which the people have made on this question that stand has been maintained, and the perfidy and insult which has been endeavoured to be perpetrated has been met, and repelled. (Cheers.)

But I look not on this question by itself alone—I look at it in connection with another question, in which the liberties of the people of this colony are almost equally concerned. A question on which, as on this, I hope the colonists will make themselves heard. I view this attempt to inflict the worst and most degrading slavery on the colony only as sequence of that oppressive tyranny which has confiscated the lands of the colony —for the benefit of a class. That class has felt our power—they are not content to get the lands alone, without labour are were worthless, and therefore they must enrich themselves with slaves. (Great cheers.)

I warn you not to be deluded by the simple aspect which the question has hitherto borne, when argued by those whose interests are involved in maintaining the system. I am for the liberty of all—and I protest not only against deluging the colony with crime, but the insidious attempt to introduce serfdom and slavery amongst us. This is not a question of the injury which the 250 felons on board the *Hashemy* will do the colony. They will perhaps cause but little evil—but it is a question—a question in which we have a right to be heard in protest—whether the inhabitants of this colony should be subjected to the contamination of trebly convicted felons, and whether we should submit to a measure which was necessary to fill up the confiscation of our lands. (Cheers.)

I therefore contend that those who brand the people of the colony with mere worldly selfishness in the part they have taken on this question do us injustice. It is not the mere fear of competition amongst operatives that now unites us on this question: it is not a mere breeches pocket question with the labouring classes, though it might be with the employers. It is a struggle for liberty—a struggle against a system which has in every country where it has prevailed been destructive of freedom. (Cheers.) Let us not be deluded by this insidious attempt. Let it go home [to England] that the people of New South Wales reject, indignantly reject, the inheritance of wealthy shame, which Great Britain holds out to us. That we spurn the gift, deceitfully gilded though it be—that we spurn the degradation however eloquently it may be glazed over. Let us send across the Pacific our emphatic declaration that we will not be slaves—that we will be free. Let us exercise the right that every English subject has—to assert our freedom. (Cheers.)

I can see from this meeting the time was not far distant when we will assert our freedom not by words alone. As in America, oppression was the parent of independence, so will it be in this colony. The tea which the Americans flung into the water rather than pay the tax upon it, was not the cause of the revolt of the American States; it was the unrighteousness of the tax—it was the degradation of submission to an unrighteous demand. And so, sure as the seed will grow into the plant, and the plant to the tree, in all times, and in all nations, so will injustice and tyranny ripen into rebellion, and rebellion into independence. (Immense cheering.)

Reproduced in full.
Transposed from indirect speech.
Source: *Sydney Morning Herald*, 12 June 1849, p. 2.

———◆———

John Dunmore Lang
The Coming Event: the United Provinces of Australia, 1850

John Dunmore Lang (1799–1878) attracted great notoriety in colonial Sydney, as both a clergyman and an outspoken politician. Born in Scotland, he arrived in Sydney in 1823 to establish a Presbyterian Church. Fiercely anti-Catholic, and dismayed by the power of the emancipists, Lang championed immigration schemes for skilled Protestants and their families. The last of these ventures landed him in jail for debt and libel. He entered parliament as a radical democrat in 1842, and he served until 1870. Lang exerted his influence through his own string of newspapers, including the *Colonist*, and was not averse to blatant self-promotion. His skill as an earnest and witty speaker was on display in April 1850 when he predicted that 'The United Provinces of Australia' were 'The Coming Event'. As Lang told his audience in Sydney's City Theatre, he had grand visions of a great republic encompassing eastern Australia and the Western Pacific.

This great political truth is universally admitted *in the abstract*: it is universally admitted that Colonies generally must some day or other become Sovereign and Independent communities; but when any attempt is made to apply this truth in any particular case, we are uniformly met with the allegation that it is merely a question of time, and that the proper time is not yet come in that particular case. Now if we may judge from the opinions and practice of Mr. Mother-country and his friends, i.e. the Government and their hangers-on at home, this time will never be allowed to have come, until the Colonies shall in all probability be compelled in self-defence to wrest their freedom and independence from the Mother-country and to set her at defiance. (Strong expressions of assent.)

Now I hold that this cannot possibly be either the natural or the proper order of things under the universal government of God. On the contrary, I maintain, without fear of contradiction, that there is a time at which Colonial communities are entitled, at the hands of the Parent State, to their entire freedom and independence, or in other words, to be placed in the rank of Sovereign and Independent States; and that this time moreover is as clearly ascertainable in the case of such communities as it is in the case of individual men.

The Mother-country cannot plead that it has planted the Colony, and incurred a large expenditure in watching over its infancy and childhood, any more than the parent can in the case of his son. All this is granted: it is the order of nature that it should be so, and the ordinance of God. But the Colony has still an undoubted and indefeasible right to complete self-government, or in other words, to entire freedom and independence, as soon as it has attained its majority, i.e., as soon as it is both able and willing to manage its own affairs, without either assistance or protection from the Mother-country.

This, I repeat it, is unquestionably the order of nature—the law of God, in reference to Colonial communities; and we may rest assured, that if this order is not observed, if this law is not obeyed, if Mr. Mother-country presumes to exercise his alleged *patria potestas*, after his son has attained his majority, and is both able and willing to maintain himself, without either assistance or protection from the Parent State, the rights of individuals will be grievously infringed; the welfare and advancement of the Colonial community will be not only retarded, but compromised and sacrificed in an endless variety of ways; while Mr. Mother-country will himself be soundly punished for his injustice in the end. In short, it was never the intention of the Great Governor among the nations to permit the establishment of universal empires upon earth, like that of Great Britain and her forty or fifty Colonies; whose wretched government, and whose backward condition, in comparison with what they might be if they were only allowed to govern themselves, are a positive disgrace to the British name, and a calamity to the civilized world.

Self-government is the inherent and indefeasible right of such communities as most of the British Colonies of the present day; and if that right is not conceded peacefully, those from whom it is unjustly withheld will only be acting in accordance with the great law of self-preservation, if they wrest it from their oppressors on the first favourable opportunity. (Great applause.)

Supposing, therefore, that Great Britain should concede entire independence and freedom to the five Australian Colonies, as I have no doubt she would on a proper representation of the case, I would recommend that the Island of New Caledonia should immediately thereafter be annexed as a separate and independent colony of the Australian Republic. There is considerable trade between Sydney and that island already. It abounds with the finest harbours in the Pacific, the finest timber and the finest land; and with a little temporary assistance from New South Wales, which it would soon be able to repay, it could easily be settled with a German if not a British population, and become one of the finest provinces in the world.

We should thus have a strong hold on the Pacific, so as to organise a powerful and beneficial influence over the numberless isles of that vast ocean; and I have no doubt we should soon be able to include under the central Government at Sydney the whole Eastern Coast of Australia, from Cape Howe to Cape York, together with all the larger islands of the Western Pacific. In short, I anticipate that the United Provinces of Australia—for I would decidedly prefer that name to the United States, both because it is equally appropriate, and because it would prevent all ambiguity, showing that we have no connection with the shop over the way (Great cheering)—will, ere long, be the great leading power of the Southern Hemisphere, and will one day exercise an influence over the civilized world not inferior to that even of the United States.

And ought not a right generous nation, like Great Britain, be proud of the honour and glory, not to speak of the commercial advantage, of being the mother of a second splendid Colonial Empire, such as the United Provinces of Australia are evidently destined to become?

As mere Colonies, we shall be the most insignificant communities on the face of the earth, unnoticed and unknown among nations. But as a series of Sovereign and Independent States, bound together in one great Federal Union, we should at once take our place among the great family of nations, our name would be known and respected in every land, and our flag on every sea; and while our land would be hailed as a City of Refuge by myriads and myriads more of the poor and destitute of the people of England, (Great cheering) our power would be beneficially felt throughout the multitude of the isles of the Western Pacific. We love with the utmost affection our mother-country, our fatherland, and we detest from our bare soul the bare idea of annexation to any other country, any other land. (Much cheering). But we do earnestly desire our entire freedom and national independence, both as being indispensably necessary to enable us to realize the glorious future that awaits our adopted land. (Loud and long-continued cheering).

Abridged.
Source: John Dunmore Lang, *The Coming Event: or, The United Provinces of Australia*, Atlas Office, Sydney, 1850, pp. 5–6, 15–16.

William Wentworth

The NSW Constitution Bill: Peerage for the Shepherd Kings, 1853

William Charles Wentworth (1790–1872) was born on Norfolk Island, the son of D'Arcy Wentworth, a respectable surgeon with a shady past, and convict Catherine Crowley. D'Arcy Wentworth flourished in the public life of New South Wales and sent his sons to England to be educated as gentlemen. His eldest, William, returned to the colony where his achievements were notable: he was in the first exploration party to cross the Blue Mountains, the first Australian-born author of a book, an occasional poet and a lawyer. Wentworth was also a potent orator—a populist rabble-rouser who championed the right of ex-convicts to live as free and loyal Australians. But Wentworth's demotic fervour vanished after he became a Legislative Councillor in 1843: he began to support, with considerable eloquence, the interests of the wealthy landowners. In 1853 a committee of the Legislative Council, chaired by Wentworth, drafted a constitution. Wentworth proposed an upper house based on a new, hereditary peerage, made up of the great pastoralists or 'Shepherd Kings'—men like himself. When he spoke on the Constitution Bill on 16 August 1853 his fellow parliamentarians vigorously opposed his proposal. The masses, who had once loved Wentworth as an inspirational patriot, would now mock his plans for a 'bunyip aristocracy'.

It was the object of the committee who framed this Bill to frame a Constitution in perpetuity for the colony—not a constitution which could be set aside, altered and shattered to pieces by every blast of popular opinion. What community of men could, I ask, be brought to live together under such a government as this would be? What security for person or the rights of property, or the administration of the law, or social order, would there be under such a Constitution?

I am firm in the conviction, that the representation of the country should be based on, or proportioned to, not the mere population, but the great interests of the country; and it should be so proportioned that no one interest shall have a preponderating influence over any other. Now, I contend, that the pastoral interest under the Electoral Act has no such preponderating influence. That interest is incomparably the largest, the most important interest in the country, and I hope it will continue so for ages. (Cheers.) I am quite confident, if the country is to continue to grow great and wealthy, this great interest must continue to flourish. It is for pastoral purposes alone that we can ever turn to successful account the illimitable wilds which exist in the interior of the colony, and which are under the system so much and so falsely cried down, producing annually millions of income to the colony. (Cheers.) Discontinue this system, give up pastoral pursuits, and this enormous amount of income will be simply destroyed. This would be a policy so preposterous that even the wildest democrat, if he understood the practical bearing of the question, would denounce it.

The wealthy class of the city consists chiefly of these men of business —these lords of the Exchange as they call or think themselves. (Great laughter.) There is my hon. friend from Darlinghurst (Mr. Barker), who is a manufacturer in a certain sense; he manufactures flour out of grain. My hon. friend the member for the Sydney Hamlets (Mr. Smart) is in the same position. Then there are some leather manufacturers, one or two brewers, an iron founder or two, and these I believe, with some trifling exceptions, are all. There is really nothing to represent here except a large mass of labour. (Great laughter.)

I sincerely hope that the Constitution the Council is about to frame will be a constitution that will be a lasting one—a conservative one—a British, not a Yankee constitution. (Loud and prolonged cheers.) I hope that it will be one under which in all times to come the people of New South Wales will repose in safety and security, and that it will assimilate in every possible respect with the constitution of the glorious fatherland. (Loud cheers.) If the Council would look to the whole range of the British colonies—throughout the West Indies and British America—and if it were considered that the nominee principle was universal throughout this extensive range—that it has ruled for nearly two centuries in some, for a great length of time in all—that, so far as can be collected from the best authorities on colonial matters, from the opinions of the local press, a single objection has never been raised against it; surely these are facts which ought to have great weight here. (Hear, hear.)

Seeing, therefore, that the form of constitution now proposed for New South Wales exists, and has long existed, in the wide range already mentioned, that no complaints (excepting those arising from the jealousies of antagonistic races) have been made against it, I would ask the Council whether this colony is now to give up the great boon which it so earnestly prayed for four years ago? (Hear, hear.)

And this brings me to the important principle involved in the hereditary clauses of the Bill. As the report of the select committee states, they are framed to a certain extent in accordance with analogous clauses to be found in the Imperial Act 3 George III, c.31, for making more effectual provision for the government of the province of Quebec. The principle of conferring an hereditary right of being summoned to the Legislative Council, upon those upon whom the Sovereign might confer hereditary titles, rank, or dignity, is therein set forth, and was maintained by Pitt, Burke, Wilberforce, and all the great statesmen of that day, except Fox, whose attempt to defeat the measure failed, and the clauses were carried, enacting that the Sovereign might confer hereditary titles upon the colonists of Quebec, coupled with seats in the Upper House, which were to descend to their sons. The design of Pitt was to establish an hereditary class in Quebec, upon the same principle as that which rules in the case of the peerage of England. But in this age of the world the committee were prompt to see that this hereditary right to seats in the Council could not be maintained, for it very often happens that the most brilliant fathers have the most stupid sons; and as talent and ability are not naturally hereditary, it could not for a moment be proposed that the seats of those upon whom hereditary titles might be conferred should descend to those who should come after them.

An Upper House framed on this principle, whilst it should be free from the objections which have been urged against the House of Lords, on the ground of the hereditary right of legislation which they exercise, would lay the foundation of an aristocracy which from their fortune, birth, leisure, and the superior education which these advantages would superinduce, would soon supply elements for the formation of an Upper House, modelled, as far as circumstances will admit, upon the analogies of the British Constitution. Now, it must be borne in mind that the principle of electing a portion of the Upper House from those holding hereditary titles is one which cannot be carried into practice for the next forty or fifty years; it is to be seen, therefore, that the committee proposed to sow the seed of an institution which will have ample time allowed it to grow to maturity. (Cheers.) And it is also to be remembered that this principle of forming a house, the one portion patented by the Sovereign, and the other elected by those holding hereditary rank, obtains at present in the House of Lords in the case of the election of Scotch and Irish peers, upon whom no hereditary right of legislation is conferred, but only the hereditary right of election. (Hear.)

When a generation having this hereditary right amongst them arises here, I (recalling the menaces of a certain portion of the colonial press, its tendencies to democracy, its recklessness of consequences) predict that it will be found a good and stable bulwark, necessary for the defence of good government and conservative institutions. A powerful body will be formed of men of wealth, property, and education—men not raised from any particular section of the community, but from every class that has the energy to aspire to rank and honour. (Hear.)

Here are no poor, no middle class, in the sense in which these words are used at home; all are rich; yet what do people aspire to here, who having accumulated perhaps £50,000 or £100,000 do not care to pursue the drudgery of money-making any longer? I will tell the Council: they aspire to a speedy migration to other lands, seeing it is better to themselves and families to build up homes where the democratic and levelling principles so rapidly increasing here are scouted; and where there are high and honorable pursuits and distinctions to which the children of the prudent may aspire. (Loud and prolonged cheers.) Who would stay here if he could avoid it? Who, with ample means, would ever return, if once he left these shores, or even identify himself with the soil, so long as selfishness, ignorance, and democracy hold sway? (Renewed cheers.)

And yet what a glorious country would this be to live in if higher and nobler principles prevailed; blessed with the most bounteous gifts of providence, it affords in its rich and illimitable tracts happy homes for millions yet unborn. (Here, hear.) With regard to the clauses in question,

I know not the opinions of hon. members, but I can only say that if they be not adopted, the colony will be virtually disfranchised. (Loud cries of hear from all sides.) Why, I ask, if titles are open to all at home, should they be denied to the colonists?

Abridged.
Source: E. K. Silvester (ed.), *Speeches in the Legislative Council of New South Wales on the Second Reading of the Bill for Framing a New Constitution for the Colony*, Sydney, 1853.[24]

———

Daniel Deniehy

Against Wentworth's 'Bunyip Aristocracy', 1853

Daniel Henry Deniehy (1828–1865) was the child of ex-convicts who rose to become successful produce merchants in Sydney. Deniehy was renowned for his diminutive height and for the wit and savagery of his tongue. The little man was a lawyer, a poet, a journalist and a sometime politician who, in his finest moments, seemed positively brilliant. On the evening of 16 August 1853 he gained celebrity at a public meeting at the Victoria Theatre. Deniehy's flamboyant speech supported a resolution against William Wentworth's Constitution Bill—which Wentworth had presented that day to Parliament. As a radical democrat, Deniehy ridiculed Wentworth's proposal that a New South Wales aristocracy be established from whose ranks the members of the upper house in the colonial parliament would be elected. The Sydney audience cheered Deniehy's argument that social standing should be a reward for achievement rather than a privilege of birth. Deniehy may have won that debate, but he lost a more vicious battle with alcoholism, which drove him to a bleak and wasteful death at the age of just thirty-seven.

Why I have been selected to speak to the present resolution I know not, save that as a native of the Colony I might naturally be expected to feel something like real interest, and to speak with something like real feeling on a question connected with the political institutions of the Colony. I will do my best to respond to that invitation to 'speak up,' and will perhaps balance deficiencies flowing from a small volume of voice by in all cases speaking plainly and calling things by their right names. (Cheers).

I protest against the present daring and unheard-of attempt to tamper with a fundamental popular right, that of having a voice in the nomination of men who are to make, or control the making of, laws binding on the community—laws perpetually shifting and changing the nature of the whole social economy of a given state, and frequently operating in the subtlest form on the very dearest interests of the citizen, on his domestic, his moral, and perhaps his religious relations. The name of Mr. Wentworth has several times been mentioned today, and upon one or two occasions with an unwise tenderness, a squeamish reluctance to speak plain English, and call certain shady deeds of Mr. Wentworth's by their usual homely appellations, simply because they were Mr. Wentworth's. Now, I for one, am nowise disposed, as preceding speakers have seemed, to tap the vast shoulders of Mr. Wentworth's political recreancies—'to damn him with faint praise and mistimed eulogy.' (Loud cheers.) I have listened from boyhood upwards to grey tradition, to Mr. Wentworth's demagogic *areopagitas* —his speeches for the liberty of the unlicensed printing *regime* of Darling; and for these and divers other deeds of a time when the honourable Member for Sydney had to the full his share of the chivalrous pugnacities of five-and-twenty, I am as much inclined to give Mr. Wentworth credit as any other man. But with those *fantasias*, those everlasting varieties on the 'Light of other Days' perpetually ringing in my ears, I am fain to inquire by what rule of moral and political appraisal it was sought to throw in a scale directly opposite to that containing the flagrant and shameless political dishonesty of years, the democratic escapades, sins long since repented of, in early youth. The subsequent political conduct, or rather the systematic political principles of Mr. Wentworth, have been of a character sufficiently outrageous to cancel the value of a century of service. (Loud cheers.)

The British Constitution has been spoken of this afternoon in terms of unbounded laudation. That stately fabric, it is true, deserves to be spoken of in terms of respect; I respect it, and no doubt you all share in that feeling. But mine is a qualified respect at best, and in all presumes assimilations of the political hypothesis of our colonial constitution-makers, I warn you not to be seduced by mere words and phrases—sheer sound and fury. Relatively, the British Constitution is only an admirable example of slowly growing and gradually elaborated political experience applied and set in action, but it is also eminent and exemplary as a long history, still evolving, of political philosophy.

But, as I have said before, it is after all but relatively good for its wonderfully successful fusion of principles the most antagonistic. Circumstances entirely alter cases, and I would again warn you not to be led away by vague associations, exhaled from the use of venerable phrases that have, what few phrases now-a-days seldom could boast, genuine meanings attached to them.

The patrician element exists in the British Constitution, as does the regal, for good reasons—it has stood in the way of all later legislational thought and operation as a great fact; as such it is handled, and in a deep and prudential spirit of conservatism it is allowed to stand; but as affecting the basis and foundation of the architecture of a constitution, the elective principles neutralize all detrimental influences, by conversion, practically, into a mere check upon the deliberations of the initiative section of the Legislature. (Loud cheers.)

And having the right to frame, to embody, to shape it as we will, with no huge stubborn facts to work upon as in England, there is nothing but the elective principle and the inalienable right and freedom of every colonist upon which to work out the whole organisation and fabric of our political institutions. But because it is the good pleasure of Mr. Wentworth, and the respectable toil of that puissant legislative body whose serpentine windings are so ridiculous, we are not permitted to form our own Constitution, but instead we are to have one and an Upper Chamber cast upon us, built upon a model to suit the taste and propriety of certain political oligarchs, who treat the people at large as if they are cattle to be bought and sold in the market, as indeed they are in American slave states, and now in the Australian colonies, where we might find bamboozled Chinese and kidnapped Coolies. (Applause.)

And being in a figurative humour, I might endeavour to cause some of the proposed nobility to pass before the stage of our imagination as the ghost of Banquo walked in the vision of Macbeth, so that we might have a fair view of these harlequin aristocrats (Laughter), these Botany Bay magnificos (Laughter), these Australian mandarins (Roars of laughter). We will have them across the stage in all the pomp and circumstance of hereditary titles. First, then, stalks the hoary Wentworth. But I cannot believe that to such a head the strawberry leaves would add any honour. (Cheers.) Next comes the full-blooded native aristocrat, Mr. James Macarthur, who would, I suppose, aspire to an earldom at least; I will therefore call him Earl of Camden, and I will suggest for his coat of arms a field vert, the heraldic term for green,—(great cheers and laughter)—and emblazoned on this field should be the rum keg of a New South Wales order of chivalry. There is also the much-starred Terence Aubrey Murray, with more crosses and orders—not orders of merit—than a state of mandarinhood. (Loud laughter). Another gentleman who claims the proud distinction of a colonial title is George Robert Nichols, the hereditary Grand Chancellor of all the Australias. (Roars of laughter). Behold him in the serene and moody dignity of that picture of Rodias that smiled on us in all the public-house parlours (Loud laughter). This was the gentleman who took Mr. Lowe to task for altering his opinions, this conqueror in the lists of jaw, this victor in the realms of gab.

It might be well to ridicule the doings of this miserable clique, yet their doings merit burning indignation; but to speak more seriously of such a project would too much resemble the Irishman 'kicking at nothing, it wrenched one horribly.' (Laughter). But though their weakness are ridiculous, I can assure you that these pigmies might work a great deal of mischief; they would bring contempt upon a country whose best interests I feel sure we all have at heart, until the meanest man that walked the streets would fling his gibe at the aristocrats of Botany Bay. I confess I find extreme difficulty in the effort to classify this mushroom order of nobility. They cannot aspire to the miserable and effete dignity of the worn-out grandees of continental Europe. (Laughter). There, even in rags, they have antiquity of birth to point to; here I would defy the most skilled naturalist to assign them a place in the great human family. But perhaps after all it is only a specimen of the remarkable contrariety which exists at the Antipodes. Here we all know that the common water-mole was transformed into the duck-billed platypus; and in some distant emulation of this degeneracy, I suppose we are to be favoured with a bunyip aristocracy. (Great laughter).

However, to be serious, I sincerely trust this is only the beginning of a more extended movement, and from its commencement I argue the happiest results. (Cheers.) A more orderly, united, and consolidated meeting I have never witnessed. I am proud of Botany Bay, even if I have to blush for some of her children. I take the name as no term of reproach when I see such a high, true, and manly sensibility on the subject of our political rights—(Cheers); that the instant the liberties of our country are threatened, we can assemble, and with one voice declare our determined and undying opposition. (Cheers). But I will remind you that this is not a mere selfish consideration, there are far wider interests at stake.

Looking at the gradually increasing pressure of political parties at home, we must, in the not distant future, prepare to open our arms to receive the fugitives from England, Ireland, and Scotland, who would hasten to the offered security and competence that were cruelly denied them in their own land. The interests of these countless thousands are involved in our decision upon this occasion, and we look, and are justly entitled to look, for a heritage befitting the dignity of free men. (Great cheering).

Bring them not here with fleeting visions and delusive hopes. Let them not find a new-fangled Brummagem aristocracy swarming and darkening these fair, free shores. (Cheers). It is ours to offer them a land where man is bountifully rewarded for his labour, and where a just law no more recognises the supremacy of a class than it does the predominance of a creed. (Great cheering). But, fellow-citizens, there is an aristocracy worthy of our respect and of our admiration. Wherever human skill and brain are eminent, wherever glorious manhood asserts its elevation, there is an aristocracy that confers eternal honour upon the land that possesses it. That is God's aristocracy, gentlemen; that is an aristocracy that will bloom and expand under free institutions, and forever bless the clime where it takes root. (Great cheering).

I hope you will take into consideration the hitherto barren condition of the country we are legislating for. I myself am a native of the soil, and I am proud of my birthplace. It is true its past is not hallowed in history by the achievements of men whose names reflect a light upon the times in which they lived. We have no long line of poets or statesmen or warriors; in this country, Art has done nothing but Nature everything. It is ours, then, alone to inaugurate the future. (Great Cheering). In no country has the attempt ever been made to successfully manufacture an aristocracy *pro re nata*. It cannot be done; we might as well expect honour to-be paid to the dusky nobles of King Kamehamaka, or to the ebony earls of the Emperor Souloque of Hayti.

The stately aristocracy of England was founded on the sword. The men who came over with the conquering Norman were the masters of the Saxons, and so became the aristocracy. The followers of Oliver Cromwell were the masters of the Irish, and so became their aristocracy. But I will inquire by what process Wentworth and his satellites have conquered the people of New South Wales (Great cheering), except by the artful dodgery of cooking up a Franchise Bill (Great laughter). If we are to be blessed with an Australian aristocracy, I should prefer it to resemble, not that of William the Bastard, but of Jack the Strapper.

But I trespass too long on your time, and would in conclusion only seek to record two things—first, my indignant denunciation of any tampering with the freedom and purity of the elective principle, the only basis upon which sound government could be built; and, secondly, I wish you to regard well the future destinies of our country. Let us, with prophetic eye, behold the troops of weary pilgrims from foreign despotism which would ere long be flocking to these shores in search of a more congenial home, and let us now give our most earnest and determined assurance that the domineering clique which made up the Wentworth party are not, and should never be, regarded as the representatives of the manliness, the spirit, and the intelligence of the freemen of New South Wales. I have sincere pleasure in seconding the resolution, confident that it will meet with unanimous support and approval.

Reproduced in full.
Transposed from indirect speech.
Sources: E. A. Martin, *The Life and Speeches of Daniel Henry Deniehy*; *Sydney Morning Herald*, 16 August 1853.[25]

Caroline Chisholm
The Families Left Behind, 1854

Caroline Chisholm (1808–1877) was a philanthropist and a tireless campaigner on behalf of single women and large families immigrating to the Australian colonies. In 1838 Chisholm accompanied her husband, Archibald, and their young sons to New South Wales. She persuaded Governor George Gipps to establish a refuge and free employment agency for single female immigrants. Chisholm advocated the settlement of families on the land, believing the violence of men living on the frontier would be mediated by the arrival of a 'God's Police' of women and children. Returning to

London in 1846, Chisholm promoted immigration to Australia and gave evidence to parliamentary committees on colonization. She feared that the discovery of gold, which drew huge numbers of male immigrants to Australia, would destabilize the colonial society she had aimed to civilize. In 1854 she arrived in Port Phillip and persuaded private and government interests to support her family immigration scheme. She set off on a tour of the Victorian goldfields. An accomplished speaker, Chisholm knew how to play to a crowd and she recognized that the novelty of a woman speaking in public could be used to good effect. On 10 November 1854 she was the special guest at a Friday evening soirée in the Hall of the mining town of Castlemaine. A band of German musicians played and tea was served before Chisholm, introduced by her supporter Mr Hitchcock, addressed a crowd of several hundred men and a handful of women. She chided diggers for neglecting their families, promised to bring more women to the almost exclusively male diggings, and looked to a future of family-run small farms. At the end of her speech, in a wave of enthusiasm among the crowd, a fund was established for a Home to accommodate single women on the goldfields.

Mr. Chairman, Ladies and Gentlemen, a cup of tea is always exceedingly pleasant and refreshing, and the one which I have been invited to partake of this evening, is particularly agreeable to me. I can assure you that I am deeply grateful for it. (Cheers.) I am sure you would not have been here this evening if what I have done had not met with your approval, and I hope that what I shall yet do, may receive your support. (Cheers.) Those whose domestic duty it is to get a cup of tea ready—as we ladies of the colony have to do—know the troubles and difficulties which such an undertaking involves—(Laughter)—and my friend Mr. Hitchcock in preparing the one of which we have just partaken, seems, from the explanation he has given, to have encountered his share.

It is, my friends, a glorious thing to live in a country and amidst a people who will not allow slander of any kind on account of religion, who will have nothing but open truth. If I could not stand a little sifting, I should not have come to the diggings. (Laughter and applause.) My character is precious and valuable to me; I hope it is even more so unto my children; and I attach some importance to it as being of some value to you. (Much applause.) And if I am jealous of my reputation it is because I feel that without character I cannot possess public confidence, and without public confidence I cannot effect any public good. Thus the sifting which I have had is a safeguard and protection, and keeps from me those who would be advocates only in words. (Applause.) Moneymaking is no part of my business. If it was, I believe I could make a fortune in many ways. During my present trip, I learnt many little ways for making money for others, but saw nothing suitable for myself. I feel there is a certain amount of work for me to do, and that I must go on, entertaining not the slightest dread for the future. Some say that I have not been sending a sufficient number of good persons to the colonies. I should like to ask those objectors if they ever did anything to help me? (Applause.) No; you will not find among the grumblers the workers. (Laughter.) I know that from experience.

It is, however, right that I should explain to you why I am here. During my fourteen years' labour I have gained among a certain class a reputation for speaking truth. I may err in judgment but not in intention. Numbers are constantly applying to me for advice, but I never seek to lead them upon the opinions of others: the rule I have always observed has been, never to go by what I hear, but to judge only from what I see. (Applause.) Consequently when many persons in Melbourne were inquiring of me, 'Shall I go to the diggings?' 'Would you advise me to go up the country?' I felt the responsibility of my position, as, if I advised them to go, and anything went wrong with them, they would blame me. My reply has invariably been, 'As soon as I can make arrangements, I shall go to the diggings, and then I will tell you.' I have delayed this for some time, though I have been under a promise, made in England, to visit the diggings.

The mission I am on is a sacred one. I have promised parents to go in search of their children — I have promised wives to make inquiries for their husbands — I have promised sisters to seek their brothers, and friends to look for friends — and oh! let me ask and implore you who have left friends at home, if you have been neglectful of your first duty, if, in your lust for gold, or in the pursuit of business, you have not written to those you have left behind, to go home this night and do your duty. Let them, too, taste of the fruits of your labors. They might be in need of your assistance. You may have left them in comfort and security, and do not think of the change that may have occurred. For they are liable to change when the strong arm that has been their natural support is withdrawn from them. Whatever their condition they must be anxious to hear from you, to know whether you are alive or not.

In a first journey like this, it is impossible to make all the arrangements that are contemplated. Still a great deal may be done — much good may be effected with present means, and if it is attempted, you will not only have me in Castlemaine again, but again and again (Applause). I shall look for you to work your own district well, and act in unison with others. I shall then have a great number of agents to help me in carrying out my objects.

The husbands who have left their wives at home, will find that I shall follow them (Laughter and applause). There are many of them about the diggings. The other day, as I was passing along, a digger whom I approached gave a sudden start, and said, 'That's Mrs. Chisholm!' I acknowledged my identity. 'Oh,' he said, 'I never thought of sending for my wife until I saw you.' Now for two years had that man been digging at Castlemaine — dig, dig, digging, and yet, as he assured me, had never thought of sending for his wife until he saw me (Cries of 'shame upon him'). There is a great number like him — equally forgetful. Now, with me as a reminder, with two or three gentlemen in Castlemaine working with me, and co-operating with a committee in England, we should soon find out these careless husbands. Will you do all you can to help me? I am sure the females will. I think the married men will. If the single men do not help me, I will not help them (Laughter and applause).

When I was in New South Wales, I thought nothing of a journey of 100 miles. I knew that I could depend upon the hospitality of the people on the line of road, to meet any want on the part of myself and the persons with me. But I was afraid, when some persons proposed to accompany me on the present occasion, that we should not meet with accommodation on the road. There is a great difference between buying a cart at fifty guineas and getting one at eleven guineas; and I had to wait till I could make things convenient. I had a pair of horses lent to me, and started on my journey.

At a public party a few days before, I met his Excellency the Lieutenant Governor. He had been informed of my intended visit to the goldfields, expressed a great desire that I should start without delay, and said he was exceedingly anxious to hear what I thought of them. My mission was known to be a domestic one; still, when I was leaving, two or three officials furnished me with letters of introduction; I had, besides, a kind of general letter, in which, in the event of my requiring any assistance, the officials on the goldfields were requested to pay me the necessary attention. Well, I did get into trouble. I broke my shaft (Laughter). I made use of the note, and the escort cart was lent to me until my own was repaired (Applause). I did not find it necessary to use my letters of introduction; for, to use the expression of my friend, Mr. Hitchcock, my object was to 'sift' the diggings, to look into the domestic wants of the diggers, and see what could be done to provide them with comfortable, happy homes (Applause).

We have been told that the heath of the Queen was drunk in this hall with 'nine times nine and one cheer more;' but what a cheer would the diggers give if the homes they go to at night were something better than the blankets under which they have to creep like dogs. Give them good homes, and if the Russians came tomorrow, the diggers would all turn out and fight in their defence like men (Applause). No man knows the strength of his arm until he raises it to defend his wife or protect his children (Applause). I was told at Bendigo that if I stayed a little while there, I should receive a large number of diggers' grievances. That is not a part of my mission. I am looking after their rights; they will have an expensive commission to redress their grievances (Applause). Numbers have complained to me very grievously of many things which they feel to press on them heavily; but I do not feel much sympathy or much pity for any body of men who pay so little respect to their own sex as to live without wives when they can so well afford to maintain them (Laughter). If I had power to do so, I would relieve of taxes all the married men, and give a bounty on all the women and children introduced into the diggers' districts (Applause and laughter).

The diggers have great grievances, but they are not competent to decide upon the remedy. It is impossible for them to act with discretion and judgment, huddled together, as they are, in fifties, listening to the evil agitator. It will be when they are really at home, with their wives and families—when they live in peace and quietness, that they will be best able to tell what they want. Then, when they can take care of the inside of their homes, and feel that the outside is protected by police, no longer regarded as an evil, their influence will be legitimately exercised (Applause).

The difficulties that impede the reunion of wives with their husbands have been much exaggerated by the men themselves. I know a case in which a man, writing home to his wife, and sending her no money, said he had met with an accident—that a tree had fallen upon him and broken his leg. Another letter narrated another fracture, and in the course of one day I have seen five different letters, each alleging fractured limbs, and written by men who, unlike the man who never thought about his wife, were thinking how to excuse themselves for not sending their partners any money (Laughter and applause).

Now I do not think so much of this would happen if the diggers had any place where they might safely deposit their gold. I think it would be a very good thing if savings banks could be established here. It might easily be done. I have no doubt that we should hear of sons sending to parents, and husbands to wives, much more frequently than at present, if they could save their money. I think that some institution of the nature of a savings bank could be attached to the Gold Commissioners' departments. There is another point, too, on which, I think, the services of the Commissioners could be made useful—that is, in giving information to people who wish to purchase lands in their respective districts. I should be glad if any gentleman would aid me in carrying this latter point out. Great good would result from it. I am constantly applied to by men with families, and perhaps £200 or £300 in cash, who want to get on land of their own. To such men the opportunity of applying to the Commissioners, and obtaining the knowledge they require, would be a great advantage.

With reference to the introduction of females here—unless the ladies of the district will come forward and co-operate in protecting those who are sent here, so that those who are good may be saved from becoming bad, it will be useless to attempt it. If you wish to prosper in this district you must encourage population; and take advantage of the present time, for it will be long before there will be a better. Wages are higher in England, and fewer people are coming out; and the love of land is so strong among those you have here, that if you do not speedily find some for them, they will dig your gold and carry it away (Much applause). I know many girls get into difficulties through being discharged from one place before they have another to go to. They seek temporary lodgings, are exposed to temptations, and generally the more innocent the girl the sooner she falls. I shall be happy to do what I can to send girls here when I know that the ladies of Castlemaine are ready to perform their part. (Applause.)

Taking the general character of the diggers of this place, I believe that anything like ordinary care and supervision over females who may arrive here, would result in good. Where there is one man among them who will annoy a respectable female, there will be found ten to protect her. (Applause.) But there must be a Home, founded in the spirit of true

Christian liberty that we all love and venerate. If, then, you will, in your district, found such a Home, I will do all I can to fill it. (Applause.) I mention this with especial reference to wives and families.

I have been informed that in this district alone there are £70,000 deposited with government, being the property of diggers; so that there does appear to be a sort of savings bank here already. But the money is yielding no interest—that would keep me awake all night! (Laughter and applause.) It belongs to working men, and ought to be worked. Government may well be short of money. I hope some of this large amount will be soon withdrawn by the working men who have placed it there, and their wives sent for. In the meantime, let them know where they may obtain lands to settle and build their own cottages on—that is an object I will arrange and forward to the utmost of my power. Just as I would endeavour to procure for you a supply of female servants to lead them into marriage, so I recommend men to dig for gold, wherewith to purchase lands and settle. (Applause.—A communication was here made to Mrs. Chisholm by Mr. Hitchcock.) I have much satisfaction in telling you that it is intended to establish, in Castlemaine, a branch of the Melbourne savings bank. (Applause.)

Abridged.
Source: *The Mount Alexander Mail* (Castlemaine), 10 November 1854, p. 3.

Peter Lalor
The Eureka Rebellion, 1854

Peter Lalor (1827–1889) was the leader of the Eureka rebellion on the Ballarat goldfields in 1854. Born in Ireland into a family of landowners who were Catholic with long-standing nationalist sympathies, Lalor trained as an engineer. In 1852 he joined the rush to the Victorian goldfields, and he soon found himself among the thousands seeking their fortunes at Ballarat. Dissatisfaction was rife among the diggers, who resented the introduction of a costly mining licence and the absence of constitutional avenues to express their grievances. Mass meetings of more than ten thousand miners were held at Bakery Hill, opposite the Government Camp. But the new Ballarat Reform League was unsuccessful in its attempts to negotiate with the government, who sent further troops to Ballarat as the unrest mounted. On 30 November the more militant of the miners gathered under the rebel 'Southern Cross' flag, and marched to the Eureka Lead. They formed a council-of-war, electing Lalor as commander, who—according to an eyewitness, Raffaello Carboni—made this stirring speech.

A make-shift stockade was erected, as the miners resolved to defend them-selves. In the early hours of Sunday 3 December police and military attacked, with about thirty stockaders killed and a further hundred taken prisoner. Martial law was declared, but after growing public support for the miners, and a commission of enquiry, most of their demands were met. Peter Lalor lost his left arm in the attack and for a time there was a price on his head, but by 1855 he had entered the first Victorian Parliament as a member of the Legislative Assembly.

Gentlemen, I find myself in the responsible position I now occupy, for this reason. The diggers, outraged at the unaccountable conduct of the Camp officials in such a wicked licence-hunt at the point of the bayonet, as the one of this morning, took it as an insult to their manhood, and a chal-lenge to the determination come to at the monster meeting of yesterday.

The diggers rushed to their tents for arms, and crowded on Bakery-hill. They wanted a leader. No one came forward, and confusion was the consequence. I mounted the stump, where you saw me, and called on the people to 'fall in' into divisions, according to the fire-arms they had got, and to chose their own captains out of the best men they had among themselves. My call was answered with unanimous acclamation, and com-plied to with willing obedience.

The result, is that I have been able to bring about that order, without which it would be folly to face the pending struggle like men. I make no pretensions to military knowledge. I have not the presumption to assume the chief command, no more than any other man who means well in the cause of the diggers. I shall be glad to see the best among us take the lead. *In fact, gentlemen, I expected some one who is really well known* (J. B. Humffray?)[26] *to come forward and direct our movement!* However, if you appoint me your commander-in-chief, I shall not shrink; I mean to do my duty as a man. I tell you, gentlemen, *if once I pledge my hand to the diggers, I will neither defile it, with treachery, nor render it contemptible by cowardice.*

Reproduced in full; original italics.
Source: Raffaello Carboni, *The Eureka Stockade.*[27]

———◆———

George Leech

A Toast to the Exploring Expedition of Robert O'Hara Burke, 1860

George Compton Leech was a book-loving barrister who lived in the bustling central Victorian gold-mining hub of Castlemaine. In July 1860 he and his fellow citizens organized a 'Complimentary Dinner' in honour of Robert O'Hara Burke (1821–1861). Burke was no stranger to many of them: until recently he had been the senior policeman and prosecutor in the nearby town of Beechworth. Now the district was buzzing with the news that Burke—despite having no exploration experience—had been chosen by the Royal Society of Victoria to lead a spectacular attempt to cross the Australian continent from south to north, departing the following month. So it was that some eighty male citizens of Castlemaine gathered in a room decorated with flags and evergreens to toast the explorer and cheer him on his way. They were not to know that Burke would prove a vain and incompetent leader nor that, within a year, he and young William Wills would be lying dead in the dry Aboriginal country of South Australia. All that lay in the future. As the gentlemen raised their glasses, Leech praised Burke as a noble son of the Anglo-Saxon race.

There has been exhibited before our eyes during this evening the prayer of 'Success to the Exploring Expedition,' and I now give to that silent supplication an audible voice by proposing it as a toast (Cheers.) The subject of exploration is one which can not fail to possess a high and sustaining interest, not only for Englishmen, but for all peoples and races. And naturally so, for no purpose, surely, can form the object of a more laudable ambition than a wish to know as much as we can of the world in which we live and in which God has placed us (Cheers.)

It seems as if up to a certain period of the Earth's history men were contented with the limits of the old world, but from the time when the first great impulse was given to the discovery of new lands, the genius of exploration was developed more and more, until at this present moment there is no quarter of the earth the research of which has not at least been entered upon. In this work of exploration, it seems that the Anglo-Saxon race is destined to take the lead (Cheers) and in this we can easily trace the wisdom of unerring Providence. There are other races which possess in a higher degree than ourselves the graces of refinement, and of elegant art, but there is in the Anglo-Saxon that sturdy independence, resolute will, and physical endurance, which qualifies us above all others to be the pioneers of civilization in the wilderness.

But better than any question of physical aptitude, is the fact that—with perhaps a few painful exceptions—the Anglo-Saxon has dealt most in the spirit of justice, forbearance, and mercy to those inferior races whom he has either conquered or approached (Hear). For this reason, although the Spaniard or the Venetian were first to discover, omniscient wisdom had ruled that our race should be the possessors and the colonisers (Cheers.)

In proposing success to the exploring expedition, I believe I am offering a prayer for the success of an enterprise whose results are fraught with immense importance not merely to ourselves, and the other Australian colonies of Britain, but to Englishmen everywhere, and to the world at large. The time has now evidently come for some mighty and persevering effort to be made to penetrate the interior of the island continent on which we have settled. Our race has occupied the coast, and the hour has arrived when we must push inwards our researches, and solve the mystery as to what kind of country it really is which forms the hidden centre of Australia (Cheers).

In this condition of things it is needless to urge the general prayer for success to the present enterprise. I not only hope for, but I have a strong belief in, its ultimate success, for it possesses in an eminent degree one of the great elements of success—a leader (Cheers) of dauntless courage, high capacity, blessed by Providence with much power of physical endurance, and with a tender and careful regard for the men placed under his command (Renewed cheers).

In the circumstances of the exploring expedition to which we are now wishing success, there is much to remind us of the history and extension of Anglo-Saxon America. You will remember how from the narrow strip ceded to, or conquered by, the early Pilgrim Fathers, mile after mile, and acre after acre of the seemingly impenetrable forest, was cleared before stout hearts and sinewy arms, until state after state, and territory after territory were added. The discovery of gold in California has led to a rapid and artificial peopling of the western shores of North America, but still for a time a vast and untrodden country lay between, until enterprises resembling the present at last locked hand-in-hand the settlers on the coast of the Pacific, and the elder people on the shores of the Atlantic— one common, mighty, and united people. Associated most memorably with one of those expeditions, was the name of Colonel Freemont, a name that is no doubt familiar to American gentlemen present (Hear, hear). The qualities which led to the fame and success of that gallant explorer are possessed in an eminent degree by Mr Burke, and must lead to similar results (Cheers).

To the result of the enterprise now being undertaken by the latter, every man in this colony—everyone in Anglo-Saxondom—must look with intense interest. Its success will hasten an issue that must one day surely happen, namely, the occupation and colonization by the European of the central part of Australia as well as its coastal regions. Of its present condition and character we know nothing. If occupied by native tribes, no better European pioneer could go thither than Mr Burke, no more worthy representative of the Anglo-Saxon race. In the post which he has filled amongst ourselves, he has with a strict regard for duty, combined the highest respect for the liberty of the subject, and the rights of his fellows —and those qualities will not be left behind him when he goes out from the quarters of civilization; he will carry them with him into the wilderness (Cheers).

Of the character of the interior we can only vaguely guess. It might have rivers, and if so, there will be the same easy materials for civilization which exist in the United States, and if there are not, why surely if the Dutch have had the energy to conquer a land from the ocean, Englishmen will be equal to reclaiming even 'a dry land where no water is' (Hear, hear).

In due time this country will become a mighty empire of many States joined in union—and will have in the now hidden and trackless interior, a federal capital, perhaps a second Washington. We might picture to ourselves a stately House of Congress, and fronting its portico a colossal statue of a man pointing with one hand to the Gulf of Carpentaria, and with the other resting on the neck of a recumbent camel, and on the pedestal the names of the intrepid men who formed the first great successful exploring expedition (Cheers.) Pointing to this, a man of a future generation explaining the history of the city to his child, will say, 'My son, this is Robert O'Hara Burke' (Loud cheers). Might the result be indeed thus successful.

You will pardon him for adding one hope by way of stimulus. There are really no accurate tidings that [the explorer Ludwig] Leichhardt has perished, and it may not be presumptuous to hope that he yet lives (Cheers.) Now we know how the search for the North-west passage was stimulated by the hope that [the explorer Sir John] Franklin and his gallant comrades might be found alive. Let us in this matter be allowed to hope that Burke may yet be the discoverer and the rescuer, perhaps from captivity, of Leichhardt. (Hear, hear.)

That the exploration might be successful and terminate in a safe, as well as a glorious issue, must be our unanimous prayer, believing as we do, that such a result will tend to the extension in Australian regions of Anglo-Saxon civilisation, enlightenment, and splendour. (Loud cheers).

Mr Leech concluded by formally giving the toast, which was enthusiastically received.

Reproduced in full.
Transposed from indirect speech.
Source: *Mount Alexander Mail* (Castlemaine), 9 July 1860, p. 5.

———

John Woolley
Founding 'New Britannia in Another World', 1861

John Woolley (1816–1866) arrived in Australia with his family in 1852 to take up the position of principal and professor of Logic and Classics at the new University of Sydney. Educated at University College, London, and Exeter College, Oxford, and ordained as a priest, Woolley was a scholar of liberal opinions. He oversaw a secularized curriculum at Sydney University, with an emphasis on the liberal arts rather than on professional courses. The role of the university, Woolley believed, was to educate the emerging colonial governing class to embrace responsible independence but to eschew destabilising radical influences. He was also passionate about the role of popular education within the wider community and was president of the Sydney Mechanics' School of Arts. An expansive and articulate lecturer who inspired both undergraduates and working men, Woolley was much admired by his students, who included Henry Parkes and William Windeyer. On 28 May 1861 he delivered an erudite public lecture entitled 'Schools of Art and Colonial Nationality' on the occasion of the opening of the Wollongong School of Arts. Woolley drew upon the history of Greek colonization in his exposition on the role of cultural institutions—particularly the Schools of Arts—as a patriotic force for the diffusion of knowledge and social unity within the Australian colonies.

It is a frequent, perhaps a just, boast that we [British] alone of Modern Peoples inherit the Greek genius for colonizing. It is a far different question 'Do we worthily wear their mantle and tread in their footsteps?' and one to which even national vanity will scarcely venture a complacent reply. Their method was simple and effectual: *a Greek settler went out for good and all.* Having once put his hand to the plough, he did not look back. He was no temporary sojourner: a stranger in a strange land: looking with contemptuous pity on its permanent inhabitants; counting the hours till he had 'made his pile,' and could compensate amidst the luxuries of the capital his weary and ungrateful exile. He sought not a squattage nor a factory, but a permanent dwelling. Once for all breaking the ties which bound him to the old, he launched himself with a courageous faith and resolved will, upon the bosom of the unknown future. From the colonies came to Athens poetry, literature and arts; during her short but brilliant empire, colonial merchants laid at her feet the wealth of the world, and colonial philosophers lectured in her schools; sometimes, even colonial princes rewarded and encouraged learning and genius which the mother country neglected or wronged.

Can we hope that Australia in a hundred years will present a counterpart to that picture? Five years ago [the beginning of colonial self-government] we should have answered with an indignant and enthusiastic affirmative. But experience has taught us humility; we have learned that no accidental impulse can precipitate an infant community into a nation. Boundless pastures, bottomless depths of alluvial soil, inexhaustible mines are not the sole conditions of greatness; material without moral resources are of less than no avail; no extension of territory and increase of population can compensate the want of a national heart. A corporate like a natural body grows only from within. Chemistry without the living soul might as easily frame a man as wise treaties and disciplined armies agglutinate an empire. The unity of a state is neither policy nor force, but the fire which comes down from heaven, kindling every hearth, and burning on the central altar, a visible symbol of an inward sacramental brotherhood. The lighting of such a Promethean torch must be greatly retarded in Australia by the absence of the Greek principle of Permanence. Neglected in prosperity, there are seasons at which this deficiency is forced upon our consciousness. All communities are subject to political and commercial crises. Trade languishes, enterprise ceases, the ardour of hope and progress is chilled by despondency and decay. Such panics are more frequent and more severe in young and uncemented societies; but besides this in old and settled countries, notwithstanding the attendant distress, they rather tend to consolidate than to weaken the bond of union. It occurs to none to fly from the danger; at least till every scheme of amelioration has failed. All men rather seek a remedy for the present, and a precaution against the future.

How different it is with us! The smallest cloud upon the horizon agitates us with doubt and fear. Every temporary check to progress, every unpleasing incident is magnified into a political or social portent; and men flee as they fled from the city of the plague, making by their desertion a slight inconvenience into a serious disaster. But it is not only at such periods that we feel the unsettled character of our population. Fluctuation is the order of the Colonies. We are yet very far from the Greek definition of colonists; we have neither given up our old homes, nor established new. A constant resident in our cities sees a perpetual succession of new faces before him like the shadows of a dream, and wearies his heart by the repeated shocks of ties broken ere they are well formed. Where are the men who built our wharves, and extended our commerce, whose courageous enterprise whitened our plains with sheep, whose genius and learning laid the foundation of our social order? Few, indeed remain amongst us. For the rest you must search amongst the squares of London and Hotels of Paris, the romantic villas of Italy, and gay watering places of Germany.

In all this there is nothing of which we have a right to complain. With the advantages and prestige of our connection with the British Empire, we must contentedly submit to some drawbacks: and amongst these will ever be numbered the temptation held out by the Imperial Capital to men, whose absence creates in their own Provinces a void which is not of the heart alone. It cannot indeed be asserted that absenteeism is an unmixed evil. It has its beneficial aspect. The presence of worthy and intelligent representatives may, and probably does tend to promote our interests; by interpreting our true position and prospects, and by removing that contemptuous indifference with which the people of the Sovereign state are too apt to regard their expatriated countrymen. We have heard how Liverpool clergymen and merchants lamented the benighted heathenism of our Queensland settlers; and only a few days ago, Roman papers announced a liberal contribution from the 'Savages in Australia'.

If this impression is wearing off, and a 'Cornstalk' is no longer imagined at home, black in colour, ape-like in form, and furnished with a tail, this is doubtless due to the increased facilities of communication, which have crowded Europe with our bold sons and blooming daughters, and may eventually teach even the Colonial Office that Adelaide is not a city of New South Wales, nor Sydney a district in Australia Felix; that aborigines do not encamp in George Street, nor bushrangers lurk in the purlieus of Hyde Park; nay, that you can traverse in a moonless night, the streets and lanes of Wollongong, without the necessity of making your will.

Yet the increasing number of those who leave us and do not return, is a just ground of uneasiness, and a bar to our social and moral, as well as our material advancement. We stagnate for want of capital. The days are happily gone when labour and capital seemed antagonistic, and scowled upon the other with greedy and jealous eyes: we know them now, not as friendly alone, but as one; one as the elder and younger brothers of the same family; one, as the past with the present and the future. The accumulation of yesterday's industry is the foster-mother of the industry of today. The source of England's elastic prosperity is the willingness of her wealthy men to contribute the hoards of a wise abstinence to schemes which, affording a present maintenance to the masses, prepare the future aggrandizement of the whole community. The remora of Australia is the slowness of her capitalists to embark in any work of local and remote utility. Then will our morning star arise, when our merchants shall not, impatient for release, look only for quick returns; when the talk in our exchange shall be of investments, not only enriching the present generation, but pregnant with blessing to remote prosperity.

The fruits of Capital we might enjoy in the absence of the possessor. It is otherwise with the political and social benefits which an independent and cultured class is qualified to confer. We call our government a democracy,—a democracy as absolute as any which has yet existed. What, then, is a democracy? It is a government in which all artificial barriers are removed from the path of merit; in which, to quote the great Napoleon, a free career is open to genius and ability. It is a country in which the whole population is fitted by education, and trained by institutions to exercise that self-government which is the privilege and burden of a moral being.

It is chiefly as an element of social refinement that we require a settled population. It is difficult to estimate the gain to morality and knowledge which might accrue from the popular diffusion of taste and art-knowledge. There is no more dangerous tempter than the listless heart-vacancy which comes upon a man, when his day's work is over, who has no occupation to stimulate and engage without fatiguing his faculties. One great object of education is to provide employment for the hours of re-creation; to prevent the demon of ennui from possessing the empty and idle chamber with his lewd rabble rout. There is no question that the inhabitants of this sunny land,—framed by Nature herself for poetry and grace,—would fully appreciate the elevating influence of such culture. Among the visitors who thronged the Industrial Exhibition, lately held in Sydney, there were many impelled by no vulgar curiosity, but an earnest desire for improvement; the contributions themselves gave evidence enough of mechanical or poetic genius in our natives or residents. But how is this latent talent to be fostered and applied to the public benefit? Our mechanics and artists labour under disadvantages which until the present year seemed well nigh insurmountable. In a young community struggling for subsistence and absorbed in material pursuits, you cannot depend upon general sympathy; nor solely upon government patronage. The eye of the nation has to be opened; and the usefulness as well as interest of these pursuits to be vindicated by experience, before we can look for the support, or even the approbation of the colony at large.

It were well if every young Australian could drink with his own lips from the spring of [England's] gracious civilization. He is a true patriot who is not tempted to linger at her shrine; but comes back from his pilgrimage not regretful and dissatisfied, but with a hopeful and patient courage, resolved to make his brothers partakers in his gain; undaunted by opposition, unwearied by delay, persevering until by God's grace he too has laid one stone in the foundation of a 'New Britannia in another world.'

Institutions like this are the surest antidote against social misunderstanding. They are so by removing the only cause of misunderstanding, mutual ignorance and isolation; by giving us work to do together, in which the chief praise is awarded to no artificial preeminence but belongs to him who labours most zealously and effectively in the common cause. The Australian Schools of Arts are, if wisely used, no less than the Palladiums of our Nationality. Some have lamented the extension which has been given to the original design of these Institutions, which were only intended by the founders to teach Mechanics the scientific principles of their trades.

But our wants are not those of England thirty years ago: we require not only skill in a section of our people, but education for all; not mere art-culture but preparation for the general duties of society. To balance the drawbacks of colonial life there is always this advantage. A colonist cannot be a mere instrument; he is not a living part of some stupendous machinery; he must think and act for himself. Nothing is so striking to a European as the handiness of dwellers in the bush; their fertility of resource, and self-dependence in the absence of those appliances by which older civilizations forestall our wishes and prevent our thought. If we are the worse artists, we are perhaps the better men; if we have not a division of labour, we have a more varied development of the individual. With time and population will come the arts of refinement,—and perhaps its impotencies. Our object is not so much to teach, as to stimulate thought and promote self-training. Our best hope is the universal diffusion of curiosity and information. This will hardly be awakened by books. He would be a real benefactor, who in such a hall as this, and before a non-political audience, should explain the principles involved in the social questions which are agitating us, in easy and familiar, but not the less exact and careful language.

In a young community and scattered population, Schools of Arts are especially beneficial by making us conscious of our brotherhood, and by giving us a common interest and occupation free from the jealousies and misunderstandings which general or local policies are apt to engender. They diffuse useful information, sharpen the intellect, and bring out obscure or unconscious genius; they create refinement; quicken our social sympathies; pull down artificial barriers, and help those who would else be strangers, to talk face to face as friends: their happy influence reaches even the sanctuary of home; and, at least indirectly the holiest affections, and cherishes the tenderest associations. May God's blessing be upon the Wollongong School of Arts, and prosper it to His Glory, and to the material, intellectual, and moral advancement of its Members, and all whom they love.

Abridged.
Source: John Woolley, *Schools of Arts and Colonial Nationality: A Lecture Delivered at the Inauguration of the Wollongong School of Arts*, 28 May 1861, Reading and Wellbank, Sydney, 1861.

———

Charles Jardine Don
The 'West of England' Election Speech, 1864

Charles Jardine Don (1820–1866) was born in Scotland and was a stonemason by trade. As a teenager, he learned radical ideas at a mutual improvement society and later took part in the Chartist movement in 1842. He was a popular street orator, especially at Edinburgh's Market Cross, and a reputable opponent in Glaswegian debating societies. Lured by gold, Don immigrated to Australia with his family in 1853. He had little success at the Ballarat diggings and returned to his trade, becoming prominent in the Stonemasons' Union, the United Trades Association and the Victorian Eight Hours Labor League. He spoke frequently on industrial issues at Melbourne's Eastern Market and was known for his fiery speeches on the pressing need for land reform. In 1859 he won the seat of Collingwood, and his radical tone continued within the Victorian legislature. But Don's political career was strained by finances, and at times he laboured as a mason on Parliament House by day and sat in it as a member at night. On 15 October 1864, seeking parliamentary re-election, he addressed a 'numerous attended meeting' at the West of England Hotel in Kerr Street, Fitzroy. In his speech, he argued that the poverty of the city was a consequence of the inequity of land distribution. The meeting concluded with a motion that Don was 'a fit and proper person' to represent Collingwood in the Legislative Assembly—a sentiment however, that was not to be echoed by the electorate.

By way of introducing the subject of the rise and progress of Victoria, I quote a passage from *Spencer's 'Conditions essential to Human Happiness'*, as follows:—'Give us a guide,' cry men to the philosopher, 'we would escape from these miseries in which we are entangled; a better state is ever present to our imagination, and we yearn after it; but all our efforts to realize it are fruitless. We are weary of perpetual failures; tell us by what rule we may attain our desire.' Now, I do not pretend to say that I am either a philosopher, or a great statesman; but simply propose to give a common-sense suggestion of what I consider would tend as a cure to existing evils.

It is necessary for the future welfare and prosperity of Victoria that a proper system of colonization be established. The present system of colonization in Victoria, New Zealand, and Tasmania, was initiated under three distinct heads, viz: 'dear land,' 'assisted immigration,' and 'free trade.' You are all aware, no doubt, to what practical use this continent was submitted at its birth; I need not tell you that it was made a penal settlement for the reception of all the rascals (if I might use so strong a term) of Scotland, England, and Ireland. In course of time, however, the soil was found to be exceedingly fertile, and the climate well adapted for settlement. It was soon found that Victoria was a country possessing great inducements to the sober and industrious man; but unfortunately it was governed by a particular system of colonization; and instead of a class of immigrants being encouraged to frequent these shores who would assist in furthering the prosperity of the country, convicts were substituted in abundance.

I refer here to the schemes propounded by Mr [Edward] Gibbon Wakefield, and to the desire of the merchant princes (viz: the squatters) to reign supreme over the length and breadth of the land. It, however, soon became patent to these men that they could not reap the benefit of their acquired possession without labor, and their raw materials being put into practical use. It was next considered that scarcity of land was a necessary condition to cheap labor, and in order to prevent the poor man who arrived from getting his portion, these already large landowners bought up the land in every direction. A system of bounty immigration was next invented, for the direct purpose of reducing the wages of those already here. Slavery with all the horrors with which it was carried out in the West Indies, was similarly initiated here. The tariff was the next thing resorted to, and it was also so arranged as to act detrimentally to the interest of the poorer colonists. And what with their assisted, and bounty immigration, they threw open the 'rag fairs of the world.' (Laughter.) But while all this was going on, these mighty princes had not the slightest conception of the vast mineral resources of the country. They could see no farther through a blue stone than a mason could. (Cheers, and laughter.) They were not conscious of the great treasures of gold which lay concealed under their sheep walks. Soon, however, they were apprised of this fact; and very soon all their attempts to keep the people from flooding the goldfields proved ineffectual. In vain were the attempts of crown rangers to turn them off; wages got higher, and the poor man at length got practical possession of this nuggetty land. (Loud cheers.)

A population was then induced to visit these shores which would not have come under the old system for the next two or three hundred years. Those parties came who by their honest and persevering habits had been enabled to save a sufficient amount to pay their passage out; they were the young, healthy, and hardworking sons of the old country. A revolution was soon effected in Victoria, the goldfields were thrown open to the people, and if such facilities had been afforded the people in regard to other things, the same results would have followed.

Reverting to the squatters' possessions, the number of sheep in the colony is in round numbers about 7,000,000, and their average worth is 10s. per head. There are 80,000 horses, and about 78,000 pigs, besides a very large number of cattle (Laughter), which is equal to £8,000,000 or £9,000,000. This is a nice little amount to be divided amongst a few squatters, and a matter which appears to have escaped altogether the attention of the people. Unfortunately, during last parliament, these merchant princes succeeded in getting a firmer grasp of the land than ever before. The labor they employ—in comparison with the agriculturalist—is lamentably insignificant, and it is in consequence of this accursed monopoly that the poor man has to submit to a town life, dragging out a miserable existence. Indeed it is hard to say how some of these men live at all. It hurt me when I stood once on Batman's hill, and contemplated the vast amount of misery existing below. Numbers were only half their time employed, and well I know it. And all this had been matured under that system of 'dear land,' 'bounty immigration,' and 'free trade.'

Do you want such a state of things to continue? (No, no.) I know of a man and his three sons who, after selling their goods at less than the English market prices, could not find employment for more than three days in the week. This was what free trade is doing, it has produced this abundance of misery, and it is slowly, but surely, defeating all other attempts to make Victoria a prosperous country. For the future, it would be to the interest of the people to support a more beneficial system, by sending into parliament men who advocated cheap land, the abolition of bounty immigration, and a tariff so arranged as to give protection to native industry. (Applause.) We ought to have a system something similar to that adopted by the people of Canada, or the United States of America; but that adopted by the inhabitants of California, is the most preferable of the three. The land there is not so productive as the land of this colony; but the population has free selection over all the land in the country. Here the Government Surveyor goes out and points out the land for use; but I think that that official, in some instances, is not a better judge than the intending purchaser; and supposing that he is—well, it is just possible that he might have his reasons for not pointing out the best land. The squatters, no doubt, always give him a warm reception, and perhaps something warm before he retires to bed. (Laughter, and hear, hear.)

Hence the preference shown to America before Australia. There the agriculturalist can get his land for three-fourths less than he can here, and the farmer can graze his sheep wherever he likes. Now, the farmer of America brings his wool into the market, and protective principles insure him against foreign competition. San Francisco and other places are now manufacturing their own cloth, and some time ago I read an advertisement inviting the weavers of Great Britain and other countries to visit the shores of America. (Cheers.) This is indeed a practical realization of a proper system of colonization. Wages become higher, and labor more plentiful. The United States tariff is becoming more and more protective every year. At the close of the revolutionary war, about the year 1782, the population of that country numbered 2,000,000; and when the last census was taken, it was found that that number had increased to 30,000,000. Towns and cities sprang up in such quick succession, and other beneficial changes followed each other with such surprising rapidity that the people began to think they had been indulging in a beautiful dream; while others were as much astonished on reading its history as a good many had been when reading 'Aladdin, and the Wonderful Lamp;' or the 'Arabian Nights' Entertainments.' (Laughter.)

Even in a British settlement like Canada, the population increased in 16 years from 500,000 to 2,500,000. All this has resulted from a free land system, backed up by a protective tariff. And it must be palpable to all that these two principles will have to be adopted here, or else Victoria will rapidly begin to decline, and the current of immigration diminish. (Hear, hear.) Property, in Collingwood particularly, is rapidly going to ruin, and instead of being re-placed by pretty little stone houses, the owners are chiefly laboring under very precarious circumstances. The theories of John Stuart Mill, Adam Smith, and others of their class, will not answer here; nor are the people of this colony going to swallow their doctrines as though they were the evangelists of trade. (Applause.) Neither are you going to be led away by a fellow who would sell his mother for twopence an acre. (Laughter.) Regarding the ministerial policy, it certainly savoured to a great extent of what the country wanted, but I do not believe in leasing the land. They propose to give the people the land at 2s. an acre for five years, and the party who purchases the land over another's head, has to pay him for improvements. I am decidedly averse to the agricultural land being sold by auction, and will endeavor to get such a system set aside.

But I do not believe we will get everything we wanted until members of parliament are paid for their services; (Hear.) and I think if this included the members of the Upper House, this principle would the sooner be adopted. I have been five years now in that House, and I have always represented the constituency to the best of my ability. If you find a better man than me, then it would be to my interest, as well as to yours, to give that man the preference; but if not I certainly would like to have an opportunity of striking a bold stroke for those liberties which we have hitherto struggled to obtain. If rejected I will always look back on the time when I was elevated from the mechanics' bench to a seat in the Assembly, with infinite pride and pleasure. I hope you will give me some consideration—'nothing extenuate, nor set down aught in malice'—let you think of me as one who had worked hard by day, and has toiled to further your interests the live-long night. (Continued cheering.)

Abridged.
Transposed from indirect speech.
Source: *The Observer and County of Bourke Intelligencer* (Collingwood), 15 October 1864, pp. 2–3.

George Higinbotham
Religion and State Education, 1867

George Higinbotham (1826–1892) was a forceful orator who rose to be a defiantly liberal Chief Justice of Victoria from 1886. Dublin born, and educated at Trinity College, Higinbotham emigrated to Melbourne in 1854, where he practised law and had a stint as editor of the *Argus* newspaper. Higinbotham then entered politics, becoming attorney-general. He was passionate about one of the great social issues of the day: government support for education. There were two great points of contention. Firstly, what role would the rival Christian denominations play in state schools? Secondly, by what right could Parliament enforce a state system of education at all? In 1866 Higinbotham chaired a Royal Commission which recommended a free, compulsory state school system, in which a kind of ecumenical Christianity was taught. Recommending his reforms in a lengthy speech to the Victorian parliament on 7 May 1867, Higinbotham began by denouncing religious bickering (which, in the event, was to thwart his reforms), then addressed the issue of whether education should be compulsory.

This, also, is a subject on which considerable difference of opinion exists, and the name, perhaps, does not convey exactly either the effect or the intention of the proposal now made. The most useful effect of a compulsory law will be, that it will extend throughout the community a sense of the importance and necessity of education. Its existence will tend to establish the sound principle that, in questions of this kind, affecting the social condition, not merely of the present, but also of future generations, the State has a right to interfere. A law rendering instruction compulsory will not belong to that class of laws which it is necessary to enforce altogether or to refrain from enforcing at all. It is not one of those many laws which should not be passed unless it is intended that they shall be universally enforced. The compulsory system now proposed is to be enforced only where circumstances render it possible for parents to comply with the requirements of the Act. It is proposed that, in the first instance, at all events, the penalty shall be of a merely nominal character, and that, where circumstances, such as the non-existence of schools, render it impossible for the parent to instruct his children, the law shall not be enforced at all.

I am aware that a strong feeling exists against any system of compulsory instruction. It is believed by many persons, both here and in England, that the State has no right to interfere with the parent in a matter of this kind. It is said that the duty of a parent to instruct his child is an imperfect obligation only, and, as we do not enforce other imperfect obligations by the criminal law, the same rule should be observed in this case. It is hard to reason against a feeling which partakes of a foregone conclusion, or prejudice, rather than of anything based on rational grounds. But I think there are some circumstances which may lead us to the conclusion that it is only reasonable that, in this matter, the State should take such steps as may be deemed proper for creating and preserving in the community at large a sense of the duty of the adult population to give adequate instruction to the young population. In England, I believe, a considerable change of opinion is growing up on this question. The increasing knowledge of the benefits of the continental systems of education appears to be producing a change in the minds of thoughtful persons. I observe that, at a meeting recently held at Manchester, where the question was fully debated, a resolution was arrived at in these terms—'That, in the opinion of this meeting, it is desirable to make complete provision for the primary instruction of the children of the poorer classes, by means of local rates under local administration, with legal power, in cases of neglect, to enforce attendance at school.' I think this resolution is of special importance, in view of the place and the meeting at which it was passed; for I may say with truth, that very many, if not all of the principal social reforms which have been carried out in England in recent years, have either been originated in Manchester or have been actively supported in that city.

Now, sir, it must be recollected that, unless some compulsory system be introduced, the class of the population for whom instruction is most required will be the very class it will be impossible to reach by any other means. There is a large class of the younger population in England—and I am sorry to say that it is a class not unknown here, and which, according to the evidence of some witnesses, is rapidly increasing amongst us—which is gradually being sunk into such a state of poverty and degradation, that the mere ordinary means of education, if these means are not enforced, will not be used by that class, and consequently any system, however complete in other respects, will not succeed in reaching them.

The committee may not be aware of the startling fact that, in the city of Melbourne and its suburbs, no fewer than 500 children—of the same class as that which is known as ragged-school children in England—are, at the present time, in attendance at schools which have been created, and which, I believe, will have to be maintained as ragged schools. These children cannot be reached by the ordinary means of education, unless the State steps in and says to the parent—'Whenever you can give your child instruction, the State providing the means, and you neglect to do so, the State will regard you as an offender against the child, just as much as if, having the means, you neglected to provide for the subsistence of that child.' I will not further trespass on the time of the committee by pressing this point. It is, no doubt, one which deserves to be carefully considered, and which should not be adopted without full discussion and mature deliberation.

These are the points which, together with those I have already referred to, constitute the main elements of the plan of the commission. I believe that plan is a wise one, and I venture to expect very great benefits from it—benefits not merely to the young, but also to the adult portion of the population. I believe that great advantages will arise if, by any means, you can induce clergymen of the different religious bodies to join in a friendly co-operation with laymen in so important and necessary an object as the education of the young. Hitherto there has been no such combination. There has been nothing but rivalry and hostility. By bringing them together you will not only effect the primary object of providing instruction for the young, but you will go a great way towards allaying those dissensions and rivalries which now exist between the sects themselves. I hope that we are not to accept as a stereotyped fact that these sects are never to cease their dissensions. I hope we may look forward to the time when the sects will become aware of their total ignorance of the very points on which they so rancorously differ. [An Honorable Member— 'When the millennium comes.']

Well, sir, I do not know when that time may be—perhaps the honorable member is better informed—but I do hope that this blot upon our civilization and upon Christian philosophy will not be perpetuated throughout all generations. At present we are concerned only with the question of the education of the young, and not with the imparting of common sense and of rational conduct to the old. The subject of the instruction of the young is one on which, I believe, all politicians can earnestly and honestly unite. I believe it is one of the few topics on which politicians of the present day with sincere and earnest opinions can unite. Opinions on the political tendencies of the times are gradually becoming stronger in individuals and classes, and are assuming every day a form of more distinctly marked hostility. I do not regret that fact, because it is an indication of growing sincerity in politics, both here and in the mother country. Apart altogether from the interests which so largely and dangerously affect public opinion, disinterested opinion itself is divided, and that division is increasing as to the effect of political changes upon society at large.

There are some persons who regard the growing tendency towards the equalization of political rights with unfeigned alarm. They believe that the world is drifting towards social and political chaos. The opposite class believes that nothing which tends towards the equalization of individual rights can issue in aught injurious to the political constitution of society. Both these classes can combine upon the subject of the education of the young. The most advanced reformer will readily admit—nay, he will be the foremost to assert—that instruction is necessary for the cultivation of the individual, and that, if men are admitted to the equal possession of political rights, then, more than ever, they require the assistance of culture, to enable them to discharge the obligations which are always co-extensive with rights, in a manner safe for themselves and safe for the community. On the other hand, the conservative, or the so-called conservative—the man of the most ancient opinions—who admires, in the highest degree, times which he believe to have gone by, will also admit that the wild human animal is capable of some culture; and that, if the human savage, who now, from the ranks of the poor, demands to be placed on a level with his wealthy and, therefore, civilized fellow citizen, can be subjected to the influence of education; if his manners can be softened; if his character can be raised, and his understanding enlightened; then the danger arising from his admission to equal political rights will not be nearly so great as if he were left destitute of instruction and culture.

It is because I believe that all classes of politicians—real politicians, not those who merely vote and speak under the influence of interest, but politicians with convictions—and all classes in this country, can unite upon a question of this kind, and that the Bill proposes a system on which all classes can sincerely agree, that I venture to bring the question forward at this advanced stage of the session.

Abridged.
Source: *Victorian Parliamentary Debates*, vol. 91, 7 May 1867, pp. 904–6.

◆

Josiah Mitchell
Rational Cultivation, 1870

Josiah Mitchell (1822–1881) was one of the leading colonial exponents of scientific horticulture and agriculture, and a gardener of skill and imagination. He was employed at the Royal Botanic Gardens in Kew, England, before emigrating to Victoria in 1853, taking up a position at the Melbourne Botanic Gardens and laying out the garden at the Melbourne General Cemetery. Mitchell established a nursery business based on 'scientific principles' and by 1863 he had leased the Experimental Farm at Melbourne's Royal Park. There he was able to apply his wide reading and observational knowledge to a series of agricultural trials aimed at improving production in the new and challenging colonial conditions. A supporter of 'practical gardens' that demonstrated the application of horticultural practices, Mitchell was instrumental in the establishment of a mutual improvement society for gardeners and was a founding member of the Victorian Farmers' Union. An articulate speaker, on 5 May 1879 Mitchell addressed members of the Victoria Agricultural Society at Heidelberg. He was disturbed by the rapidity with which colonial farming practices led to exhaustion of the soil and he foresaw that the too-small blocks allocated to selectors would lead to both economic and environmental disaster. The introduction of agricultural education, the adoption of scientific methods and the politicization of farmers were the remedies that Mitchell sought under the radical banner of 'rational cultivation'— an early term for sustainable agriculture.

There are a large number of people who imagine that farming, or the cultivation of plants for the sustenance of man and the higher orders of animals, is a sort of business that anyone having the land may pick up and carry on without the slightest previous training or education to fit them for it; and as for there being an irrational as well as a rational mode of cultivation — why, such a thing is never dreamt of in their philosophy! 'To plough and sow, and reap and mow,' in the words of the old song, that, in their opinion, is to be a farmer. Many entertaining this absurd notion of farming are now being 'settled' on the land, and of course, become farmers.

But in addition to the class already pointed out, we have also in the country districts a large and ever-increasing number of Australian born youths, fast growing up to manhood. Those young men and boys will learn, whether we take the trouble to teach them or not. Their education, such as it is, relative to agriculture, is going on daily. It is imbibed from the practice they see carried on around them, and in which they are engaged. This being the case, from the nature of our prevailing practice of agriculture, it is much to be feared that those coming men into whose hands the cultivation of the land must fall in the course of time, will also become possessed of the erroneous notion that ploughing, sowing, &c., constitutes the sum total of cultivation. Their fathers, let us hope, they consider rational men; they will therefore naturally conclude that the farm practice carried on by them must be perfectly rational too, even although it may consist of growing 'wheat after wheat,' or successive grain crops and nothing else.

Let it not, however, be supposed that those two are the only classes interested in this important question. It affects the interests of the entire community. Yet strange to say, we drive along or 'go-a-head' as it is termed, at such pace that we have hitherto taken no time to inquire whether the seemingly prosperous course we have been pursuing is a rational one, or only the shortest road to ruin. We are rushing up our social edifice, putting in it, true, a lot, of 'scamped' work; paying much attention to 'schools of design;' to the technical education of the mechanic and the artisan, but with a blind and fatuous disregard as to whether the foundations of the structure are resting on the treacherous sands of avarice and speculation, or on the solid rock of rational agriculture, and honest industry. In all this hurry and hubbub to become a great and wealthy nation, the education of the agriculturist to fit him for carrying out his most important duties in connection with the State has been left to chance; no one seeming to trouble about it.

In the first place then; the growth of the same crop year after year on the same land, 'wheat after wheat' for instance; the production of successive grain crops without any manure, and with only an occasional bare fallow when the land becomes foul; burning straw instead of converting it into manure by the aid of stock, and restoring it again to the land; the laying down of land to grass after it has been exhausted by the growth of grain — these are some of our practices that are not rational because opposed to the laws of nature—rotation and restitution—which govern the growth of plants and the continued fertility of the soil. Rotation, I have said, is a law of nature that governs the growth of plants; it compels change of soil or situation. No plant will thrive continuously on the same spot. This applies as well to oak and pine forests as it does to wheat, oats, or any of our cultivated crops. The necessity for rotation or change of crop is caused, partly by exhaustion in the soil of elements essential for the healthy growth of the plant, and partly in consequence of the excretory matter thrown off by the roots rendering the soil unfit for its further growth. Yet one plant by its death and decay from these causes makes the most suitable preparation for the healthy growth of some other plant belonging to a different order. In this way the great globe we inhabit has been converted out of barren rocks into the thing of beauty we now see it, and became fitted for the sustenance of man. It is upon this law that the modern practice of British agriculture is founded, and no system of cultivation can be deemed rational if it does not embrace some rotation of crops. We now know that in conjunction with rotation we must also have restitution, or compensation, if we would maintain the fertility of the soil and avoid barrenness. Restitution and rotation should be the watchword, the creed, not merely as a matter of faith, but the every day practice of all who desire to cultivate rationally. We cannot go on ploughing and sowing, reaping and mowing, taking all away, and giving nothing back to replace the mineral substances removed from the land. We cannot, I say, long continue this system of robbery, even with some sort of rotation, without being brought face to face in the long run with one of these two alternatives, restitution or barrenness.

Nay, not only does the State look with indifference on the present system of spoliation without making any attempt to introduce a more rational one, but it actually, by 'settling the people,' as we are pleased to call it, on too small portions of land, renders an exhaustive practice compulsory on the part of the poor settler. We read of an exodus of farmers from already exhausted districts of South Australia, coming to Victoria to take the benefit of our recent Land Bill, and, of course, to pursue the same system here that has led to the necessity of their leaving South Australia. We are told by the *Hamilton Spectator* of farmers in the Western district, who having exhausted their own freeholds are now renting land on short lease at a high rent for the purpose, no doubt, of carrying on the same exhaustive practice. Meantime they have laid their own farms down to grass, to recover the lost fertility. Delusive hope! With the Government selections of 80-acre lots, how can we expect any attention to be paid to the natural laws of restitution and rotation, or any attempt at rational cultivation?

It is not my intention to attempt to lay down any course of cropping. Everyone must decide this matter for himself according to circumstances, climatic conditions and local requirements. In one part of the colony it may be dairy stock in conjunction with grain growing; in another, sheep;

in a third, the purchase of phosphatic manures, and the ploughing in of an occasional crop of green manure. But this I may say, that whatever system may be adopted it must be based on the laws of restitution and rotation. In colonial agriculture generally the natural tendency seems to be to begin at the wrong end. Instead of starting from grass and the depasturing of stock, the production of grain is made the starting point. By the continued production of grain alone the land becomes exhausted, and thereby unable to produce grass except of the most worthless and innutritious description. Now, the rational course would be to start from grass as a basis, and in conjunction with this, through green crops, stock, and manure, advance to grain; then, in the course of any rotation, back again to grass. The first step, however, towards the initiation of such a course of practice is the subdivision of farms into fields; the next, keeping stock and taking care of the muck; after that rotation of crops, and last, but most important of all, restitution.

That a system of rational cultivation will not pay in this colony I deny. The truth in this matter is not left without witnesses. For, although an exhaustive practice is the prevailing one, and tenant farmers can hardly be expected to follow any other, yet I know several farmers who cultivate their own freeholds on a rational system, and who make it pay too. It is also a cheering sign of the times that many are now impressed with the necessity of some change, and anxious to adopt a more enduring system.

First on the list of things that would tend to promote rational agriculture, I will venture to mention farmers' clubs, such as this society has had the honor of introducing to the colony, or, as they might be called, farmers' schools for grown up pupils, 'Where each by turn is teacher and is taught.' They are the most readily available and practicable means of agricultural education that we have at hand. These clubs and the national shows of the Royal and Highland Societies have done more to advance British agriculture to its present position of high excellence, than anything else. They have taught the British farmer to think, and to express his thoughts. I can assure you, although you may not think it, I read with far more interest and profit the papers and discussions of some of those farmers' clubs in the old country, than I do even the parliamentary debates in our own. Through these clubs, and the agency of the Press in diffusing the knowledge gleaned at their meetings, and by that strength which such union gives, the British farmer is fast becoming a power in the State.

Now, if farmers' clubs can effect such revolutions as they have done, in the practice, in the social and intellectual position, and in the political influence of the farmer at home, why should they not produce the same results in this country? Farmers' clubs are a far greater necessity as a means of collecting and diffusing information in a new country like this, than in an old one. Here we have a climate so widely different from that of the old country, that we have as it were to begin afresh, and elaborate a practice in accordance with climatic and local requirements. Nothing can aid us more in doing this, and in devising some course of rational cultivation, than periodical meetings of farmers, to 'reason together' on questions affecting their interests and the progress of their art. By such means many valuable facts derived from practical experience, and that would otherwise be lost, will be collected and recorded. It is from farmers' clubs that some scheme for the education of young farmers should emanate, and the neglect of their education, as I have already pointed out, may be attended with injurious consequences to the State. I hope soon to see them flourishing in every district in the colony, and I feel sure their establishment will be attended by good results to farmers themselves, and to the community at large.

Abridged.
Source: *The Leader*, 14 May 1870, pp. 6–7.

———◆———

Thomas Fellows
Against Compulsory and Secular Education, 1872

Thomas Howard Fellows (1822–1878) was educated at Eton and arrived in Melbourne aged thirty. He became a prominent citizen of Melbourne, carving out a career in the law, in politics, and as a judge of the Supreme Court of Victoria. Fellows was conservative on social issues, and so was inclined to support the interests of the large land owners and to mistrust the spirit of egalitarianism. As a member of Victoria's Legislative Council, he was greatly discomforted in 1872 when the parliament introduced a system of secular, compulsory and free education. In effect, this Education Act laid the basis on which government schools still operate today. But when the Bill came before Victoria's upper house, Fellows was torn between his mistrust of state coercion and his fear of an uneducated under-class. As a pious Anglican, he was also dismayed by the exclusion of religion from the curriculum of government schools. Fellows resolved his discomfiture by proposing a system of state aid to private schools. He was, in effect, an early advocate of 'choice' as more important than equality in the state funding of education.

What right has the State to interfere on the subject of education? That appears to me to lie on the threshold of every proposition of this nature, because, until we have ascertained what that right is, it is utterly impossible to deal with the question. Abstractedly, I contend that the State has no right at all to interfere with education, any more than with a man's religion, or his food, or his clothing. Practically, I will admit the right, but only, I wish it to be understood, when the matter is regarded as one of police, pure and simple. That ignorance is a prolific source of crime is an axiom nobody can be more fully inclined to accept than I am, and it appears to me that only to that extent has the State a right to interfere with the question of education.

That point established, the next that arises is how and to what extent that interference is justifiable, consistently with the maintenance of the proposition, already placed on our statute-book, involving the existence here of perfect civil and religious liberty and equality. If any system of education involving religious teaching is insisted upon by the State, there is, of course, at once a palpable violation of the civil and religious liberty of the subject; and if, on the other hand, it is made compulsory to abstain utterly from all religious teaching, the liberty of those who think that religious teaching ought to form part of all instruction is at once infringed. This appears to me to be the great difficulty in considering the Bill before us.

I perfectly agree with the Government, that the State has a right to compel education to a certain extent—an extent which it and all other bodies can recognize, namely, that of the elementary and primary education hinted at—but for persons to be compelled to educate their children in the manner which the State may deem requisite, is quite another thing. If education is enforced up to a certain standard, the difficulty which at once strikes me is, the mode in which that standard is to be attained. I understand the Legislature declaring that all children shall be educated up to a certain standard, but not the justice of establishing the mode in which it is to be done. When the State interferes to compel parents to educate their children in a certain manner, it appears to me that the civil liberty of the subject is infringed. I was somewhat surprised when the Attorney-General stated that he considered this a party question, because it struck me he was imperceptibly allowing himself to be dragged into the common herd of those who are too apt to make onslaughts on the personal liberty of the people of this country.

Mr. Longmore.—Who are they?

Mr. Fellows.—Those who, like many honorable members of this House, are inclined to interfere with personal liberty. We have other instances of it. I alluded to one at the time this question was dealt with on a former occasion. The Permissive Bill is another. A man has a right to do what he pleases. Whether he abstains or whether he drinks, it is his own look out, and no one else's; and any attempt to thwart him by legislation, or to force him to do one or the other, is to interfere with his personal liberty.

Mr. Casey.—Why stop him from gambling?

Mr. Fellows.—Because that is a crime of itself. Drunkenness is also a crime, and I am quite prepared to punish those who get drunk whenever and wherever they get drunk; but that is not the object of nor the question involved in the Permissive Bill. When we find a man like the Attorney-General allowing himself imperceptibly to be dragged in with those who are inclined to tyrannize over others, it is high time to beware of persons who do not occupy the position which he does. That is the light in which

I view this Bill. If the education of all children up to a certain point is to be paid for by the State, I can understand the proposition; but I want to know why it should not be admitted, also, that a person who brings into the market an article in the shape of education equal to that procurable in any Government school, but which has not been derived from sources provided by the State, ought to be paid for it?

I want to know why, in point of fact, we should establish Government schools at all, except in outlying districts, where the population is sparse and small? Why in thickly populated districts there should be Government schools at all I cannot understand. If the State pays for schools, it gives a certain amount of money to be divided among those who are to be educated, according to their number. That amount is, in effect, divisible by the number to be taught. Why, then, if a certain sum is appropriated to each child for the purpose of his education, should the Government not let the quota of money be spent wherever the person or persons concerned please? If some such principle were engrafted on this Bill, it would remove many of the objections entertained to it.

It may be said that engrafting such a principle on this Bill will be to initiate or rather continue denominational education. Suppose that is the effect; who suffers? If people choose, whether through whim, fancy, or prejudice, to indulge in that kind of education, why should they not have their wish? If, on the other hand, they choose to have schools in which all religious teaching is abolished, why should they not be at perfect liberty to do so? I ask honorable members to consider, as a question of personal liberty, whether the objections entertained against the measure may not, in this way, be satisfactorily dissipated? Perfect equality will then exist. The right of each person or each child to receive his portion of the State benefaction for the purpose of education will be conceded; and, that point settled, he can spend the money how he pleases—on this condition, that the money is only paid when the education comes up to a certain standard, which fact can be ascertained by authorized Government inspectors. I merely wish honorable members to keep this broad principle in view before they come to consider the Bill at its second reading—to ask themselves whether they are willing to enforce throughout the country a system of education in which all people cannot equally and conscientiously participate.

AN HONORABLE MEMBER.—Why?

MR. FELLOWS.—I don't want to know why. I don't care why. It is an infraction of personal liberty to ask why. It is their will, and they choose it to be so—that is why. As to education being free, that is a new view into which I do not wish to go now. I agree to education being compulsory, provided the mode does not involve an infraction of personal liberty.

I have already said that education must be regarded to a certain extent as a matter of police, otherwise the State would have no right to interfere at all. To that extent I am quite prepared to vote for compulsory education, provided the mode is left to the choice of those who are compelled to be taught. As to the secular division of the question, it is just as tyrannical to compel secular education as to compel religious education. When a child is compelled to submit to religious education it is tyranny.

I hope the House will not lose sight of the principle which I maintain, and which is assailed in all directions—that of personal liberty. That principle may be laughed at now, but the time will come when people will be glad to recognize it, and be sorry that, when they had the opportunity, they did not do so more effectually. I make these remarks now because I am satisfied that that principle is being lost sight of. I have no great affection for one system of education more than another, but I say let each man do as he pleases; and if the State is going to pay for all, let each one get his proportion of payment in the way that suits him, so long as he gives to the State what it pays for. To go beyond that will raise up in this country an acrimonious feeling which it will take a long time to get rid of, particularly when, as on the present occasion, the question is introduced as one that must be discussed in a party spirit.

Abridged.
Source: *Victorian Parliamentary Debates*, vol. 15, 12 September 1872, pp. 1355–7.

Charles Pearson
Land Tax, 1877

Charles Henry Pearson (1830–1894) was a historian, a journalist, a politician and an educational reformer. Born in London, he attended King's College, London, and Oxford University and between 1855 and 1864 he was professor of Modern History at the former. In 1864 diagnosis of a 'sluggish liver' sent him to South Australia, where he bought a sheep run at Mount Remarkable and lived on the land during a period of extended drought. Pearson returned to an academic post at Trinity College, Cambridge and published on the history of England, pioneering the historical use of maps. But he was back in South Australia in 1871, married, and eventually secured a lectureship at the University of Melbourne in History and Political Economy. He established the university debating club as a lively forum on social and political questions. In 1855 Pearson became headmaster of the new Presbyterian Ladies' College, and was outspoken on the rights of women to participate in higher education. His interests were extending to wider debates about colonial government, including a more equitable system of land ownership. At the invitation of the National Reform and Protection League—which opposed the political and economic power of pastoral and commercial interests—he addressed a 'monster meeting' at the Princess Theatre on 19 February 1877. Pearson called for the introduction of a progressive land tax. The lecture's impact was immediate: Pearson was branded a 'class traitor' in the press and forced to resign from Presbyterian Ladies' College. He then turned to a career in politics, entering the Legislative Assembly and conducting a major enquiry into education.

I well understand the reason of the old Greek law which enacts that in times of civil strife all men shall show themselves in the street and take part on either one side or the other. It is considered better that heads shall be counted in this rough way than that the minority should afterwards say they had not brought their full force into the field. (Cheers.) That is one of the reasons why the people as a body should speak out at the present general election, and, speaking as a Liberal, I think you should have no fear of the result. (Cheers.)

There is, I might say, scarcely anything more loudly—and I might say, more impudently—denied than that large estates in land are being concentrated to any great extent in Victoria. I think that if I quote the case of England it will not be considered an unfair illustration to guide political economists in our colony.

Accepting this comparison then, we find that a Doomsday book has been published last year in England, stating exactly the extent of the landed property in the country, and the manner in which it is distributed amongst the people. At the same time in this colony there is, for purposes of comparison, the admirable returns of Mr. Hayter, the Government statistician, showing exactly how the land is distributed in Victoria. What is the result of the comparison? We find that in England the whole of the soil is at present divided amongst 4,500 proprietors, whilst in Victoria one half of the public estate is in the hands of 700 proprietors. (Cheers.) If we go on alienating the public estate in future at the same rate as it has been alienated in the past, by the time that all the available land in Victoria is alienated—of course I left out of my calculation all the land that is not considered of any value—you will find an extent of country, half as large as England, has passed into the hands of not 4,500 persons, as in England—but less than 2,000 landowners. (Cheers.) This colony has only been in existence about 40 years, instead of centuries, and what has been the work of centuries in England has not only been effected, but exaggerated, in Victoria within that short time. (Applause.)

There is no reason that can be urged to show that the tendency to accumulation is less now than at any former time, because we cannot shut our eyes to what is passing outside our boundaries. Without wishing to criticise the policy of the neighbouring colony of New South Wales, we cannot but see that New South Wales is parting with large tracts of land at a very small price, and it is equally well known that the principal purchasers of these large properties in Riverina are men who have small freeholds in Victoria ranging from 20,000 to 100,000 acres. ('Hear, hear,' and laughter.) It is therefore rather unfair to suppose that the tendency to the accumulation of land in this colony is stopped, or even checked, even for a time, because even rich men, backed up by the banks, cannot buy in

Victoria and in other places at the same time. (Applause.) I hope, however, that the electors of Victoria will see the danger that threatened us in the future by the accumulation of those large estates, not only in our own colony, but also in New South Wales and South Australia. On this question the interests of all Australians are the same. (Cheers.).

I think, however, that before such an audience as this present one, it is unnecessary for me to disclaim any hostility to the rich. (Hear, hear.) Any man avowing communist sentiments in Victoria would be like a wolf amongst sheep, because the people of this colony are distinguished for their law-abiding spirit and their respect for property. (Cheers.) I profoundly respect those rich men who regard themselves as the trustees of their property for the good of mankind, such as Cornell and Peabody, but I cannot say that I will leave to the judgment of all rich men the disposal of all our riches. A few Rothschilds owning 25 millions sterling of money would not prove a great danger, but a few Rothschilds owning the same amount in land would prove a great principle of danger in the country where they exist. It is certainly not right to invest in the rich such powers as we have seen them posses in other countries, neither the power to deny permission for the erection of churches or schools, and neither is it good for the poor that they should be shut out from rights, which lowers their self-respect.

But I know that to men of English temperament—men reverencing law almost pedantically—nothing speaks like a precedent, and fortunately we have precedents in the English constitution for interference with the proprietorship of land much more violent than any that have been proposed here. Some 600 years ago it was feared by the King of England and the barons that the church was acquiring too large a portion of the soil of the country. There was no feeling against the church at that time. The King was a crusader, and the barons were all interested in monasteries and churches. Nonetheless did Parliament pass a law so stringent that our modern Conservatives would shrink from the mere mention of it. The name of that statute is an instructive one; it is called the statute of mortmain, or the dead-hand, because those corporations holding large tracts of land were supposed to hold them with the stiff, unrelenting grasp of a dead man. Although that was 600 years ago, the law then passed is still in force in England.

The law which the National Reform League proposes will tend to have the effect of a very moderate mortmain law, and we may go back to a constitutional custom of 600 years ago, dating from Edward I and continuing to the present time, and approved by all historians, and consecrated by usage, as their authority. (Cheers.) But there are more modern precedents too. Thirty years ago it was found that a number of estates in Ireland were heavily encumbered. Parliament dealt with Ireland a little more mercilessly perhaps than it would have dealt with England. (Laughter.) A law was passed creating a court, under which these estates were sold, and that court in 10 years actually disposed of 3,000 estates, or one seventh of the landed property of the kingdom. In the opinion of an

Irish lawyer that law was the most revolutionary interference with the rights of property that has ever been attempted. Lastly, within seven years another act has been passed extending the Ulster tenant right, more or less, to other parts of Ireland, giving the peasant a right in his labour and improvements. Surely we might here follow the example of the most conservative country in the world. (Cheers)

I urge, in conclusion, that this question of a land tax be made a test question with all candidates. (Cheers.) I beg you to remember that, although men might ring the changes on land, property, and income tax, there is really no connection whatever between a land and an income tax. An income tax is a tax upon labour and earnings, and has the effect of taxing again those who have been already taxed once in the way we like best through the tariff. (Cheers.) The shibboleth of all political liberals should therefore be 'a land-tax, pure and simple.'

The final point to which I will allude has lately been raised by an able letter from one of the landowners, viz., 'That inasmuch as when the squatters bought their land no mention was made of a land tax being imposed, they were therefore entitled to be free from a land tax for all time to come.' (Laughter.) Well, I will not then go into the question of policy—upon which we are all pretty well agreed; I will only say it is now the duty, and a question of simple honesty, of all liberals to see that in all future land sales there should be no mistake on that point. (Cheers and laughter.) The sooner a mistake of this kind is corrected, the sooner those who bought land know that it is not exempted, as nothing else in the country is exempted, the better it will be for all classes. Meanwhile the landowners must comfort themselves by reflecting that if the tax is not mentioned in the conditions of sale, neither is the 10 to 20 million [pounds] which the state has spent in improving their properties by railways and other works. (Loud cheers.)

Abridged.
Transposed from indirect speech.
Source: *Argus*, 20 February 1877, p. 6.

—————•—————

Redmond Barry
The Sentencing of Ned Kelly, 1880

Redmond Barry (1813–1880) was an Anglo–Irish lawyer who emigrated to the township of Melbourne in 1839 and thereafter made a vigorous contribution to the development of cultural institutions as the settlement evolved into a bustling, modern metropolis. He was the first Chancellor of the University of Melbourne, was founder of the Public Library and Art Gallery and was influential in copious social and philanthropic activities. In 1851 Barry became the colony's inaugural solicitor-general, and a year later he was appointed a Judge of the Supreme Court. On the bench Barry was known for his logical, if sometimes sanctimonious, summaries of legal cases. His judgments were conservative and, in criminal cases, often harsh; he was a decisive believer in the need for order in 'new' societies. On 28–29 October 1880 Barry presided over the most infamous trial of his career when Edward 'Ned' Kelly (1855–80) was charged with the murder of Thomas Lonigan. The alleged incident had occurred two years earlier at Stringybark Creek, when Kelly and his gang fatally ambushed a group of police. They were to become Australia's most legendary bushrangers, going on to rob a bank at Euroa, bail up the residents of Jerilderie, New South Wales, and in June 1880 face the police in a blazing shoot-out at Glenrowan. Kelly, the only survivor, was arrested wearing home-made metal armour. His exploits —symbolizing a democratic resistance to authority and injustice, and highlighting the plight of impoverished small farmers, especially of the Catholic Irish 'underclass'— had transformed him into a popular hero. The trial proceedings were highly charged but the jury took a mere thirty minutes to agree on a verdict of guilty. When asked by Barry whether he wished to make a statement, Kelly responded:

Well it is rather too late for me to speak now … It is not that I fear death; I fear it as little as to drink a cup of tea … On the evidence that has been given, no juryman could have given any other verdict … I lay blame on myself that I did not get up yesterday and examine the witnesses, but I thought that if I did so, it would look like bravado and flashiness.

Barry then addressed the court, with some interjections from Kelly, before pronouncing the death sentence. Kelly was hanged in Melbourne on 11 November 1880—and Barry was to die following a short illness only twelve days later.

Barry
The facts are so numerous, and so convincing, not only as regards the original offence with which you are charged, but with respect to a long series of transactions covering a period of 18 months, that no rational person would hesitate to arrive at any other conclusion but that the verdict of the jury is irresistible, and that it is right. I have no desire whatever to inflict upon you any personal remarks. It is not becoming that I should endeavour to aggravate the sufferings with which your mind must be sincerely agitated.

Kelly
No, I don't think that. My mind is as easy as the mind of any man in this world as I am prepared to show before God and man.

Barry
It is blasphemous for you to say that. You appear to revel in the idea of having put men to death.

Kelly
More men than me have put men to death, but I am the last man in the world that would take a man's life. Two years ago, even if my own life was

at stake, and I am confident I thought a man would shoot me, I would give him a chance of keeping his life and I would rather part with my own. But if I knew that through him innocent persons' lives were at stake I certainly would have to shoot him if he forced me to do so, but I would want to know that he was really going to take innocent life.

Barry
Your statement involves a cruelly wicked charge of perjury against a phalanx of witnesses.

Kelly
I dare say, but a day shall come at a bigger court than this when we shall see which is right and which is wrong. No matter how long a man lives, he is bound to come to judgement somewhere, and as well here as anywhere. It will be different the next time they have a Kelly trial, for they are not all killed. It would have been for the good of the Crown had I examined the witnesses and I would have stopped a lot of the reward, I can assure you; and I do not know if I will do it yet, if allowed.

Barry
An offence of this kind is of no ordinary character. Murders have been discovered which had been committed under circumstances of great atrocity. They proceeded from motives other than that which actuated you. They have had their origin in many sources. Some have been committed from a sordid desire to take from others the property they had acquired, some from jealousy, some from a desire for revenge, but yours is a more aggravated crime, and one of larger proportions, for with a party of men you took up arms against society, organised as it is for mutual protection, and for respect of law.

Kelly
That is the way the evidence came out here. It appeared that I deliberately took up arms of my own accord, and induced the other three men to join me for the purpose of dong nothing but shooting down the police.

Barry
In new communities, when the bonds of society are not so well linked together as in older countries, there is unfortunately a class which disregards the evil consequences of crime. Foolish, inconsiderate, ill-conducted, unprincipled youth unfortunately abound, and unless they are made to consider the consequences of crime, they are led to imitate notorious felons whom they regard as self-made heroes. It is right therefore that they should be asked to consider and reflect upon what the life of a felon is. A felon who has cut himself off from all decencies, all the affections, charities and all the obligations of society is as helpless and degraded as a wild beast of the field. He has nowhere to lay his head, he has no one to prepare for him the comforts of life, he suspects his friends, he dreads his enemies, he is in constant alarm lest his pursuers should reach him, and his only hope is that he might use his life in what he considers a glorious struggle for existence.

That is the life of the outlaw or felon, and it would be well for those young men who are so foolish as to consider that it is brave of a man to sacrifice the lives of his fellow creatures in carrying out his own wild ideas to see that it is a life to be avoided by every possible means, and to reflect that the unfortunate termination of your life is a miserable death. New South Wales joined with Victoria in providing ample inducement to persons to assist in having you and your companions apprehended, but by some spell which I cannot understand—a spell which exists in all lawless communities more or less—which may be attributed either to a sympathy for the outlaws, or a dread of the consequences which would result from the performance of their duty—no persons were found who would be tempted by the reward. The love of country, the love of order, the love obedience to law, have been set aside for reasons difficult to explain, and there is something extremely wrong in a country where a lawless band of men are able to live for 18 months disturbing society. During your short life you have stolen, according to your own statements, over 200 horses.

Kelly
Who proves that?

Barry
More than one witness has testified that you made the statement on several occasions.

Kelly
That charge has never been proved against me, and it is held in English law that a man is innocent until he is found guilty.

Barry
You are self-accused. The statement was made voluntarily by yourself. Then you and your companions committed attacks on two banks and appropriated therefrom large sums of money, amounting to several thousands of pound. Further, I cannot conceal from myself the fact that an expenditure of £50,000 has been rendered necessary in consequence of the acts with which you and your party have been connected. We have had samples of felons and their careers, such as those of Bradly and O'Connor, Clark, Gardiner, Melville, Morgan, Scott, and Smith, all of whom have come to ignominious deaths; still the effect expected from their punishment has not been produced. This is much to be deplored. When such examples as these are so often repeated society must be reorganised, or it must soon be seriously affected. Your unfortunate and miserable companions have died a death which probably you might rather envy, but you are not afforded the opportunity—.

Kelly
I don't think there is much proof that they did die that death.

Barry
In your case the law will be carried out by its officers. The gentlemen of the jury have done their duty. My duty will be to forward to the proper

quarter the notes of your trial and to lay, as I am required to do, before the Executive any circumstances connected with your trial that my be required. I can hold out to you no hope. I do not see that I can entertain the slightest reason for saying you can expect anything. I desire to spare you any more pain, and I absolve myself from anything said willingly in any of my utterances that may have unnecessarily increased the agitation for your mind. I have now to pronounce your sentence.

Justice Barry then sentenced the prisoner to death in the usual form, ending with the usual words, 'May the Lord have mercy on your soul'.

Kelly
I will go a little further than that, and say that I will see you where I go.

Reproduced in full.
Source: *Argus*, 30 October 1880, p. 8.

———————

William Windeyer
The Mt Rennie Rape Case, 1886

William Charles Windeyer (1834–1897) was a Sydney-based barrister and politician committed to law reform and education. Appointed a judge of the New South Wales Supreme Court in 1879, Windeyer held strong views on the rights of women and children, was a supporter of law and order, and had no fear of controversy. On 9 September 1886 around twenty men, mostly teenagers, had participated in or been present at the brutal rape (or 'outrage', as it was known) of sixteen-year-old Mary Jane Hicks—who, as a consequence, attempted suicide. The crime occurred in the bushy wasteland of Mt Rennie, now the site of Moore Park Golf course in inner Sydney. Eleven men were brought to trial amid a furore of press debate and cries of moral outrage at the criminal behaviour of the notorious Sydney 'pushes' or gangs. The Mt Rennie case had been preceded by serial rapes of women in the impoverished suburbs of Woolloomooloo and Waterloo. Although in these cases 'push' members had been brought to trial, juries were reluctant to convict because the crime of rape attracted a mandatory death sentence in New South Wales. But Windeyer's conduct of the Mt Rennie trial became newsworthy. Intent on a speedy decision, the court sat as late as 3.30 a.m., with many of the accused falling asleep. On the sixth day Windeyer addressed the jury for an extraordinary period of ten hours without a break, in one of the longest summing-up speeches in the history of the British judicial system. The jury found nine men guilty, and Windeyer sentenced the accused in a stern and emotive address.

Huge public meetings expressed opposition to these mass executions. Under pressure, the government commuted the sentences of five men. The remaining four —Martin, Duffy, Boyce and Read—were hanged before a crowd of more than two thousand people at Darlinghurst Gaol in January 1887. One outcome of the landmark Mt Rennie rape case, with its focus on the problems of youth crime, was the formation of workingmen's clubs. Yet, at the same time, young working-class males only became more suspicious of a legal system seen to favour the wealthy, and juries were even less likely to pronounce men charged with rape as guilty.

Prisoners, you have been convicted of a most atrocious crime, a crime so horrible that every lover of his country must feel that it is a disgrace to our civilisation. I am glad to find that this case has been tried by a jury that has had the intelligence to see through the perjury upon perjury that has been committed on your behalf, and the courage to declare the truth as they see it. It is terrible to think that we should have amongst us in this city a class worse than savages, lower in their instincts than the brutes below us. No language could express the abhorrence of right-thinking men of a scene such as that described by witness after witness in this case, as this poor defenceless girl, friendless and alone, is, like some wild animal, hunted down by a set of savages, who spring upon her and outrage her until she lies a lifeless thing before them, and then, when returning consciousness brings with it the terror of further outrage, she, in frenzy, seeks in such opportunity of death as seems to present itself a refuge from the horrors of her life.

I warn you to prepare for death. No hope of mercy can I extend you. Be sure no weakness of the [Legislative] Executive, no maudlin feeling of pity, will save you from the death you so richly deserve. Those who are charged with the administration of our affairs, to whose keeping is confided the safety of the public, will remember there are things more precious to society than life itself—the honour of our women and the safety of our families, compared with which the wretched lives of criminals such as you are of no account.

It is true that you are young, but the remembrance of that fact is coupled with the recollection that not twice nor thrice has public feeling been horrified by the perpetration of similar crimes by young men like yourselves. The present outrage is, I believe, the outcome of the past, and I solemnly express my belief that this culminating atrocity has been brought about by the immunity from the death penalty which your class has so long enjoyed upon the ground of your youth.

I hold in my hand a list of crimes similar to this which have been perpetrated during the last few years. The first is an outrage that was committed by a number of young men upon a girl in the neighbourhood of Parramatta-street, but by some mischance a gross miscarriage of justice, as I believe, took place in the acquittal of the men. The difficulty of proving such cases is often great, and false evidence is always ready, too ready, at hand to throw its protecting shield around criminals of your class. This outrage was followed by an outrage upon a young woman at North Shore, and the perpetrators escaped the death penalty on account of their youth. After this an outrage took place upon an old woman in the neighbourhood of Ultimo, and I have not the slightest hesitation in saying that a miscarriage of justice took place there in the acquittal of the prisoners, young men like yourselves—an acquittal which amazed me, as the evidence was of the clearest kind. This was followed by another, where the wretched woman was done to death somewhere in the neighbourhood of the locality now made infamous by this crime; and again, as I believe, a miscarriage of justice took place in the entire acquittal of all concerned. This was followed up by another frightful outrage in Woolloomooloo, where the wretched creature was found lying dead, like a dog, naked in the street, under circumstances of outrage too horrible to mention. Only one of the ruffians who outraged her was brought to justice, but escaped with his life. Again, last year I tried eight men for a concerted outrage of this kind upon an old woman under circumstances too disgusting to refer to. They escaped the death penalty too, and the outcome of all this mistaken leniency, and failure to convict, is this culminating horror.

You cannot expect that those who are charged with the execution of the law will hesitate under all these circumstances in handing you over to the death which you most righteously deserve. Outrages such as this are not committed on the daughters of the rich, the surroundings of whose life give their children protection, but upon the daughters of the people, who in the pursuit of their honest avocations are compelled to go about alone exposed to attacks of such gangs of ruffians as choose to assault them. Under all those circumstances be sure no pity will be extended to you; our pity must be reserved for the homes that are desolated and the victims who are wrecked for life by outrages such as these.

I warn you not to waste your time in idle protestations of your innocence. I advise you to prepare to meet your Maker; and if you are capable of understanding the position in which you stand, remember that your time is short. The recommendation to mercy which the jury have made in your favour it will be my duty to convey to the Executive. Your fate rests with them, not with me; but I can hold out no hope that this recommendation will be acted upon after all that has taken place of late years in this country. The time has come when a terrible example must be made of those who seem to be restrained by no pity for their victims, no sense of shame, no dread of the loathing of their fellows. Crimes such as yours it is too clear can only be restrained by the fear of death, the fate which awaits you. I have now but one duty to discharge, and that is to pass upon you the last dread sentence of the law.

[Silence having been called, His HONOR, naming each of the prisoners, said]: The sentence of the Court is that you be taken hence to the place from whence you came, and thence, on a day hereafter to be named by the Governor in Council, to the place of execution, and that there you be severally hanged by the neck until your bodies be dead. God help you to repent of this crime.

Reproduced in full.
Source: *Sydney Morning Herald*, 29 November 1886, p. 5.

The Bulletin

A Centennial Oration: Eureka—The Day We Ought to Celebrate, 1888

The *Bulletin* (1880–) was in rebellious mood in January 1888, as many citizens of New South Wales prepared to celebrate the centenary of the arrival of the First Fleet in Sydney Cove. Under the editorship of J. F. Archibald the newspaper had swiftly become an influential vehicle for a 'school' of nationalist writers who advanced the cause of popular democracy and republicanism. In an imaginary 'Centennial Oration', the biggest selling weekly in Australia denounced 26 January as a shameful anniversary. The pages of convict history, said the *Bulletin*, 'smell of the gaol; they are marked with the rust-prints of gyves; they are bruised and branded with the lash'. The event that all true democrats *ought* to celebrate, it announced, was the miners' revolt at the Eureka Stockade on 3 December 1854. For this was the fight in which Australians had died defying the British Empire and giving voice to their own democratic will. The story of Eureka, according to the *Bulletin's* imaginary speechmaker, went like this:

When gold was found, all the brawn and brain of Europe flocked to the port of Melbourne. These were men who came in search of wealth 'tis true, but men who dared danger and death and loved adventurous enterprise, many of them, as much as they loved gold. They were not as the commercial thieves and titled spongers who visit the colonies in later degenerate days. These gold-searchers were the fathers of Victoria, and almost the first thing that happened after their multitudinous invasion was collision with the cut-and-dried system of government provided so generously by England and copied so slavishly from the fusty pattern furnished by the alleged 'mother colony.'

The Victorian Legislative Council, composed partly of nominee and partly of presumedly-elected members, knew not the people—the diggers. Those sons of toil were not represented in the official-filled and squatter-bossed councils of the State. They paid an exorbitant fine for the privilege of working. They were hounded like dogs by the insolent brats who wore the Government uniform. Digger-hunting was huge sport. Miners were chained up by the 50 like a road-gang, and dragged to the police-court to be fined. Two days every week were devoted by the authorities to hunting for unlicensed diggers.

By and by a man named Scobie was killed in a brawl at Ballarat, and his murderer was acquitted by the police magistrate who tried the case. The enraged diggers burnt down the assassin's hotel, and MacIntyre, Westerly and Fletcher were imprisoned for the act. A demand was made by their comrades for their release, and it was refused.

The soldiers marched up from Melbourne to keep order and were harassed by the diggers who hung upon their trail. Then came the weekly hunt for unlicensed miners, with the red-coated rabble to support the police.

The diggers resisted and enrolled themselves in a citizen army under the leadership of Peter Lalor, noblest of diggers and of opponents to the first manifestation of aggressive Imperialism in Victoria. On 3 December 1854—the day we ought to celebrate—met this little representative Democracy and the paid bloodhounds of unjust authority. It was Sunday morning, the day upon which Officialism was wont to repair to church, and to pray with sycophantic snuffle for the evangelical replenishment of their most Sovereign Lady, Queen Victoria, and the prospering with all happiness of that multifarious entity euphemistically described in the church service of an obedient people, as 'all the Royal Family.' It was Sunday morning when a prayer was put up to Liberty by a digger, and the responses were sung by the rattle of side-arms and the whistle of death-dealing bullets.

Two hundred and seventy-six men in the pay of a foreign power, including a strong body of cavalry, stole forward in the grey mist of morning to carry by assault the miners' frail embattlement. They fire alternately—the diggers and the docile instruments of military force. The men behind the stockade give a ringing cheer, and fire again. Then there is a dash on the part of the hirelings of authority and the first line of defence is crossed; the police rush the inner line, and uproot the flag-staff, and tear down the banner of rebellious Labour.

On come the soldiers, close in the wake of the police, but Captain Wise, of the 40th, and Lieutenant Paul, of the 12th Regiments, are wounded, the former mortally. The military rush headlong over the barricade, carrying the tiny redoubt at the point of the bayonet.

But the insurgents behave gamely to the last. Thirty of them lie dead in the entrenchment, 125 are disabled, and taken prisoners; the district is placed under martial law, the tents of the diggers are burnt and razed to the ground. And all this happened while the good people of Melbourne were sleepily preparing to go to church, and pray for their Gracious Sovereign Lady, Queen Victoria!

Peter Lalor, left for dead in the Eureka Stockade, escaped with the loss of his arm, and, like his lieutenants—Vern and Black—defied the cunning of the police, though a reward of £100 was offered for his capture, alive or dead.

In the following year, Mr Lalor and Mr Humffray, also a rebellious miner, represented the Ballarat diggers in the Government of the country. The State had condoned rebellion, and was compelled to recognize the will of the people. Revolt is the parent of reform; and, though Eureka Stockade fades into insignificance when placed beside Bunker's Hill, the meaning and the impulse in each case of armed resistance were the same. In the dusky dawn, when the hired soldiers of Imperialism crept forward to take by storm the rude barricade erected by the insurgent citizens; when the ringing voice of Lalor thundered out upon the damp air of the morning; when, with the glistening dew beading their unshorn beards, the stalwart diggers gripped with brown hands or swung aloft with brawny naked arms the clubbed musket; then—then was heard in each heart an echo of the shot fired by the New England farmer which won a nation's freedom and gave mankind another lease of hope. Then was heard that voice in the crack of the miner's rifle that rang out in the lines of [the Reverend John Dunmore] Lang when he wrote to Earl Grey with scathing invective, and warned him that for three years had that unwitting noble-man been knocking at the gates of Futurity for the President of the United States of Australia.

The spirit of Lalor and of Lang is the spirit that we long for in our public men, but it is the spirit that seems to have taken flight with the men who gave it birth. Lang is dead; Lalor has retired from public life. As with America so with Australia. Washington, Lincoln—Cleveland; Lang, Lalor—Parkes. In America of the past, heroes, patriots, farmers. In America of the present, capitalists and their human property. In Australia of yesterday, pioneers, diggers, Democrats. In Australia of today, toadies, grovellers, lick-spittles.

The old impulse is not dead, however, though the land-thief and the labour-thief rig our markets and shark our estates; though our politicians sell us for an empty distinction and barter our birthright for a mess less than royal pottage. The people of Australia—the true, the genuine Demo-crats, the Australians—refuse to celebrate the landing of Phillip; they look across the Murray for the one representative act of their nationality; they look across the ocean for the one representative utterance which foretells their future, and they find their exemplars in the rebellious miner, Lalor, and the irritable parson Lang. The one, by his heroic action in heading the diggers in revolt against unjust and tyrannical authority, furnished forth a precedent to Australia, which all Australians worthy of the name should inscribe in letters of indelible print within the red-leaved tablets of their hearts. The other, by his magnificent pertinacity and splendid daring, snatched a grand territory from convict-loving Official-dom and gave it to the free settler.

Their deeds will speak ever louder than tablets of brass or monuments of marble, but if there is one thing the people of Australia could, with beautiful propriety, perform, it is to place in the Fortitude Valley, Brisbane, in the very locality in which Lang's first free settlers took up their first abode, a memorial of this genuine worker and true Australian. The Ballarat monument still remains to be erected, but alas! the race of men in Ballarat of today are not the stalwart heroes of fifty-four. They huckster about a Stock Exchange, and their most magnificent effort at apprecia-tion of merit is a statue to a Guelphic and foreign Sovereign. Let it pass. The men who fought for liberty are not of the brand to be pleased with flattery. Their deeds live on in default of tablets. The shouts of diggers are in the air, the ping of the rifle-bullet is heard overhead, there is a clash of steel and a hurtling of arms; a flag with the insignia of labour—the pick and the shovel—flaunts proudly in the morning breeze above us.... 'Tis a memory of the day that Australia set her teeth in the face of the British Lion, 3 December 1854 — the Day We Ought to Celebrate.

Abridged.
Source: *Bulletin*, 21 January 1888, p. 5.

———◆———

Louisa Lawson
Women's Suffrage, 1889

Louisa Albury Lawson (1848–1920) grew up near Mudgee and at the age of eighteen married Niels 'Peter' Larsen, a Norwegian sailor. The couple had five children. After many difficult years on the goldfields and a failing farm, the marriage disintegrated and Lawson moved to Sydney. In 1887 she acquired a printing press and published the *Republican* newspaper, assisted by her eldest son, Henry Lawson. In May 1888 Louisa Lawson established *The Dawn: A Journal for Australian Women*. Produced by an all-female staff, *The Dawn* had a wide circulation in the city and country, appealing to readers through its wide coverage of political issues, fashion, household hints and fiction. Lawson, forceful, fiercely intelligent and direct, advocated the need for women's economic independence and saw women as the leaders of moral and social reform. On 23 May 1889 she called a meeting at the Forresters' Hall, Sydney, with two aims: forming an association to discuss all issues of relevance to women and encouraging public speaking. The Dawn Club was established and began gathering fortnightly at the tearooms of benefactor and business identity Mei Quong Tart. In this inaugural address to the Dawn Club, Lawson launched her campaign for women's suffrage, drawing upon international examples of women's political and economic activity as she urged Australian women to agitate for the vote.

The popular idea of an advocate of women's rights is this: — she is an angular hard-featured withered creature with a shrill, harsh voice, no pretence to comeliness, spectacles on nose, and the repulsive title, 'blue-stocking' visible all over her. Metaphorically she is supposed to hang half way over the bar which separates the sexes, shaking her skinny fist at men and all their works.

I don't think it will be difficult to unseat this idea as soon as we can get people to think about the subject at all, for it is remarkable that almost every thinking man who does investigate the topic seriously, at once hands in his allegiance. For as a clever American woman has said: — 'There are no arguments against women's suffrage — only "objections".'

Now as we have no time to be elaborate or diffuse, we must be methodical and we will take first the reasons why women claim the right to vote; then we will pick up the objections one by one and turn them inside out to show their entire vacuity, and finally review briefly what women are doing now in other countries in order to show how woefully we in New South Wales are behind the times. For the thoughts we entertain on this and other sections of the Woman's question are merely scattered unshaped blocks lying rough in the quarry, while in America and England they are already squared and set together in the foundations of that new social edifice which the 19th century is building.

The whole principle of the justice of the woman's vote agitation may be compressed into a question:—'Who ordained that men only should make the laws to which both men and women have to conform?'

No strong faction however honorable they might be, ever yet looked at the rights and interests of a weaker party with quite the same consideration as they bestowed on their own concerns; no parliament responsible only to men voters can ever take any but a purely masculine view of things, although both men and women are equally concerned, and in fairness the reasons of both sides should be heard. Pray why should one half of the world govern the other half? Is it just to first ensure the silence of the weaker half by depriving them of a citizen's status, and then inform them that by the laws of the stronger section this is the way they must act and this is the way the world may legally use them. A woman's opinions are useless to her, she may suffer unjustly, she may be wronged, but she has no power to weightily petition against man's laws, no representatives to urge her views, her only method to procure release, redress, or change, is to ceaselessly agitate with the hope that after many years the sense of justice in the majority of her rulers may be stirred and some tardy concession be granted perhaps in time to benefit her grand-daughters.

Lucy Stone in an article on 'Lobsters, Crows and Women' reminds us that in Maine the lobster question, important to fishermen, was discussed in Parliament and duly passed in committee; a price was set on the heads of the crows on the plea of the men voters; the gipsies robbed the fowl yards and straight on the motion of men who, having votes, had power, the laws were made more stringent; but when the women of Arkansas sent in a petition that temperance might be taught in the State schools they promptly had leave to withdraw. The Bill was hardly presented before a resolution to table it was carried without discussion; the women had no votes so what did their desires and opinions matter?

The form of liberal government is a government in accordance with the wishes of the majority; these wishes are written down and put in a ballot box for convenience in counting and in thus taking the sense of the community certain classes by tacit consent are omitted from participation in the right. We always omit minors, felons, idiots, and women; why women? What kind of liberal government or government by a majority is this? Does housekeeping or any other woman's employment make anyone more unfit to conscientiously and usefully record a vote than bricklaying or writing up a ledger? It is not the right to rule which women want; they have no desire to change places with men; they only claim the right to record an opinion, a right difficult one would think to justly deny an intelligent creature. Here in New South Wales every man may vote, let his character be bad, his judgment purchasable, and his intellect of the weakest, but an honorable thoughtful and good woman may be laughed at by such men, they can carry what laws they please in spite of her.

It cannot be urged that women have no need to vote because justice is always done even though they are silent. It is only since 1886 that a mother's right to share in the guardianship of her children has been legally admitted; even now in some places the husband may separate the children from their mother if he wills to do so. Not alone as a citizen but even as a mother a woman has not full legal recognition. In divorce men are protected from infidelity—not women. In intestate estates women do not share equally with men. In educational endowments and facilities they have not the same privileges. Wives may still be forced to live in the same house with a husband whom they hate or fear. Have women no need of a vote to protect them in these things and in the multitude of other interests affecting women and children; to say nothing of the larger questions of vice and drunkenness in which the happiness of women and children is always closely involved?

But the vote in these things is not all. The expression of women's desires leads to a change in public opinion which is far more powerful than law. It leads moreover to the development of thought in women, and to the purification of governing bodies; for women in the mass will never vote for corrupt or dishonourable representatives.

They say that if women vote we shall have an effeminate nation, but those nations are strongest where the women are most free. How can it be otherwise while the principle of heritage remains a universal truth? Children inherit from both parents and are most influenced in their training by their mothers. From thoughtful women will come noble sons, and the enfranchisement of women must make the thoughts of women wider, their interests less selfish, their ambitions ampler and more noble. With a share in the national life they will learn to care for the good of other homes and other affairs than their own.

As to the effect of women's influence on government we can turn from theory to fact. In Kansas with women voting and the prohibition law in force, more than half the state gaols are now without prisoners. In Wyoming women have had the right to vote since 1869 and the Speaker of the House of Representatives there has been asked to give the results of his experience. This is what he says:—'I started with the strongest prejudice against women's suffrage and was decidedly opposed to it at all points, but on its introduction I became a close observer of its practical results. I have been twice Speaker of the House of Representatives, and I have had opportunities of forming judgment upon the circumstances. I can now say that the more I have seen of the results of women's suffrage the less have my objections been realized and the more has the thing commended itself to my judgment and good opinion, and I must frankly acknowledge, after all my distrust, that it has worked well and been productive of much good to the Territory and of no evil that I am aware of.'

He then refers to the influence of women's suffrage in inducing both parties to choose respectable men as their candidates, and adds, that the interest taken by women in politics since their admission to the franchise, has led to 'No domestic trouble, or made any of us speak slightingly of women.'

Now we will consider the objections made to Women's Suffrage. I have collected all which I have ever heard or read.

Some say:—'If you want to share men's rights you must share their responsibilities too: men have to fight for their country, are the women also ready to do the same?' This objection cuts both ways—if rights and responsibilities must be exactly halved, the men must help to mind the children and do the cooking. But seriously, if the ability to fight is the one necessary qualification enabling citizens to have a voice in the making of the laws under which they live, you must disqualify all old men, and the lame, and the feeble, for they are as unfit to be soldiers as women are. You must also exclude clergymen, and Members of Parliament, for they don't fight—except amongst themselves.

Another objection urged is that women have no knowledge of politics and that to vote will interfere with their domestic duties. It seems to me that a very large proportion of men voters use their vote without any previous close study of politics; moreover that a knowledge of the burning questions of the day is very quickly learned even if it is not thrust upon the attention of all reading and thinking people. And inasmuch as both men and women suspend their occupations at odd times on various pretexts without upsetting the order of things, the little time taken by the recording of a vote will not seriously disturb the conditions of domestic life.

Some say that women have no commercial training and cannot therefore understand political and economical questions. Now we know that in the trading classes in France, and in the working classes in English speaking nations the financial affairs of the whole household are usually left in the wife's hands. We know that there are thousands of women managing business institutions, and hundreds of thousands of women commercially employed, and therefore getting political training—if this is what commercial training means.

As to women being inherently destitute of average talent, there is so much evidence to the contrary that the objection is hardly worth answering. It is usual to allege that the instances relied on are instances of quite phenomenal women, but when we see so many thousands of women holding high places in all varieties of vocations it is transparently clear, that, if women have any stimulus to work, and fair chances to develop, their talent reaches nearly as high an average as man's. We could weary anyone to death with instances, but taking merely a few more recent papers and records we find these fragmentary facts in evidence and they show what the sum total of women's public work to-day would be, if the statistics could be collected. In England we read in the few papers from which these facts are culled—that during the three years between 1885 and 1888, six women were elected to serve on school boards.

Women were elected on the New County Councils but the law decides they are ineligible. The London Council elected Miss Emma Cons to be an Alderman of the City but she will also probably be disqualified. Two women have been elected by the Council to act on the Committee on the housing of the poor. Women have inaugurated and are managing Trades Unions among working women.

They are managing hospitals, asylums and schools, they are appointed as Inspectors under the Poor Laws Act. They compete on even terms with men as artists, musicians, journalists, dentists, photographers, farmers, storekeepers, and their successes in literature are numberless.

Two lady students took the highest prizes for descriptive and practical anatomy at the Irish, Royal College of Surgeons. The report of the Dublin University shows that in 1888 one woman took the degree of LLD [Doctor of Laws], two took the MA degree, and 18 the BA degree. At the London University, one woman has taken the LLD degree, two that of Doctor of Science, six the MA degree, 20 the degree of B.Sc., over 150 the degree of BA. At Oxford and Cambridge they have done as well, but at those Colleges no degrees are conferred.

Recent papers from America, not complete statistics I must remind you, mention that no less that 2500 women hold first class diplomas from duly incorporated medical colleges. There are 60 women dentists. Reference is made to two women who are licensed commanders of steam vessels on the Mississippi, to two women sculptors, and to several women editing newspapers. The Vassar College is founding a Chair of Astronomy in honour of Professor Maria Mitchell who has long worked in the department of Astronomy at that College; Mrs Braman is Commissioner of Deeds in New York; Mrs Russel is a Prison Commissioner. Dr. Sarah Millsop has been appointed by the Southern Homœopathic Association to the Chairmanship of a section. Miss Hayden has just beaten fifteen young men in an original architectural design at the Institute of Technology, Boston. There are 213 clubs of women formed in New Orleans for the study of political economy.

There are 16 women doctors in Paris and at the recent Medical Congress in St. Petersburg 162 women doctors attended. The Professor of Literature at Stockholm is a woman, so also is the Professor of Pathology at Pisa.

If these and the thousands of other instances are all cases of phenomenal women there must be a great many exceptions to the 'Smaller brain' theory.

Women serve as jurors in Washington Territory [USA], and this is what Chief Justice Greene says of them: 'Twelve terms of Court I have held in which women have served as grand and petit jurors, and as a fact beyond dispute no other twelve terms so salutary for the restraint of crime have ever been held in this territory. For 15 years I have been trying to do what a Judge ought, but have never, till the last six months felt underneath and around me in the degree that every judge has a right a feel it, the up buoying weight of the people in line of full and enforcement of the law.' Women have been managing (as Mayor and Council) a town of 2000 inhabitants in Kansas.

Thus facts against theories show nothing to woman's disadvantage; they are I am glad to say, a happy presage of a better future.

Twenty-five years ago women (with insignificant exceptions) could not vote anywhere. To-day they have school suffrage in 15 of the American States, municipal suffrage in Kansas, and full suffrage at Wyoming. In Ontario, New Brunswick, Nova Scotia and British Columbia they have the municipal suffrage, and last January two million women voted in England, Scotland and Wales at the election of County Councils under the new system of local government.

They only need one step more, while we are far behind. It remains for the women of Australia to say how long they will lag in the rear of the great onward march of liberal thought and women's advance. We have examples: now we only need our own efforts.

Abridged.
Source: *The Dawn: A Journal for Australian Women*, Sydney, 1 July 1889, pp. 9, 12, 13.

———

Henry Parkes
The Tenterfield Oration, 1889

Henry Parkes (1815–1896) is a towering political figure of nineteenth-century Australia, serving in the New South Wales Legislative Assembly from 1856 to 1895 and as premier five times. Born in Warwickshire, the son of a dispossessed tenant farmer, Parkes received little formal education and emigrated with his wife to New South Wales in 1839. After a period of initial hardship he became established as an ivory turner, an importer and a newspaper proprietor although his business interests were always dogged by insolvency. Parkes had literary aspirations, wrote poetry and was a strong speaker who pitched to the 'ordinary' person. His many political achievements included the introduction of compulsory education, free trade, immigration restrictions and the creation of national parks. At an inter-colonial conference in 1880–81 Parkes called for greater unification of the Australian colonies. But the path was blocked by the reluctance of New South Wales, as the bastion of free trade, to join protectionist Victoria and other colonies in a federal council. On 24 October 1889, en route from Brisbane to Sydney, Parkes stopped at the border town of Tenterfield and delivered this landmark oration, perhaps less striking for its language than for its sentiment. Parkes called for a strong national government to be developed through a council representing all the colonies. He was to preside over the first Federal Convention held in Sydney in 1891. But in 1896 the 'Father of Federation', now retired from politics and in reduced circumstances, died—four years before his vision was realized.

The Imperial general who inspected the troops of the colony has recommended that the whole of the forces of Australia should be united into one army. It would be pleasing if we could rely on being safe without taking military precautions at all, but as this is impossible, we must take measures to defend ourselves. The knowledge of the fact that we are in this condition of security will spread all over the world, and make us additionally secure. There are two very important questions towards which I ought to direct your attention.

You must have heard something of the Federal Council in which New South Wales has not yet taken a place: if we are to carry out the recommendations of General Edwards, it is absolutely necessary for us to have something more than the Federal Council. We need one central executive authority, which is able to bring all the forces of the different colonies into one national army. Some colonial statesmen have said that this might be done by means of the Federal Council, but this Federal Council has no power to do anything of the sort, as it has no executive function; and, moreover, is not an elected body, but merely a body appointed by the Governments of the various colonies. It does not, therefore, carry with it the support of the people. It is constitutionally weak, and, under the Imperial Act which created it, no such tremendous power was given as that which the exigencies of Australia might demand.

It has been suggested that the Imperial Parliament should be asked to pass a measure authorising the troops of the colonies to unite in one federal army. But even if this were done, there would be an absence of the necessary central executive Government. Each of the colonies would object to the army being under the control of the Imperial Government, and no one of the colonies could direct it. The great question which we have to consider is whether the time has not now come for the creation on this Australian continent of an Australian Government as distinct from the local Governments now in existence. (Applause.) In other words, to make myself as plain as possible, Australia has now a population of three and a half millions, and the American people numbered only between three and four millions when they formed the great commonwealth of the

United States. The numbers were about the same, and surely what the Americans did by war, the Australians can bring about in peace—without breaking the ties that hold us to the mother country. (Cheers.)

Believing as I do that it is essential to preserve the security and integrity of these colonies that the whole of our forces should be amalgamated into one great federal army, whenever necessary,—feeling this, and seeing no other means of attaining that end, it seems to me that the time is close at hand when we ought to set about creating this great national Government for all Australia. This subject brings us face to face with another subject. We have now, from South Australia to Queensland, a stretch of about 2,000 miles of railway, and if the four colonies can only combine to adopt a uniform gauge, it will be an immense advantage in the movement of troops, as well as in the operations of commerce and the various pursuits of society. These are the two great national questions which I wish to lay before you.

I have just returned from Brisbane, and the object of my visit was not to force my advice on the authorities there but to discuss with them these matters. Unfortunately, owing to the illness of the head of the Ministry, my communications were rather more of a private character than otherwise; but, without disclosing any confidences, I think that I can state I understand both sides in politics sympathise warmly and closely with the views I expressed. As to the steps which should be taken to bring this about, a conference of the Governments has been pointed to, but we must take broader views in the initiation of the movement than has been taken hitherto. We must appoint a convention of leading men from all the colonies—delegates appointed by the authority of Parliament, who would fully represent the opinion of the different Parliaments of the colonies. This convention will have to devise the constitution which would be necessary for bringing into existence a Federal Government with a Federal Parliament for the conduct of the national business. (Applause.) The only argument which could be advanced in opposition to the views I have put forward is that the time has not yet come, and we must remain isolated colonies just in the same way as we are now. I believe, however, that the time has come. In the words of Brunton Stephens, I would ask—

> Not yet her day. How long 'not yet'?
> There comes the flush of violet!
> And heavenward faces, all aflame
> With sanguine imminence of morn,
> Wait but the sun-kiss to proclaim
> The day of the Dominion born.

(Applause.) I believe that the time has come, and if two Governments set an example, the others must soon of necessity follow, and we will have an uprising in this fair land of a goodly fabric of free Government. And all great national questions of magnitude affecting the welfare of the colonies will be disposed of by a fully authorised constitutional authority, which will be the only one which can give satisfaction to the people it represents. This means a distinct executive and a distinct parliamentary power, a Government for the whole of Australia. And it means a Parliament of two Houses, a house of commons and a senate, which will legislate on all great subjects. The Government and Parliament of New South Wales will be just as effective as now in all local matters, as will the Government and Parliament of Queensland. All great questions will be dealt with in a broad light and with a view to the interests of the whole country.

I, therefore, take advantage of this opportunity which has arisen for the consideration of this great subject, for I believe that the time is at hand when the thing will be done. One great thing to be accomplished is the massing together of our military forces, whenever necessary, and this cannot be effected by any other power than one representing all the colonies. In conclusion, I thank you for the kindness you have shown me. I have no fear but the Federal Parliament will rise to a just conception of the necessities of the wider sphere of political existence. This great thing will have to be done, and to put it off will only tend to make the difficulties which stand in the way greater. In the meantime, there is this substantial work of defence to be carried out, which we can not do by any other means—which cannot be done by any existing machinery.

Reproduced in full.
Transposed from indirect speech.
Source: H. Parkes, *The Federal Government of Australasia*.[28]

James Chisholm

Visit of Lord Sheffield's English Cricket Team, 1891

James Kinghorne Chisholm (1830–1908) was descended from a Scottish family whose association with Australia dated from the 1790s. A prominent pastoralist at Camden, New South Wales—the district where John Macarthur had established his famous merino stud—Chisholm was a community leader, president of the local Agricultural Society and a keen spectator of cricket. English cricket teams had visited Australia from the 1860s. In the summer of 1891–92 Lord Sheffield, a stout little man who loved cricket but who wilted in hot weather, sponsored an English cricket tour. At the time, Australian cricket was in the doldrums: spectators were wearied by seven years of squabbling and defeat. But the English team was led by a celebrity—the grey-whiskered Dr W. G. Grace, whom Lord Sheffield had lured with a fee of £1500 and a promise of all the wine he could drink. In the colonies, people flocked to see the great man bat. On 16 December 1891 the rival teams were entertained at Camden where Chisholm welcomed the tourists. Although he was a sheep baron, Chisholm sang the praises of an Australian egalitarianism which was exemplified on the cricket field. Australia was to win this series against England, 2–1, signalling a revival in the local game. Lord Sheffield was so pleased with the success of the tour that he donated 150 guineas for the advancement of Australian cricket, allowing the purchase of the Sheffield Shield, a trophy for inter-colonial competition.

Gentlemen,—

It is now my pleasant duty to propose the health of our English visitors, who have done us the honour of coming to our district and accepting a challenge from our local players. I much regret that through indisposition Lord Sheffield has been prevented from accompanying his team; his reputation of being a most enthusiastic patron of cricket has preceded him to the colonies, and Australians who have represented us in the old country have reason to feel grateful to him for much courtesy and hospitality. On the present occasion we are especially grateful to him for inducing Dr. Grace, the greatest hero of the cricket field, to pay us a visit, and thus affording us an opportunity of witnessing his remarkable prowess with the bat.

I have much pleasure, gentlemen, in welcoming you to the district, which you now see under exceptionally favourable circumstances; for at this season of the year our hills are not always 'with verdure clad' as at present, and our pastures occasionally present a parched and less luxuriant appearance. Our Sydney cousins are sometimes credited with a disposition to blow about their beautiful harbour, and I think they may be excused so amiable a weakness. We, too, are vain enough to think our district contains some picturesque beauty, and that in some of its physical aspects it resembles portions of the dear old country from which many of us rejoice to think we have descended. We are also fond of emphasising the fact that a historic interest attaches to it, since it was selected by Mr. John Macarthur, the great grandfather of our young Onslow friends, who are playing in the present match, for the first successful experiment in fine-wool-growing ever tried in Australia. It was here he demonstrated the remarkable fitness of our climate and our pastures for the growth of wool of the finest quality, and started an industry which now constitutes the chief source of the wealth and prosperity of these great colonies. Some idea of its magnitude may be inferred from the fact that we now have in New South Wales alone upwards of sixty million sheep, yielding wool of an annual export value of about twelve millions.

But I am not going to weary you with details of this kind, which are scarcely in order at a cricket match. This is the second time we have been honoured by a visit from an English team. For the first we were indebted to the enterprise of our then townsman, Mr. Joseph Toll, who about five years ago induced Mr. Shaw's team to play a match with our own men; but the weather proved most unfavourable, and in every way it turned out an unsuccessful venture. I thought at that time it was a bold proposal on the part of our players; but when I heard they were challenging so formidable a team as the present, it seemed to savour almost of temerity. It showed, however, that our Camden youth have inherited much of the pluck and indomitable energy of their British ancestors, and are not afraid to face a most formidable set of opponents. I will not be so rash as to venture on any prediction as regards the result of the game; I would merely tender our players one word of advice, 'stick to your guns, and keep your powder dry.'

I am old enough to recollect when it was considered a very important event in the annals of cricket for a team to come from Maitland, a distance of eighty or ninety miles, to play against a Sydney club. It was the first match of the kind ever played in the colony, and although it is now nearly fifty years ago, one or two little incidents happened on the occasion which helped to fix it indelibly in my recollection. The game was played on Hyde Park, close to St. James' Church. At the time I was a pupil in the old Sydney College (now the Sydney Grammar School), and we applied to the head master for a holiday; but I suppose he was not a cricketer, for he peremptorily refused our application. (So unlike our present paternal government, which never refuses to proclaim a public holiday for a horse-race, a game of football, or a tennis match—they might even be induced to grant one for a Punch and Judy Show.) However, about thirty of us were determined not to be disappointed, and we banded ourselves together to play truant, and thus become witnesses of the game. Play had scarcely commenced when I had the misfortune to get hit on the head with a cricket-ball which sent me reeling—a judgment no doubt for my misconduct; and to mend matters it turned out a wet day, and a more miserable one I never remember to have passed. On our return to school we found ourselves in sad disgrace, and as a punishment for our misdeeds were ordered to learn five hundred lines of Virgil each, in order to improve our acquaintance with the classics.

In those days the 'demon' bowler had not been developed. Runs were known as notches, and it was considered no ball if the hand was raised above the waist, bowling being literally all along the ground. Cricket has certainly made marvellous progress since that time; and thanks to the wonderful facilities of travel which now exist, we have here to-day in our little village of Camden one of the most powerful teams of England.

We have been hearing much lately of the waning of the popularity of cricket, and various reasons have been assigned for the decline of the game, amongst which prominence has been given to stonewalling; but however objectionable the practice may be in Parliament, it is justifiable in the cricket-field. What would be thought of a General in command of an army who recklessly ordered his troops to charge the enemy, when common prudence should have suggested the wiser course of acting on the defensive? Defeat might have followed the former method; caution in the latter secured a victory. No doubt the practice of stonewalling in cricket detracts much from the interest of the game, and often proves very wearisome to spectators; but it may be the only chance of weak players against a powerful antagonist, and cricketers, as a rule, play for victory and not merely for the amusement of spectators. I think, however, if there is any decline in cricket, which I much doubt, the cause will be found in the many counter-attractions which now exist—tennis, football, and other sports which have become popular in the country. These have all tended to divide the interest of the public, and have undoubtedly drawn away many from the cricket field who might have excelled in the game had they given their undivided attention to it.

Notwithstanding all that has been said of the decline of the noble game of cricket, I feel sure that it will continue to retain a pre-eminent place in the regard of all true lovers of athletic sports. Other games may have much to commend them as manly exercises, but there is none so good as cricket for schooling the temper, and fostering habits of self-control and self-reliance. There is also no other game so suitable for all ranks and stations in society, in which representatives of every class may join on principles of social equality. It is a game for the peer and the peasant, the parson and the parishioner; and here on the present occasion we have a most powerful team from the old country, championed by a distinguished English nobleman, whilst amongst our local players may be observed the young lord of the manor and a number of his employees, together with the parson of the church and several of his parishioners, all on terms of fraternity and equality. Recently I have seen the Primate of our church—who is an ardent admirer of the game—playing in the neighbourhood, but episcopal garments are certainly not well adapted for athletic sports. Lord Jersey, I understand, is also to play in a match at Bowral in the course of next week.

All honour to them in their distinguished patronage! While cricket receives such practical encouragement from those in high positions, I do not think there is much fear of its declining in popular estimation. Such international games as we are now engaged in do much to render the colonies and the parent country better acquainted, and promote those kindly feelings which should be maintained in every community, irrespective of class or creed; and whatever may be the result of the present contest, I feel assured it will give a great impetus to cricket in the district, and rekindle an enthusiasm for the game.

Reproduced in full.
Source: J. K. Chisholm, *Speeches and Reminiscences*.[29]

William Spence

The Ethics of New Unionism, 1892

William Guthrie Spence (1846–1926) emigrated with his family from the Orkney Islands in 1853 to settle near Creswick, Victoria. With no formal education, he was working in the mines from the age of twelve. Attracted to miners' unionism in 1874, in just four years Spence was secretary general of the Amalgamated Miners Association, which evolved under his leadership into the largest inter-colonial union of its time. In 1886, in a major feat of mass organization, the new Amalgamated Shearers' Union of Australasia was formed, with Spence as president. But the bitterly contested Maritime Strike of 1890, and the unsuccessful shearers' strikes which followed, left the union movement in disarray. Spence played a prominent role during these years of tumult, economic depression and unemployment. During 1892, he gave public lectures about his vision of 'the new unionism', wherein all workers, regardless of sex or occupation, would be embraced by an industrial–political organization that preached an ethic of co-operation and common humanity. While this ambitious and utopian revolution came to nothing, in later years the Australian Workers' Union, with Spence at its helm, was to play a key role in the formation of the Labor Party in New South Wales. On 12 June 1892 Spence outlined his plan under the auspices of the Australian Socialist League in Leigh House, Sydney.

Mr. Chairman and Fellow-workers—It is said to be a scientific axiom that all present forms take their character from those which lie behind. Throughout the whole of nature there is undoubtedly a spirit of evolution working, and working in a very definite direction. Specialising the various forms of life, adapting them to their environment. Humanity must, of course, be regarded as part of Nature, and are also influenced by this spirit of evolution. We have been placed at the very apex of the pyramid of created things. We have, by the exercise of our superior intelligence been able to control many of the forces of Nature and utilise them for our own good. We have been able, to a greater degree than any of the lower forms of life, to take advantage of co-operation, or of forming alliances for mutual benefit.

In this great movement called 'Trades Unionism,' or the 'Labor Movement,' or any other term they choose to apply to it we find the same evolutionary spirit has been at work. When machinery began to be introduced we find the first great division of men into the two classes in which we find them today. At that time men began to be employed in groups, or bodies, and then commenced the departure from individualism and the joining together for greater self-protection. Shortly afterwards, seeing the combination effected among the men, the employers began to unite and form joint stock enterprises and the vast syndicates which are so patent to us to-day. The employers recognised that large enterprises would be far more effective than smaller concerns, and the truth of that is exemplified by the power they wield in our midst today.

When they came under the pressure of competition and felt the grinding of the competitive system, the two parties—employers and employees—came into conflict. It was, and is now to the interest of the employer to produce as cheaply as possible, and he naturally only employs men if by so doing he can make a profit out of the result of their labors. During the last fifty years there has been, as you know, a very rapid trend towards the displacement of men by machinery and the crushing out of smaller concerns by the larger syndicates, as they can produce much more cheaply, and by the employment of less manual labor. We find ourselves faced by an ever increasing mass of men who have no work to do although eager and willing to work.

In the days of what we call the old unionism there was a certain amount of antagonism among the members. But these old unions or organisations confined their attention solely to what was called obtaining reasonable wages and hours of labor, or as good a wage as they could get, and to a resistance of the crushing tendencies of the employers. (Cheers). They did not, or could not take much interest or do anything for those outside their own ranks or amongst the great masses of the unemployed. They could not and did not find work for those who were idle for want of it. They refused to touch political matters at all, or have anything to do with either party in Parliament.

Matters have changed during the last few years and the unions ought to change also. Labor bodies have become federated and the employers seeing that feel alarmed because to them the federation of labor, if conducted upon the old lines, means an attack on their self-interest. In the meantime there is spreading amongst unionists this idea—whether socialistic or not—that they cannot effect the improvement they desire by dealing only with the mere question of hours and wages. And so comes what has been termed the 'new unionism'—a unionism wide and broad in its aim, and one which will certainly be far-reaching in its effects. We are aiming now at securing an improvement by social and political reforms—and by that means alone a revolution will undoubtedly be effected in time. When I use the word revolution—do not misunderstand me—I mean a quiet one. It will be a change from one condition to another, which almost deserves the name of 'revolution.' I feel certain it will come about steadily and surely and rapidly if we take the proper stand, the only stand—that of common humanity. (Cheers.)

I want you to look at our social system and the evils connected with it and are created by it, and then you will better understand how far 'new unionism' may be expected to bring about the desired change. We have now on the one side production on socialistic lines altogether. We have distribution on individualistic lines. We have on the one side the controlling class. They hold a monopoly. They have as a class power in controlling other men. Any individual or any body of men given supreme control over his fellows is almost certain to not unjustly. And no body of men ought to be trusted with uncontrolled power over their fellows. (Cheers.) I need not reason out how it is that a class has control of the sources of production—ownership of the land, and ownership of the people practically. (Hear, hear.) All that they aim at is producing for profit.

Now take the commercial ethics of this life, and does it not develop the worst side of human nature? (Hear, hear.) It develops too much of that instinct which distinguishes the savage. The savage is noted for the exercise of cunning. It is a question of what he can take, and is not that one of the faculties developed in all forms of business? Scheming, cunning, lying, and dishonesty are associated with our commercial enterprise. We have fraud perpetrated by men of intelligence who ought and do know better. There is in commercial life a system of ethics which will not stand setting up side by side with the Decalogue. You cannot get along sometimes without telling lies. Adulteration of goods is very common. The gospel of cheapness has such a hold upon people, and the pressure of competition so keen that if you are to make your way in the commercial world, as in other walks of life, you are forced, I insist, to give way if you are to succeed. To get on you must do as other people do—or you will go down. We have surrounded our commercial men in such an entanglement that they cannot be expected to do right. I do not look at what men should do, but what it is reasonable to expect them to do under the circumstances in which they are placed. (Hear, hear.) I say that if we have a set of conditions under which it is impossible for men and women to do right we are responsible for them.

On the workers' side the evils are, perhaps, more felt. We have on their side enforced idleness and poverty. Poverty with all its wretched surroundings—the most degrading things in all the world. We have unworthy dealings, and all the discontent engendered thereby. Always crushing downwards—the man losing all self-respect as he goes. How can you expect a man to stand against the influences surrounding him? The strong stand for a time, but we have no right to put the weak in a position that will compel them to go down. We have the evils of ignorance amongst those less fortunate than ourselves in not knowing right from wrong. We have coarseness, lack of refinement, even brutality. You cannot expect the working classes—especially those who are crushed most low—to be so polished and nice as those who have nothing else to do but study how to be polished and nice. The weaker men and the women suffer. Women undoubtedly suffer most. At one time it was the boast of the Anglo-Saxon race—in the ages of chivalry—that they would defend their women. Today our sisters are shut out and degraded to the lowest of all depths, even to prostitution. Those who know most about that say that there is not one in a thousand of them who ever chose that life. They have been driven to it—driven to it for want of bread. I am charging this to the social system we have set up. It is physically and morally degrading to the human race. (Hear, hear.)

Well, then co-operation instead of competition is one of the aims of the New Unionism; giving equality of right, equality of opportunity, and equality of justice to all men. The destruction, so to speak—annihilation if you like it better—the doing away of that abnormal growth the aristocracy of land possession, and setting up in its place an aristocracy of character, genius, and intellect. (Cheers.) That is the principle of the New Unionism. Under the old Unionism men sank their individualism for the common good of their own class. New Unionism asks the masses to sink individuality for the common good, to unite on the common platform when they speak, and when they vote to vote for the reforms that are necessary. (Cheers.) Many of the unions or Labor organisations that are in existence have adopted the 'new unionism' out and out, taking part in political questions and giving effect to their wishes at the ballot box. But 'new unionism' means more than mere labor organisation.

It recognises those who are non-unionists. An organisation of labor, constituted on the lines of 'new unionism,' will have to abolish entrance fees and contributions to the lowest sum at which it can possibly carry on. (Cheers.) The aim in this case is, so to speak, to go outside a particular organisation and take in all workers, no matter what their occupation. Women workers will also be included, for the spirit of 'new unionism' makes no distinction of sex. Our present social system is altogether against the weak and certainly in favor of the strong. The weak are crushed down and on their prostrate bodies rise to eminence the unprincipled men, who crush them. (Cheers.) New Unionism is to-day looking beyond the employer and fixing its hatred upon the system, (cheers) which is bad not alone for the workman but for the employer—which forces the employer to act unjustly even if he did not wish to do so. (Renewed cheers.) It is a system which produces the non-unionists and all other matters of which the unionists have had reason—and justifiable reason—to complain. We must take in the whole of them if we are to do any good, to accomplish what we desire.

Humanity is divided into two classes, the employers and the employed. The employees can only work at the will of other men, and whether they are employed or not depends upon whether they can be paid. It is certain that there will be always an ever increasing army of those who will be idle. What we have now is one large syndicate controlling one line of industry. Now, if the people were the owners of that industry this would be all right. Those who are wealthy today cannot be happy or enjoy life under present conditions. Every wealthy man is afraid when he goes to bed at night that he will pick up his newspaper in the morning and find it telling him that his bank has broken or that something else has happened to deprive him of his wealth. There is no happiness anywhere—'Uneasy lies the head that wears a crown.' All the way down through life there is this struggle which makes life not worth living. Numerous young men and women have said to me that there is nothing for them worth living for and that they would almost as soon die. How long is this condition of things to remain with us?

You cannot have success in any movement unless it is morally and ethically correct. This social system of ours is wrong in every stage. In the future things must be done in the mass. There must be unity and co-operation if we are to rise and take upon ourselves the responsibility of proving that we, as an Australian people, can under the favorable conditions we have around us—setting before us the ideal of being the first people to accomplish what they are aiming at in all parts of the civilised world—to find the solution of what is called the labor problem. I think that we can do it. We can if we set our minds upon it. We can never do it if we are apathetic or careless, nor unless we are an organised party, nor if we do not drop those petty differences existing between us. (Cheers.)

We have special advantages in this young country, and if we make use of them we can accomplish all we desire. We shall then have the satisfaction of having made the world a little better than it was when we came into it. A satisfaction greater and nobler than the satisfaction of a man who dies leaving his children a mass of wealth. That does not bring the satisfaction to a man that doing good for his fellow-men does. Let us have the unselfish spirit that the New Unionism teaches us—the willingness to subscribe to the will of the majority, even though we believe the majority to be wrong—to have sufficient love for our fellow-men to take them on, no matter what they may be or what position in life they may occupy. I expect to see economics advance, and I expect to see what will be really a revolution in our social system in Australia. Let us set up a system that the rest of the world will not be slow to follow. We have certainly, so far, had a good name and held our own in the world in modern social movements. I am anxious that we as a people should be able to do this great work, and that we should be able to give the rest of the world something to imitate, and they will quickly follow in our steps. (Loud cheers).

Abridged.
Source: W. G. Spence, *The Ethics of New Unionism*, Martin and Grose, Creswick, 1892 (pamphlet).

George Simpson
Protection of Settlers, 1892

George Thomas Simpson (1856–1906) was born in Sydney and educated there and in Dunedin, New Zealand. He abandoned early hopes of entering the law and worked as a miner and a grain agent in New Zealand before relocating to Broken Hill in 1883. From this point Simpson launched into a successful career as a speculator and a stockbroker, moving to Western Australia in 1888 to become the first

secretary of the Perth Stock Exchange. Western Australia was in the throes of a
gold boom, and Simpson became a prominent investor on the Southern Cross
goldfields. He entered the Western Australian Legislative Assembly in 1891 as the
member for Geraldton, and became known for his scathing powers of oratory. In
January 1892 the parliament hotly debated government protection of settlers from
Aboriginal attack. On the violent Kimberley frontier, drought had led to unprecedented
Aboriginal spearings of stock. Black–white relations were characterized by extended
guerrilla warfare and massacres of Aboriginal people. In a torrent of racist rhetoric,
Simpson defended the rights of settlers in the Kimberley to be 'their own police',
advocating that 'justice be done with an iron hand'.

To my mind this question is beginning to assume rather ugly proportions.
If we take the history of the colony for the last six months, it seems to me
we have a stream of blood gurgling away from Kimberley to the Irwin—
the blood of settlers 'done to death' by natives. First of all there was poor
Miller done to death at Kimberley. Within the last few days another death
has been recorded, which I am sure has enlisted the sympathies of the
members of this House, on the Ashburton. Then we have young Waldeck,
on the Irwin, also done to death by natives.

I think the best way to proceed in this matter is to start on the basis of
teaching these natives the sacredness of human life. I do not address
myself so particularly to the property aspect of the case, but human life
must be held sacred at any price. We must bear in mind that the development of our colony depends largely on pioneering. Men go out, not in
armed bands, or protected by the police, but with their lives in their
hands, to discover and develop the pastoral, the agricultural, and the
mineral resources of the colony; and the least we can do is to extend them
some protection.

We must bear in mind the proportions which this native difficulty is
assuming. It seems to me to suggest that these pioneer settlers may be
done to death at any minute by an absolutely useless nigger. The whole
thing seems to me to resolve itself into what was once said by a distinguished Australian statesman, Sir Samuel Griffith; we must look the
matter in the face, and decide whether the country where these native
depredations are committed is to be a white or a black man's country. Men
who reside there, and whose word is their bond, tell me they have known
niggers spearing their cattle simply for the fun of the thing. Not because
they were driven to it by drought or by hunger, but simply for fun. Rather
ugly fun for the squatter, the man who has surrendered all the comforts of
civilised life and faced the dangers and drawbacks of this almost torrid
country. When these depredations are committed, these natives simply
laugh at you. They know they are masters of the situation. There is, of
course, the possibility of their being captured, but one must have a very
large imagination to realise that possibility. But, if they are captured, what
is the prospect opened out to them? A temporary but pleasant seaside
sojourn at Rottnest. I think that Rottnest establishment is about the

most grandmotherly thing, and the most silly thing, this colony can show, with its sleek and well-fed niggers.

I may say that the last time I was out in that Never-Never country I saw a native prisoner who had started out with better clothes on than myself, but either the cut of them was not to his tastes, or perhaps they were a little too warm, and he first pitched away his coat, and later on his trousers. He had the decency to retain an undergarment which a paternal Government or the Aborigines Protection Board had supplied him with. He had some flour, also presented to him by the State, and that nigger, after capturing a few lizards, sat down to enjoy his repast, absolutely king, and supremely indifferent to our laws. He naturally felt the utmost contempt for the rights of property or the sacredness of human life, so far as the white man was concerned, and looked forward with positive gusto to the prospects of another sojourn in that agreeable retreat at Rottnest.

I do not wish to use any bloodthirsty arguments about natives. I have seen good natives and bad natives, and I have a strong opinion about them. I think it will be a happy day for Western Australia, and for Australia at large when the natives and the kangaroo disappear. So far as their service on stations is concerned, although I know they are employed by some very level-headed men engaged in pastoral pursuits, still I think when those men come to make up their ledgers and reckon the cost of this kind of labor, the difficulty of management so as to get any satisfactory results, and the methods of conciliation one has to use, it is a question whether those engaged in pastoral pursuits would not do better without this class of labor, and employ some other form of labor more useful.

My own idea about this native difficulty—I throw it out with all due deference to more experienced heads than my own, and to the Ministry—but my own idea is that in these sparsely settled, out of the way districts, the settlers should distinctly understand that when they go there they have to be their own police. I do not think this colony has revenue enough to establish an extensive system of police protection in these far-away districts. I think all of us know that in the settlers in that part of the country where these depredations are committed we have a good class of settlers —a high stamp of men.

I say sitting here as the representative of a constituency largely connected with pastoral pursuits, I should be only too happy to put into the hands of a board, appointed by the Government power to administer justice to natives in that part of the colony, without bringing these natives all the way to Perth. Let this board be composed of men in whom the Government would have confidence. I would also protect the natives. I would ask the Government to appoint a Native Defender in these districts, whose duty it would be to protect the natives, to see that however emaciated or decrepit a native might be he should be properly protected and receive British justice. I think this would be an economical and a good way of dealing with these natives.

There is another point in connection with this native question: I would suggest for the consideration of the Government that the time has come when these natives should be distinctly told that they are to remain on the reserves set apart for them, and that if they go outside those reserves they do so at the risk of suffering pains and penalties. I think that would infuse the native mind with respect for the white man. We are told that it is because of the drought—at least it has been so suggested—that these depredations are committed. I have known droughts, so far as food is concerned, in cities; I have known it in Melbourne and Sydney. But I have never heard it suggested that this scarcity of food warranted a white man to steal a leg of mutton out of a butcher's shop, without being punished for it. If a bad or a dry season is to establish the rule that a nigger may kill a sheep or a bullock with impunity, I do not know where we are going to draw the line. The killing of one sheep or of one bullock or of twenty, or a hundred, is only a question of degree.

I think that in dealing with this matter all maudlin sentiment should be abolished. The time has come for drastic, exact, and positive measures, administered not with a light hand. The Government of the colony should accept the position without flinching and see that justice is done with an iron hand; and let the natives realise that while we are ready to treat them kindly and well so long as they behave themselves, they must also be made to understand that they must show an absolute respect for human life and property.

Abridged.
Source: *Western Australian Parliamentary Debates*, vol. 2, 1891–1892, 14 January 1892, pp. 255–6.

———◆———

Edward Hutton
Duty and Honour, 1894

Major General Sir Edward 'Curly' Hutton (1848–1923) was an energetic and autocratic British officer who swashbuckled his way through several African campaigns, including the Zulu War and the first Anglo–Boer War. In 1888 he returned to Britain, where he developed the mounted infantry, anticipating the 'light horse' units he would later set up in Australia. He married the daughter of a lord and in 1892 became aide-de-camp to Queen Victoria. That same year he was appointed commandant of the New South Wales military forces. With the rank of major-general, he galloped vast distances through the colony, addressing public meetings on patriotism and army recruitment. As Federation approached, he began organizing the Australian Army; he envisaged a citizen force capable of fighting anywhere in the service of the Empire. In December 1894 Hutton was invited to distribute the prizes and to present the Speech Day address at the exclusive all-boys Sydney Church of England Grammar School. Hutton knew his audience well: they were chaps of his own stamp, the future leaders of a British Australia.

I am a soldier. And as a soldier I am not in the habit of talking very much. But for the sake of the recollections I entertain of my early school days at Eton, I wish to say a few words to you today. Soldiers are proud of two watchwords and the boys in this great school who wish to become great Englishmen must learn to maintain these watchwords.

They are *duty* and *honour*. (Applause.) Duty—to yourselves, to your parents, to your friends. And honour—your own honour, and the honour of your county. (Applause.)

These two watchwords we, as soldiers, cherish. And I would ask you boys, who sit before me here today—members of the rising generation of a great British Empire—to also cherish these words, if you are going to follow in the broad footsteps of those who have made these words mean what they do today. (Applause.)

As regards that important word, *duty*—you are being taught your duty as boys at school and I advise you, in the life after school, to be firm in carrying out that duty. Take to yourselves the line that duty dictates, and then, cost what it may, carry out that line. (Applause). Your headmaster has touched a chord in his recollection of his own public school days. He referred to 'old boy feeling', for he too is an old boy of Eton College. To give you an idea of the enormous bond which unites Etonians in all parts of the world, I will relate an anecdote.

At the battle of Langs Nek when the British troops were following rapidly after the Boers, there were three Etonians at the head of the regiment. In the heat of the moment one of the Etonians pushed past his commander waving his sword on high. At that moment he was struck by a bullet from the Boers, which soon proved fatal. He still continued to wave his sword, and turning round to his commander cried, *'Floreat Etona!'* (Applause.)

Those athletic games, cricket, football, rowing, and everything that the English are so proud of, have helped to make the British race what it is today. It has given us determination, perseverance, and that upright character which marks Englishmen in all parts of the world—and makes the British Empire what it is. (Applause.)

To give you an illustration of what I mean by determination, I will acquaint you with the fact that I have just left the Association Cricket Ground. I saw United Australia for the first time playing a magnificent innings for 586 runs. (Loud applause.) The Englishmen had gone in against that great score, and made 386 in the first innings and 437 in the second, and that was through pluck, determination, and perseverance, and the Englishmen, by the skin of their teeth, won by ten runs. (Applause.)

In speaking to you boys, I feel that I am addressing the men of the future. You boys in Australia are in a proud position indeed. You are the inheritors of a great birthright. But in New South Wales you have a very small notion what that inheritance is. Not until you travel the world—and visit India, the Mediterranean, Africa, Canada, Burma[h], will you realise what it is to be an Englishman. (Loud cheers.)

You have to maintain that birthright, and it is not to be maintained except by cultivating all the highest instincts that are required to make a man. You all know the feelings experienced when a son does not maintain the prestige of his father or the family. You, as Australian boys, are part of the great family of the British race. Though you are only one portion of that race, it is a portion which in the future will play a very important part in the world's affairs. In conclusion, I ask you to remember the responsibilities you have inherited in being Australian natives and British subjects.

Reproduced in full.
Transposed from indirect speech.
Source: Sydney Church of England Grammar School, *Major-General Hutton's Speech, December 21st, 1894* (pamphlet), Mitchell Library, State Library of New South Wales (ML ref. 179.9 H).

Frank Madden

If Women Had the Vote They Would Abolish Manly Games, 1895

Sir Frank Madden (1847–1921) was born in Cork, Ireland, and when he was ten years old emigrated with his family to Melbourne. He trained as a solicitor and set up offices in Collins Street, soon becoming a well-known figure in the colony's legal circles. In 1894 Madden won a seat in the Legislative Assembly representing the Eastern Suburbs, and here he expounded his extreme conservative views. Even those on his ideological side of politics often found him 'impossible', as he pugnaciously stated his opposition to state support for education, the eight-hour day and any cause that smacked of socialism. Not surprisingly, he was suspicious of the women's suffrage movement, which had already secured votes for women in the neighbouring colony of South Australia in 1894. In this 1895 speech to the Victorian parliament Madden argued that if women were able to vote they would side with 'socialists' and undermine the masculinity of the British Empire. In 1902 the Commonwealth parliament decreed that all Australian citizens, regardless of their sex, could vote in federal elections. Victoria, birthplace of the women's suffrage movement, became the last state to grant that right in 1908.

During the recess I attended a meeting in my electorate which was convened by the association supporting women's suffrage. This meeting was addressed by various speakers of ability, both male and female.

The ladies I lately heard were cultured matrons of mature age, who were as little hysterical on the subject as the impulsive nature of woman would allow, and who convinced me beyond a shadow of a doubt—if I had needed convincing in that direction—that the granting of the franchise to women would be a terrible mistake.

The objects and aspirations of these ladies are pure, noble—and impossible. These ladies have not commenced to understand what a wicked world we live in, and while in their language and conduct they show how wide a charity moves their hearts; they also show us how utterly unqualified they are to deal with the great questions with which they propose to grapple.

Their first proposal, as I understand it, is to do away with soldiers and war. Now, that involves the total regeneration and reconstruction of the human race. Unless all nations are induced to cease to grow and train soldiers, for any one nation to do so would be simply to lay itself open to the first marauding enemy that chose to come down on it. Where would the glory of the British race—the glory of brave men and chaste women—go to if we do not train our boys to fight for hearths and homes? What would be the use of passing laws fixing the consent age in girls if we are powerless to protect those girls from ravishment by soldiers of a foreign nation?

And how would these good ladies set about doing away with soldiers? They tell us they would abolish racing, hunting, football, cricket, and all such manly games as rouse the combative spirit of emulation among our boys and young men. Although these ladies are not warriors, they agree with Wellington that the battles of England are won in the school-yards and hunting fields of England. And yet they would abolish that manly spirit which makes true women proud of their natural defenders. Have they forgotten the siege of Lucknow, and its relief by brave Havelock and his Highlanders? Would they prefer to have had their English sisters left to the mercy of the infuriated Indians, drunk with European blood, by whom they were surrounded?

But why pick out instances when the only difficulty is to choose from the multitude which occur to one's memory? Take the last occasion on which England made her enemies feel the weight of her hand. When a few of our countrymen were shut up in Chitral, besieged by some of the most bloodthirsty savages in India, was the danger and difficulty of the road considered by our countrymen or our brave Indian subjects who have been proud to acquire that martial spirit and military training which distinguish our arms in the East? No! Chitral was to be relieved, and they relieved it. They had to travel over almost impassable roads. They had to cross broad and rushing rivers without bridges or boats. They had to march for miles up to their knees in snow. They were harassed by day and by night by the active and hostile tribesmen who knew every rock and every turn of the road which gave cover from which to fire. But our men did not halt or falter. Some were blinded by the snow, some were crippled with frost-bite, many were shot; but they relieved Chitral, and they made the tribesmen feel that difficulties and dangers only make a British soldier more determined to conquer or to die.

And this is the spirit these good ladies would like to see eliminated from the British race. Would it be wise to double the present number of voters if the new half of them hold views like these? That in itself is, to my mind, an answer to the question. But there were other proposals which were mentioned and approved of at the meeting to which I have alluded. It was there stated, and the statement was applauded by the promoters of the meeting, that in the state of Wyoming, in America, where women have an equal franchise with men, the consent age of girls has been raised to 21. This shows the lengths that some women would go. It is simply entering into a conflict with human nature to pass any such law, and the approval of such a proposal by women shows how unqualified they are to deal with great questions in a broad and statesmanlike manner. They know so little of politics that they imagine they can change people's natures by Act of Parliament.

There is no man here who would go further than I to protect our girls in the early years of their womanhood. But, while protecting girls, I am not afraid to be just to the men. Since the consent age was raised to sixteen here we have seen what a terrible weapon has been placed in the hands of certain designing young vixens. It is but a few months ago since a Judge in a certain case stated from the bench—'That such a girl under sixteen years was more likely to seduce than to be seduced.' In another case we saw that but for the skilful cross-examination of Mr. Maxwell a low-minded slut under sixteen was prepared to swear away a man's life. She is now suffering the penalty for perjury. But what may not occur if we raise the age to 21? Well, I don't know if the good St. Anthony was a citizen of the United States and came from Wyoming, but I do know we don't grow many St. Anthonys here, and I can plainly see an infinity of misery if such a law were passed in Victoria. And these good ladies who want the franchise would pass it if they could.

There are two distinct classes of women who are clamouring for the franchise. There is the chaste honest amiable matron, whose charity outruns her discretion, and whose knowledge of politics is so small that she or that her good-nature is being made use of by a section of the community which is struggling for power by every conceivable method. It is well as a further test of the capacity of these ladies for political life to see what section of the political public they associate with and by whom they are supported. We find that on every platform they are supported by socialists. Not the amiable amateur socialist, who really does not know the meaning of the term or the views of the party; but the pronounced determined eloquent socialist, of the type of Mr. Champion and the Rev. Dr. Strong.

And if the franchise was granted to women it is by just such men as these they would be led—polished educated gentlemen, whom women could respect for their pure and honorable lives. They are men without a stain upon them, but more dangerous to the community than the most foul-mouthed demagogue who ever preached sedition on the banks of the Yarra.

These worthy ladies look everywhere for arguments to support their cause, and bring forward one quotation from Genesis in support of their view:—'So God created man in his own image, in the image of God he created him: male and female he created them.' This is a general statement in the first chapter, and does not, I consider, bear the interpretation the good ladies place upon it; but if they would look a little further into the Book they will find the following:—'Unto the woman he said.... Thy desire shall be to thy husband, and he shall rule over thee.' That law is clear and plain, and has been acted on ever since it was given.

I have dealt with one class of women who claim the franchise in order to enable them to set up a social despotism, and now I will deal with 'the women who did,' and who are making strenuous efforts to gain power for themselves by bringing forward false arguments and specious pleas on behalf of the women 'who didn't' and who 'don't intend to.' The former are the shrieking women to whom I alluded when last I spoke on the subject in this House. These are the creatures who write the vilest of modern literature to show how manly they become when they are mannish. These are the worst form of socialists. Their idea of freedom is polyandry, free love, lease marriages, and so on.

Are these the qualifications for the franchise? Are we going to allow women who would sap the very foundation of a nation who do not understand the meaning of the holy word 'Home' to have a voice in the government of the country? No; let them have the divided skirt if they please. That is as near the manly costume as they dare to come, and when they wear that they break the law which says—'The woman shall not wear that which pertaineth unto a man, neither shall a man put on a woman's garment. For all that do so are an abomination to the Lord thy God.'

Abridged.
Source: *Victorian Parliamentary Debates*, Session 1895–6, vol. 79, Legislative Assembly, 25 November 1895, pp. 3495–7.

John Forrest
Water to the Coolgardie Goldfields, 1896

John Forrest (1847–1918) was born in Bunbury, Western Australia, and spent the first half of his adult life as a gritty and enquiring explorer of Western Australia. A popular figure who spoke ably 'on his feet', Forrest was elected the colony's first premier (in 1890) and was to be a strong supporter of Federation. Throughout the

1890s 'Big John' borrowed courageously to finance large government projects in a visionary development of major infrastructure in Western Australia, then experiencing the gold boom. On 21 July 1896 Forrest outlined to Parliament his ambitious £2.5 million scheme to supply water to the thirsty goldfields of Coolgardie and Kalgoorlie. The five-hundred-kilometre pipeline and its pumping stations were to be meticulously designed by the colony's Chief Engineer, C. Y. O'Connor. O'Connor and Forrest agreed that local contractors were too slipshod and greedy to be trusted with the scheme: instead, construction would be carried out entirely by government employees. O'Connor's private-sector enemies retaliated with a slur campaign so vicious that it drove O'Connor to suicide before the work was finished. Forrest opened the pipeline at Kalgoorlie on 24 January 1903, and it still operates today. Forrest recommended the proposed pipeline to Parliament in the following terms.

First, then, as to whether this water supply is necessary. I do not think it requires very much argument to prove this point. No one probably will get up in his place in this House and say that the water question is not the great question that requires solving in regard to the Coolgardie and Yilgarn goldfields. Everyone I think agrees in regard to this. If anyone, however, has any doubt on this point I should only wish that he had travelled as I did over the Coolgardie goldfields in December last. There was not sufficient water for crushing anywhere. Water was being sold at the condensers at from fourpence to sixpence a gallon. It cost a pound to water my five horses. I do not know what small sum it would cost—I can hardly calculate it—for doing the same thing if the scheme we propose were carried out. It certainly would not cost more than a penny or twopence to do what cost a pound in December last.

What did I see during my visit to those goldfields in December last? Absence of water everywhere. I found a numerous population of hard-working men, as dirty as ever they could be. No water to wash in—scarcely enough to drink. At one place called Bardoc, I got there early in the forenoon, and found about fifty men waiting at a small inn, and I asked if there was any water. They said that there was not, and that they did not expect any till evening, when a team was coming in with water, but when it would actually arrive they did not know. They were in the greatest straits for want of water to drink. The only mines at work on the goldfields at that time were three at Kalgoorlie and one at Broad Arrow, at a mine called Hill End, and they scarcely had sufficient water to go on with the work on that mine, which has turned out some of the richest quartz in the district. They had to carry salt water several miles in order to crush with it, and then could only obtain a small quantity at very great cost. Things are very little better at the present time on the fields than they were in December, excepting that there has been some rainfall, but I have no doubt that anyone who visits the Coolgardie goldfields in December next will find very little difference as compared with the state of things I experienced there last year.

I will ask this House if this state of things is to continue. Are the large centres of Coolgardie and Kalgoorlie to depend on condensed water at twopence or threepence[cf below] per gallon forever? These two large towns, if they develop in the way we all hope to see them develop, will want at least three-quarters of a million gallons each for domestic purposes; and if the population we expect goes there, and the mines prosper, as we believe they will, how are these three-quarters of a million gallons of good fresh water to be obtained for the towns of Coolgardie and Kalgoorlie? Are they to be obtained by condensing even at a half-penny a gallon? Is that to be the state of affairs that is to go on forever? Is that to be the permanent water supply for that country? I hope not. No stock could be kept in all that territory in December last. I did not see a single hoof except it was round a condenser, or a small number of sheep kept for killing purposes. I did see, however, and it was painful to see it, horses left on the roads tired and jaded, left to die in the wilderness, and it was only at the Government tanks, where the water lasted—and there were very few of them—that these animals could get a drink. It was only while there was water in the Government tanks that there was any chance of these poor animals getting a drink, as no one else, except the Government, would give them a drink for nothing. There were no stock paddocks—not a single stock paddock in all that country; and if there had been there was no water to sustain the stock, unless owners were prepared to pay for water at fourpence or sixpence a gallon. The stock required for the meat supply was sent up by rail, as far as the railway ran, and was killed as quickly as possible.

There is no doubt about it—I speak from experience, and there are other experienced men in this House who will support me—that there is in the eastern portion of this colony, and in Central Australia generally, a very small and uncertain rainfall. It is an absolute certainty that it is a droughty country. We do not want anyone to tell us that. Those of us who have lived here, and had any experience in travelling in the interior of Australia, know that as we go to the eastward, when we get over the coastal ranges, the rainfall decreases. Even in our own eastern districts, at our very doors, we know there is almost always 10 inches difference in the rainfall as compared with the rainfall in the Darling Ranges, and as you go further eastward we know from experience that the rainfall is more uncertain and in smaller quantity.

Some people will say, and have said whilst this matter has been under discussion, that we can depend upon the rainfall in the interior for the water supply on the goldfields. Have we not had seven years' experience of Southern Cross and four years' experience of Coolgardie? We know with what result—that there is not a single drop of fresh water at Southern Cross unless it is caught from the heavens, or unless it is condensed, and if you catch all the rain it is possible to secure there will not be nearly enough. During the seven years that we have known Southern Cross, the rainfall has not averaged more than five inches, and we know from experience the tanks that we have had constructed are never full, that the tank at the '13 mile' from Southern Cross, which has a good catchment, has never been half full, and it has been constructed two or three years. The tank at New Zealand Gully has never been half full, and all along the line, although these tanks have been constructed with splendid catchments, in very few instances have they been altogether full. The average rainfall of the interior is not likely to exceed five inches. It is five inches so far as our information goes, and it is not likely year by year to exceed five inches. [An Hon. Member: It may be less.] Yes; it may be less at times and it may be more on some few occasions. Of course thunderstorms will come, but they are uncertain, and cannot be depended on. Where are the catchments, and where is the rain to fill them?

What I wish to say is that there is no certainty, and that all experience shows that the annual rainfall you have to depend upon is not likely to exceed five inches. It is my opinion, founded on some experience, that no scheme based on the rainfall in the interior of Australia can be depended upon as a permanent water supply for a large population. I have some experience of these matters. In 1874 I crossed from Champion Bay to the overland telegraph line, from Adelaide to Port Darwin, and on that route we passed places which were named as places where permanent water was to be found. These were Windich Springs, Weld Springs, Fort Müeller, Beare's Creek, and Lungley's Gully, four places where there was running water. We thought that season was a very dry one, and declared that these places had permanent water, but we have heard that the beautiful running streams we saw were dry the year before last, and that a surveyor who visited Weld Springs had to dig for water. He found some by digging. Fort Müeller, we know, has been absolutely dry, from the experience of some explorers who have visited it since I was there. Beare's Creek, in the Musgrave Ranges, where we could hear the hum of running water half a mile off, has since been dry, and explorers have had to dig 20 feet to get a drink. At Lungley's Gully, a stream that we saw running between high hills, and which had every appearance of permanency, has been altogether dry since.

We need not go so far into the interior as the places I have been speaking of. My friends, the hon. members for the De Grey, and for Beverley, who have had experience in the Nor'-West in pastoral pursuits, and where there are immense pools with every semblance of permanency—have they not found them all dry on some occasions? What about other places? We can go to the Gascoyne or elsewhere in this country, and even in the Northern settled districts within range of the coastal rainfall, and what is the evidence? We find there are droughts, and long droughts. On a station on the coast, belonging to my friend the Attorney-General, only a total of five inches of rain fell during five years, or an average of about one inch a year. So it is wherever you look, even comparatively near the coast. Well, then, if these things have occurred even close to the sea, how much more will they occur away in the interior, where there are no mountain ranges and no rivers, for it must be always remembered that there is no river system in the whole of Central Australia? Surely these are evidences that the House will not set aside.

In 1869, when I travelled along by Lake Barlee and Mount Margaret, through country which has since become famous goldfields, there were an abundance of marsupials in that country; but where are they now? When I asked the aboriginals what had become of the kangaroos and other marsupials they told me that drought had killed them all. Soon after I was in the Coolgardie goldfields, viz., in January last, every tank belonging to the Government was dry. There was not a drop of fresh water throughout the goldfields in any catchment from the rainfall, and the people had to depend upon condensed water for their sustenance. Notwithstanding all this knowledge of my own, and the evidence of others, people who have had no experience in these things in this colony have come to me and propounded schemes, saying they were prepared to raise funds in the British market to carry out the work of erecting reservoirs in the interior of these goldfields, and from those catchments to supply the large and increasing populations that are going to these fields, and also to provide the mines with water. I am not going to be led astray by people of that sort. I have my own knowledge and the knowledge of other people, and I am convinced that any scheme based upon the rainfall in the Coolgardie goldfields is not one that we can place dependence upon, but is one that would probably lead us into great difficulty and great disaster.

I now come to another point that I wish to place before hon. members, and that is the question of private enterprise. I have told you that, unless this project is to be carried out as a Government work, the alternative is that we must hand it over to private enterprise, because the work must be done. I stand here to-night opposed to private enterprise in regard to this great work. I am not, however, opposed to minor works being undertaken by private enterprise, but I am opposed to a great project like this, which would mean the necessities, the conveniences, and even the lives of people on these goldfields being handed over to private control. I am opposed to that altogether.

I will ask this House again, and will ask the people of this colony, whether this great auriferous country that we have to the eastward shall be handed over to private speculators, to provide a water supply; whether we shall hand over that great work to a pack of speculators, who cannot manage it as well or as cheaply as we can. Have we not had enough of these promoters offering to do our public works yet in this country? [MR. SIMPSON: No.] The experience I have had with such persons has all been unsatisfactory. I never had any good experience in connection with their projects. There is one that we will perhaps have to deal with in a few days; one of these projects which has been carried out by private enterprise, and which the Government will now be asked to buy up in the interests of the people. That is what it comes to in the end. The Midland Railway, also the Great Southern Railway, are not giving that satisfaction which the people of this colony were led to expect; and do you want more of these private projects? These promoters make plenty of promises when they come before you. They profess they will do anything, and sometimes they do make a start; but after making a start they often get into difficulties and have to come to the Government for assistance. Delay ensues. There is then perhaps a reconstruction, then obstruction, then threats to injure the credit of the colony, and the last act of the play is that we have to buy them out.

You were told by the hon. member for Geraldton that some mining experts—and he named one friend of mine—had expressed opinions adverse to the Government scheme; but what do they propose in place of it? Nothing. They propose to wait upon Providence, trusting to the rainfall. They propose to trust to boring in the earth, and to many other things; but I have an idea that those gentlemen as a rule are interested in or have a little project of their own to carry out, which this scheme of the Government will interfere with. Well, if they have, I cannot help it, and do not care a straw what they say. I am not here as an advocate of private enterprise for a great project like this. I am here not only as the advocate for the people of Coolgardie, but for the people of the whole colony.

I think I said the chief opponents [of this pipeline scheme] were those who have a little water scheme of their own to promote. However that may be, there are other opponents, there are other good honest men in this country who are opponents. They are timid and afraid. They have not been accustomed to great projects. I find no fault with these people, as I know them to be honorably inclined, but it seems to me that if they had had their way during the last six years, since the introduction of Responsible Government, the colony would not be in the position it is in today.

To these good men who are my friends, I say we are not afraid. The members of the Government and the supporters of the Government are not adventurers, we have something to lose, and we believe that this is a great and urgent work, and we also believe that it will pay. I will ask hon. members whether they have found us very much in the wrong during the six years we have been working together for the good of the colony. And if we have not been wrong in the past, is it not probable that we shall be right in this matter, as we have been in many other projects that we have had difficulty in carrying through this House? I wish hon. members to remember that the expansion of the revenue and the increase in the value of land, which is enormous, especially in the city of Perth—the good market for the producers—and I appeal to producers especially and ask all those who have producing interests in the colony to rally round the Government and support this scheme, because we are going to provide markets in the interior, which will be sufficient for all you can supply for a very long time—and the general prosperity of the colony are all very largely due to the goldfields. Besides these things we have been able to build railways, construct the Fremantle harbor works, and we propose to establish a deep sewerage scheme in Perth and Fremantle, all of which are works you so much desire, but none of them could have been carried out before the discovery of gold in this colony. Let us all remember these things in dealing with this question, and help that industry which has been helping every other industry in the colony. What is there to be afraid of? I suppose I am more intimately associated with the finances of this colony than anyone else. I have to look after them from year to year, and know their details, and I am not afraid of this scheme, which will be a self-supporting one and will assist the agricultural and every other industry in the colony. I think that when hon. members come to reflect upon this matter and consider it in the way I have considered it they will be convinced that there is no alternative. There is really no alternative but to adopt it. The proposal for conserving rainfall as a permanent supply for the fields is in my opinion quite out of the question.

In conclusion, I would like to emphasise this point, that not only are the mines languishing for the want of water, and the output of gold is being retarded, but our fellow-colonists who are trying to build up this country are also languishing—living in discomfort, without even the necessaries of life in regard to water. And when we remember that dirt and disease are fostered by the want of water, where health and cleanliness should prevail, surely a strong case is made out in favor of this scheme. I say, sir, the scheme which I have had the pleasure and honor of placing before the members of this House, and before my fellow-colonists, is a project worthy of an enterprising people. I believe, if we carry out this great work, not only will the goldfields flourish, and not only shall we be relieved from our present anxiety in regard to the water question, but we shall also be repaid a hundred fold. Future generations, I am quite certain, will think of us and bless us for our far-seeing patriotism, and it will be said of us as Isaiah said of old: 'They made a way in the wilderness, and rivers in the desert.'

Abridged.
Source: *Western Australian Parliamentary Debates*, Legislative Assembly, 21 July 1896, pp. 130–51.

———————

Isaac Isaacs

Federation and States Rights, 1897

Isaac Alfred Isaacs (1855–1948) was born into a Jewish immigrant family in Melbourne and spent his early years in towns in north-eastern Victoria. He qualified as a teacher before completing a first-class honours degree in law at the University of Melbourne. By the 1890s he was well established as a barrister, with a reputation for the clarity and authority of his legal briefs. Isaacs reportedly had a photographic memory, and was a forceful speaker and debater whose analysis of fine technicalities was often adorned with literary quotations. In the 1892 Victorian election he was returned as a member of the Legislative Assembly for Bogong, representing the rural constituency of his youth, and later served as attorney general. He reformed

Victoria's company law, supported the Factories Acts to eliminate sweatshops and set fair wages, was sympathetic to women's suffrage and welcomed Federation. In 1897 he was elected as a Victorian delegate to the Federal Convention which met over several months in Adelaide, Sydney and Melbourne. There, he drew upon his extensive learning in constitutional law to make speeches that were lengthy and pedantic, and so antagonized his fellow delegates that he was excluded from the committee that drafted the Constitution. Isaacs was a strong defender of the rights of the populous larger states in the Federal Agreement. He claimed he awaited the day when Federation would be achieved, for then he could say 'I am an Australian'. In the new Commonwealth he served in the federal parliament and as a judge of the High Court, and as chief justice, before becoming the first native-born Governor-General in 1931. On 13 April 1897 Isaacs outlined what he saw as the distinctions between Commonwealth and state responsibilities.

I feel that we have arrived at a point where the tension is of the greatest, and I feel that within the next hour or so the fate for the present at all events, of the Federation question in Australia will be determined. The people of Victoria, and indeed of all Australia, desire that there should be Federation. They see that amongst the various powers, authorities, and rights that their several governments wield and exercise there are some that concern them, and this is the root of the matter which interests them, not as individuals of different States, but as the people of the whole continent of Australia. They see the disadvantages, the folly, the expense, and the danger of remaining separated on certain questions, and with that before them, and uniting with their material considerations a public sentiment of the highest possible nature, they desire that their separate existences as States with regard to those collective interests should cease now and for ever, and that they should hence-forth be regarded as one united people. I was very much surprised to hear my hon. friend Mr. McMillan refer to what he called the ignorant feeling on the part of the people of Australia; but so far as I have had the privilege of coming into contact with the people on this question. I find that the feeling, so far from being ignorant, has been of slow growth; it is deep rooted, clear, and is the result of a long and careful education. I believe there is nothing they would prize more at the present moment than to see these arbitrary marks and divisions that now exist in regard to certain matters entirely obliterated.

When we are asked to make what are termed concessions, I ask have we not already made more concessions than the justice of the case warrants? Let us ask ourselves what is the meaning of this Federation. Let us consider for a moment what it seems to me has been entirely lost sight of: the reason of this Federation and the meaning of it. We possess as separate and distinct colonies a host of powers and authorities. Most of these are purely of local concern. Most of these can be best worked out by us as we now stand as different and distinct identities. With most of these things no one State is concerned with the management of the other, but there are certain matters—such as defence, quarantine, and various other things—we generally agree upon, in which we as a people say we are concerned, not as residents of Victoria, Tasmania, or any other colony, but because our interests and our desires are united. We say there is henceforth to be no distinction between us; let us blot out of our future history and out of our future politics the arbitrary fact that we are residents of different colonies, and if we start with that and we select these subjects, it is on the distinct basis that our interests are identical.

If our interests are identical why do we have it continually thrown in our face that the diversity of State interests in these matters is to be protected? We select these subjects on which we are agreed; there is by this very hypothesis no diversity of interests in these matters, and the residuary powers are retained by the States. As to these they have their State rights, and the federal authority cannot enter into the sphere one single inch. It is outside the sphere of Federation altogether, but when we have selected these subjects on which our interests are presumably identical the States, as such, have equally little claim to enter. It is because we assume as a starting point that there is no divergence of interest that we attempt to federate at all, and we are doing something self-contradictory when we say in one breath that we federate on these subjects as one united people with regard to State distinctions because our interests are identical in these matters, and in the next breath turn round and say we must have equal representation in the Senate because we must protect the diversity of our interests in these matters. If our interests are not identical, do not federate. If they are diverse and repugnant let us remain as we are, but do not let us be inconsistent and illogical with ourselves by saying one moment: We federate in these matters, and select them from the mass of our present possessions—we place on one side all those subjects that concern us as one people, as Australians, not as residents of separate colonies, and we deal with these under a Federal Government—that as to these questions we regard ourselves as a nation, and yet the next instant, with forgetfulness of the true position, that in the very collective interests we must still protect our State rights.

This is the starting point of the matter. The State rights are conserved by the exclusion of the subjects which are still retained for State government. Such interest in the matters that are appropriated to the Federation are admitted to be identical, or else we would not federate. If they are not identical, if they do not concern us generally, why do we federate upon them at all? Therefore it is because we say: Henceforth let us be one nation in those regards, let us contribute man for man throughout Australasia with regard to them, let us regulate them as one people—that we have determined to enter upon this scheme. For that reason we have the House of Representatives on the basis of proportional representation, and we have a Second Chamber as they have in America for the purpose of what has been called the sober second thought of the people, elected in a different manner for a different term, and without the power of dissolution; but it is only the fear, the ill-grounded fear, of the smaller American States that led them after that was determined on to say 'We must have equal representation.' It was denied by the Federalists, insisted upon by the Particularists, and here we have the same fight 100 years afterwards. This principle is foreign to Federation. The only units in a true Federation are the people. Outside the sphere of the Federation we have the States, and their people owe allegiance to them, but the allegiance of the peoples to the States can only be in regard to the matters which are not conferred upon the federal authority. The allegiance of the people to the federal authority is beyond all question free of the allegiance of the people to the States in that connection.

That is the key of the whole position. A State is not a unit in a true Federation. That is an important principle, and to my mind it is the vital question when we are considering the question of equal representation. It is because the people have come to the conclusion that certain matters heretofore carried on by the States as such should not longer be so, but should be massed together and worked in the interests of the people as a whole, that we have determined to federate at all. Once we have arrived at that conclusion we exclude State interference in their particular range. We are told—never mind the logic of the position—that equal representation is essential. I believed, and within certain limitations I believe it still, that equal representation is right to protect the smaller States from fears which are groundless, but, as I have said before, and I hope may repeat without presumption, are not unreasonable in certain minds. But I am not willing that that equal representation shall be coupled with co-ordinate powers. If you have co-ordinate powers, or what are tantamount to co-ordinate powers, you have no need for equal representation.

Abridged.
Source: *Australian Federal Convention Debates*, Adelaide, 13 April 1897, vol. 3, pp. 542–5.

———◆———

George Reid
'Yes–No' for Federation, 1898

George Houstoun Reid (1845–1918) emigrated to Australia with his Scottish Presbyterian clerical family in 1852 and began his working life as a junior clerk for a Sydney merchant at the age of thirteen. His autobiography charts his rise from 'no triumphs' as a schoolboy to his flowering in young men's debating societies, where he recognized that his 'thick skin' and perseverance were ideal qualities for a political orator.[30] After a career in the public service and admittance to the Bar, Reid realized his political ambitions when he entered the New South Wales parliament in

1880. By 1894 he was the 'Free Trade Premier', overhauling the public service, introducing fiscal reforms, and raising revenue for the colony via direct land and income
taxes. Reid was wary that Federation would force New South Wales to surrender free
trade to the protectionist interests of Victoria and the other colonies. But he played
a key role in bringing the colonial premiers together in Hobart in early 1895, and in
the Federal Convention of 1897–98 where he disagreed with aspects of the draft
constitution that would disadvantage New South Wales. With the ratification of the
Bill to be decided by a referendum, Reid addressed his constituency at Sydney Town
Hall on 28 March 1898. The packed audience of five thousand included those for
and against Federation, all uncertain of Reid's position. Reid was an extraordinary
platform speaker, the surety and wit of his words matched by his overpowering and
corpulent presence. With the declared 'impartiality of a judge addressing a jury', he
quickly discarded notes and for two hours advanced the pros and cons of the Bill.
Only in his concluding remarks was Reid's support clear, and the meeting dissolved
amid cheering and disappointment. The colony's failure to pass the Bill was blamed
on Reid's confusing message, but in the new and ultimately successful negotiations
over Federation greater concessions were granted to New South Wales. Reid's pre-
varicator's speech earned him the nickname of 'Yes–No Reid' for the remainder of
his political career, including a term as Australia's third prime minister.

In Conclusion:– Looking beyond this instrument, and believing that in
every word of this bill there is an effort, with which every man with ordinary feelings of patriotism will cordially sympathise, I say that the whole
of this enterprise with all its drawbacks and faults has a noble side to it. If
there is written on the book of destiny one fact clearer and more signifi-
cantly than any other, in reference to these southern lands, it is the fact
that soon or later, by one sort of contrivance or another, the whole of the
boundaries that separate Australian from Australian must come down.
(Cheers.) Divided strength and varying, and sometimes intensely conflict-
ing purposes now radiate from five or six centres of political thought, and
government and legislation must someday be united, and the whole manhood, intellect, and power of all the colonies must be crowned by an act of
union. (Cheers.)

I feel myself under a peculiarly deep sense of responsibility. I, with my
colleagues, brought the government of Australia together in an effort at
last on the broadest democratic grounds to carry this work to a happy conclusion. The colonies responded to the invitation, and passed laws which
brought into existence a convention framed on a basis which was well
known before the Convention was summoned. It was too late [for] us to
criticise the fact that in this Convention so many people's representatives
could outvote the representatives of so many others. That was known
beforehand, and so with equal representation in the Senate. In many
respects no man had greater repugnance than I to such a provision, but I
looked on it as a thing without which federation seemed to be an impossible dream. I, knowing these things, entered upon the responsible leadership of this movement as a political movement outside the Convention. I
also knew that there was only too much room for fear; that in the great

crisis of a nation's destiny the voice of the people might be strangled. (A voice — 'So it will be.') I hope it will not be so.

I ask you in New South Wales: I implore after you have fully realised the grandeur of the thing in view, and after you have fully realised the absolute necessity of some day, and some day soon, being one nation; I ask you to look at this bill honestly and fearlessly, and to decide for yourselves on your own conscience. So far as I am concerned, with all the criticisms I have levelled at the bill, with all the fears I have for the future, I feel I cannot become a deserter to the cause of federation. (Great cheering.) I cannot take up this bill with enthusiasm. I see serious blots on it, which have put a cruel strain on me. I have not made up my mind about this without great deal of painful and anxious thought. Great as nationhood is great as Australian union is, I admit we ought to have a more democratic constitution. (Cheers.) I fought hard to bring this bill more into harmony with my views. I sometimes succeeded, and I often failed. Looking back on the Convention now that the fight is over, I frankly and honestly say they were a body of men who acted honourably, and a voted according to their judgement. Now, having opened up my mind, having shown the dark places as well as the light places in this constitution, I put it on every man in this country without coercion or interference from me to judge for himself. So far as I am concerned, I consider my duty to Australia demands me to record a vote in favour of this bill.

'Conclusion' to the speech reproduced in full.
Sources: *Argus*, 29 March 1898 pp. 5–6; *Sydney Morning Herald*, 19 March 1898, p. 4.

———————◆———————

William Holman
Against Sending Troops to South Africa, 1899

William Arthur Holman (1871–1934) emigrated to Melbourne in 1888 with his actor parents. After the Bijou Theatre (where the senior Holmans were engaged) was destroyed by fire, the family relocated to Sydney and Holman obtained employment as a cabinetmaker. A prodigious reader and intellectual, he became active in debating and discussion groups at the Sydney Mechanics' School of Arts, where he met Edmund Barton and Billy Hughes. Holman joined the fledgling Australian Labor Party, attracted by its socialist ideals, and worked within the union movement, demonstrating a flair for grass-roots political organization. In 1898 he won the seat of Grenfell in the New South Wales Legislative Assembly. Holman viewed Federation as a distraction and channelled his energies towards strengthening the Labor Party in New South Wales. Known for his charismatic presence and melodious voice, he achieved a reputation for outstanding eloquence both in and out of Parliament. In October 1899, the New South Wales Government was in fierce debate about whether to send a contingent to fight alongside British troops against the Boer republics in the great struggle for control of southern Africa. Taking a minority position, Holman argued against the war in a speech that drew upon recent history and aroused jingoism and forceful interjections from his fellow parliamentarians.

We are asked to arm and equip 375 of our fellow-colonists, and to send them to another country to shoot men down. A very bitter responsibility will rest upon the head of every man in this Assembly if a single man is killed by our action in sending away this contingent, and it can be shown afterwards that we were mistaken, and threw in our weight with the wrong side in an unjust and unrighteous quarrel.

I say that there are no people in the world who have no grievances, and I admit that the Uitlanders have grievances. Their grievances amount to this: that the Transvaal Government refuses to permit the Uitlander, the alien, the stranger within its gates, to take any part in the political life of the country until he becomes naturalised. But the grievance exists in full force in our midst to-day. There are men in my own electorate who, although they have been in this country for fifteen years, have never had a vote and never will have a vote, no matter how long they may live in the colony, or how industrious may be their share in the work of the colony, unless they throw off their allegiance to their native land and swear allegiance to the Queen of Great Britain and Ireland. But they do not want to do that, and, therefore, we, as a self-governing colony, refuse to allow them the political rights that we enjoy. The position is the same in the Transvaal.

The time has now come to speak plainly, and to throw all the pretence that this is an affair of the empire to the winds. I do not know whether it is necessary for me to say that I am loyal to the empire. I happen to have been born in England, and come of solid and patriotic English stock, and I say that I have a profound respect for my own nation. Whilst I am loyal to the empire, I see with emotions of shame and indignation which I can hardly express, the name and reputation of that empire being dragged in the dust at the behest of a little gang of swindling speculators on the Rand.

We know that this affair is no movement of the empire at all. We know how the whole trouble between the Dutch and the British races at the Cape has been stirred up since that masterly and statesmanlike pacification was brought about by the greatest Englishman of the century. Every time there has been a rift in the lute at Cape Colony a revival of the old hatred between the Dutch on the one side and the English on the other— every time it has been possible to create trouble there at once we trace the hand of Cecil Rhodes pulling the string that sets everything in motion. I say that he is the man at whose behest we are now asked to send our gallant but misguided men to fight in the Transvaal.

I must for a minute ask the House to consider what has happened since 1890. There is the key to the situation. In 1887 gold was discovered in the Rand, and an inrush of Uitlanders commenced. In 1890 special legislation was introduced in the Volksraad by Kruger to deal with the new position of affairs. What did that legislation embrace? First, liberalisation of the mining laws, so that the new-comers would be well looked after. It embraced a proposal for building railways, so that the heavy freight which had to be paid to Cape Colony could be dispensed with, and it finally embraced legislation to effect the reduction of the term necessary for naturalisation. That was in 1890, when the amalgamation of the two races was in rapid progress, and when there was comparatively little danger of any outbreak.

A few months later a change in the political affairs of Cape Colony put Cecil Rhodes at the head of the Government as administrator, and there the Governor was Sir Henry Loch, who was previously Governor of the adjoining colony of Victoria, but who was a weak and incapable administrator in the troubled waters of South African politics. And those two men between them, Rhodes acting in the joint capacity of managing director of the chartered company and Premier of the colony, with the pliant tool, Loch, in his hands, advanced steadily from one intrigue to another, every one of which had the object of ultimately obtaining the Rand gold-field as a private property of the company.

Trouble came up in Swaziland. One of the most solemn agreements ever entered into by the Imperial Government was deliberately broken within six years of its being signed; it was thrown to the winds, and all the business of Swaziland was settled without regard to the wishes of the Dutch republic after they had had the assurance that their wishes would be supreme. That was done under the influence of Cecil Rhodes. The Matabele war was a step taken to influence the sale of the chartered company's stock. Things were slack; they wanted new territory, and they could only get it by stirring up war. They stirred up a war against the Matabele by means of lying telegrams and despatches. They had a man there living in the country. He lived in Buluwayo, so peaceful was the country and free from suggestions of any attack upon the British settlement that he lived in the Matabele country—in Lobengula's own kraal at Buluwayo. He lived there, and from there sent out day by day despatches to the order of the Rhodes gang at Capetown, describing the formation of Matabele impis and the marching of regiments north and south. These dispatches were not published in the local papers at Johannesburg or Cape-town, where they might have been criticised; but they were sent straight through, without reaching any local centres, to the columns of the London *Times* and *Standard*. They worked up a feeling against the Matabeles, and the suggestion was conveyed to the English public that we were leaving a handful of settlers to be overwhelmed and crushed by the impending hordes of Matabeles, and that steps must be taken immediately. The word was given at last that the administrator there, Dr. Jameson, could do whatever he thought necessary to protect the interests of white settlers, and that most infamous war was entered upon immediately.

When all has been said, what does all this vague clamour against Boer rule amount to? No overt act has been charged against them. Suppose they had broken the convention, it is from the Dutch, and not from the English, that the offer to proceed to arbitration has come. The English Government say they have broken the agreement. The Boers say, 'Show us in what way.' The English say that they cannot show them; but that the agreement having been broken they will disregard it, and advance by force of arms.

The Uitlander then goes into a country which the Chief Justice of England declares to be an independent and autonomous country, and he goes there at his own risk. He goes there and submits himself to the conditions, legal and physical, which are in force there, and if every word which is alleged to-night, in this vague and unsubstantial way, were founded upon a genuine and undeniable fact, if the very ravings of the maddest jingo in New South Wales were true, and every grievance that has ever been imagined for the Uitlander were a reality, the answer to it all would be this—that the country is not a gaol, that if a man does not like it he is free to leave it to-morrow. When a man goes into another country he goes there at his own will. Kruger did not bring these men there; he did not invite them there. The Dutch did not want them to go there. They were forced to let them go there by the superior power of the British Empire. That provision was forced upon an unwilling republic, and the Uitlanders, being there, are there entirely at their own risk.

It is a well-known fact that at the bicycle works in Germany there are many thousands of English artisans employed. That is the case in certain large cities in Germany where this is the leading industry. Those men are foreigners in a foreign country. They have to submit to the German law. They cannot speak their own language in the courts; they cannot have their own language used in official documents. They have no votes. Why does not the hon. gentleman propose to send 375 men to coerce the German Government to grant the rights for these men that are demanded on behalf of Uitlanders from the Transvaal Government?

That is not oppression in Germany which is oppression in the Transvaal.

That in the captain's but a choleric word, Which in the soldier is flat blasphemy.

That is not oppression in Germany, because the Germans are too big, too formidable, to be coerced. But with an insignificant little state like the Transvaal every patriot in the House, swelling into importance with the jingo emotions which possess his little twopenny-halfpenny soul, feels called upon in the interests of humanity and freedom to go to the relief of his oppressed and down trodden countrymen. There was a time indeed when to belong to the English race and to fight under the English flag was an honor.

That was a time when England stood up and alone withstood in the interests of freedom the might of conquering France. In those days it was, perhaps, a fair thing to say that England did stand up on behalf of liberty and freedom. There was a time when English statesmen and English politicians did not fear—I will not say to draw the sword—but, at all events, to measure their forces with the proudest and mightiest empires on the Continent. Within this century England has been within measurable distance of war with France, when France was at its highest. It has made war with Russia. It has exchanged defiances with almost all the powers of Europe. But today the English race has fallen on a time when apparently the utmost it can do is to bully weak and struggling powers. England can threaten a country like Venezuela; it can send an expedition into the Soudan. It can fight the Zulu; and it can now, after a long process of negotiation, finally draw the sword against the Boer.

Whilst my country is fighting in a just cause I hope I shall be as ready to support its claims as any other member. But as I believe from the bottom of my heart that this is the most iniquitous, most immoral war ever waged with any race, I hope that England may be defeated.

[The House was interrupted with Cries of Shame! Shame! Bunkum! Bunkum! until Order was restored].

The English Empire has done much, and is undoubtedly a large civilising factor. That is a fact which we delight in, and which none of us deny. But the Englishman has no rights in the world peculiar to himself. The heaven-born Englishman is entirely an invention of the jingo press. We are not called upon to set right the other countries of the world, and to instruct them in the management of their affairs, and to dictate to them in their own internal concerns. No doubt we have a right to interfere on behalf of our fellow-subjects when those fellow-subjects are really oppressed, when those fellow-subjects have no other hope of redress of grievances under which they languish save the armed intervention of their country. But that that is the case in the present instance will not be alleged for an instant by the other side. The majority of then Uitlanders have not asked for assistance, they are under no grievances which are not common to all aliens living in foreign countries. These men are not oppressed, they are not slaves, they are not robbed. It is free to them to find shelter in friendly British territory not 100 miles away. They do not wish to do so, they elect to stay there, because on the whole they are better off in the Transvaal in spite of all their disabilities than they would be in Natal.

From the broader standpoint of humanity we are told that, after all, these things are merely the working out of a law of nature; that here we have once more an instance of the survival of the fittest; and that the vigorous and illustrious English race is now about to step in and wipe out this effete and crumbling power, which has too long cumbered the ground.

The law of the survival of the fittest is, of course, a fact; but it is a fact which it has been the crowing triumph of civilisation to make more and more conformable to the requirements of justice and of equity. Here the fittest does not survive. The man with the loudest voice, with the strongest determination, with the most impudent disregard for the rights of his fellow-men, is not the man who gets the ear of the Chairman when a deli-cate point of order is to be decided; but justice is done, and the rules of the House are carried out. To-day, while the fittest survives, it is the fittest, not in endowment of brute force, but of social equipment. The man who survives in the struggle for existence to-day is not the man who goes forth, as Dr. Jameson went forth on his raid, with his pistols in his belt and his sabre at his side, prepared to ride roughshod over humanity, but the man who conforms to the usages of society; and the fittest nation to survive is that nation which, in all its dealings with its fellow-nations, is actuated by the highest regard for every jot and tittle of international law. Just as to-day the robber, the burglar, and the bushranger, in spite of their courage and energy, are held down and thrust into the outer darkness, and have to meet the punishment which justly waits upon them at the bidding of society at large, so, with nations, the day of buccaneering has gone by; and it is the duty of every man who values human progress to build up more and more an understanding between the peoples of the world; to turn the human race into one gigantic nation, with a community of laws and of intellect, so that questions of difference, instead of being settled by the sword, may be settled by the humane and peaceful method of arbitration.

Abridged.
Source: *NSW Parliamentary Debates*, Legislative Assembly, vols 100–102, 18 October 1899, pp. 1460–70.

PART TWO

Part Two: 1900–1949

When the bewhiskered members of the new Australian parliament took their seats in 1901, they launched the history of federal law-making by debating the great question that confronts all societies: Who belongs— and who are the outsiders? The government, having decided that this was to be a white Australia, raised popular fears of alien values and alleged Asian diseases. And Labor members added the declaration that no Asian or Pacific Islander should be permitted to undermine the wages of Australian workers. So it was that the first substantive law enacted by the Parliament of Australia was the Immigration Restriction Act 1901—the 'White Australia Policy'.

The 1890s had been a traumatic decade in eastern Australia. Corrupt politicians and reckless speculators had sent a boom economy crashing into depression, inflicting the miseries of unemployment and hunger on working-class families. At the same time, many Australian workers had begun to organize themselves into militant trade unions. The combination was so inflammatory that social chaos—or revolution—seemed imminent. These upheavals radicalized a generation of middle-class liberals, who sided with Labor to devise a prototype of the welfare state. The champion of this innovation was the liberal Prime Minister, Alfred Deakin. In fact, it's not unreasonable to see the brand-new Australia of the early 1900s as a massive social experiment, one in which the state modified the harshness of capitalism to provide pensions for nursing mothers, the old and the sick, and to ensure that working-class men received—as the saying went—'a fair day's pay for a fair day's work'. At the same time, industries that did pay fair wages were insulated from Asian competition by tariffs and subsidies. This precursor to America's New Deal was known as New Protection. In 1907 the famous Harvester Case established a principle that held sway in Australia for eighty years: the minimum acceptable male wage was a living wage—enough to support a working man and his family in 'frugal comfort'.

Aborigines scarcely figured in the government's plans for the future; they were not even counted in the census. Many indigenous communities now lived in missions or state reserves. In outback Australia, some Aboriginal groups had come to an understanding with the European sheep or cattlemen and worked on their stations for subsistence wages while maintaining their culture in their traditional country. But as the decades of the new century passed, Aboriginal resistance formalized the demand that the nation recognize their right to be citizens and end the discrimination that had begun with that 'Day of Mourning' when the whites arrived in 1788.

The new federation of states was overwhelmingly a British Australia. In fact, looking back, the trappings of Australian nationalism can be a little hard to detect. At Federation there was no national flag and no national anthem. And, although the Constitution was ratified by the people of Australia in a referendum, it was passed into law by the *British* Parliament. When Britain marched into World War I in 1914, most Australians accepted without question that it was the entire Empire that was at war. They joined in a jaunty wartime song in which they assured Britain that 'Australia will be there!' But the misery of the war, and the eventual death of sixty thousand men, tore Australia apart. Many families lost fathers, husbands and sons; others found themselves trying to nurse back to health the broken minds and bodies of their soldier–boys. In the face of the horror and suffering, many Australians began to denounce the war as wicked and obscene. But others were unable to imagine that the carnage was in vain: they waved the flags of Empire more valiantly and sang 'God Save the King' more staunchly—as if patriotism were an antidote to grief. Meanwhile, Prime Minister Billy Hughes realized that the cannons were growing impatient, and he made two attempts to introduce conscription by popular referendum. The campaigns became bitter, as imperialists, radicals and anti-Empire Catholics unleashed their vitriol against each other. The divisions they inflicted on Australian society took decades to heal.

As a result, the decade after the war—the 1920s—was a period of great vitality set against bitterness and ideological chaos. It was a time when vicious industrial relations contrasted with the joyful abandon of the youthful jazz culture, when Australians took pride in national icons like Dame Nellie Melba, and literary critics and writers spoke proudly of the growth of a unique Australian literature. It was a time when hundreds of defiant communists were opposed by millions of Empire loyalists. A time when defiant libertarianism was countered by oppressive policing and grim censorship laws. A time of gramophones and motor cars and talking pictures—when liberated 'new women' dared to smoke, ride motorbikes and dance till dawn. In the aftermath of the war, this was a bruised Australia attempting to modernize and cure itself—a society convulsed by grief, fear and desire.

It was also the period in which Australian myth-makers, led by the prolific historian C. E. W. Bean, set about creating the sad and triumphal legend of the Anzacs. This story celebrated young Australian soldiers as egalitarian, brave, resourceful and delightfully disrespectful of authority. It affirmed a version of Australian manhood that had its origins in the frontiers of the previous century—a version that had begun to set the

Australian armed forces apart from the English, whether counterparts or superiors. And, in every Australian community, Gallipoli was solemnly remembered on Anzac Day.

During the 1920s Australia borrowed heavily in London, to finance the building and the investment in trade summed up in Prime Minister Stanley Bruce's slogan 'Men, Money, Markets'. When Wall Street crashed in October 1929 the debt-laden economy of Australia tumbled into the abyss of the Great Depression. Social divisions widened as people with comfortable bank accounts benefited from the crash: their ability to buy property or labour was actually enhanced by the rising value of the pound. What few members of the share-holding class appreciated was that around two in five breadwinners in the country were either unemployed or chronically under-employed. Many working families lost their homes; mothers were left with children who often went hungry; while thousands of fathers and sons were forced onto the roads, moving from one short-term government relief project to the next. It was little wonder that increasing numbers of radical Australians began to give speeches extolling a fairer society.

Many of these radicals were seduced into believing that the murderous dictator Stalin was actually a benign and caring father figure. The same radicals were quicker to realize that Hitler and the Nazis were assaulting human decency. But marches against war and fascism won no support from those conservatives who admired Hitler and Mussolini as men of vision, strength and national purpose.

In 1939, when war broke out in Europe, Australia once again joined in. The official reason was simple. As Prime Minister Robert Menzies put it: Britain was at war—and as a result Australia was also at war. But on the home front many Australians remained far removed from the anguish of the conflict in Europe. The mood changed when the Japanese launched their savage assault on the region in December 1941. Australians had long believed that the mighty navies of Britain would patrol their sea lanes and send any Asiatic invader packing. But the great British naval base at Singapore crumpled before the Japanese advance. Thousands of allied troops were marched away to Japanese prison-camps. And as Japanese bombs exploded in Darwin, Australians realized their 'Mother Country' had deserted them: England had its own battles to fight, nearer home.

Labor's John Curtin was a frail man made mighty by the urgency of the hour. Displacing Menzies as prime minister, Curtin introduced sweeping government controls over the economy and the labour force. He spurned British demands for more Australian troops and called on the United States to come to Australia's aid. America urgently required a secure base from which to wage the Pacific War—and before long, Australian cities were playing host to our new American allies. It was the Americans who savaged the Japanese in the decisive Battle of the Coral Sea and it was the Americans who brought the war to its ghastly end, with the annihilation of Hiroshima. In time, these events would convince Australians that their natural ally was no longer Britain; it was now the United States. And some in Australia would look with hope to the new international organization of the United Nations to maintain peace in the post-war world.

For Australia, the 1941–45 war with Japan was a nightmare come true. Australians had long been taught to fear that the 'starving hordes of Asia' were eyeing the vast open spaces of Australia. And they had long believed the argument that their best defence was population. Even before the war ended, the Labor Government began preparing for post-war reconstruction under the slogan 'Populate or perish'. A team of brilliant young Canberra mandarins, led by 'Nugget' Coombs, planned the expansion of a centralized Australian economy. They were to build a labour force through a massive program of assisted immigration from Britain and Europe. And they continued the policy of excluding Asian competition with a rampart of tariffs and subsidies. At the same time, the welfare system was expanded and now included unemployment benefits. Labor's guiding principle, said Prime Minister Ben Chifley in a famous phrase, was 'the light on the hill'. However some of Labor's socialist innovations were more sweeping than the electorate—or the press—were prepared to tolerate. Labor lost office in 1949.

The winner was Robert Menzies. This grandiloquent champion of the Empire had used his time in opposition to great effect. He had developed a new, forward-looking brand of liberalism that championed individual effort and valorized the middle class as the true nation-building class of Australia. At the same time, he renovated anti-Labor politics by forming the modern Liberal Party. Once in power, his Liberals were to dominate a rapidly expanding Australia for the next twenty-three years.

Alfred Deakin

White Australia, 1901

Alfred Deakin (1856–1919) was a remarkable statesman, a key figure in the formation of Federation, and three times prime minister of Australia. Melbourne born and
educated, with a degree in law, the young and dreamy Deakin was attracted to
spiritualism. He read voraciously and became a talented journalist with the *Age*
newspaper. He launched his lengthy political career in 1879 when he became a
successful Liberal candidate for the Victorian parliament, and he was to serve in
successive coalition governments. A believer in democratic social reform, Deakin
embodied the values of colonial liberalism. His political style was courteous and
conciliatory: 'Affable Alfred' was a skilled negotiator, a pragmatic idealist and a
native-born nationalist with imperial loyalties. But despite his brilliant career, Deakin
was increasingly plagued with self-doubt, particularly after suffering financial losses
in the economic crash of the late 1880s. He redirected his energies to the great
national cause of Federation—as a campaigner, a delegate at the Federal conventions, a member of the constitutional drafting committee and a colonial representative in London. Tall, darkly handsome and with a rich voice, Deakin was an
outstanding orator. His speeches, articulated clearly despite the speed and enthusiasm of his delivery, were incisive and literary; he understood the beauty and power
of language. These skills were on display during the second reading of the Immigration Restriction Bill in the new Commonwealth parliament on 12 September
1901. The first substantive federal legislation to be passed, the 'White Australia
Policy' built upon the colonial view that non-European immigration should be
restricted. As attorney general in the government of Edmund Barton, Deakin spoke
of a racially cohesive Australia that would protect itself from unwanted immigrants
through the mechanism of a dictation test. His claim that it was the 'good' qualities
of the Japanese that required their exclusion was, not surprisingly, met with displeasure from Japan.

We here find ourselves touching the profoundest instinct of individual or
nation—the instinct of self-preservation—for it is nothing less than the
national manhood, the national character, and the national future that are
at stake. At this early period of our history we find ourselves confronted
with difficulties which have not been occasioned by union, but to deal
with which this union was established. No motive power operated more
universally on this continent or in the beautiful island of Tasmania, and
certainly no motive operated more powerfully in dissolving the technical
and arbitrary political divisions which previously separated us than did
the desire that we should be one people and remain one people without
the admixture of other races. It is not necessary to reflect upon them even
by implication. It is only necessary to say that they do not and cannot
blend with us; that we do not, cannot, and ought not to blend with them.

This was the motive power which swayed tens of thousands who take little interest in contemporary politics—this was the note that touched particularly the Australian born, who felt themselves endowed with a heritage not only of political freedom, but of an ample area within which the race might expand, and an obligation consequent upon such an endowment—the obligation to pass on to their children and the generations after them that territory undiminished and uninvaded. A coloured occupation would make a practical diminution of its extent of the most serious kind. It was this aspiration which nerved them to undertake the great labour of conquering the sectional differences that divided us.

The programme of a 'white Australia' means not merely its preservation for the future—it means the consideration of those who cannot be classed within the category of whites, but who have found their way into our midst. I should say that at a very moderate estimate, based on reference to the last census, there are from 70,000 to 80,000 aliens already in Australia. A certain number of these may be naturalized, and a certain number may have been British subjects before they came here. Of these probably less than one half are Chinese, and apparently about 9,000 are Polynesians. The remainder are recruited from a variety of people, mainly those of the neighbouring countries of Asia.

It was with a full recognition of those facts that the first plank in the Government platform, as submitted at Maitland, and emphasized at every opportunity since, was the plank which for ease of reference was called the declaration for a 'White Australia.' It was for this reason that so much stress was laid on this issue, and it is for this reason that since the Government took office, no question has more frequently or more seriously occupied their attention, not only because of this one proposal now before the House, but with regard to executive acts that have been and will be necessary. There have been determinations which hereafter may have important consequences arising out of our administration, as well as other measures which will be submitted to Parliament, all having in view the accomplishment of the same end. That end, put in plain and [un]equivocal terms, as the House and the country are entitled to have it put, means the prohibition of all alien coloured immigration, and more, it means at the earliest time, by reasonable and just means, the deportation or reduction of the number of aliens now in our midst. The two things go hand in hand, and are the necessary complement of a single policy—the policy of securing a 'white Australia.'

The origin—the source of our action—requires some little exposition to those who look at us with old world eyes. One can well understand the attitude of the statesmen of Europe, absorbed in their own affairs, and in the control of large populations within comparatively narrow areas, approaching amazement when they regard what appears to be the arrogance of a handful of white men, most of them clustered on the eastern littoral of this immense continent, adopted before they have effectively occupied a quarter of the continent, and with the great bulk of its immense extent little more than explored, or with a sparse settlement.

Those European statesmen may well view with surprise the anxiety exhibited here in this respect. There are those who mock at the demand of a white Australia, and who point to what they consider our boundless opportunities for absorbing a far greater population than we at present possess, who dwell, if commercially-minded, on the opportunities for business we are neglecting by failing to import the cheapest labour to develop portions of our continent which have not as yet been put to use. But the apprehensions of those abroad, even when cursorily examined, are soon seen to proceed from a far narrower outlook than that which belongs to those who feel themselves charged with the future of this country.

Cost what it may, we are compelled at the very earliest hour of our national existence—at the very first opportunity when united action becomes possible—to make it positively clear that so far as in us lies, however limited we may be for a time by self-imposed restrictions upon settlement—however much we may sacrifice in the way of immediate monetary gain—however much we may retard the development of the remote and tropical portions of our territory—those sacrifices for the future of Australia are little, and are, indeed, nothing when compared with a compensating freedom from the trials, sufferings, and losses that nearly wrecked the great republic of the west, still left with the heritage in their midst of a population which, no matter how splendid it may be in many qualities, is not being assimilated, and apparently is never to be assimilated in the nation of which they are politically and nominally a part.

The unity of Australia is nothing, if that does not imply a united race. A united race means not only that its members can intermix, intermarry and associate without degradation on either side, but implies one inspired by the same ideas, and an aspiration towards the same ideals, of a people possessing the same general cast of character, tone of thought—the same constitutional training and traditions—a people qualified to live under this Constitution—the broadest and the most liberal perhaps the world has yet seen reduced to writing—a people qualified to use without abusing it, and to develop themselves under it to the full height and extent of their capacity. Unity of race is an absolute essential to the unity of Australia. It is more, actually more in the last resort, than any other unity.

Here we begin to pass from a general consideration of the question to the particular consideration of the form of this Bill. Honorable members who are aware of what the policy of the Government is, and who know how they have realized from the very first moment the importance of this issue, have asked from time to time during this debate why the Government adopted the particular form of this measure, and why they have not put upon the face of it a prohibition of the particular Asiatic people whom it is desired to exclude?

The most recent communication which has been made public property in which the attitude of the British Government is defined, is the despatch which accompanied the Queensland Central Sugar Mills Bill, when it was returned within the last two or three months. The measure contained a provision which named, as it is desired we should name in the

Bill, the classes of persons whom it was sought to exclude by colour, and race. It was taken exception to. Mr. Chamberlain says [in 1897 to the colonial Premiers]—

> In the first place it embodies a disqualification based on a place of origin—that is, practically a distinction of race and colour. Any attempt to impose disqualifications on the base of such distinctions, besides being offensive to a friendly power, is contrary to the general conceptions of equality which have been guiding principles of British rule throughout the Empire. Disqualifications by educational tests, such as are embodied in the immigration laws of various colonies, is not a measure to which the Government of Japan or any other Government can take exception on behalf of its subjects; and if the particular tests in these laws are not regarded as sufficiently stringent, there is no reason why more stringent and effective ones of a similar character should not be adopted.

This is a most signal sentence—nothing could be plainer. If honorable members consider that the test of writing 50 words in the English tongue will not exclude those whom we are determined to exclude, it is open to us to increase the educational test, with the hearty approbation of the British Government. Mr. Chamberlain then repeats—

> But disqualification for certain employments on the sole ground of place of origin is a measure to which any Government concerned may reasonably object; and in the present Bill the aboriginal natives of two continents and of the Pacific Islands are disqualified solely on that ground.

Then he adds—

> In the second place, besides being contrary to the general policy on which the British Empire is based, the Bill is objectionable as embodying a provision which is peculiarly offensive to Japan, a power with which His Majesty's Government is, and earnestly desires to remain on friendly terms. It not only excludes Japanese from certain employment; but in excluding them it places them in the general category of Asiatic races, without any consideration being paid to their state of civilization.

Referring for a moment to the Empire of Japan, it has never been my privilege to visit that country or to become acquainted with its inhabitants, but we all know, from the merest acquaintance with current news and with critical literature, how high a position that nation occupies in art and letters, and how worthy they are of the place, in our estimation, generally conceded to the highest and most civilized among the nations of the world. Japan is justified in resenting any unnecessarily offensive legislation on the part of another nation, just as we might object to being classed with the peoples of the Pacific Islands, as if the Polynesian residents of those islands and ourselves were on the same plane. When it becomes necessary for us to exclude people like the Japanese it is reasonable that we should exclude them in the most considerate manner possible, and without conveying any idea that we have confused them with the many uneducated races of Asia and untutored savages who visit our shores. To lump all these people together as Asiatics and undesirables would naturally be offensive to a high-spirited people like the Japanese, and surely without any request from the British Government or without any representations from the Japanese people mere courtesy, such as should exist between one civilized people and another, should lead us to make this distinction. Considerations of simple politeness, such as honorable members extend to each other in this House, should at least govern the actions of civilized nations in their dealings with one another.

I contend that the Japanese require to be excluded because of their high abilities. The Japanese are the most dangerous because they most nearly approach us, and would, therefore, be our most formidable competitors. It is not the bad qualities, but the good qualities of these Asian races that make them so dangerous to us. It is their inexhaustible energy, their power of applying themselves to new tasks, their endurance, and their low standard of living that make them such competitors. It is the business qualities, the business aptitude, and the general capacity of these peoples that makes them dangerous, and the fact that while they remain an element in our population, they are incapable of being assimilated, makes them all the more to be feared. The Japanese represent the highest class of those who seek to come here, and they are people who are capable of being dealt with on the same footing as any other civilised power.

Abridged.
Source: *Commonwealth Parliamentary Debates*, vol. 4, 3 October 1901, pp. 4804–12.

Edmund Barton

Britons of the Empire, 1903

Australia's first prime minister, Edmund Barton (1849–1920) was a key figure in the push for Federation and later became a judge of the High Court. Barton was born in Sydney's inner suburb of Glebe and graduated in Arts from the University of Sydney. He went on to balance a career in law with one in politics, becoming a member of the New South Wales Lower House in 1879. 'Toby Tosspot' Barton gained a reputation for his genial self-indulgence. But he was a sharp constitutional lawyer and played an important role in the drafting of the Federal Constitution. As a younger man, he was diffident about his ability as a public speaker, but he developed skills as a logical and impressive debater, and these served him well as leader of the Federal Convention (1887–88) and at the helm of the inaugural Commonwealth parliament. The new government faced the gruelling task of establishing foundational legislation covering areas such as the judiciary, immigration, customs tax and defence. When it came to the formation of an independent Australian navy, Barton was aware that there were insufficient funds and argued that—for the time being—Australia should contribute to, and continue to rely upon, the protection of the British Admiralty. In his parliamentary speech on the Naval Bill on 7 July 1903, he invoked the organic ties of an international community of British heritage in which patriotic Australians were nonetheless 'Britons of the Empire'.

Let us call ourselves Britons. In using the term Britons in Australia, I wish it to be as clear as possible that, in my belief, we have not forfeited, by our emigration, or by that of our fathers, any of the rights of Britishers at home, or any of our share in either the glory or the material prosperity of the Empire. We are Britons of the Empire. We did not sever ourselves from the rest of the Empire when we came here, neither did the fathers of those of us, who like myself are natives of the soil, do so. We retain our heritage, and with it our responsibilities. We cannot have the one, and say 'no' to the other, because the thing is impossible, and because we should be poor Britons if we did. Surely, the consciousness that we are at least making a small attempt towards the equalization of these burdens is 'something to show' for our expenditure.

With regard to the next objection, that the agreement does not satisfy our local aspirations, or give proper scope to our patriotism, I recognise to the full the importance of this contention, and have always endeavoured to so mould the Constitution and the legislation of the Commonwealth as to give fuller scope for the national aspirations of Australians. But this is a case where our patriotic feelings towards the Empire of which Australia forms a part must express themselves, because we regard the Empire as one for purposes of naval defence. If we do not take that view, we must accept the alternative, that the Empire must operate by scattered units, and lose the power of concentration, and its Navy be by so much the more open to defeat and capture in detail.

We must look at the great question of naval defence from the point of view of citizens of the Empire. Heaven forbid that I should ask any one to relinquish his feeling of local patriotism, or to do anything which would be unjust to his fellow citizens in Australia. But we can be just to Australia and still meet our obligations to the Empire so long as we recognise them. On the day when we cease to recognise them, we should be honest, and say to the mother country, 'We want to go.' Just as we look at Federal questions as Australians rather than as citizens of the States, so we must look at questions of Empire as citizens of the Empire rather than as citizens of Australia. I do not wish to use the word 'Imperial,' because in some men's ears it carries the far-off sound of absolute despotism and domination, but we may speak of the Empire because we have no other name to give it. It is an aggregation of free men in free lands, and while we belong to it we must look at questions of Empire as citizens of the Empire, just as we look at Australian questions as citizens of Australia.

If we wished to cut the painter—and no one is proposing to do so—we could rid ourselves of these obligations. But at what price? We should be independent, but we should be much more exposed to the insults and intrusions of foreign Powers than we are now, when there is a shield of protection thrown over us which has taken the Empire ages to make, and such as we could not make apart. We cannot make this ægis for ourselves, and we cannot put on ready made the garb of Empire, because we do not want the 'slop clothes' of Empire. We are, I take it, content with our position as a free self-governing portion of the Empire. We are content to maintain it at a reasonable expenditure—at an expenditure much less than we should have to make if we shared in the defence of any other Empire; and for a purpose which means this: Take one portion away from the Empire and you may as well take another. Be a party to its disintegration, even by abstention from what is right, and you make that disintegration easier. The principle surely should be this: Touch one of us and you touch us all. What was our answer when South Africa was attacked? Were we wrong in making that answer? To my dying day I shall not believe so. What was at stake? Not only perhaps the most important of the trade routes of the Empire, which provided the material solace to our action. We decided to act when it was too early to think of that, but we believed that success against England meant the disintegration of the Empire at one point, which we thought almost as much against our interests as if some other portion of the Empire, or we ourselves, were cut off from it.

What, then, is the right principle to adopt in regard to the defence of the Empire? The principle that by common action we must keep every portion of it intact. By going on our own initiative in various directions, we leave every portion of it open to attack. I do not think that there is anything in our local aspirations which entitles us to give the lie to that principle. Our 'patriotic' feelings, if I may use a word which is sometimes derided, must find expression in our acts. We may maintain the name of our attachment to the Empire, and do nothing; but that seems to be a fair way of getting ourselves branded, not only as mean men, but as hypocrites.

Under this agreement we shall give Australia better protection than we could if we adopted the alternative of an Australian Navy, unless we went to a cost which, in our present stage, is prohibitive. There can be no want of loyalty in giving Australia adequate defence at a much lower rate than it would otherwise cost. While we remain part of the Empire, there will arise questions of Imperial rather than of local importance, and they will arise even if we turn away and shut our eyes. But it is our duty to have regard to these questions so long as we remain in the Empire, and to recognise what our position requires of us, not to the extent of slavish adherence to everything done by others, but to the extent of realizing that with participation in the advantages of the Empire comes reciprocal obligation. Holding the views we do as to the sound principle of naval defence, we are unable to subscribe to the theory that our loyalty to Australia calls upon us to set up a separate Navy.

Abridged.
Source: *Commonwealth Parliamentary Debates*, vol. 14, 7 July 1903, pp. 1797–9.

King O'Malley
Bombala for the National Capital, 1903

King O'Malley (1858?–1953) emigrated around 1888 to Melbourne from the United States, where he had had a successful career as an insurance salesman. Once in Australia, he was quickly established as an insurance agent and speculator, most notably in the mining towns of Tasmania and Western Australia. In 1896 O'Malley's interests turned to politics and he secured a seat for a term in the South Australian parliament. Returning to Tasmania, O'Malley campaigned successfully among the miners of the west coast and entered the first federal House of Representatives. Initially an independent member, he soon joined the Labor Party and had a keen interest in the site of the new federal capital. O'Malley was later to play a pivotal role in the urban planning of Canberra. But in October 1903 he defended in Parliament, with characteristic wit and verbal force, a small town in the New South Wales Southern Tablelands as having the perfect 'cold climate of hope' for the seat of national government.

We have listened to some extraordinary speeches; and it appears to me as though honorable members are suddenly prepared to vote now that Bombala is apparently 'out of the running.' There is collusion somewhere, but I cannot get on to its track. If ever there was a spot set apart by the Creator to be the Capital of this great Australia—the pivot around which Australian civilization should revolve—it is Bombala.

The Americans, in fixing upon Washington, selected a site close to the eastern seas. The result is that to-day members of Congress have to travel 4,000 miles from Oregon, and they are paid 10 cents, or 6d. per mile, as expenses. It is a selfish and ungodly state of things when men arrive at the stage of thinking only of themselves; the curse of the world to-day is selfishness. We are legislating now for countless millions still unborn, we are legislating for centuries hence, and posterity will rise in its might and curse us if we select the wrong site. It will be a black crime against posterity if we select any place but Bombala.

A number of honorable members have asked how honorable members will reach the seat of government, if it be fixed at Bombala. Why, the leader of the Opposition, for instance, could step on a steamer in Melbourne and next morning be at Twofold Bay, whence he might be wafted to the scene of his legislative labours in the buckets of an aerial railway. It is not two years since I met the leader of the Opposition fishing in the Snowy River, and it is that stream and not the Murray which is the national river of Australia. The Snowy River is fed by Heaven from the eternal snows of the mountains. In the very beginning the Garden of Eden was laid to the eastward; and when I reached the hills, after having climbed Black Jack and entered Monaro, I thought of the story of Adam and Eve. I looked back over 6,000 years, and, in fancy, I could almost see the Garden of Eden at Bombala. I could see Adam and Eve leaving after they had eaten of the tree of life—for the tree of life is growing there to-day.

The Royal Commission seems to me to have been like some bulldozed Commission from South Carolina or Georgia. The result is sometimes peculiar when pressure is put on a man; the pressure may not be from without but from within, and yet it has the same effect. The history of the world shows that cold climates have produced the greatest geniuses, all of whom were born north of a certain degree. I have heard some remarks about a 'toy State,' but how big is Scotland, whose sons are all over the earth? How big is Rhode Island, whose sons can make wooden nutmegs? How big is the State of Maine? That State is not as big as Bombala, and yet it gave birth to Longfellow. How big was Greece or Sparta? There are more people to-day around Bombala than there were in Greece and Sparta when Miltiades won the liberty of mankind on the field of Marathon. There are more people round Eden and Bombala to-day than were gathered on all the seven hills of Rome when she commenced a sway which afterwards embraced the whole earth.

It is all nonsense to talk about population and size; the history of the world shows that small territories and small republics have produced the greatest men. It will be the same to-day. This is the first opportunity we have had of establishing a great city of our own, where we can experiment with our socialism, as it is called. Socialism is going to rule this earth, and to destroy the selfishness and the misery that has come into the world through the greed and avarice of humanity.

In conclusion, let me say this: Look where we like, it will be found that wherever a hot climate prevails, the country is revolutionary. Take the sons of some of the greatest men in the world, and put them into a hot climate like Tumut or Albury, and in three generations their lineal descendants will be degenerate. I found them in San Domingo on a Sabbath morning going to a cock-fight with a rooster under each arm, and a sombrero on their heads. I want to have a cold climate chosen for the capital of this Commonwealth ... I want to have a climate where men can hope.

We cannot have hope in hot countries. When I go down the streets of this city [of Melbourne] on a hot summer's day, and see the people in a melting condition, I look upon them with sorrow, and wish I were away in healthy Tasmania. I hope that the site selected will be Bombala, and that the children of our children will see an Australian Federal city that will rival London in population, Paris in beauty, Athens in culture, and Chicago in enterprise.

Abridged.
Source: *Commonwealth Parliamentary Debates*, vol. 17, 8 October 1903, pp. 5933–4.

———

Henry Bournes Higgins
A Fair and Reasonable Wage, 1907

Henry Bournes Higgins (1851–1929) was a politician and the judge responsible for the creation of the 'sufficient' or basic wage for workers in Australia. Higgins emigrated from Ireland to Melbourne with his family in 1870. He worked as a teacher and studied at the University of Melbourne, demonstrating an outstanding ability at languages and overcoming a stammer through involvement in the debating society. From a successful career at the Bar, Higgins became active in political causes, including support for Irish Home Rule, and entered the Victorian parliament as a liberal. A delegate to the 1897 Federal Convention, he ensured that the arbitration of interstate industrial disputes would be within the powers of the new Commonwealth. But Higgins was to oppose both Federation and the Boer War, and as a consequence he lost his state parliamentary seat and gained a reputation as a radical. He was elected to Federal Parliament as a supporter of the Labor Party, was appointed to the High Court in 1906, and one year later assumed the presidency of the Commonwealth Court of Conciliation and Arbitration. In his first case, Higgins had to decide whether H. V. McKay—the anti-union proprietor of the Sunshine Harvester agricultural machinery works—was paying his workers 'a fair and reasonable wage'. The hearing stretched over a month, and Higgins considered evidence from workers and their wives. His judgment was delivered on 8 November. The landmark Harvester case was welcomed by the trade unions and resisted by employers—including McKay, who lodged a successful appeal to the High Court.

The provision for fair and reasonable remuneration is obviously designed for the benefit of the employees in the industry; and it must be meant to secure to them something which they cannot get by the ordinary system of individual bargaining with employers. If Parliament meant that the conditions shall be such as they can get by individual bargaining—if it meant that those conditions are to be fair and reasonable, which employees will accept and employers will give, in contracts of service—there would have been no need for this provision. The remuneration could safely have been left to the usual, but unequal, contest, the 'haggling of the market' for labour, with the pressure for bread on one side, and the pressure for profits on the other. The standard of 'fair and reasonable' must, therefore, be something else; and I cannot think of any other standard appropriate than the normal needs of the average employee, regarded as a human being living in a civilized community.

If, instead of individual bargaining, one can conceive of a collective agreement—an agreement between all the employers in a given trade on the one side, and all the employees on the other—it seems to me that the framers of the agreement would have to take, as the first and dominant factor, the cost of living as a civilized being. If A lets B have the use of his horses, on the terms that he give them fair and reasonable treatment, I have no doubt that it is B's duty to give them proper food and water, and such shelter and rest as they need; and, as wages are the means of obtaining commodities, surely the State, in stipulating for fair and reasonable remuneration for the employees, means that the wages shall be sufficient to provide these things, and clothing, and a condition of frugal comfort estimated by current human standards.

I come now to consider the remuneration of the employees mentioned in this application. I propose to take unskilled labourers first. The standard wage—the wage paid to the most of the labourers by the applicant—is 6s. per day of eight hours, with no extra allowance for overtime; but there is one man receiving only 5s. 6d. There is no constancy of employment, as the employer has to put a considerable number of men off in the intervals between the seasons. The seed-drill and plough season, I am told, is in the earlier part of the year, about April; but the busiest time is the harvester season, about August to November. But even if the employment were constant and uninterrupted, is a wage of 36s. per week fair and reasonable, in view of the cost of living in Victoria? I have tried to ascertain the cost of living—the amount which has to be paid for food, shelter, clothing, for an average labourer with normal wants, and under normal conditions. Some very interesting evidence has been given, by working men's wives and others; and the evidence has been absolutely undisputed.

There is no doubt that there has been, during the last year or two, a progressive rise in rents, and in the price of meat, and in the price of many of the modest requirements or the worker's household. The usual rent paid by a labourer, as distinguished from an artisan, appears to be 7s.; and, taking the rent at 7s., the necessary average weekly expenditure for a labourer's home of about five persons would seem to be about £1 12s. 5d. The lists of expenditure submitted to me vary not only in amounts, but in bases of computation. But I have confined the figures to rent, groceries, bread, milk, fuel, vegetables, and fruit; and the average of the list of nine housekeeping women is £1 12s. 5d. This expenditure does not cover light (some of the lists omitted light), clothes, boots, furniture, utensils (being casual, not weekly expenditure), rates, life insurance, savings, accident or benefit societies, loss of employment, union pay, books and newspapers, tram and train fares, sewing machine, mangle, school requisites, amusements and holidays, intoxicating liquors, tobacco, sickness and death, domestic help, or any expenditure for unusual contingencies, religion, or charity. If the wages are 36s. per week, the amount left to pay for all these things is only 3s. 7d.; and the area is rather large for 3s. 7d. to cover—even in the case of total abstainers and non-smokers—the case of most of the men in question. One witness, the wife of one who was formerly a vatman in candle works, says that in the days when her husband was working at the vat at 36s. a week, she was unable to provide meat for him on about three days in the week. This inability to procure sustaining food—whatever kind may be selected—is certainly not conducive to the maintenance of the worker in industrial efficiency. Then, on looking at the rates ruling elsewhere, I find that the public bodies which do not aim at profit, but which are responsible to electors or others for economy, very generally pay 7s.

My hesitation has been chiefly between 7s. and 7s. 6d.; but I put the minimum at 7s., as I do not think that I could refuse to declare an employer's remuneration to be fair and reasonable, if I find him paying 7s. Under the circumstances, I cannot declare that the applicant's conditions of remuneration are fair and reasonable to his labourers.

Abridged.
Source: *Commonwealth Arbitration Reports*, 1907–1908, vol. 2, H. V. McKay *ex parte*, 8 November 1907, pp. 3–7.

———

Joseph Cook
A Righteous War, 1914

Joseph Cook (1860–1947) served as Australian prime minister for a mere fifteen months, but during this period World War I broke out and Australia joined Britain at war. However, it was the leader of the Labor Opposition, Andrew Fisher (1862–1928), who, in a speech made in the Victorian wheat-town of Horsham, was to utter the phrase that famously summed up Australia's pledge: '... we Australians will help and defend her [Britain] to our last man and last shilling'.[31]

Cook, born into a Staffordshire coalmining community, was a pit-boy at the age of nine, becoming the family breadwinner after his father was killed in an industrial accident. He emigrated to Australia in 1887 and settled in the New South Wales coal town of Lithgow, where he was drawn into local union politics. By 1891 he was in Parliament, serving briefly as Labor leader before breaking away to join the free-trade ministry of George Reid. Cook admired Reid deeply, following him into Federal Parliament and in 1908 as the leader of the free-traders. By now, many years out of the mines and ensconced in the most exclusive suburb of his electorate, the self-made Cook had abandoned his working-class origins. A conservative and staunch imperialist, he was a steady rather than brilliant figure of influence within non-Labor politics and a dogged political survivor. And, after years as a Primitive Methodist lay preacher and a politician, Cook was a very capable, if somewhat pugnacious, public speaker who was fond of ornamenting an argument with quotations. In September 1914 Cook was ousted as Liberal prime minister. Now he was leader of the Opposition, giving a parliamentary speech on 14 October where he graciously endorsed the Fisher Labor government's war policy.

If ever there was a righteous war, this, I believe, is one. The Empire is at war today after the most strenuous efforts for peace. Sir Edward Grey was patient almost to weakness in the preliminary negotiations preceding the outbreak of the war. If ever a man solemnly and earnestly strove to preserve the peace of Europe, he did so. Indeed, I am not sure that there was not point in the remarks of some of the Allies that, had he stated a little earlier that Great Britain would join with them in case of war, Germany might have been made to hesitate. But I am glad that did not happen. It is better to take the job on now than to have waited until the German Navy had grown stronger. A few years hence we might have had a very different proposition to tackle. The war has been inevitable for years past. Anyone who has read anything of the preparations that have been going on must know that it would have been impossible to have kept it much longer from breaking out. It is better to fight when we have a fighting chance than to have waited until Germany had grown stronger, as she intended to do, and could attack us under more favorable circumstances for her.

The arresting feature of the present situation is the determination of Germany to secure the hegemony of Europe. It was intended to prostrate Europe before the almightiness of Germany, which, I believe, aimed at securing world power. If the statements that have been attributed to the German Emperor are true, his associating of himself with the Almighty and his claim to a monopoly of the Almighty's favour and assistance amount almost to blasphemy. For years past the motto hung up in the German naval quarters has been '*Delenda est Britannia*' ['Britain must be destroyed']. It must, therefore be a fight to a finish. We must beat Germany, or Germany will beat us. It has been suggested that for the time being our motto should be '*Delenda est Germania*,' at any rate, so far as the military oligarchy of the country is concerned. In regard to the German people, I have no such feeling. I believe that a great many of them are as sincerely desirous of peace as we are.

This war has driven us back to the fundamental passions of human nature. The Socialists in Germany, the Socialists in France, and the Socialists in other countries are fighting each other to extermination. Evidently, nationality is stronger than socialistic brotherhood. We have a long way to go before the millennium of which we speak in our ecstatic moods is realized. War is a tragedy in many ways; it means a set-back to the higher aspirations of the nation, and to many of those things to which we look for the uplift of civilization, no matter from which nation they may emanate; and when we are fighting a nation so nearly akin to us in blood, race, and literature, one that is leading the world in many paths of civilization, we cannot but regret it as one of the great tragedies of the world. But we are not fighting these qualities in Germany; we are fighting Prussian Junkerdom, which is always the enemy to the higher civilization of Europe and the world.

In all these matters we have to apply a practical test. Culture is as culture does; culture separated from conduct is an empty and barren thing. Applying these tests to German culture, I venture to say it leaves very much to be desired in this war. If culture means the breaking of international treaties, the violation of international good faith, and hacking one's way through agreements voluntarily entered into, I know little about that sort of culture; it is a culture not worth preserving, and I hope that we shall not cease our preparations nor our fighting until that kind of thing is made impossible, at any rate for many years to come. There are many indications in connexion with the history of this war which prove that Germany is violating all the ethics of international relationships. It was said the other day by Archibald Hurd that it had been proved up to the hilt that Germany has sown mines in the international highways of commerce 50 miles from the coastline. There is not much culture about that: there is not much about international ethics in it; there is only pure, perfected barbarism in an action of that kind.

The other day I read a statement by the German poet Schiller—

> *The nation is worth nothing that does not joyfully stake all on its honour.*

That statement is worth quoting in these days. I wish that the poet would commend it to his own rulers, for they have violated the honour of their nation, and have violated their solemn pledges given to the world many years ago. Now that we are in this fight our attitude should be that of Polonius when he says—

> *Beware of entrance to a quarrel; but, being in, Bear't that the opposer may beware of thee.*

We must make them[Germany] beware how they hack their way through solemn treaties, and violate the neutrality of small kingdoms who had every claim to their protection and support! Sir, I believe that war is not all bad. It is bad enough. There are, however, more things in war than those that are ineradicably and unmistakably bad. When one comes to think that out of many a war in the past has come the great fillip to the freedom of the various peoples of the world one can only hope that some such result may come from this war.

So far as we in Australia are concerned, I believe that the sentiment expressed the other day by Harold Begbie is our own, and that we—

War for the end of war:
Fighting that fighting may cease.
Why do our cannons roar?
For a thousand years of peace.

We cannot hope to get a thousand years of peace, but we can hope for a peace which will last for many years to come when this tremendous war is over.

There is another consideration, and with this I shall conclude. War is a great leveller. Liberal, Labour, Home Ruler, Unionist, rich and poor, all are together, side by side. The other day we read that there were seventy members of the House of Commons and the House of Lords at the front fighting in this battle. I hope that in this war we are doing more than fighting for the capitalist. I hope that all sections are banded together and, setting aside all fratricidal feelings, which had already got too far ahead in many of these countries, that all are combining to fight for the principles of freedom and liberty which are the birthright of all of us, and which are worth any cost in preserving in Europe and the rest of the world. Instead of seeking points of difference, I should like to say that these words fill the bill very much better—

He, to-day, that sheds his blood with me shall be my brother; be
he ne'er so vile, this day shall gentle his condition. [Henry V,
Act 4, Sc. 3]

I should like most of all to see that this war shall put an end to that class strife which has been so rife in recent years, and that we shall all begin from now to try to understand each other's position and put ourselves in each other's place, to consolidate our resources in order to fight our natural enemies, instead of fighting through all the regions of political and social existence in the fratricidal way we have done for so many years. May we not hope that war is like an earthquake, which, when the convulsions are active, sends out fertilizing streams which spread themselves over the land and beget in later years rich harvests of the rarest products. I hope that as a result of this war we shall gain rich fruits of liberty and freedom in Australia. For this, above all, is our own war. If we lose it, we risk the loss of Australia. I hope we shall feel right through to the bitter end, if need be, that we are fighting for the liberties of Australia, for the social ideals of this home of ours, as well as for the homes of the kingdoms over the sea. I wish to say to the Government that we shall be behind them most cordially with our best support—and not critical support—in prosecuting this war right to the end, and in financing it to the full in every legitimate and reasonable way.

Abridged.
Source: *Commonwealth Parliamentary Debates*, vol. 75, 14 October 1914, pp. 171–3.

———————➤———————

Robert Moore
Sermon on the Moral Choice of Nation, 1916

Robert Henry Moore (1872–1964) was born in County Westmeath, Ireland, and after reading theology at Trinity College, Dublin, became an Anglican priest in a crowded Belfast parish. He emigrated in 1897, following an appeal for clergy to minister to the unruly populations of the Western Australian goldfields, where he spent over a decade in parish work. Recognition of Moore's energy and leadership led to his appointment as a canon at St George's Cathedral, Perth. It was from the cathedral's pulpit in late 1916, after Australian troops had suffered losses at the battle of Pozières on the Somme, that Moore advised his congregation to vote 'Yes' to the referendum—introduced by Prime Minister Billy Hughes—that conscription be introduced for overseas military service. Australia was divided by the question, and Moore believed that the Church could not be neutral in the debate. He took as his text Matthew 18: 7: 'Woe unto the world because of occasions of stumbling, for it must needs be that the occasions come, but woe to that man through whom the occasion cometh!' In October 1916 the Australian people would reject conscription, as they would in a second referendum held the following year. By this time, Moore had taken up a commission as chaplain in the Australian Imperial Force and served with the Light Horse Brigade in the Middle East.

'Woe unto the world because of occasions of stumbling'—it is an exclamation more of sorrow and pity than of denunciation, for it is in the nature of things—'it must needs be that the occasions come'—but they are the result of the wilful and responsible actions of evil or ignorant men who, while indeed they involve the world around them in sorrow, will not escape the just reward of their deeds. But the scripture teaching goes deeper still to point out that these troubles have an immediate effect which is not altogether bad; if indeed they bring sorrow to many innocent people in the world, and if most certain judgment will dog the steps of those through whose sin the trouble comes, yet these very deeds of evil will have the effect of showing up the good and the true. Just as the darkness emphasises the brightness of the lighted lamp, so the sin and misery of the world help to throw into relief the deeds of kindness and self-sacrifice of which often that misery is the occasion and opportunity. 'How far that little candle throws its beams, so shines a good deed in a naughty world.'

How wonderfully these days of judgment and trial through which the world has been passing have illustrated this thought. How have they not 'made manifest' the great and beautiful qualities of heroism, devotion, sympathy, in contrast to the loathly brutality of those whose vaulting ambition wilfully plotted for years the ruin of their neighbours so that they might seize their goods! Who believed two years ago that the sons and daughters of this sunny land were capable of the patriotism, self-sacrifice, patience, discipline, cool unfaltering courage, and generous sympathy our soldiers have shown in the battlefield, and that their mothers, wives, and daughters have shown in the patient watching and service at home? When we look back and compare our old outlook upon life and the philosophy of the 'market place' of two years ago with the facts of life as we see them today, it seems almost as if some vast transformation had been worked upon us. Few believed that we were capable of submitting to discipline or of making any serious sacrifice which might interfere with our pursuit of pleasure, until this 'day of judgment' came upon us like a bolt from the blue. Then we saw how men of peace could submit themselves to rigorous training, and were capable of the grandest sacrifices and noblest heroism, like Zebulun and Naphtali, 'a people that jeoparded their lives unto the death in the high places of the field.' But there have been

Ugly Jarring Notes

in our national life, which in the days before the war often gave us cause for anxiety; voices that preached material gain as the sole aim of life, and discounted honest industry; which counselled less and slower work and ever more and more pay and leisure; which emphasised class distinctions and openly preached class war. The national danger of the great conflict, we believed, had all but silenced this clamour; the spectacle of rich and poor serving in the ranks together against the common foe of our national liberties would, we believed, bridge the chasm which the days of selfish peace had tended to widen between them; the common sacrifice, the common service for the State in the great crisis of her fight for life, was certain, we thought, to breed a community of interest that would stand the test of time. And no doubt there will be a great move forward in this direction; but meantime those disintegrating forces are again making themselves heard, in, perhaps, it may be a final effort to assert themselves and wreck society. Australia, who has proved herself capable of such great things in the past two years, is now called upon in her corporate capacity to set her seal to the sacrifice and heroism that her individual sons and daughters have so lavishly shown. It is incredible that she will draw back and it is well to remember that every alleged reason for her doing so is equally a reason why we should not have entered on the path of duty in the first place. And, further, there is

No Mistaking the Quarter

from which the objections to national service are coming. We may leave out of account the 'conscientious objector.' For him, if he is genuine, there are many non-combatant services which give him ample scope for self-sacrifice and heroism. But the political objector is none other than a wrecker of the present social order who is seizing on this great call to the nation as an opportunity for spreading the poison of class hatred and keeping alive the dying embers of class war. His type of mind is amply illustrated in the sordid meanness of some of the objections to National Service, which he puts forward and the lying insinuation contained in others. It is not a question as to whether or not there are millions of men elsewhere, but is Australia—fighting as she is for her life—to draw back now because immediate danger seems to be passing, and to leave it to other races, Englishmen, Russians or Indians may be, to do the fighting for her? The men who made Australia's name glorious on Gallipoli and at Pozieres were not cast in this mould. It is not a question of some deep laid scheme of capitalists that has made the founders and builders of Australian Democracy make this call to the nation, but the national need of the freest democracy in the world, if she is to make good her claim to hold her glorious heritage. It seems as if we could not properly appreciate the truth without having its opposite placed in contrast, the true inwardness of beauty is emphasised by the horror of that which is hideous. There are some who think that the Church should not touch on these matters, but if religion is to teach us how to live now she must take up her burden to educate men to see the truth, and while she can have nothing to do with mere party politics she is bound to speak out where questions arise which affect

The Moral Choice of the Nation

as a whole. And at this moment we stand at the parting of the ways. On the one hand we are bidden to look down into the pit of destruction in which writhe the slimy forms of selfishness, indifference, wilful and obstinate ignorance, and the un-brotherliness of narrow sectional and class interests; on the other hand, there towers before us the mountain peaks of sacrifice—not the pushing of my brother into the fray while I stay at home at ease as is their unheroic jibe, but the sacrifice of self for the sake of our free Australia for the sake of our Empire, for the sake of the liberties of the world. There is no need at this time to elaborate it all again, for it is common knowledge that we have arrived at 'day of judgment' for the world, when there are being revealed the ideals of truth and liberty and justice for nations as for individuals; and in addition to that we here in Australia have arrived at the greatest crisis of our national life, when it will be known whether we are a people worthy of the sacrifice so many have made, worthy of a lasting and honourable place among peoples of the earth, or whether we are a degenerate and craven race, hasting to miserable and ignoble dissolution. It cannot be that such is our fate! This occasion of stumbling may bring us trouble and woe, but its effect will surely be to reveal us steadfast in holding on along the path of truth, and swift and certain judgment will surely seek out those by whom the occasion of stumbling has arisen. Let us see to it that no specious arguments drawn from days of peace, nor cunning insinuations, deflect us from our duty.

Abridged.
Sources: Marian Aveling (ed.), *Westralian Voices: Documents in Western Australian History*;[32] original documents in the Robert Henry Moore papers, Sermon Notebook 1916, Battye Library, 1210A.

———◆———

Vida Goldstein
Against War, 1917

Vida Jane Mary Goldstein (1869–1949) was a prominent feminist and peace activist who epitomized the late nineteenth-century 'new woman' with her independent spirit, confident intelligence and stylish appearance. She grew up in Melbourne in a family committed to reformist ideas and philanthropic actions, becoming the youthful leader of the United Council for Women's Suffrage. A delegate to the International Women's Suffrage Conference in Washington DC in 1902, Goldstein was also influential in international suffrage circles. She formed the non-party-aligned Women's Political Association, then ran for the Senate in 1903—the first woman in the British Empire to stand for Federal Parliament. Goldstein continued to contest national seats over the next two decades and, while unsuccessful, was feted in the press. A charismatic platform speaker, Goldstein was noted for her clarity and witty repartee. With the outbreak of World War I, her commitment to pacifism became paramount (even though her only brother was to be killed at the Western Front). Indeed, her unflinching anti-war stand was to rupture the women's alliance she had worked to build and she was expelled from the National Council of Women. Undaunted, Goldstein founded the Women's Peace Army and spoke at anti-war and anti-conscriptionist demonstrations, addressing crowds of more than eighty thousand at Melbourne's Yarra Bank. She was also involved in a 'commune' to assist the families of striking maritime workers. On the evening of 1 November 1917 Goldstein gave a fundraising speech on 'War and Industrial Democracy' at the Mechanics Institute in the Victorian town of Bacchus Marsh. Among the small, orderly audience was Detective Olholm of the military police, and he carefully recorded Goldstein's words.

Ladies and Gentlemen, I am very glad to be here tonight and especially to see so many women. I remember on one occasion [when] I addressed the people in a place called Mansfield there were nearly all men present—that was, I believe, mainly because the women had to stay home and mind the babies! So I am glad to see both men and women here tonight.

Our organisation [the Women's Political Association] was formed in 1902. We have always been opposed to war—that is one of the planks of our programme. Every time I stood for parliament I have always stood as an advocate of international arbitration. We do not think anything can be settled by the sword. We have gone right on until the present day, [and] we have absolutely presented an unbroken front to those who support the war. In 1915 we decided to form a Women's Peace Army of which you hear a good deal recently. We formed this little association to help the women and children.

There are a great many people who do not approve of our non-party policy, [and] we have got nothing to do with the conservative section of politicians. We are in favour of international peace arbitration. I would like to refer to the disturbances that took place in the early part of the war. We were held up to public scorn. We were called pro-Germans, disloyalists and everything else because we held meetings on the Yarra Bank!

We have never caused any trouble on the Yarra Bank, [although] there was once a little disturbance between some soldiers and civilians, but that was not due to us. As far as the soldiers are concerned, we respect those who have gone to fight for their country. We know that they have gone to do what they consider a sacred duty, and we respect them just as much as we expect those who differ from us to respect us. There were other disturbances that came into conflict with the soldiers. The soldiers know very well there are black sheep in every flock, [and] there were some of those black sheep who came along and tried to break up our meetings. I do not think they would have done it if they had not been inflamed by the press.

At the time of the Boer war, I was held up to public scorn as a pro-Boer, because I dared say what I believed to be correct. [Can] you tell me one war that has ever achieved anything, that has not left destruction, ruin and misery upon the people? As Lord Northcliffe said: there must be wars, it was inevitable, [so] there must be a war between Germany and England. When we speak about trade wars we do not say this is wholly a trade war, we say all wars are more or less trade wars. What brings the countries into conflict with one another is that their competition these days for markets is so keen, [that] they look with jealous eyes to other countries. Germany, of course, was making tremendous headway commercially—she has wonderful business methods, [and] some people think we as a nation [should] copy her methods. Great Britain is going to be entirely run in the interests of the financiers and capitalists of Great Britain.

Well, friends, these are the things that are going to make other wars in the future. There are one hundred and one different things that cause war. You know if two men have a fight, it is extremely difficult to find out the right side: one says one thing, and one says another, so it is very hard to get the real facts as to who is right and who is wrong. Supposing the press were doing what we are trying to do with this little body of ours, do you not think the press would be a mighty instrument? But no, they make bitter startling head lines on what we are trying to do. After this war I hope the people will have learned a lesson and will have a press of their own, run in the interests of the people.

You talk about fighting for democracy, fighting for the rights of the people. Well, friends, we maintain that if conscription is brought in [then] the people are enslaved, because no man is free if he has to go away against his will. Friends, what has happened? For one hundred years the great glory of England was that no man need fight against his will. Australia is the only country of the world where there is liberty today, long may it be maintained.

Talking about peace, they say we fanatical women want peace at any price. Our price is a very high price, [for] it is a peace with democratic principles. What we are striving for is true industrial democracy, [and] what we mean by that is the control of industry in the interests of the people as a whole. The workers who produce things never get the full reward of their labour, [for] that simply goes to the capitalistic section of society. In every country—in every belligerent country—these principles are making headway.

Talking of poverty and distress, there are two and three families living in [ie sharing] some homes in different parts of Melbourne. That is not brought about by drink or gambling. It is brought about by the slavery of the wage system, [for] when men get out of work for a few weeks it is difficult for them to pull up again. When this strike occurred in Sydney we saw what was happening. And when the wharf labourers strike occurred here [in Melbourne], we saw what would happen. We made up our minds that we would not see the women and children punished in this industrial fight as they had been in the past. So at the Guild Hall [the headquarters of the Women's Peace Army] we provided food for as many as five hundred women and children in one day. We also have two boot shops, and a barbers saloon where the men can get a free shave and hair cut.

We say the people have got the power in their hands if they choose to use it—[but] if they do not choose to use it they must take the full consequences. Remember that the members of parliament are your servants, [and] not your masters as they make themselves. They are the elected servants of the people. I do not blame them altogether for using that power, because the people allow them to do so. I say we must have a world run in the interests of the people.

Before concluding I ask you to give as liberally as you can to the wives and children of those who are suffering in this present strike.

Reproduced in full.
From transcript of speech produced by Detective Olholm, Victorian Police.
Source: Australian Archives (Melbourne), MP 16/1, Attorney General's Department, Intelligence Section Records 1914–23, File No. 15/3/1371.[33]

Daniel Mannix

No to Conscription and Sectarian Bigots, 1917

Daniel Patrick Mannix (1864–1963), the legendary Catholic Archbishop of Melbourne, was a controversial church leader for half a century. Born in Ireland on a tenant farm, he showed a strong scholarly drive that led him to a doctorate in Divinity and appointments as professor of Moral Theology, then president, at the National University of Ireland, Maynooth. Mannix was appointed coadjutor to Melbourne's ageing Archbishop Thomas Carr in 1913 (whom he succeeded in 1917) and arrived on Easter Sunday to an enthusiastic welcome at St Patrick's Cathedral. He approved of Australia's entry into World War I, arguing that the voluntary enlistment of Catholics should be recognized through State aid to Catholic schools. As the war progressed, anti-Catholic and anti-Irish feeling became more pronounced in Australia, with Catholics unfairly accused of shirking their duty. Mannix deplored the way British troops had turned their guns against Irish nationalists during the 1916 Easter Uprising in Dublin. His claim that Australians were fighting 'an ordinary, sordid trade war'[34] and his opposition to conscription led Prime Minister Billy Hughes to question his loyalty. But Mannix's outspoken leadership had turned him into a popular hero—in November 1917 a 'monster' crowd of a hundred thousand assembled at John Wren's racecourse in Richmond to hear the Archbishop speak on 'Irish Home Rule'.[35] One month later, in the lead-up to the second referendum on conscription, Mannix addressed some twenty thousand people at Melbourne's Exhibition Building. The Archbishop was a great orator, who combined the moral authority conveyed by his position with a sharp wit; his opening lines dubbed Hughes the 'Little Czar' of Australian politics. At the conclusion of the speech, all at the great meeting sang a rousing rendition of 'God Save Ireland'.

Conscriptionists will not be satisfied until Australia is denuded of her manhood. Australia, they think, has not done her part. Now, returned soldiers have told me, they have seen big strapping Englishmen walking about the streets of London and other English cities. I suppose these Englishmen are waiting to see the Australians take the places they could fill themselves at the front. (Cheers). I am not able to tell the truth of these statements, but I believe the returned soldiers as readily as I would the Prime Minister. (Applause). We are told over and over again that we are not doing our share, but I say that we have done more than our share compared to other parts of the Empire. (Applause). We have done more than all of the Dominions, and more than England itself if all things are taken into account. (Applause).

I am opposed to the conscription of Australians for service overseas in any form—(applause)—and in no circumstances will I ever stand on a recruiting platform. (Applause.) At the beginning of the war, I made up my mind that the recruiting platform was not the place for a Catholic priest or a Catholic Bishop. (Applause.) Non-Catholic clergymen are entitled to do their own business according to their lights. I have no quarrel with them, if they think it their duty to become recruiting agents. But I am under no obligation to follow their example, and I have no intention of doing so. (Applause.)

I have made it perfectly clear that England and the Allies were quite justified in coming to the rescue of Belgium and other small nations. Of that I am absolutely convinced, and I wish I could be equally certain that there were not ulterior motives of which no just man could approve. At all events, I have never blamed the English people for coming to the rescue of Belgium, and I have never blamed the French people for defending themselves and endeavouring to save Belgium. (Applause.) Within the last two or three days the Minister for Defence said I had changed my attitude, and that I had just said for the first time that England was justified in coming to the rescue of Belgium. Well, if I said this once, I suppose I have said it dozens of times. (Applause.) But, while there was every justification for England's coming into the war to protect Belgium and France, and to protect herself, there was—and is—no justification for that country to go into the war or to remain at war for the purpose of securing the economic domination of the world. (Applause.) When we can say we have vindicated the rights of the small nations, and secured ourselves from aggression, we should think of making peace, even though we had not secured the economic domination of the world. (Applause.)

Australia is part of the Empire, and, like England, and for legitimate ends, Australia has been justified in coming to the help of the small nations. (Applause.) Our men at the front are not likely to be deserted by the Australians, but it would be disastrous to give Mr. Hughes or Sir William Irvine a blank cheque to continue the war indefinitely for such aims as they may have in view. (Applause.) We should be clearly told what we are fighting for. If the fight is for the economic domination of the world, then, as far as I am concerned, I am totally opposed to the war and to enlistment. (Applause.) Let our aims be clearly defined, and then we shall know where we are. But we shall remain uncompromisingly opposed to conscription. (Applause.)

I advised the authorities before, but they disregarded my advice, that recruiting would necessarily suffer while sectarian bigots were allowed on the platforms. (Applause.) These bigots had antagonised a large section of the community by their abuse and their insults. Their abuse, as far as I am concerned, does not give me a moment's thought, but I particularly refer to the insults heaped upon the Catholic people. (Applause.) In abusing me, they have hurt the Catholic people more than they have hurt me. (Applause.) If it is desired, by voluntary recruiting, to do the fair thing by the men at the front, the sectarians should be shunted off the platforms. (Applause.) When they were gone, and the platforms were purified and disinfected, those engaged in recruiting might expect to get a more calm and patient hearing from a large section of the Australian people. (Loud applause.)

Moreover, let us at least have the truth. I say deliberately that it is a great exaggeration for Mr. Hughes to state that 7,000 men are required to be sent to the front monthly from Australia. At the very outside, the military authorities should not need more than 5,000, and I am inclined to believe that perhaps 4,000 would be enough. (Applause.) I have just as reliable information on this point as Mr. Hughes. (Loud applause.) A regulation has been passed for the imposition of dire penalties on persons who do not speak the truth during this campaign. (Laughter and applause.) I have no difficulty in submitting to the regulation, because I have always told the truth. (Loud applause.) All I ask is that the regulations be applied to Mr. Hughes. (Laughter and applause.)

The Australian people should be treated fairly, and should be told the truth, whether it be palatable or not. If this course be followed, I know the Australians will continue to do their duty, as they have done it throughout the war. (Applause.) The people want a fair and square deal. (Applause.) If the appeal for recruits to help the Australians at the front is made by reputable people, and not by sectarian bigots, and if the people can feel sure that the war was made for just ends, and these only, I am sure that Australians will respond in sufficient numbers. (Applause.)

My last word is to advise you to keep the little power you have, and to vote No on December 20th. (Loud applause.) You will be acting in your own interests, and in the true interests of the Empire, by keeping Australia free, and not giving a blank cheque to Mr. Hughes or anybody else. (Applause.) If you surrender your freedom by accepting conscription, what assurance have you that the rights you give away will be used to the best advantage of Australia? (Applause.) You can do your duty without conscription, as you have so far done it nobly and generously. (Applause.) I have conceived it my duty to oppose conscription. (Applause.) If conscription be carried I shall be able to absolve myself from blame for the consequences which I foresee and which Australia will have time to regret. (Loud applause.)

Abridged.
Source: *The Advocate*, 8 December 1917, pp. 13–14.

———

Billy Hughes
Australia and World Peace, 1919

One of the most notable orators of early twentieth-century Australia, William Morris 'Billy' Hughes (1862–1952), was a quick-witted little man with a shrewd sense of political theatre. Born in London, with a childhood spent in Wales, he arrived in Australia as an assisted migrant in 1884. After a period working as a labourer, and experiencing hard times, Hughes opened a small shop in the Sydney suburb of Balmain. A wily socialist and labour organizer, Hughes entered the New South Wales parliament in 1894, switched to federal politics in 1901, and became Labor prime minister in 1915. He believed passionately that World War I was a battle between British civilization and Germanic barbarism. After visiting the Australian Diggers in France he was determined that their toil and sacrifice should be supported by conscription at home. It was a policy to which most of his colleagues were bitterly opposed and it resulted in his expulsion from the Labor Party. It is a mark of his political shrewdness that Hughes emerged from the political brawl still holding the position of prime minister: he now led a coalition of pro-war MPs, most of them conservatives, and formed a new Nationalist Party in 1917. When the war ended, Hughes was a tenacious defender of independent Australian interests at the international Versailles Conference, which established the terms of the peace. He browbeat the delegates into granting Australia the power to administer New Guinea (thereby wresting it from German control). He fought for an Australian share in war reparations and he insisted that Australia be permitted to enforce its White Australia Policy on immigration. On his return to Australia, Hughes explained his actions at Versailles in a virtuoso speech to Parliament on 10 September 1919.

When I ask this Parliament to approve of this Treaty, I have a right, as the spokesman for Australia to speak proudly of what Australia has done through her soldiers, her sailors, and all those who have striven, each in their own way, to serve their country in its hour of peril—the women, the nurses of Australia, and those who went out to serve their country, even in the manufacture of munitions, and aid in every possible way in the great conflict which has shaken the world to its very foundations. There never was, in the history of the world before this war, a record like that of this young community of five million people. We sent out a greater Army than Great Britain herself had ever sent out before, and we transported it over 12,000 miles of ocean. We maintained five divisions of fighting men at the front line, men who will stand comparison with the finest and bravest soldiers of any of the Allied and Associated Powers. We need not claim more distinction than that. It is sufficient, if we are able to say that on the land, and on the sea, and in the air, in every theatre of war—in Europe, in Asia, in the Pacific—Australia played her part, and that, in the great victory that has been achieved, Australia has done well, or, rather, her soldiers have done well for her. They have done great things, and have given to all of us freedom and safety. They have assured to us forever the possibility of realizing all those ideals which we cherish above life itself. Only we ourselves, by being recreant to the cause for which they fought and died, can now destroy this temple of our liberties, the keys of which they have handed to us stained with their hearts' blood.

It was abundantly evident to my colleague and to myself, as well as to the representatives of other Dominions, that Australia must have separate representation at the Peace Conference. Consider the vastness of the Empire, and the diversity of interests represented. Look at it geographically, industrially, politically, or how you will, and it will be seen that no one can speak for Australia but those who speak as representatives of Australia herself. Great Britain could not, in the very nature of things, speak for us. Britain has very many interests to consider besides ours, and some of those interests do not always coincide with ours. It was necessary, therefore—and the same applies to other Dominions—that we should be represented. Not as at first suggested, in a British panel, where we would take our place in rotation, but with separate representation like other belligerent nations. Separate and direct representation was at length conceded to Australia and to every other self-governing Dominion.

By this recognition Australia became a nation, and entered into a family of nations on a footing of equality. We had earned that, or rather, our soldiers had earned it for us. In the achievement of victory they had played their part, and no nation had a better right to be represented than Australia. This representation was vital to us, particularly when we consider that at this world Conference thirty-two nations and over a billion people were directly represented. It was a Conference of representatives of the people of the whole world, excepting only Germany, the other enemy Powers, Russia, and a few minor nations. In this world Conference, the voice of this young community of five million people had to make itself heard. In this gathering of men representing nations with diverse and clashing interests, Australia had to press her views, and to endeavour to insist upon their acceptance by other nations.

Let me give honorable members some idea of the Conference, which consisted of more than seventy delegates—about as many as there are honorable members of this Chamber—men of all colours, and from every part of the world. There were representatives from China, Japan, Liberia, Hayti, Siam, Brazil, America, Britain, India, Roumania, Poland, and Greece. There were men speaking diverse tongues, and having ideals as far asunder as the poles. There were interests which had their origin in thousands of years of tradition, and in race and geographical position. Here was Australia, an outpost of the Empire, a great continent peopled by a handful of men, called upon to defend, amongst other things, a policy which could not be understood, and which was not understood, by those with whom we consorted. I speak of the policy of a White Australia. Imaging the difficulties of the position, and the clashing of warring interests; for, while the world changes, human nature remains ever the same. While there was a sincere desire to obtain a just Peace, each nation's conception of justice differed. Each nation desired what it considered necessary for its own salvation, though it might trench on the liberties, rights, or material welfare of others.

Honorable members who have travelled in the East or in Europe will be able to understand with what difficulty this world assemblage of men, gathered from all the corners of the earth—men representing four hundred million Chinese, men representing Japan, men representing India, Siam, Hayti, and Liberia; men representing partially coloured populations —were able to appreciate this ideal of those five million people who had dared to say, not only that this great continent was theirs, but that none should enter in except such as they chose. I venture to say, therefore, that perhaps the greatest thing which we have achieved, under such circumstances and in such an assemblage, is the policy of a White Australia. On this matter I know that I speak for most, if not all, of the people of Australia. There are some at the two extreme poles of political opinion who do not hold those views, but their numbers, thank God! are quite insignificant, and their influence, I hope, even less important. Remember that this is the only community in the Empire, if not, indeed, in the world, where there is so little admixture of race. Do you realize that, if you go in England from one county to another, men speak with a different accent; that if you go a few miles men speak with a different tongue; that if you go from one part of France to another, men can hardly understand one another? Yet you can go from Perth to Sydney, and from Hobart to Cape York, and find men speaking the same tongue, with the same accent. Place on that bench men from Alice Springs, Cape York, Hobart, and Adelaide, and you cannot distinguish them in speech, form, or feature. We are all of the same race, and speak the same tongue in the same way. That cannot be said of any other Dominion in the Empire, except New Zealand, where, after all, it can be said only with reservations, because that country has a large population of Maoris. We are more British than the people of Great Britain, and we hold firmly to the great principle of the White Australia, because we know what we know. We have these liberties, and we believe in our race and in ourselves, and in our capacity to achieve our great destiny, which is to hold this vast continent in trust for those of our race who come after us, and who stand with us in the battle of freedom. The White Australia is yours. You may do with it what you please; but, at any rate, the soldiers have achieved the victory, and my colleague and I have brought that great principle back to you from the Conference. Here it is, at least as safe as it was on the day when it was first adopted by this Parliament.

What has been won? If the fruits of victory are to be measured by national safety and liberty, and the high ideals for which these boys died, the sacrifice has not been in vain. They died for the safety of Australia. Australia is safe. They died for liberty, and liberty is now assured to us and to all men. They have made for themselves and their country a name that will not die.

Looking back, through the vista of years of trial, tribulation and turmoil, into that Valley of the Shadow of Death into which we and all the free peoples of the earth were plunged, we may now lift up our voices, and thank God that, through their sacrifice, we have been brought safely into the green pastures of peace.

We turn now from war to peace. We live in a new world; a world bled white by the cruel wounds of war. Victory is ours, but the price of victory is heavy. The whole earth has been shaken to its very core. Upon the foundations of victory we would build the new temple of our choice.

Industrially, socially, politically, we cannot, any more than other nations, escape the consequences of the war. The whole world lies bleeding and exhausted from the frightful struggle. There is no way of salvation, save by the gospel of work. Those who endeavour to set class against class, or to destroy wealth, are counsellors of destruction. There is hope for this free Australia of ours only if we put aside our differences, strive to emulate the deeds of those who by their valour and sacrifice have given us liberty and safety, and resolve to be worthy of them and the cause for which they fought.

Abridged.
Source: *Commonwealth Parliamentary Debates*, vol. 89, 10 September 1919, pp. 12166–79.

Nellie Melba and Stanley Melbourne Bruce

Farewell to Grand Opera, 1924

Dame Nellie Melba (1861–1931) was Australia's beloved grand diva, and in her own words 'put Australia on the map' internationally. From a privileged Melbourne childhood, early marriage and motherhood, and many years of musical training, Melba rose to command the world operatic stage. Her international career of an extraordinary thirty-eight years spanned stretches in the opera houses of London, Milan, Paris and New York, and her clear pitch and perfect trills were brought to new audiences through her recordings for the gramophone. Despite her international acclaim, Melba never abandoned her birthplace. In 1909 she undertook a bush tour that covered 16,000 kilometres, and in Melbourne she contributed to the development of musical education and financial support for rising Australian artists. Melba spent World War I entertaining the Allied troops and bolstering morale, including through a promotional film clip with Charlie Chaplin made in Hollywood, and was singing at Covent Garden in the first season of peace. Her retirement from the stage was a protracted affair. On 13 October 1924, in the role of Mimi in Puccini's *La Bohème*, Melba bid adieu to Grand Opera at His Majesty's Theatre in Melbourne. This concert, which was broadcast live, raised £18,000 for limbless soldiers. Melba's farewell speech was followed by an eloquent tribute by the 'silvertail' Prime Minister Stanley Melbourne Bruce (1883–1967), who cast Melba as a national treasure and commended her for her patriotism. Melba's gracious goodbye was premature, as she was to continue performing at farewell concerts around Australia and overseas for the next three years—introducing the phrase 'doing a Melba' into the Australian language.

Nellie Melba:

To-night the curtain falls on my last operatic appearance in Australia, and I have to say to you the most difficult word in life—Good-bye. I shall try to say it with a smile, not only on my lips, but with my heart, a smile that comes not from the memory of achievement, but from the knowledge that I have done my best and that I have tried to keep faith with my art. For all that Australia has done for me, for all the beauty that she has shown me, for all the love she has offered, I wish to say, thank you from the bottom of my heart. (Great Acclamation).

What shall I say? My heart is breaking, but I am happy, so happy, that you are honouring me in this way. I am happy too, to think that the darling soldiers, who gave everything, will receive a very large sum of money through your kindness and hard work in this appeal. It is a thing I shall never forget. (Cheers). But you cannot expect me to say too much—you do not want me to break down. (Cheers). You want me to go away with a smiling face, and I am determined to do that. (Prolonged cheers). I thank you more than I can say for your kindness, your fidelity, and your loyalty to me. I cannot express one half that I feel. All that I can say is 'Thank you, from the bottom of my heart.' And I never was prouder than I am to-night to be an Australian woman.

Stanley Melbourne Bruce:

I have been set a task impossible of accomplishment by any living person. I have been asked to render to you, Dame Nellie, on behalf of the people of Australia, a tribute which may make you understand how much we think of you, and in what surpassing affection you are held. (Cheers.) There is no language in which anybody could frame words with which to express our admiration and esteem for you. To-night, which is your farewell to the operatic stage at the summit of a great career, the people of Australia pay their tribute with greater feeling, because to-night you have done something that is emblematic of your career. You have associated yourself in your triumph with the maimed soldiers of Australia, and it will be to the people of the Commonwealth a new inspiration. It will enshrine you the more surely in their hearts when they think that on this last great night you have devoted yourself to the stricken soldiers. (Cheers.)

Tonight we must remember that art knows no nationality. There are no barriers to race. So tonight it is not only the people of Australia bidding farewell to Melba on their operatic stage, but it is the peoples of the whole civilised races of the world. (Cheers.) They all desire to render their tribute. The people of Australia think that it is peculiarly fitting that this great honour should be theirs to-night, and they feel that they are entitled, on behalf of the people of the world, to express their regard for you. (Applause.) What you have done for Australia no man can say. Long before the Australian soldiers had blazoned the name of Australia throughout the world you were her great ambassadress. (Cheers.) You have done great things. After a triumphant career, when the nations of the world have given you all the honours they could bestow, your ambition has been to try to give to the people of Australia the art you know and love. You have succeeded wonderfully. You are an inspiration and an example to all of us. (Cheers.)

And at this time, when it behoves Australians more than ever to believe in their own country, I think in your patriotism you will find you wrought better than you knew. (Cheers.) With your power undiminished, your career unfurnished, you now leave the operatic stage in a blaze of glory for that retirement which you have richly earned. You will carry with you the good wishes of the people of Australia and of the whole civilised world. On behalf of the people of Australia I render you the homage of a great nation. (Prolonged cheers.)

Reproduced in full.
Source: *Argus*, 14 October 1924, p. 11.

———

John Monash
Anzac Day: Remember Gallipoli, 1927

John Monash (1865–1931) was Australia's pre-eminent World War I military leader. Born in Melbourne of German–Jewish origin, Monash graduated from that city's university in Engineering, Law and Arts and combined work in engineering with part-time soldiering. He led the 4th Brigade of the Australian Imperial Forces at Gallipoli, was in charge of the new 3rd Division and was promoted to commander of the Australian corps on the Western Front. Monash was a modern general whose strengths lay in his administrative capacities and in his emphasis on the preparation of troops and careful military planning. On his return to Melbourne, he was regarded as the greatest living Australian. He became active in the organization of Anzac Day, which in 1927 fell during the visit of the Duke of York (George VI). Monash led a parade of some thirty thousand ex-servicemen through the city, watched by a crowd of at least half a million—the largest Anzac Day turnout ever seen. After the march a commemoration service was held at the Exhibition Building. This was Monash's moment, for as he mounted the podium a spontaneous burst of applause rang out, dying away suddenly as he raised his hand. From his commanding position as the Great War leader, he spoke with simple authority about the meaning of Gallipoli to the nation.

The passage of another year, comrades, has brought us together once again to join in this commemoration service in honour of Anzac Day. This annual commemoration has grown from a small beginning until it has reached the mighty demonstration which has been today. Although Armistice Day is recognised throughout the Empire as a day of national mourning and a commemoration of the sacrifice and service of all the nations, yet April 25 is a day specially dedicated by the people of this southern land on which the whole nation mourns its dead and honours their memory.

Anzac Day makes a special appeal to the hearts of all of us because of the special place it holds in our history, for it was on this day 12 years ago that the flower of Australia's youth flung itself against the beetling cliffs of Gallipoli and performed a memorable feat of arms which instantly welded the people of Australia into a nation, and proved to the entire world that our men and women were not unworthy of their sires. It was on this day that was born the tradition of the Australian Imperial Forces, a tradition which carried the A.I.F. through four long years of the horror and turmoil of war.

The single exhortation, 'Remember Gallipoli,' became the watchword of the A.I.F, in France, in Palestine, and on all the battlefronts for the remainder of the war, and that same exhortation, 'Remember Gallipoli', is destined to become the watchword of the Australian people. If any proof were needed that our returned sailors and soldiers and the people of this country respect this day, that they do not forget what it stands for, that they are alive to the traditions of sacrifice, loyalty, and comradeship which were born on this day, then I think this great assembly, the wonderful concourse of people that thronged the streets of this city, and the reverent homage at the Cenotaph would supply the answer.

But this anniversary is marked by a special significance, for we are honoured by the presence of His Royal Highness the Duke of York who, we know, shares in full sympathy all the feelings that inspire our minds on this occasion—of sorrow for our lost comrades, sympathy for all those who mourn them, and pride in the great national tradition for which they gave their lives. Australia's toll of dead in the war was 60,000 men. Every one of us here had friends and dear comrades in that host. There are many here, indeed, who had close and immediate relatives, and to all of them our heartfelt thoughts go out in deepest sympathy.

It is not too much that the people should pause for one day in the year to do homage to those men and to keep alive the spirit which animated that host of departed friends. But our duty does not end there. On us who have survived the stress of war and who have been safely restored to our homeland is laid the duty of helping to restore to Australia the mighty loss of that legion of men by devoting our lives and energies to that class of nation building in which they would have shared had they been spared. Remember, in war those who came out of battle had to carry on the fight in reduced numbers, so we who have been fortunate enough by the blessing of Providence to survive the war must now do our part, but not only our part; we must take up the burden of those we left behind. Only so can we worthily honour their memory.

Anzac Day stands for one other ideal—the ideal of comradeship, a comradeship which consoled us on many a distant battlefield, a comradeship which, I hope, will endure till the last of us has gone to his rest, a comradeship which must never be allowed to fade, a comradeship which must hold us together in the same patriotic spirit in these days of peace that bound us shoulder to shoulder in the years of war. But after all, when the A.I.F. has passed away, let us hope that the Australian people will for all time keep sacred the memory of this day.

Reproduced in full.
Source: *Argus*, 26 April 1927, p. 12.

John Anderson
Censorship of Literature, 1928

John Anderson (1893–1962) was Australia's most prominent philosopher during the first half of the twentieth century. After an early career in Scotland, in 1927 Anderson took up the Challis Chair of Philosophy at the University of Sydney. A charismatic teacher who attracted disciples, Anderson influenced students over several generations and was a central force in Sydney's libertarian Push—a group of bohemians, writers and artists associated with Sydney University after World War II. He was deeply committed to philosophy as a way of life and, under the banner of 'free thought', promoted values of pluralism and liberty in opposition to the 'illusions' of organised religion, uniformity and orthodoxy. Anderson's university appointment coincided with the decades in which Australia was blinkered by a regime of official censorship. There was a ban on the import of novels dealing with sex, books on birth control and publications advocating radical or communist ideas. In 1928 Anderson travelled interstate to address the University of Melbourne Graduates Association, arguing that censorship was the enemy of 'an adult and independent outlook'. One year later, James Joyce's *Ulysses* was banned in Australia. Anderson gave action to his words by illegally importing a copy of *Ulysses*, bound as a Bible, and circulating it to colleagues and students at the University of Sydney.

It is not perhaps generally known, the newspapers having carefully refrained from discussing the matter, that there exists in Australia a political censorship of imported literature, and that practically all publications dealing otherwise than unfavourably with Russian affairs and with Communism in general are thereby excluded. It is natural enough that if the ventilation of views is not recognised as a primary social requirement, the acts of Governments themselves should not be offered for, and subjected to, the closest possible scrutiny.

The case against prohibition (with special reference to the question with which the name has come to be most closely associated) has seldom been more forcibly stated than by Wells in 'The New Machiavelli.' It is put forward by the hero, Remington, as an expression, ironically enough, of his dissatisfaction with the policy of the Liberal party, to which he had hitherto adhered. Prevention, he points out, is an indirect method of dealing with a situation; it consists of stopping one thing because it will stop another; it takes, or aims at taking a step which is *sufficient* to remove a certain danger, but does not pause to consider whether or not the step is *necessary*. Abolish ropes, and no one will be able to hang himself! Or to take Wells' own examples 'we shall presently want to stop the sale of ink and paper because those things tempt man to forgery. We do not threaten the privacy of the post because of betting touts' letters. The drift of all that kind of thing is narrow, unimaginative, mischievous, stupid.' 'But prevention,' comes the 'liberal' protest, 'is the essence of our work.' To which Remington replies, 'There's no prevention but education. There's no antiseptics in life but love and fine thinking.' Prohibition, as the phrase goes, does not prohibit; it is not even sufficient. Education is, of course, itself a subject of the same sort of controversy, and the educator's work is often represented as that of a censor.

Education, properly so-called, is not preceptive or moralistic but aesthetic; only so can it be co-operative and creative. This fact is obscurely conveyed by Remington's slogan, 'Love and fine thinking'. 'Make people fine, make fine people,' besides its suggestion of that very moulding which it was intended to combat, is too sentimental and exclusive to be acceptable as a working principle. The slogan of the 'shrivelled don,' marshalling opposition to Remington, is in some ways more to the point: 'Hate and coarse thinking.' Seize hold of things, hammer out the issues, abjure dilettantism in any shape. This is the true attitude of the artist, whose mind is superior to the squirming refinements and sensitive shrinkings of the 'aesthete', the *arbiter elegantiarum*, and who permits no ideals or taboos to come between him and a direct handling of things themselves. No sentimental attachments, no higher meanings, no irrelevant antecedents or consequences, are allowed to affect the positive treatment of things, their presentation as a balance of forces or sequence of phases. The artist is the best educator because he speaks only to those who are willing to share his work and do not beg to have their prejudices respected and, in general, to have things made easy for them. 'This ought not to be, therefore avoid it' says the moralist. 'This is, therefore, grasp it' says the artist. The issue, it appears, is between directness and indirectness. Now when any direct interest in certain subjects is forbidden, they are almost bound to be misunderstood not only by the ward but also by the guardian. If he knows them well enough to be able to pronounce finally upon them, the question naturally arises, 'What harm has his acquaintance with them done him?' Are we to judge that, since it has enabled him to take up the higher moral stand, it has done him good? Or is he to be reduced to the exquisitely hypocritical position of wanting to save the children from his own moral degeneration? He may say, indeed, that he desires first of all to inculcate such principles as will enable the recipient to meet the perils unafraid and to pass by them unsmirched. But to what can he appeal in the absence of understanding of these principles; in what way can he approach the subject? All that the moralist can do, and what he actually does, is to employ the 'awful consequences' argument. But what are the consequences of this argument itself? Fear and credulity; the spreading of vague notions of fearfulness and shamefulness and un-speakableness as attaching to things which can themselves be only vaguely known. Accordingly the protected persons, not even knowing what they are prevented against, are powerless in the face of any situation which is not on the index. 'The road to hell is paved with good intentions.'

Society, with all due respect to Socrates, cannot be founded on guardianship, even if we could assume that our constituted guardians were trained in 'dialectic'. Ruling, conceived as the transmission of virtues to the ruled, is a pious fiction; unless the governing body is itself expressive of the virtues of the many, it can rule only by force or fraud—that is to say, in either event, by fraud.

What, then, is the force of law in the community? Are we reduced in our defence of liberty to a defence of anarchy? This is a question to be faced like any other. We may begin by asking what anarchy is? It is presumably something like Hobbes' 'war of all against all'. Now why, as a matter of fact, do not all war against all? Is it because they have made a prudential contract to evade the consequences of mutual hostility, by giving up so much of their liberty? Not at all; no such state of hostility has ever existed. If it had, the compact could never have been made. Again, assuming it to have been made, it would not work—the demonstration of this being one of the notable features of the 'Republic'. With each person trying to give up as little and to get as much as possible, even the appearance of concord could not be maintained. The fact is that people find co-operation natural and enjoyable, not because of the dangers that it averts but because they are made that way. Otherwise they would never have discovered that it averted dangers. Allowing, as we must, that there are other motives than the co-operative, we cannot overlook the defects of a utilitarian conception of evolution. It is, in fact, merely a confused teleology, and does not allow for the spontaneous operation of human motives. Thus we cannot assign even to taboos a merely precautionary basis. But in addition to laws based on and issuing in fear there must always have been definite modes of co-operative activity, making possible both the recognition, in the course of time, of rules whereby the work might go forward, and the modification of rules previously established. Doubtless there are no rules which cannot be so perverted as to take the mandatory form. But they are indefensible in that form, since it is required that their basis and working shall not be examined. The only logical defence of them consists in showing what motives they promote and express; a demonstration which requires that they should be operated in a critical fashion. To admit that they have to be defended by censorship and the demand for obedience, instead of by ventilation and the recognition of things themselves, is to admit that they do not work. An institution or a country which, in such a predicament, falls back on 'tradition', adopting an exclusive attitude and attributing all its ills to external and accidental influences, is like the neurotic accusing 'fate' instead of his own repressions. Educators and Governments cannot do people's thinking and living for them, and a censorious attitude on their part shows that they do not understand their functions.

Liberty, then, is the ability to take things artistically, to pursue them for their own sake. It cannot be supported except by itself; there is no other motive to it than those free activities already in existence, in others and in a man's own self. It demands publicity and is opposed to all obscuring and confusing of issues. We might almost say that its greatest foe in English-speaking countries is the law of libel, based on the ridiculous conception of 'reputation'. A free society on the other hand, would be concerned with things only as they are. Its attitude towards repressive and obsessional activities would be to provide channels through which they could express themselves as criticism of existing arrangements or as demands for material upon which to work. It would recognise that a certain amount of opposition is a good thing—instead of demanding unanimity and expressions of 'loyalty' to particular policies, as was done, with great social damage, during the late war. When opposition goes so far as to attack the basis of co-operation itself, it must be rooted out; but this is best accomplished under conditions of the fullest possible publicity. And the need will least often arise when the upholders of co-operation have themselves continually examined, exposed and expounded its foundations. Censorship, in short, is anti-social and is never 'in the public interest.'

Abridged.
Source: Address published in *Schooling*, vol. XI, no. 4, August 1928.

Jack Lang
Opening of the Sydney Harbour Bridge, 1932

John Thomas 'Jack' Lang (1876–1975) was a real estate agent who became a defiant Labor reformer. During his first term as premier of New South Wales (1925–27), Lang introduced a swag of reforms, including child endowment, widows' pensions and a shorter working week. But his second term (1930–32) was cursed by the misery and unrest of the Great Depression. As Labor supporters fought bitterly about how to revive the economy, Lang led a splinter party known as 'Lang Labor'. He opposed the payment of interest to British bond-holders, arguing that the payment of the 'dole' to the unemployed was a more pressing priority. At the same time, proto-fascist militia, including the 'New Guard', were fearful that a revolution led by the unemployed and communists was imminent and they developed plans to overturn both Lang and Labor Prime Minister Jim Scullin. Amid the hunger and conflict, Sydneysiders watched the two great spans of their new Harbour Bridge reach out to each other across the water. The opening of the Bridge, on 19 March 1932, was spectacular. Massive crowds cheered marching bands, colourful floats, a twenty-one–gun salute and a procession of ships. Lang made a conciliatory speech, finishing just moments before one of the most spectacular disruptions of a public event in Australian history was to occur.

The achievement of this bridge is symbolical of the things Australians strive for, but have not yet attained.

The bridge itself unites people who have similar aims and ideals, but are divided by physical and geographical boundaries. This unity is brought about by a harmonious blending of English and Australian resources. The engineering brains and the financial facilities of the centre of the Empire have combined with the skill, the labour, and the determination of the Australian people.

This amalgamation has produced an edifice that it is of great utility to the people of New South Wales. It is an adornment to the city to which it belongs, and above that is a pride to the whole Empire. It is the fulfilment of a dream entertained by many of our pioneers, who, unfortunately, have not lived to see its realisation.

The Sydney Harbour Bridge has been many years building. Long before the engineer drew the plans, or the labourer turned the sod, the people of Sydney dreamed about, worked for, and fought over, the bridge which is about to be made available to them. Just as Sydney has completed this material bridge which will unite her people, so will Australia ultimately perfect the bridge which it commenced just 30 years ago. The statesmen of that period set out to build a bridge of common understanding, that would serve the whole of the people of our great continent. That bridge, unlike this, is still building.

The builders of that bridge, as the builders of this bridge, meet with disappointments, which make the task difficult sometimes—often delicate. But that bridge of understanding among the Australian people will yet be built, and will carry her on to that glorious destination which every man who loves our native, feels is in store for her.

I now officially declare Sydney Harbour Bridge open for traffic, and by pressing this button, will unveil a tablet recording this fact. (Cheers.)

At the conclusion of these proceedings I shall complete the opening ceremony by severing the ribbon stretched across the highway and duplicated on the Bridge itself. (Cheers.)

The *Sydney Morning Herald* reported how, at this point, a horseman in military uniform intervened in the ceremony and deprived Lang of the honour of officially opening the Sydney Harbour Bridge:

'The Premier's voice was carried by amplifiers to the dais where the ribbon stretched across the bridge, and, shortly after he had finished his speech, the man spurred his horse up to the ribbon and with an under-hand swish of his sword at the ribbon shouted: "On behalf of decent and loyal citizens of New South Wales, I now declare this bridge open".'

The protestor was New Guardsman Francis de Groot. He was dragged from his horse by Superintendent Mackay and later fined £5 plus £4 costs for offensive behaviour and maliciously damaging one ribbon.

Source: *Sydney Morning Herald*, 21 March 1932, pp. 11, 15.

Vance Palmer
Fishing Along the Great Barrier Reef, 1932

Edward Vivian 'Vance' Palmer (1885–1959) was a writer and an influential literary critic, perhaps best known by the Australian public for his reviews of local and inter-national books broadcast fortnightly on ABC radio between 1941 and 1956. Born in Bundaberg, Queensland, Palmer left school at sixteen and began writing soon after. The author of potboilers, essays, poetry, plays and short stories, Palmer wanted, above all, to be a great novelist. But while he wrote numerous novels—and these were respectfully received by contemporaries—Palmer's posthumous reputation is built on his literary criticism and finely crafted short stories. Through his involvement in literary circles in Australia and England, and a period spent on a Queensland cattle station, Palmer developed the view that a sophisticated national culture should enrich the lives of ordinary people. He favoured 'bush values' over a supposed suburban insularity. He admired Henry Lawson and Joseph Furphy, and his *Legend of the Nineties* (1954) celebrated the writing associated with the *Bulletin* School. In 1914 he had married Nettie Higgins, thus starting the most famous literary partner-ship in Australia. The couple supported their family through journalism and broad-casting, attempting to buy time for more 'serious' writing. For eight months in 1932 they camped on Green Island, near Cairns, on the North Queensland coast. Palmer had a deep and almost mystical appreciation of the Australian environment and on his return to Melbourne gave a series of radio talks on his island experiences. Part travelogue for southern city audiences, Palmer's account of fishing on the Great Barrier Reef romantically portrays northern Australia as offering an inter-racial 'democratic independent life' for Asian, white and Indigenous fishermen. He also made an early case for conservation of the Reef's varied marine life.

One of the features of life along the Reef is the number of fishing-boats that are always to be seen around the little cays and islands—particularly in the neighbourhood of Cairns. There is small possibility of netting in those coral-infested waters, so nearly all fish have to be taken on the line. That makes work for a large number of fishermen—black and white—for the fish are plentiful enough, and the market is there. Winter is the chief fishing-time, for during the summer there is always the danger of cyclones if the boats go too far afield, and there is little shelter among the outlying reefs. So all winter, provided with a good stock of ice and stores, the boats make out from their home ports, sometimes for two or three days, sometimes for a week or longer. There is not much profit for the boat unless it comes back with at least half-a-ton of fish.

Countless varieties of fish make their home among the coral growths, of course—emperor, trevalli, parrot-fish, rock-cod, coral-cod—but the staple reef-fish is the cod, which is caught in all sizes, from the smallish coral-variety, to the enormous groper that may turn the scale at several hundred pounds. The fishermen net their bait from the shoals of sardines and hardihead that swarm in some of the lagoons, and make for favourite spots along the reef, fishing by night, sleeping by day. Very often they make for an anchored lugger, for fish have a keen sense of smell, and are often found in large shoals round a lugger where the work of curing beche-de-mer is going on. But the usual method for a boat to collect the fish around it is to burley—that is, to cast out little packages of minced-up sardines that burst when they reach the bottom and form ground-bait. For though fish may be plentiful, the extent of possible feeding-grounds is enormous, and it is hard to hit the exact spot where they are to be found in great numbers. The only way is to attract them around your boat.

A peculiar class of fishermen has arisen in the North—men who are particularly adept in the handling of small boats and who know the reefs even better than the lugger-boys. They are a very mixed lot in origin, belonging to no one social class—one boat may be owned by an ex-officer in the Navy, and the one working with it by a Darnley Islander, with a strong strain of Malayan blood in him. For it is a democratic independent life, and attracts all types of men. Malaytown, on the outskirts of Cairns, is the centre of perhaps the biggest fishing-fleet in the North, and it is interesting to prowl about the little bays and mangrove-creeks and note the swarms of boats at anchor there, with their variegated crews. But by far the greater number of them are owned by white men, and white men are, as a rule, more successful fishermen than black. They use their intelligence more in speculating about methods and feeding-grounds, and they are less likely to lie up for a spell after they have made on good catch.

Yet it is an uncertain life, at the best of times, this living not on the net but on the line, for there is the factor of the weather to be taken into account. All winter the south-east trades blow up the reef, and in spite of the protection of the Barrier it can grow very rough there for small boats. Often they have to lie in the shelter of some island or other for days at a time; sometimes they have to beat back to port with their ice-boxes empty. Then there is the peculiar fact (most amateur fishermen have noticed it) that though there may be swarms of fish around they won't, for some obscure reason, take a bait. Perhaps something in the weather-conditions has put them off their food; perhaps they have come upon large natural supplies; at any rate they contemptuously turn down any bait that is offered them. Whole tribes of fish are, of course, perpetual vegetarians. Others again, like the beautiful and plentiful parrot-fish, live on the coral polyps, and have too small a mouth, anyhow, to take a hook much bigger than a bent pin. So it comes about that, often when the dealers are clamouring for fish the fishermen find it impossible to catch them in any quantity.

Now comes the chance of the dynamiter, a pest to all those who really care for preserving the fishing-grounds along the reef. He can burley in some good spot, attract a lot of various kinds of fish around him, then drop down his plug of explosive. Usually he carries a couple of native boys to dive for him, for dynamited fish don't often float. Without much effort he can fill up his boat and make back to where there is a ready market awaiting him.

For some time there has been a struggle going on along the reef between the genuine fisherman and the dynamiter. The genuine fisherman know that though dynamiting may bring immediate results it will ultimately destroy the fishing-grounds, for like most promiscuous methods, it kills many more than it secures. Besides it destroys the spawn along the breeding-grounds. In many places where dynamiting has been practised for a long time there are practically no fish today. Besides, even as a practical matter, the method handicaps the white fisherman in his competition against the black; few white men care to practise naked diving in a dozen fathoms to gather up their haul. Of course dynamiting fish along the Reef is illegal, but it is hard for even an experienced inspector to detect whether a load of fish has been caught with the hook or with dynamite, and unscrupulous dealers don't care as long as they get a supply for their market.

Fishing in Barrier waters takes on its most exciting aspect when the kingfish come swarming up the Reef at the beginning June. This great fighting-fish is the delight of amateurs, the great stand-by of the professionals who look upon the easy money it brings them as a reward for the lean months. The kingfish is mainly taken by trolling. A boat goes out with four strong lines trailing behind it, two stretched from the stern, one at either end of long poles placed amidships. The hooks are baited with garfish, or with peeled lily-root, anything in fact that makes a white flash in the water when it twirls, for the kingfish, swimming through the water, has not time to look very closely at the bait. He leaps at it like a tiger on his prey, and when a boat gets among a school of kingfish it is usually a matter of 'all hands on the lines' for a lively half-hour or so.

I remember being anchored in a fishing-boat at the end of last winter off Low Island, where the Yonge expedition made its head-quarters a few years ago. A little before daylight the skipper roused us and got the engines going, for dawn is supposed to be the time when the kingfish bites most strongly. Round and round the island we went a couple of times without any luck, and then just as we were leaving for Snapper Island, six miles away, there was the leap of a silvery shape in the air. 'Kingfish ahoy!' It was the signal for as exciting a half-hour as I have ever spent. No sooner was a hook baited and trailed out behind than there was a tug on another line, and it meant an incessant hauling, with a jerk at the end to swing the hooked fish over the rails. Then another baited hook had to be seized from the hatch and snapped on to the swivel, there being not time to free the hook from the mouth of the last one. Before an hour was out, we had passed through the shoal and in spite of all our circling round and round we could not pick them up again. But on the decks there were forty or fifty fish, a yard long, and averaging twenty pounds in weight, and the skipper had enough to make it worth while running home.

Watching the countless beautiful vari-coloured fish along the reef I have often wished that some authority would do for our fish what men like Neville Cayley have done for our birds. In *What Bird is That?* Mr Cayley has made it possible for the merest tyro to identify every bird in the country, but so many fish along the reef have only vague generic names or none at all. 'That's some sort of weed-fish,' I have heard men say of a beautiful specimen decked in startling hues of green and peacock-blue. It's a pity we can't do better than that, for half the pleasure in watching fish comes from being able to identify them and give them a name.

Abridged.
Source: Vance Palmer, 'Fishing Along the Reef', 1932, ABC Radio broadcast script; National Library of Australia, Vance and Nettie Palmer Papers, MS 1174, Series 18, Box 89, by permission of the National Library of Australia.

Jean Devanny

Deportation of Egon Kisch; For Humanity and Spain, 1934, 1938

Jean Devanny (1892–1962) grew up in New Zealand, where she achieved notoriety after her first novel *The Butcher Shop* was banned because of its frank exploration of sexuality and violence. She emigrated to Sydney in 1929 and soon joined the Communist Party of Australia. The patriarchal Party authorities viewed Devanny with some caution, particularly in relation to her liberated sexual politics, and paid small heed to her substantial literary output. But Devanny was an outstanding political organizer and a popular and effective orator who travelled tirelessly throughout the eastern states to address rallies and meetings. Her style was both dramatic and direct, with a rich use of language and an uncompromising line of argument. In 1934, the Czech journalist and communist Egon Kisch was invited to Australia to speak at an anti-fascist conference. In an attempt to evade immigration officers, Kisch jumped from his ship in Melbourne, and broke his leg. Kisch was then convicted as an illegal immigrant after he failed an official dictation test—administered in Gaelic! He was freed by the High Court, on the grounds that Gaelic was not an appropriate European language for the test. The case attracted much publicity, and Kisch became a left-wing hero. Devanny spoke at a huge protest meeting against Kisch's intial conviction held at the Sydney Domain in late November 1934.

Seeing Comrade Kisch carried on to the ground brought back to me an occasion on which I had seen another great working-class fighter carried into a working-class gathering—Clare Zetkin, to the W.I.R. Congress in Berlin. I had been moved by hearing from Comrade Kisch that many of the leading fighters in the workers' cause whom I had met on terms of comradeship in Germany had been tortured to death in the Fascist cells of Hitler Germany.

And beside it another picture came to my mind—the picture of the building on the banks of the Neva, in Leningrad, of a huge palace to house the political refugees from foreign lands. The three hundred *Schutzbunders*, refugees from the Fascist terror of Austria, were now honoured Soviet citizens. In the one country, Fascist Germany, the Fascist terror, in the other country, refuge for Fascism's victims.

The victims of the bloodiest and most barbarous terror of modern times, victims of a ruling class which in its dying struggles moves back to the methods of dead historical epochs, realising again in the twentieth century all that is dead and rotten in the past—these victims called to the Australian workers for international solidarity.

And in reply to their cries from the torture cells of Germany, Italy, Spain and Austria, we must extend to them, not only the open hand of international friendship and goodwill, but also the shut fist of an irrevocable determination to fight against the forces of Fascism in Australia, so that those who have written with their blood a most glorious page upon the book of working-class history will know that their struggles have not been in vain.

Devanny was also outspoken in her support for the Republican cause in the Spanish Civil War, and spoke tirelessly at fund-raising meetings for the 'popular front' Spanish Relief Committee. At an address given in March 1938, her impassioned pleas of sympathy for the Spain's women and children are a fine example of the heightened rhetoric of radical agitators.

You fuss, and when your man comes home from work you hurry to him anxious and alarmed and tell him: 'Our baby is not well.' Then he too gets worried, and together you do all in your power to cure your baby's little aches and pains. I know, because I've done it so many times myself.

Over in Barcelona Spanish mothers are seeking THEIR babies, crazed, babbling with terror; mothers are clinging to husbands as crazy, seeking tiny tots in the ruins of school buildings, beneath wreckage in the streets.

Over in Barcelona it is just as though Franco—just to type the name horrifying—with the claws of his own horrible hands tore the living flesh from the breasts of Spanish mothers. All their joy in mothering, in giving suck to the tiny pink mouths at their breasts, is turned to shuddering terror and desolation.

And when they have found their little ones—IF they find them—then there is no food, no warmth. Mothers even then have to hug half-skeleton frames to their breasts, trying with sheer love to satisfy hunger, striving to warm tiny bodies with the ashes of their grief.

Only the workers can feel the deep wrongs of others. Only the workers are loving and compassionate. Only the workers will take the Christ from his Cross. The mother and babes of Spain are CHRIST ON THE CROSS! Lend a hand to take the nails from little limbs, the thorns from childish brows.

Money for the Spanish Relief!

Abridged.
Sources: *Workers' Weekly*, 23 November 1934, p. 6; *Workers' Weekly*, 25 March 1938, p. 4.[36]

Nettie Palmer
The National Face: Lipless, 1934

Janet Gertrude 'Nettie' Higgins Palmer (1885–1964) was a leading literary critic who played a unique role in the development of Australian culture. Her writing, journalism, lectures and broadcasts over several decades were instrumental in defining, and awakening an appreciation for, an Australian national literature. Palmer was educated at private girls' schools before graduating with a BA, then MA from the University of Melbourne in 1912. Two years later, in London, she married writer Vance Palmer and the couple returned to Australia following the outbreak of World War I. Nettie Palmer contributed to the financial support of her husband and two daughters by writing professionally—not only literary criticism but poetry, biography and essays. Her landmark *Modern Australian Literature* was published in 1924 and she established a wide network of contacts with writers and intellectuals in Australia and overseas and actively encouraged younger Australian writers. In the late 1930s, after a period in Europe, she became increasingly politicized, opposing the rise of fascism and speaking publicly in support of the Spanish Republican cause and the 'defence of culture'. Palmer's enthusiasm for people and causes were admired by her contemporaries; she was an animated and warm speaker who used both words and tone to embrace her audience. In 1934 she was approached by the ABC radio station 3AR to deliver a series of broadcasts called 'In the Looking Glass', which examined distinctive Australian characteristics. Palmer brought her deep knowledge of literature to the topic of 'the national face', demonstrating her considerable skills in presenting cultural criticism as provocative, amusing and accessible. Her emphasis on pioneer legacies and the potential for a 'dead mediocrity' to exert a hold on Australian life were consistent themes within Palmer's broader intellectual advocacy of a national culture that fostered both social justice and a vibrant creative spirit.

Does the looking-glass say that by this time we have evolved a national face at all? This means, I suppose, the question: if we met some men at the North Pole, and one or two were Australians, would we be likely to pick them out? Would we recognise them by their faces as easily as by their way of speaking, or more easily? Do people mean anything definite when they say they recognised an Australian soldier in London easily during the War —of course without waiting to distinguish the uniform? Was it the face, or the figure, or after all the voice?

Is there an Australian face? With great regrets, I find I must restrict the scope of this artless enquiry to the masculine face. As for the feminine Australian face, like the feminine face all over the world, it has retreated behind a more or less complete mask. When people discuss the looks of Australian girls today, they are generally to be found examining the success of the girls' chemist or whatever tradesman it is that undertakes to guarantee the anonymously immaculate look that is considered necessary. In speaking of the national face, I feel it is necessary to discuss only the men, who are carrying on its succession.

For the sake of argument, let us take it that there is an Australian face developed by this time; because it is seventy years at least since Marcus Clarke discussed the same thing and made some very dogmatic statements and some more dogmatic predictions. If Marcus Clarke could make his wide guesses as to our developing dark complexion and our future look and stature that would be like that of the Greeks because of our love of the open air and sport, today there are writers who draw their ideas on the subject, not from any theorising but from conservation. When D. H. Lawrence was here ten years ago, and afterwards wrote about us in two novels, it was his observation of landscape and the look of people here that were the most valuable and unexpected gift from him. You will remember what he said about the landscape that was so utterly unlike anything he had seen in the Sicily or Mexico or England he knew so well: but as for the Australian face—do you remember his saying, casually but emphatically, that the Australian man's face was lipless? Lipless.

That doesn't sound much of a definition, but it is certainly a clue, and just as I was thinking it over lately I came upon something in support of it that makes it seem more significant. In a new complex and brilliantly written novel by a young Queenslander, *Landtakers* by Brian Penton, there is a more searching analysis of the characteristic Australian face as it developed in the early and very difficult days. *Landtakers* is the story of an Englishman from an orthodox family in Dorset who comes to the ramshackle Moreton Bay settlement in 1844, intent on making some sort of a fortune. The life on Moreton Bay and in the place up country where he takes his land so successfully is a very hard life, and after twenty years of it he decides never to go back to Dorset where his brothers are chasing tame stag across the moors for ten mile on horseback and calling that hunting. Twenty years—and what has happened to his face in that time?

Taking [his hero] Cabell, the author looks first at a daguerreotype taken after his arrival in Sydney and sent home to his people in Dorset. It shows him in his colonial clothes—a pair of Wellingtons, loose trousers, light coat and open shirt, with a broad brimmed hat in his hand. One sees Cabell's young face against the background of the country. There is the full, sensual lower lip that was a family characteristic, the plump, olive cheeks, thrown up vividly by the blackness of the hair and the thick eyebrows. In the Byronic fashion his hair falls into a curling sidelever on each cheek. There is something dandified about this that seems out of place in the businesslike clothes; deliberately, defiantly dandified. 'What surprised me most' (the author goes on) 'was the contrast between this youthful face and the face of old man Cabell as I knew him. In sixty-five years life seemed to have changed even the bones under the flesh. The nose, which in old Cabell was predatory, hooked, with splayed, enormous nostrils—a cruel beak—in the young man was straight, with a sensitive bridge and a delicate womanish septum. The youth had a chin more rounded than otherwise, neither weak not particularly strong, whereas the old man's jaw looked like three pieces of roughly cast iron clamped together and hinged under his ears on a huge bulge of muscle that swelled and relaxed continually as he sat thinking. The sensual lower lip, so prominent in the youth as to mark, one would have thought, a permanent trait, had disappeared in the old man whose tightly repressed mouth seemed to have no lips at all, giving him an air of Calvinistic severity.'

'Seemed to have no lips at all'. There is Lawrence's assertion all over again! Of course in the case of Cabell we are faced partly with the inevitable contrast of age and youth. What had happened to bring about this change? To make this pioneer looks so toughened, so hard-bitten? You can read the novel for yourself, but the difference between the life Cabell led in Moreton Bay and the kind he would have led in Dorset was enough to make any man's contours change. 'Where a man's had his hard times, there he stays', and he settles down with his descendants, [who] it seems, inherit (as they aren't exactly supposed to do so) his acquired characteristic of lipless mouth and even a predatory beak.

These characteristics form the typical Anzac face, though they can in many instances be modified by a personal gentleness. Take the Light Horseman in George Lambert's well-known study in the Melbourne Gallery. I think you would agree that it is a face you would recognise anywhere as Australian. Why? How? Is it a matter of colour at all, of complexion, as Marcus Clarke foretold, with his emphasis on the fact that Melbourne's latitude was the same as that of Athens? Well, that Light Horseman probably didn't come from as far South as Melbourne, though many Light Horsemen did; but he doesn't even help out the argument by being dark. He happens to be ruddy, almost sandy, though of course sun-burnt, one hopes not too painfully, by the desert and its glare. It isn't a matter of colouring in this case at all; in his colour this Anzac would pass if need be for an Englishman. But not in his features, not in his expression, not in his attitude. Why then do we know he is an Australian? Without being at all tragic or worn out or overstrained, this young man has that characteristic lipless look in some degree; he has those hawk-like features allied with gentleness and a generous look and, in his attitude, the way his head turns to look over his shoulder, a casual look.

This results in that famous casualness and acceptance of a certain equality among Australians which is visible to the observer from overseas even when we ignore it ourselves. Equality among men because they are all equal in face of their common opponent, call it nature or the Bush, which can at times be a friendly enemy while at other times it is full of treasons, stratagems and spoils, such as grasshoppers. It is all hands to the pumps when these common troubles arise and are shared by all; there is not time, there has not been time, for emphasising or even for discovering social distinctions. There is the Anzac face, we recognise it, we accept it, but we couldn't for the life of us guess whether the owner of it was in one class or another. Even if he is a private, you feel that is just an accident; he may well have a brother who is a major. You can hardly tell whether he comes from the bush or the city.

But here I seem to hear a protest. That Anzac, you are saying, is a bush type, and it is that that makes him recognisable at once as an Australian. We know more or less what an Australian bushman looks like; but why should our generalisations about the Australian's looks be based always on the bushman who after [all] isn't as numerous, in recent decades, as the city man. Why not begin the other end? What about the face of the man in the Australian city? Is it distinguishable from the face of the man in New York, Liverpool or Berlin? Well, I'm sorry to come back to the same thing, but in every country the type is mysteriously set by the man who is nearest to the soil and to the struggle with it. The city life later on can pare down the distinctions and make for a sort of generalisation. The bushman brings his features and his expression into the life of the town generations; call him the bushman, the experimenter, the pioneer—if you are not quite too tired of the word. Without having been born among bush things, without being a pioneer except perhaps among a few ideas or plans for such matters as education, an Australian city man in Brisbane or Melbourne will mysteriously have in his face the something that marks the pioneer—a certain carelessness of appearances that isn't slovenliness but suggests a kind of energy and concentration on the particular matter in hand.

The freedom that is the boon of Australians has also its reverse side in a degree of dead mediocrity that resents what is distinguished personally as it would resent what was set apart socially. Hence it comes that often the Australian does not make the most of his appearance—or of his voice—for fear of showing off. A man with definite possibilities of impressiveness in his appearance will feel that as for grace, as for personal style, which after all can correspond to the thing we call character—as for all these qualities, he will leave them to some subtle foreigner, a Spaniard perhaps, or at nearest an Englishman with that once-and-for-all attention to his appearance that an Australian distrusts much more than he should.

The Australian face, and not only the bushman's face, is recognisable for a certain nearness to life, a certain refusal to recognise what came socially between a man and the actualities about him. He has the qualities and defects of the unpretentious. As for colour, in spite of Lambert's blond Light Horseman, and in spite of countless instances that may occur to you, the Australian on the whole can be recognised as a dark type, with the skin even in a fair man well pigmented against the sun. His eyes are not round and wide open like those of Englishmen and still more of Germans; they are wind-wrinkled quite early, and this helps to make him look more whimsical, more questioning, more sceptical, more penetrating than he often actually is.

Abridged.
Source: Nettie Palmer, 'In the Looking Glass. The National Face', 1934, 3AR, Radio broadcast script, National Library of Australia, Vance and Nettie Palmer Papers, MS 1174, Series 25, Box 11, by permission of the National Library of Australia.

Yarra Bank Orators
'Scabs' and Capitalists, 1936

The Yarra Bank—at times both the north and south bank of the river, on the eastern side of Princes Bridge—was the place in Melbourne where public speakers from the 1920s to the 1960s took their ladders or their soap boxes and shouted their messages of resistance and dissent. It was at this open-air and turbulent 'university' that many of the key figures of Australian politics learnt the art of oratory and debate. By 1925 the Melbourne City Council had installed small mounds and planted elm groves in recognition of the needs of those gathered at the 'people's forum'. Sometimes, among the crowds large and small that gathered to hear these speakers during the interwar years, there appeared a man who took shorthand notes. He was an undercover officer working with the Victorian Police Force's Criminal Investigation Branch. Thanks to these records, we can capture a little of what these defiant Yarra Bank orators had to say in the early months of 1936, before their words vanished into the air, like the gulls.

On 5 January 1936 at 5 p.m. Edward Gentry (identified by the undercover policeman as a communist) got up to address a crowd of angry seamen who were on strike against a tough new award which put them on a longer 56–hour week. The union leadership recommended that the men accept the award. But the rank-and-file backed the strike. Gentry spoke up for the workers.

Comrades, It is good to be amongst the fighting seamen. Three years ago I was a member of the Seamen's Union and since that time I have been connected with the struggles of the unemployed. We see in this an attack by the Government on one of the strongest unions in Australia. They have made an attack on the miners and failed and I am satisfied that the seamen will win this war. We have to point out that the seamen are solid and will not go back to work under these conditions and the same can be said of the unemployed. They will not go to work and take the seamen's jobs.

The next day Joseph Keenan (described as a communist) addressed the strikers, telling them the new award was intolerable. This was a violent era in Australian industrial relations—a time when unionists and strike-breakers often traded blows, and when the police themselves would sometimes take truncheons to workers on a picket line. Keenan stirred up the strikers, assuring them that the strike-breakers would soon learn what it meant to cross the Seamen's Union.

A boat arrives in Sydney. Some of the scabs come ashore for a drink. Even scabs can drink. Some of the seamen who are on the shore at the moment saw them going into a bar and the reception committee was immediately formed. After the reception the scabs gave the press an interview. 'We are members of the Royal Australian Navy, it will take more than a couple of punches to make us give up our jobs.' Well anyhow four of them went to hospital. One I believed swallowed eight teeth. I think that eight teeth in one's inside would be apt to cause a little bit inconvenience. Even in order to maintain their morale they did not come on shore. The company said, 'If you want a drink we will bring it down to you.' They bought down four dozen bottles to the scabs. If we take a bottle of beer on board we are guilty of misconduct and fined ten pounds. But the poor, poor little scabs. You do not read in the press, of course, of what is being meted out to them. I myself have no intention of saying over much. Sufficient to say that in Newcastle there are eleven scabs in hospital. I do not know what happened to them but they are in hospital. The majority of them are suffering from haemorrhage of the stomach. The complaint I understand is both painful and often results in your sudden demise. Of course there will be no tears shed if the scabs pass out.

A few days later Alfred Watt of the radical newspaper Workers' Voice told the crowd that the economy, banks and the press were controlled by a few powerful families such as Syme, Fairfax and Baillieu.

The Baillieu family sit on the Board of Directors of no less than 250 different companies. These companies are not little developments; remember that these companies are like the Melbourne Electric Supply.

There is not a rise in the price of any single product; there is not a reduction in the wages of any worker, there is not a worsening of conditions in a single group of workers that does not benefit the B.H.P. and the small body of bloodsuckers who have control of this capitalism-ridden, fortune-producing country ...

The use of the *Crimes Act* against the Communist Party; the use of the *Transport Workers Act* against the seamen; yes, even every change of Government is brought into operation in the boardroom of Broken Hill Pty Ltd. This is as powerful a group of capitalists, faced by us in this country, as the working class in any country face. A powerful monopoly, capitalism has taken the same course in this country as in every other part of the world. We have got to fashion our weapons. We have got to build them stronger. We have got to make them more powerful before we can be successful and sweep this of thieves off the face of the earth for once and for all.

On 3 April 1936, the young communist thinker Ralph Gibson addressed a rally of the Movement Against War and Fascism, in which he predicted that Hitler would attempt to strike at the Soviet Union and warned that many British capitalists were pro-Hitler.

Unquestionably the German Fascist rulers are the main instigators of war in the world at the present moment. They are at the end of their tether. Their country is ruined and bankrupt and they are prepared to stake all on war which is the last chance that it left for political gamblers in a desperate situation.

Gibson saw quite early that the coming war was a battle against a new evil, German Fascism. But George Franks, a militant organizer with the Carpenters' Union, believed that the war would be a conflict in which rival capitalists sent their workers into battle to kill each other in the quest for markets: the pattern of the previous war would simply repeat itself.

England needs markets. The markets they have got are not big enough and they want you to get out of this country and fight so that they can extend their markets and everyone knows that England is in that position today. France is in that position, so is America and many of the other countries. So, comrades we are in the same position—the working class of this country are in the some position and the same dangers—as the people of Germany, and the people of any other country of the world today. We are in the same danger from Fascism unless we are prepared to organise and set up a united front in this country to drive back the onslaught of the capitalist class on the working class.

On other days during the opening months of 1936, a visitor to the Yarra Bank might have heard speeches on behalf of the Friends of the Soviet Union, the Spanish Relief Committee, the Anti-Conscription Celebration League (marking the twentieth anniversary of the struggle against conscription) and any number of trade union and other radical causes.

The text of all speeches quoted is taken directly from transcripts compiled by the police. Source: Victorian Police Force, Box 807/1158, Public Record Office of Victoria.[37]

Frederic Wood Jones

Medical Men, Universities and the Spirit of Adventure, 1937

Frederic Wood Jones (1879–1954) was an anatomist, embryologist and anthro-pologist who became an influential medical educator and public figure in Australia during the interwar years. A graduate of the University of London, Wood Jones served as a medical officer in the Cocos-Keeling Islands and on an archaeological survey in Nubia, and held a series of academic teaching posts in England. In 1919 he was appointed professor of Anatomy at the University of Adelaide, where he strengthened the department, wrote a handbook on South Australian mammals and was outspoken on the need to improve conditions for Aborigines. As a member of the Royal Society, and an internationally acclaimed scientist, Wood Jones was often controversial: his view of evolution was firmly anti-Darwinian. By 1930, after a brief period at the University of Hawaii, he was lured to the chair of Anatomy at the University of Melbourne. His teaching was legendary. Lectures were innovative in their breadth of sources and copious illustrations (often his own). Wood Jones was a prodigious scholar, with a passion for fieldwork, and he believed that within uni-versities there should be no separation of teaching and research activities. Larger than life, he was a dynamic and popular writer and public speaker who could reach audiences well beyond the scientific community and contributed to radio broadcasts and the press. On 5 August 1937 Wood Jones presented a public lecture at the Medi-cal Congress in Adelaide where he challenged his audience to embrace the spirit of intellectual adventure that should be the driving force within Australian universities.

That the medical profession is unique in that it is protean in the ways in which it may be followed, should ever be in the minds of those who are called upon to give young people advice as to their choice of a career. Once a man has become possessed of a medical degree or of a registrable quali-fication, almost any mode of life is open to him. He may aspire to the city life of the fashionable consultant, or he may be drawn to the simplicity of life in the country. He may prefer the shelter of institutional routine, or look forward to the struggle of competition in industrial districts. He may care to be a soldier or a sailor—either road is open to him—or he may lean towards the mode of life of the civil servant. He may come as near to being a priest or a sportsman as fancy takes him, or he may devote his life to pure scientific research within the four walls of a laboratory. He may become an explorer, a pioneer, a criminologist, a naturalist or an administrator, and be well paid for living the life of his own choosing. A thoroughly incom-petent lawyer or a hopelessly inefficient engineer could not look forward to a very successful professional career; but a medical graduate, who would certainly be a conspicuous failure in the active practice of his profession, may yet have happiness and a competence, and attain to considerable repute in one of the many scientific bypaths that are open to him.

But I am afraid we are bound to confess that no matter how high were the student's hopes of adventure upon entering on the medical course, the number of potential adventurers is considerably reduced after the ceremony of the conferring of degrees has been performed. It is depressing to discover that nearly every good student, in the later years of his curriculum and at his graduation, has as his ideal the affixing of a brass plate to the door of one of the professional rabbit-warrens in the fashionable medical street of the capital city wherein he had his training. To achieve this end he is prepared to make sacrifices by way of being crammed still fuller with details of the professional curriculum in order that he may write more or higher-sounding letters after his name. He is even prepared to go overseas to suffer still further cramming and to acquire more authoritative or more exotic professional badges, as the tourist who sticks the labels of foreign hotels upon his trunks.

It is a regrettable fact that there is a tendency for most of our best-equipped graduates to look upon practice in even the larger provincial towns as a career to be entered on only as an unavoidable necessity when the period of waiting for practice in a capital city cannot be faced. Still less are they inclined to go to country towns, even when these are the centres of large populations scattered through the surrounding rural districts. A great many of the purely professional problems that are at present of very pressing reality in Australia, for instance, would be capable of solution if only well-equipped men, or teams of men, were willing to go further afield and adventure into regions more remote from our university towns. It is perhaps a fortunate thing that, at a time when it is difficult to find well-qualified young medical men willing to apply for posts in the army, the navy, the public health services or in the mandated territories, there should be what might almost be termed a boom in 'flying doctors'. As a high adventure in the service of mankind, the life of a flying doctor should make strong appeal to the youth of the medical profession.

In a young country such as Australia, we are able to contemplate the results of more than half a century of free, compulsory and universal education. I think it may be said with truth that the first half-century of universal school education has produced few original thinkers, few rebels, few seekers after truth in the general mass of the 'educated' population. A universally literate population is doubtless a triumph for universal free education; but a population that is prepared to accept its every opinion ready-made from the printed page is surely not a wholly desirable factor in democracy. If this be the result that our present educational system is producing, it is high time a corrective were applied; for it would be easy to instance several races of mankind which, though held in some contempt by the so-called higher races, could justly boast that the average adult, literate or illiterate, has a far wider aesthetic experience in intellectual adventure than has the average educated European.

Even if this undesirable result appears to be the almost inevitable outcome of our present system of school education, it is a fortunate thing that what should be the natural remedy is to-day within the reach of most young people. For the natural antidote to the indigestion caused by school cramming is the university—the real university. If our universities cannot provide this stimulus for the mentally jaded, and intellectually surfeited, young scholars who seek their help, they are failing in their only important function. In the ideal university the professor should be the leader of an expedition into the most exciting and most romantic of all regions— the region of the intellectually unknown. The members of his staff should be his officers, who with him seek to ensure that the equipment of the expedition and the plan of campaign are adequate for the successful carrying out of the enterprise. His students should be his eager followers, prepared to share in the hardships, the excitements and the triumphs of the adventure. The wonder of the child who bred silkworms should be aroused again; the enterprise of the child who dissected the clockwork toy should be reawakened. They should be encouraged to go afield, campaigning adventurously with those who can help them on the road. Can it be justly claimed that our universities are providing the antidote that seems to be so necessary for a school education, which consists in the routine teaching of a certain range of detailed facts? Or are they, perhaps, only carrying on the melancholy business to further stages? This question must be answered one way or the other before long; and it must be answered very frankly.

Changes are taking place with some rapidity in the educational life of the country, and these changes may easily determine the ultimate fate of our universities. More and more, governments and institutions are becoming alive to the necessity of conducting research into our most vital national problems. Money is becoming more freely available for research into scientific, industrial and medical problems as they are presented under present-day conditions. Where and by whom are these researches to be undertaken?

The university in which an original quest after intellectual adventure is being undertaken in its schools is the nerve-centre of the intellectual life of the community in which it is situated. It will be the source of generation after generation of young men and women who will enter upon life and citizenship eager to undertake intellectual adventure in any walk of life that may fall to their lot. It will be the fountain-head from which will flow an endless stream of young minds, ready to question, to examine and to criticize the condition of things as they find them, and willing to search for remedies when remedies are needed. The university whose sole concern is the further teaching of individuals past school age can hope to achieve but little more than a standardized and mass-produced product. Its degrees imply no more than that the graduate is certified to have attained to a requisite standard of proficiency in remembering for a defined period a prescribed range of assorted dicta upon some subject or other. It is only by mere chance that, despite the system, anything other than an uninquiring individual, devoid altogether of a desire for intellectual adventure, will emerge from the academic ordeal.

Are we to have research institutions in which a few workers will devote their whole time to our problems? Or are we to make it possible for the staffs of our universities to conduct research in our university departments?

If we, by reducing the burden of teaching and administrative duties, make it possible for real and continued research to be undertaken by the staffs of our universities, we shall, I think, achieve much that is of pressing importance in the world to-day. We shall be able to attract first-class men to our universities, and we shall beget generations of students who conceive themselves to be part and parcel of a real organization for undertaking original work. Inquiry will be undertaken by the many, and into every department of learning, instead of by the few, and into circumscribed problems only.

Surely this is the most desirable result that can be achieved by expenditure on education? And to achieve this end no mere endowment of research, however well intended, can ever be effective. It is useless to endow research if the research worker is not at hand, or if, being at hand, he has no sufficient time at his disposal in which to conduct research. The problem is a domestic one for government and universities, and for those who are able to provide endowment funds. Its solution lies in providing sufficient staff and equipment in our universities to guarantee that the research worker shall have ample facilities for conducting research, and at the same time shall be able to train the students in his department. In this way only shall we be able to attract first-class men to our university chairs and be in a position to produce students who will go out into the world prepared to take up the quest of intellectual adventure in every walk of life.

Abridged.
Source: Frederic Wood Jones, 'The Spirit of Adventure', Public Lecture, Medical Congress, Adelaide, 5 August 1937.[38]

———◆———

William Macmahon Ball
Report on Sachsenhausen Concentration Camp, 1938

William Macmahon Ball (1901–86) was a leading public intellectual during the middle decades of the twentieth century, with a career that spanned the spheres of journalism, public service, diplomacy and academia. After graduating from the University of Melbourne in 1923, 'Mac Ball' lectured in Psychology and in the fledgling department of Political Science, where he was to become foundation professor in 1949. It was during the 1930s that Ball became well known for his analysis of international affairs in the press, and he began a long association with the then Australian Broadcasting Commission as a political commentator. In 1938 Ball was on a study tour in Europe at the time of the Munich Agreement, which annexed the Sudenten German territories in Czechoslovakia to Germany. He travelled with Hitler's army to Sudentenland and later, from Berlin, visited the Sachsenhausen concentration camp. The visit had been arranged by a German friend who had become influential in the Nazi Party and who wanted Ball to view the 'achievements' of National Socialism. These experiences were to have a profound impact on Ball, transforming his stance from one of pacifism to an acceptance that war was inevitable, and indeed necessary, as a response to oppression. Through ABC radio he shared his experiences of Nazi Germany with Australian audiences. There was no direct broadcasting service, so Ball sent his 'talks' by airmail, and they were read by ABC announcers in Melbourne and Sydney. The written report on Sachsenhausen is dated 22 October 1938 and was first broadcast in early November and repeated several times. Ball's account of his horror at the camp is a remarkable historical document, demonstrating that Australians had access to first-hand accounts of the situation in National Socialist Germany in the lead-up to World War II.

Last Thursday I spent three hours in a Concentration Camp. I was told that I was the first foreigner to be allowed in such a camp for some years, and my visit was only made possible by the personal consent of Herr Himmler, the head of the German police; and then only because a German friend of mine gave the fullest assurances that I could be relied upon to give a completely fair and unbiased account of what I saw; that, in spite of my being a guest to the Political Police, the S.S. officers who were my hosts. They were not only courteous and hospitable, but put their own car and chauffeur at my disposal for the day. Most important of all, I feel that it is essential in my serious examination of the relations between Germany and Britain today to keep the discussion of such things as Concentration Camps in Germany or British prisons in India in their proper secondary place. Yet there is, of course, a real connection between the Nazi attitude to their political opponents at home and their attitude to democratic nations like Britain which they feel to be so much under the control of Socialists and Jews. It was mainly because I thought a Concentration Camp might throw some light on the world attitude, as distinct from the domestic policy, of the German Government, that I wanted to see one. I was not in search of atrocities. I knew that if they did occur, I would not be likely to see them, and if they do not occur, then I would still be without proof of this.

The camp I visited is near Sachsenhausen, a village near the town of Oranienburg about twenty-five miles from Berlin. As we neared the camp we found S.S. Guards holding their rifles ready, lining the roadside at intervals of about 30 yards. A ring of these men had been thrown around a field in which prisoners were at work chopping wood. Our driver said, perhaps to comfort us, that although this stretch of road could be used by the public the guards were empowered to fire instantly on any car which stopped, without making preliminary investigations. At the outer gate of the camp was another group of armed guards, some with sub-machine guns instead of rifles. These S.S. men are very impressive specimens of the might of the Nazi party. The Brown Shirts—the S.A.—hardly count now as a political force in Germany. All political police work is done by S.S., men of outstanding physique and unquestionable loyalty, disciplined on severe military lines.

Inside the outer gates I found a stretch of neat lawns and trees amongst which the offices and living quarters of the Guards had been built. I was then introduced to the Camp Commandant, and his adjutant than indicated that he was at my service for the morning.

Our guide took us to the inner gates, from where we could see the lay-out of the camp. It is built in the form of a semi-circle or fan, these main gates being in the centre of the diameter. Above the gates is a concrete watch-tower from which three machine guns on swivels command first the parade ground in front, and than all of the alley ways between the huts, which are built in straight lines radiating from the central guard's house. There are other smaller watch-towers round the arc of the semi-circle, so that every spot inside the camp is continuously commanded by a machine gun. Inside the boundary fence there is a path about eight feet wide. If any prisoner puts his feet on this path, he is instantly shot at. On the outer side of the path there are tiers of barbed wire rising to the high wire fence which is electrically charged and flood-lit at night. The scheme is so efficiently planned that it is not surprising that there are only 200 guards for the nine thousand (9,000) prisoners. Last May there were only three thousand (3,000) prisoners at Sachsenhausen, but a big police drive in June and July trebled the members in two months.

The prisoners are classified in accordance with the nature of their offences, and each class wears a different badge and is most of the time separated from the other classes. The Jews have a special badge. The biggest class was made up of those rather vaguely described as 'work shy and Anti-Social'. I tried hard to find out exactly what this term means. In what precise circumstances was a 'work shy' man sent into concentration? What particular offences were considered anti-social? But at the end of all my questions I could get no clear idea of the nature of this classification.

Second, there are the 'political' prisoners, those found guilty of a specific political offence; third, the straight out criminals, those convicted of house-breaking or forgery; fourth, the 'Bible students' whose conviction prevent them from giving allegiance to the National Socialist State; and, lastly, a few perverts of various kinds.

When my guide, the adjutant, took me alone to any man at work inside the camp, the prisoner with very quick movements would snatch off his cap, and stand very rigidly to attention, hands and fingers taut and outstretched down his side, and stay like this while we passed. Sometimes the officer would sharply summon a prisoner: 'Come here'! The prisoner would run to us as fast as he could and again click to attention. 'Why are you here'? The officer would rap out. 'Preparing high treason, sir' the answer would come with quick mechanical certainty. 'What was your crime?' was the next question. And in several cases the answer came.

'Distributing Communist literature, sir'. There were, of course, the political prisoners. In one case when the officer asked, 'What is your crime?' the prisoner replied 'I don't know, sir'. 'What,' said the officer, 'you don't know your crime?' 'No, sir'. We passed quickly on, and it seemed to me that the officer was faintly annoyed. A little later I asked him how it was that the prisoner did not know his crime. He replied that he had not taken the incident seriously, and that, by looking at the man's papers he could at once see what his crime was. I nevertheless felt quite certain that this man would have given a clear answer if he had known what answer he was expected to give.

Everything in the prisoners quarters was scrupulously clean and most efficiently hygienic. They were well built and well ventilated; the bunks looked comfortable; the kitchens and shower rooms were all splendidly planned. I was told that 62 pfennigs per day was spent on each prisoners' food; in comparison with 65 pfennigs spent on the food of each man in a Labour Service Camp. I ate the prisoners lunch, which that day was whale,[39] potatoes and a small portion of fat. I did not find it exactly appetising, but it was well cooked and the whale was not at all bad.

The prisoners' day begins at 5 a.m. After breakfast hard labour begins at 6 and goes till 11.30. Then two hours for roll call, lunch and minor duties. The afternoon's labour is from 1.30 till 5 p.m. I was told that in the evening the men had two to three hours leisure before lights out at 9.

I was told that each prisoner, unless he is under special discipline, may receive money from his family and use it to buy extras from the tuck-shop or tobacco. Smoking is allowed in certain leisure periods, but not inside the huts. Those who do receive money generally share it with their fellows. I saw some German newspapers and there is a lending library of perhaps 2,000 books.

There is also some self-administration by the prisoners. In most of the huts there are no permanent guards during the night. A senior prisoner is entrusted with a key, and if there is any disturbance in his hut, he turns this key in a lock in the wall. This switches on a blue light above the hut which is seen at once by the guards in the watch-towers. Then there is a small office where five or six prisoners do the clerical work of keeping prisoners' records; these records being quite distinct from those kept by the political police. The chief clerk in this office is the head prisoner of the camp. We talked with him for some minutes. He was formerly a prominent official of the Social Democratic Party and a member of the Reichstag. He impressed me as a man of intelligence, culture and character.

So far I have been writing only of externals. But the thing wanted most to see was the kind of men in a concentration camp, their expression, and the relationship between guards and men.

I have never seen before, and never believed it possible to see, a group of men so cowed, so completely deprived of the rudimentary personal dignities that I have always felt belong to human beings. The way in which these men responded to orders was something quite different from the mechanical precision of military discipline; it showed the quick, shrinking nervousness of animals that have been utterly subdued. Of the hundreds of men whom I saw at close quarters, there were perhaps five or six senior prisoners who I was told would soon be released who did not look frightened and cowed. In the eyes of most there was deep misery; when addressed by an officer the misery was mixed with fright, and at least in some cases terror is not too strong a word. In one of the huts a prisoner was ordered to open a cupboard for me to see; he ran to obey the order but, in his excitement, fumbled for an instant with the lock. 'Quick'! the officer rapped out. And this the man gave a jump and quiver that shook his body and told his nervous condition quite clearly. In describing the demeanor of these prisoners I am not writing as a psychologist; I am writing as an observer with normal eyesight.

The prisoners differed a great deal in appearance. Many in the 'criminal' class had the degenerate look that is sometimes noticed in habitual criminals anywhere in the world. Some of the 'work shy and anti-Social class' seemed to me to be well below average intelligence. I think we would class them as morons. There were also some with physical disabilities. I noticed two cripples, and one blind man. But amongst the 'political' and the 'work-shy' prisoners I saw many faces which I thought showed character, sensitiveness and intelligence. It certainly takes more than average courage to engage in Communist or Socialist activities in Germany today. The officer who took me round and the younger officers I saw in camp, did not in any way look coarse or gross types of men. My own guide, in his manner and appearance, impressed me as being like any good type of officer in the British Army or the London Police Force. He said that neither he nor his comrade relished the job of guarding the Concentration Camp, but it was just one of the jobs that somebody had to do in the interest of the State. He would only be on camp work for perhaps three or six months as it was not the policy of this Government to keep men permanently on Concentration Camp duties. But this same officer did not think it strange to call up, address, and dismiss prisoners in a manner more peremptory and impersonal than that usually adopted to animals. He saw nothing strange in three men standing facing a wall while they waited outside the camp hospital for medical attention. It was a fresh morning, but these three men, in their ordinary prison jackets, stood rigidly to attention here in the sharp breeze for at least half an hour—I don't know how much longer—while they awaited medical attention. One of these prisoners was shaking pitifully, and was unable, with the most desperate effort, to get out any coherent answer to the officer's question. Yet apparently the officer thought I would be, if not pleased, at least reassured by my visit to the camp. It is a difference of outlook hard to understand. It was put to me that many of the prisoners had never worked decently or submitted to any discipline in their lives, and that it was hoped that for these the stay in camp would have great educational value. I could not follow this argument, for I saw no training in any trade or profession, nor any other sort of educational work. Since sentences moreover, are indeterminate, I cannot understand when and why a prisoner is released.

My guide was anxious for me to hear the camp singing which takes place on the huge parade ground after midday roll call. We waited at the main gates while the prisoners marched in. As the last section entered, the gates were closed and armed guards formed in front of it, while the three machine guns were manned in the watch tower above. We stood in the centre of those 9,000 prisoners on parade. Then the choir-master climbed up on to his wooden platform to conduct the singing. No political songs, but German folk songs. I walked among the ranks as they sang. Many did not sing at all; other moved their lips when I looked at them, but thousands lifted their voices loud and clear. And they sang as only Germans can. There were the machine guns watching them, the barbed wire round them, and each man's future quite unknown; but I felt that so long as they could sing like that there must be somewhere deep inside them a faith and a courage that had not been killed.

Slightly abridged.
Source: Lee Kersten, 'W Macmahon Ball's report on the Sachsenhausen concentration camp'.[40]

——◆——

Brian Penton
The Propaganda Machine, 1940

Brian Con Penton (1904–1951) was a writer, a social commentator and a newspaper editor who delighted in raising the hackles of authority and provoking the Australian public with new intellectual ideas. Born and educated in Brisbane, Penton began his career as a journalist with the *Brisbane Courier*, and later achieved notoriety through his daily reports on the federal parliament for the *Sydney Morning Herald*. In 1929 he went to London, where he began work on his first novel, *Landtakers* (1934), an historical account of the greed of pioneers in colonial Queensland. Penton joined the staff of Sydney's *Daily Telegraph* in 1931, assuming editorship of the newspaper in 1941. He was strongly opposed to the moral censorship of art and literature enforced in Australia during the interwar years and with the outbreak of World War II he came into conflict with the censorship authorities. He was also interested in the political uses of propaganda, as evident in Nazi Germany. Could propaganda be employed 'constructively' or 'democratically'? In late January 1940 Penton was invited to speak on the topic to 'men of influence' from academia, business, law and politics at the Australian Institute of Political Science in Canberra. He began by claiming that it was 'false' to presume that the British people were 'eager and unified' in their response to the current war, pointing out both the necessity of propaganda and its effects on liberties. Penton concluded his speech with 'a bit of alarmed tub-thumping'.

No educated man can regard the machinery of modern propaganda without loathing and fear. The more he knows of his Goethe, his Schiller, his Thomas Mann, his Beethoven, Mozart, Bach, and a hundred and one other fine minds, whose philosophies are woven into the consciousness of the German people, the more will he be intimidated by the history of Germany in the last few years, its inane racial theories, its persecution of men like Einstein and Freud, its submission to men like Hitler and Himmler.

Even now many of us find it hard to believe that grown-up, civilised, educated people are really disposed to tolerate some of the things which we are told of Germany. Our respect for human intelligence makes us believe that these manifestations of half-wittedness are overstressed, and that the mass of the German people is only waiting for an opportunity to resume its place among the free and enlightened nations of the world.

We are, alas! deceiving ourselves. The German people have accepted the jackboot, the concentration camps, and the philosophical fanfaronades of Fascism with a fantastic ardor. The astute use of propaganda upon a mind discouraged and fatigued by years of suffering has brought this to pass, as we all know.

Only the most insular and fatuous optimist could fail to be infected by alarm when he turns his eyes from the German scene to our backyard. 'Our ingrained British love of liberty prevents such things from happening here,' we say. Beautiful thought, but what is it worth?

History provides many examples of the voluntary surrender of liberty by people in whom the love of it was supposed to be ingrained. Even democracies accept an overpowering number of restrictions on ideas and expression. 'We believe that some ideas are too poisonous to be propagated, some too true and sacred to be criticised,' says Amber White.

To extend these bans and censorships needs only the acquiescence men will readily give in a national crisis which inflames their anxiety and puts their reasons to sleep. If the crisis lasts long enough, the new restrictions become accepted as the ordinary way of things. The history of many restrictions on individual liberty applied during the last war demonstrates this.

Such bits of Government interference as six o'clock closing of pubs in our land, and, in England, the dozen and one absurd prohibitions applied under the Defence of the Realm Act, ostensibly for the duration of the last war, continue still, and are accepted, though we would have fought tooth-and-nail if anyone had tried to impose them before the war started.

If this thesis is true, and any Government has only to seize the ripe amount of anxiety to apply the heat of the modern propaganda machine in order to persuade the people that an autocratic regime is best for them and that all the liberties they previously enjoyed were effete and unworthy, then the outlook for democracy is gloomy indeed.

I hear your objection—that no British Government would wish to do such a thing a moment longer than the 'exigencies of the situation' demanded. But who can say where the 'exigencies of the situation' in which we are landed will end? Certainly not with the peace.

Mr. Chamberlain has rightly said that the winning of the peace is going to be more difficult than victory in the war. Those who hold power when the post-war economic mess is being sorted will be sorely tempted to continue the repression of individual liberties; especially liberties of critical expression.

The question is whether the people will allow them to continue it. A pessimist by nature, I think they will, because I think that the propaganda machine will have degraded their minds and unfitted them to think critically or to wish to think critically.

Propaganda must be always emotional, and often untruthful, and by feeding lies to the people and inflaming their emotions we make it difficult to restart the process of rational education. Nothing is so tentative, so unstable, as the ability to reason objectively. It deserts the most intelligent in moments of small, let alone great, stress, and is given to none without years of education and discipline. The democracies still find themselves suffocated by people who remain mentally childish all their lives. Obviously it is only too easy to enlarge this already oppressive infantilism.

And what then? Will it matter much if the sun still fails to set on the British Empire, and the rentier smokes his Partagas Cabinet cigars again, and a little man with a Charlie Chaplin moustache is under the sod? The lights will have gone out over Europe. There will be no more Einsteins, Manns, Schnabels, Bertrand Russells, or Lowes Dickinsons, because such minds do not develop in the darkness.

There will be only a new crop of ridiculously posturing leaders, blaring nonsense from loud-speakers, and you and I perhaps, sodden by years of such balderdash, will lift up our voices and applaud.

We are not sodden yet. Before the blight descends there is still time to realise that the true division of society is horizontal, not vertical, that intelligent Frenchmen, Norwegians, Russians, Germans, and Turks have more in common with each other than with stupid members of their own communities.

I have a feeling that if this obvious fact could be universally admitted the war would collapse instantly on both sides. Ah! but what an admission. Yes, I fear I let a false note of optimism creep in there. But it has this much to it—you know—if we don't try to make the admission, then we deserve to lie and rot in the long night that is approaching.

And we will.

Abridged.
Source: *Sydney Morning Herald*, 4 February 1940, p. 3.

Mary Grant Bruce

The Soul of England, 1940

Mary Grant Bruce (1878–1958) was the author of the much loved 'Billabong' series of children's books, written between 1910 and 1942 and selling over two million copies. Born in Sale, Victoria, Bruce worked as a journalist in Melbourne and England. With her second cousin, George Bruce, whom she married in 1914, she lived for some years in Ireland before returning to Australia. Like many artists of her generation, Bruce was torn between her dedication to the New World and her longing for the Old. In 1927 Bruce and her family moved to Ireland. Shortly after they arrived, one of her two boys accidentally shot himself and died. The grieving family spent the next twelve years travelling and working on the Continent and in the south of England, and Bruce found comfort in 'thought-breathing' and a philosophy of self-help. In 1939 they returned to Australia, where Bruce soon became a leading figure in the voluntary Australian Imperial Force Women's Association. She had the soul of a campaigner, with her passions including a fierce regard for the dignity of other women and the importance of patriotism. Throughout World War II, she was one of the many Australian public figures who gave morale-boosting talks on ABC radio. Her broadcast on 25 August 1940, written as the Battle of Britain raged, was potent with nostalgia for an idealized England and called to Australians to support un-reservedly the war effort 'back home'.

There are many of us in Australia who know and love England—the England that we knew; sleepy, perhaps, set in its ancient ways of peace, never fully aware of the thunder-clouds rolling up over Europe until— almost—too late. It is hard for us to picture it changed. I lived there for twelve years, and now when hour by hour we wait for news of the Battle of Britain, it seems that half of me is there still; seeing the winding loveliness of Devonshire lanes, the heather-clad majesty of Yorkshire moors, the dreaming beauty of Sussex-by-the-Sea. I have picnicked often in Ashdown Forest, where the Germans dropped one of the first bombs that shattered English soil; where we used to watch squirrels rustling the golden-brown beech leaves of autumn that carpeted the ground. My home was not far from Hastings. The raiders have been there twice. I wonder if our house is standing yet, or just a heap of ruins.

People say to me, 'You're lucky to be in Australia', and since Australia is my own land I know that's true. Yet ... there are many times when I would gladly give up the peace and safety of Australia and the joy of being again with its people, to be back in the new England that has become the last rampart of civilisation. I want to see England awake, as she is to-day, her people united as never before in the face of a danger common to all.

I should be happier, I believe, than when I was there in the last war. Then we sat at home in comparative ease; the war raged across the Channel, but except for the mild air-raids of those days life went on much as usual. Great fortunes were made, while day by day the ships carried our soldiers to France—and brought back the broken men who had fought for us. There was a shortage of shells and equipment; we were not ready, of course, and—as was bitterly said—we got ready behind a rampart of the bodies of two million young men. I was closely in touch with soldiers. It was not an easy thing to see them go, half-trained, badly armed, marching away singing, to the hell that awaited them.

No, I'd rather be there to-day, in that new England where men and women are shoulder to shoulder, sharing work and risk and death; sharing them in the British fashion, dogged and cheerful, turning most things into a joke—but underneath all, the fierce flame of patriotism that counts death a little thing in the defence of British soil. There are the huntin' and the fishin' and the shootin' men, so often the subject of jests—do you realise their value now? I can picture them, those men of trained vision and clear sight, who know every yard of the country, of the sea-lochs, of the Scottish moors. Hardy, tough men, dead shots, keen-eyed; game-keeper or duke, old age will not keep them now from the long places where they watch for parachute troops. Many of their women will be with them, just as women are in the thick of Britain's battle everywhere. There can be no sitting at home in ease now, but there is something better. For the spirit of Britain is awake, as never before, and it is an awakening that may change the face of the world.

A wise Englishman said to me years ago, 'A country becomes great in proportion to the *group-soul* of its people. That is something that develops through the centuries, through unity of faith and service and love of country. America has not grown hers yet—she is too big, too scattered; a mixture of races. Australia has not had time to grow hers. Ireland's was shattered at the Battle of the Boyne. New Zealand, I think,' he added, 'has more; she is set apart, a small country, and her people are united. But of all countries England's group-soul is strongest, for it has grown from all who have lived and died for her: an unseen, spiritual force, becoming potent at any time of crisis. You saw it work in the last war; you saw it work at the time of the abdication. When the great crisis comes you will see it in full force.'

I think of that prophecy today, when every news-bulletin brings its talk of heroism and selfless service, when my letters from England tell of the men and women who work and endure day and night; of the children, trained to sing marching songs as they file calmly to air-raid shelters when the sirens scream warnings that the bombers are near. 'We had lots of jokes in the shelter', one woman wrote—'thank goodness *those* can't be rationed!' Old men and women have renewed their youth in helping others; class distinctions and privileges once jealously guarded have vanished. In that fortress which is Britain the group-soul nerves and stiffens its people in a way only possible to a spiritual force, fighting against the dark legions of cruelty and oppression. And there are many in England who believe they do not fight alone; that with them are warriors of the unseen, the souls of those 'who lived and died for England and gladly went their way.'

Who shall say that that garrison is not 'encompassed about by a cloud of witnesses?' Throughout the centuries the sons of Britain have served her well; and her glory and honour have been more to them than individual profit. Soldiers, sailors, explorers, they have taken the British flag to the ends of the earth, choosing always the hard path, the way of adventure and peril; giving health and life itself, revelling in danger—and so building up an Empire. Not many of their names are remembered. Here and there an immortal phrase speaks for a son of England, as in Captain Scott's last words, written as he lay dying in the Antarctic, 'For my own sake I do not regret this journey which has shown that Englishmen can endure hardship, help one another, and meet death, with as great a fortitude as ever in the past.' But for the most part they have been undistinguished men, men who did their job in the quiet British way and did it well; just as well as did the country-men of Britain, those quiet, slow-spoken, hard-working men who have held the little farms for generation after generation; the yeomen of England, who are its backbone. Generation after generation, century after century, they have built up the group-soul that guards the beleaguered fortress of Britain now. And because it is a spiritual force we can believe that nothing can stand against it.

We in Australia can share in that great spiritual force. Like our brothers overseas we have heard the cry of the stricken nations; the blood of the slaughtered refugees of Belgium and France has called to every generous and selfless instinct in our young men. In proportion as we cast out self, giving ourselves freely in support of their sacrifice, we become inheritors of the honour of the British race, fit to take our place beside those who defend Britain—the unseen hosts of the Lord as well as the common men and women like ourselves, who are facing death with a smile and a joke. Such man were the life-boat crew of Rye, who died to a man in the great storm that swept the south of England in 1928. Their epitaph has been written by Sir Henry Newbolt—it stands for the common man and woman of Britain today:-

'These men of Rye Harbour, crew of the life-boat Hary-Stanford, having confirmed by the habit of a noble service the courage handed down to them by their fathers, were quick to hear the cry of humanity above the roaring of the sea. In the darkness of their supreme hour they stayed not to weigh doubt or danger, but freely offering their portion in this life for the ransom of men whom they had never known, went boldly into the last of all their storms. Their names are recorded in acknowledgment that we have received the memory of their faithfulness and loving-kindness, in trust for England.'

Reproduced in full.
Source: Mary Grant Bruce, 'The Soul of England', 25 August 1940, ABC Radio broadcast script; Australian Archives (NSW), Series SP300/1.

Pearl Gibbs

Citizenship for Aborigines, 1941

Pearl Mary Gibbs (Gambanyi) (1901–1983) was an astute and dedicated campaigner for Aboriginal rights and a persuasive public speaker who sought to inform and influence the opinion of white Australia. Her early education occurred in a segregated classroom at the Mount Carmel convent in Yass and she was later denied entry to government schools in rural New South Wales. From 1910 Gibbs's family worked on a pastoral station near Bourke and at sixteen she entered domestic service in Sydney. During the 1920s Gibbs began agitating on behalf of indentured Aboriginal women workers. A casualty of the Depression, she lived for a period at the Unemployed Workers' Camp at La Perouse before pea-picking at Nowra, where she sought to improve conditions for agricultural labourers. Gibbs's politicization was influenced by her observations at Wallaga Lake Aboriginal Station. In 1937 she joined the Aborigines' Progressive Association and a year later she was prominent in the Australia Day protest. She participated in parliamentary and ministerial delegations, wrote for the press and spoke to the wider community. Gibbs was the first Aboriginal person to present her own scripted talk on Australian radio.[41] On 8 June 1941 listeners of Radio 2GB Sydney and 2WL Wollongong heard Gibbs's exposé of the discrimination faced by Aboriginal people in an address that drew upon her own experiences and outlined Aboriginal claims for citizenship.

I wish to express my deepest gratitude to the Theosophical Society of Sydney in granting me this privilege of being on the air this evening. It is the first time in the history of Australia that an Aboriginal woman has broadcast an appeal for her people. I am more than happy to be that woman. My grandmother was a full-blood Aborigine. Of that fact I am most proud. The admixture of white blood makes me a quarter-caste Aborigine. I am a member of the Committee for Aboriginal Citizenship.

My people have had 153 years of the white man's and white woman's cruelty and injustice and unchristian treatment imposed upon us. My race is fast vanishing. There are only 800 full-bloods now in New South Wales due to the maladministration of previous governments. However, intelligent and educated Aborigines, with the aid of good white friends, are protesting against these conditions. I myself have been reared independently of the Aborigines Protection Board now known as the Aborigines Welfare Board. I have lived and worked amongst white people all my life. I've been in close contact with Aborigines and I have been on Aboriginal stations in New South Wales for a few weeks and months at a time. I often visit them. Therefore I claim to have a thorough knowledge of both the Aboriginal and white viewpoints. I know the difference between the status of Aborigines and white men. When I say 'white man' I mean white women also. There are different statuses for different castes. A person in whom the Aborigine blood predominates is not entitled to an old-age, invalid or returned soldier's pension. There are about thirty full-blooded returned men in this state whom I believe are not entitled to the old-age pension.

A woman in whom the Aborigine blood predominates is not entitled to a baby bonus.

Our girls and boys are exploited ruthlessly. They are apprenticed out by the Aborigines Welfare Board at the shocking wage of a shilling to three and six per week pocket money and from two and six to six shillings per week is paid into a trust fund at the end of four years. This is done from fourteen years to the age of eighteen. At the end of four years a girl would, with pocket money and money from the trust, have earned £60 and a boy £90. Many girls have great difficulty in getting their trust money. Others say they have never been paid.

Girls often arrive home with white babies. I do not know of one case where the Aborigines Welfare Board has taken steps to compel the white father to support his child. The child has to grow up as an unwanted member of an apparently unwanted race. Aboriginal girls are no less human than my white sisters. The pitiful small wage encourages immorality. Women living on the stations do not handle endowment money, but the managers write out orders. The orders are made payable to one store in the nearest town—in most cases a mixed drapery and grocery store. So you will see that in most cases the mother cannot buy extra meat, fruit or vegetables. When rations and blankets are issued to the children, the value is taken from the endowment money. The men work sixteen hours per week for rations worth five and six-pence. The bad housing, poor water supply, appalling sanitary conditions and the lack of right food, together with unsympathetic managers, make life not worth living for my unfortunate people.

It has now become impossible for many reasons for a full-blood to own land in his own country. On the government settlements and in camps around the country towns, the town people often object to our children attending the school that white children attend. This is the unkindest and cruellest action I know. Many of the white people call us vile names and say that our children are not fit to associate with white children. If this is so, then the white people must also take their share of the blame. I'm very concerned about the 194 full-blooded Aboriginal children left in this State. What is going to happen to them? Are you going to give them a chance to be properly educated and grow up as good Australian citizens or just outcasts? Aborigines are roped off in some of the picture halls, churches and other places. Various papers make crude jokes about us. We are slighted in all sorts of mean and petty ways. When I say that we are Australia's untouchables you must agree with me.

You will also agree with me that Australia would not and could not have been opened up successfully without my people's help and guidance of the white explorers. Hundreds of white men, woman and children owe their very lives to Aborigine trackers and runners—tracking lost people. Quite a few airmen owe their lives to Aboriginals. I want you to remember that men of my race served in the Boer War, more so in the 1914–18 War and today hundreds of full-bloods, near full-bloods and half-castes are overseas with the AIF. More are joining each day. My own son is somewhere on the high seas serving with the Australian Navy. Many women of Aborigine blood are helping with war charities. Many are WRANS.

We the Aborigines are proving to the world that we are not only helping to protect Australia but also the British Empire. New South Wales is the mother State and therefore should act as an inspiration to the rest of Australia. So we are asking for full citizenship and the status to be granted to us. We are asking that the 800 full-bloods in New South Wales be included in the claim—all those who are deprived of all federal social services to be granted, through the state, the old age pension and the maternity bonus until this injustice can be reformed by a federal law. We want an equal number of Aborigines as whites on the [Aborigines] Welfare Board.

My friends, I am asking for friendship. We Aborigines need help and encouragement, the same as you white people. We need to be cheered and encouraged to the ideals of citizenship. We ask help, education, encouragement from your white government. But the Aborigines Welfare [Board] gives us the stone of officialdom. Please remember, we don't want your pity, but practical help. This you can do by writing to the Hon. Chief Secretary, Mr. Baddeley, MLA Parliament House, Sydney and ask that our claim be granted as soon as possible. Also that more white men who understand my people, such as the chairman, Mr Michael Sawtell, be appointed to the Board—not merely government officials. We expect more reforms from the new government.

By doing this you will help to pay off the great debt that you, the white race, owe to my Aboriginal people. I would urge, may I beg you, to hand my Aboriginal people the democracy and the Christianity that you, the white nation of Australia, so proudly boast of. I challenge the white nation to make these boasts good. I'm asking your practical help for a new and better deal for my race. Remember we, the Aboriginal people, are the creditors. Do not let it be said of you that we have asked in vain. Will my appeal for practical humanity be in vain? I leave the answer to each and every one of you.

Reproduced in full.
Source: Kevin Gilbert, *Because a White Man'll Never Do It*.[42]

Ian Clunies Ross

Heirs of the Pioneers: Science, Agriculture and Markets, 1941

(William) Ian Clunies Ross (1899–1959) was a veterinary scientist with expertise in parasites. He played a central role as an administrator and promoter of scientific research in Australia. Clunies Ross graduated from the University of Sydney in 1921 and undertook further study in England before joining the Commonwealth Scientific and Industrial Research Organisation (CSIRO). He spent a year in a Tokyo laboratory, toured North China and Korea and from 1937 served as chair of the International Wool Secretariat in London. These experiences expanded his outlook, and he believed in international co-operation in agriculture and the necessity for Australia to develop its relations with Asia. At the outbreak of World War II, Clunies Ross returned to the University of Sydney as professor of Veterinary Science. He advised the Commonwealth Government on the wartime employment of scientific personnel and delivered broadcasts and talks on international affairs. A popular and willing public speaker, Clunies Ross was skilled at addressing diverse audiences and adapting his message, and humour, to suit formal and informal occasions. He recognized that it was imperative to communicate scientific matters in an accessible way and excelled as a publicist for science during the 1950s when he was director of the CSIRO. On 23 August 1941 Clunies Ross delivered the annual Pioneers' Memorial Oration at Wangaratta, Victoria. Peppered in the crowd were descendants of original white settlers in the region. In outlining the responsibilities of the 'heirs of the pioneers', Clunies Ross's speech roamed widely—from the history of frontier violence to the 'practical science' of agriculture and animal husbandry, and from national primary production to international markets.

Tonight we commemorate those brave men and women who a century ago began the development of North-Eastern Victoria. We remember with pride the courage, the resolution and independence of that small band of pioneers who crossed the Murray and so extended the frontiers of settlement. I think that we Australians recall too seldom the deeds and qualities of our forbears.

How different was their world from ours. How different and yet in many ways how much more simple in spite of the hardships and dangers from hostile natives, and from famine, flood and fire. You remember how at the outset, settlement in this region was threatened by an attack by aboriginals, which cost nine lives, and how two years later, in 1840, Dr. Mackay [an original settler] lost his home, his stores, his horses and almost all his stock. As a result of the great exertions necessary to recover his cattle and to build life anew his health was seriously and permanently affected.

Why then do we say that life was more simple and straight-forward? Because for these pioneers the future had no limitations except those imposed by nature, and these they were resolved to overcome. For then there were no doubts that Australia would grow and expand, and that internal and external demand for her primary products could have no predictable limits. It is true that for the moment their export markets were limited. Only wool, tallow, hides and wheat could be exported in any quantities, but there was faith in the inevitability of Australia's population growing, a faith which appeared more than justified when, following the finding of gold, the country's population leapt from 200,000 in 1840 to over one million by 1860, while that of Victoria grew more than sevenfold in ten years; from 70,000 in 1850 to 500,000 in 1860.

In those days the foundations of society appeared firm and unshaken, and society whatever its defects was organised on a rational and understandable basis. If men starved they did so because there was a dearth of food to eat, if they went ill-clad they did so because of a shortage of raw materials. The pioneers could not have conceived that the day might come when it would be said that there was no room for further production in Australia, or that millions should die of starvation in a world in which foodstuffs were burnt or ploughed into the ground. In their day, when, from natural or economic causes, prices crashed and their fortunes tumbled these were regarded as manifestations of a temporary disorder only, with the passing of which the world's progress would continue. There was no doubt that they would pass.

The Australia they then knew, as the fringe of a continent with its 200,000 people has grown to a country with 7,000,000 people, with its sheep flocks amounting to 123,000,000, with its production and export of wool more than twice as great as any other country in the world. They would find it second in the export of mutton and lamb, one of the greatest exporters of butter and a not unimportant factor in the world's wheat market, and all this after feeding and clothing its own people at as high a standard as any other country.

The land which the pioneers settled was virgin country so far as domesticated stock and their diseases were concerned. But as settlement became established and pastures were grazed from year to year, the diseases introduced in imported livestock and disseminated even more widely in the train of the advancing flocks and herds began to enact a steadily increasing toil.

For many years we were content to apply the results of work done elsewhere in the control of such familiar diseases as anthrax and tetanus and the commoner forms of parasitic disease. Many too we succeeded in keeping out through intelligent quarantine methods. But over the last twenty years we have begun to make an increasingly effective attack by the development of scientific research in this country, and Australian research has some notable achievements to its credit, which have been recognised the world over.

Take the spectacular work of black disease and its allied problem of liver fluke infection, previously such a scourge throughout the tablelands of New South Wales, much of Victorian and of South-Eastern South Australia. There has been no more fascinating story in research and none with more clean cut and decisive economic results. It is a romance all the way. By a clear appreciation of the life history of the fluke parasite under Australian conditions and the elaboration of preventive vaccine against the black disease organism, it has been possible to devise methods of control which have reduced losses from this cause to a tiny fraction of their former toll.

Take again another and more recent classic; the cause and control of footrot of sheep. Here was a condition which had invited research in almost every country where sheep raising was carried out. Here too the solution was found by a young Australian, the son of a pastoralist, who had been drawn to research. No less striking has been the advance in knowledge of the control of other bacterial infections of the bowel of young sheep, particularly fat lambs run on improved pastures, and of the obscure nutritional diseases due to minute deficiencies of certain mineral elements.

Yes, so far as disease control is concerned we should have a very satisfactory record to place before the pioneers. But when they began to probe a little deeper, I fancy they would express surprise that we had not made equal progress that in other directions of no less importance to the primary industries.

Our methods of breeding in all important respects are identical with those which the pioneers followed one hundred years ago; of selection of mating like with like, of avoiding any close degree of inbreeding. Only here and there are there individual herd flock masters who have even a rudimentary knowledge of the scientific principles which underlie their craft.

Here we come to another and very serious defect in our agricultural organization, namely, the failure to apply the methods of scientific analysis to the economic problems of the industry. The science of agricultural economics has been virtually disregarded in this country, whether in regard to the problems of the individual farmer, or those of a district or an industry or of the country as a whole.

Well we may assure the pioneers, I hope, that we are going to close many of the gaps in our defences as soon as possible, that we are going to push on with research into our animal husbandry as distinct from our disease problems; that we are going to develop our extension services very greatly, and, finally that we are going to provide the machinery for investigation the whole economic structure of the industry through the setting up of State and Federal bureaux of Agricultural Economics. We hope that the pioneers would have certain of their fears allayed in regard to these matters, but finally, I believe, they would come to the most disturbing, the most incomprehensible thing of all. What would be their concern to learn that we had begun to doubt the future, that we have lost our faith in the certainty of the progress and development of the primary industries?

Is there any alternative? There is, and if we show the courage and resolution of the pioneers in adapting ourselves to new conditions, in going forward to fresh achievements, not back, we can find a road which will lead us to an era of a great progress as that which lies between the pioneers and ourselves. What then is necessary? First, to realise that our salvation and that of the primary industries lies in raising standards of living not only in this country, but in the world. Secondly, to see that this can only come by replacing the system of unrestricted economic warfare, which has led to war and the prospect of an uncertain and limited future, by a system of economic co-operation based on the recognition of the mutual dependence of all countries. Thirdly, for this country to press for a policy of conscious and continuous co-operation and investment by all advanced industrial countries to develop world demand, so that following the war there will be stimulated a rapid demand for peace-time goods to assist in the economic demobilisation which will present a post-war problem of the first magnitude. There is no alternative to this deliberate and planned development of a greater volume of world trade but world-wide economic collapse, when at the end of the war every industrialised country is forced to look beyond its own boundaries, for the full-time employment of its swollen industries.

Finally, let us resolve to be worthy of the pioneers by never doubting that the future lies in our hands, as it lay in theirs, if we have but the vision, the will and the courage to shape a new world for our children.

Abridged.
Source: Ian Clunies Ross, *The Fourth Annual Pioneers' Memorial Oration*, 23 August 1941, Wangaratta, 1941 (pamphlet).

———◆———

John Curtin
Men and Women of the United States, Men and Women of Britain, 1942

John Curtin (1885–1945) was Australia's heroic prime minister of World War II. Curtin had grown up in the Melbourne working-class suburb of Brunswick, became involved in union politics, joined the Victorian Socialist Party and learned public speaking as a 'red-ragger' at Melbourne's Yarra Bank and Eastern Market. In 1917 he moved to Western Australia, married, and assumed the editorship of the *Westralian Worker* before entering Federal Parliament in 1928 as the Member for Fremantle. From 1935, as leader of the Opposition, Curtin set about rebuilding a shattered Australian Labor Party. In August 1941 Prime Minister Robert Menzies was forced to resign and by October Curtin had assumed national leadership (which he held until 1945). On 8 December the Japanese bombed Pearl Harbor and began a swift advance through South-East Asia towards Australia. The nation faced its 'darkest hour', and on 27 December Curtin delivered his famous New Year message to the nation: 'I make it quite clear that Australia looks to America, free of any pangs as to our traditional links or kinship with the United Kingdom'.[43]

Despite Winston Churchill's displeasure, Curtin recalled Australian troops home from the Middle East and fully supported United States General Douglas MacArthur's Australian-based command of Allied operations in the Asia–Pacific. Singapore fell to the Japanese on 15 February 1942, and four days later Japanese planes bombed Darwin. Australia was in a state of national crisis when Curtin made an eloquent broadcast to the American people. Delivered on 14 March, on the eve of a visit to the United States by H. V. Evatt, Minister for External Affairs, Curtin warned that Australia stood as 'the last bastion' between the United States and Japan. One month later, Curtin's broadcast to the 'Men and Women of Great Britain' provided assurances that, despite Australia's new military partnership with the United States, the older loyalties of Empire were unbroken. Curtin spoke with intense sincerity and passion, even though his voice was raspy from years of chain smoking and open-air public-speaking. Churchill and Roosevelt's priority was to defeat Hitler in Europe and, although Curtin's advocacy of Australian interests had limited influence on Allied military strategy, the symbolic power of his 'looking to America' has resonated throughout Australian foreign policy and culture in succeeding decades.

Broadcast to the United States (14 March 1942)

Men and women of the United States:

I speak to you from Australia. I speak from a united people to a united people, and my speech is aimed to serve all the people of the nations united in the struggle to save mankind.

On the great waters of the Pacific Ocean war now breathes its bloody steam. From the skies of the Pacific pours down a deathly hail. In the countless islands of the Pacific the tide of war flows madly. For you in America; for us in Australia, it is flowing badly.

Let me then address you as comrades in this war and tell you a little of Australia and Australians.

I am not speaking to your Government. We have long been admirers of Mr. Roosevelt and have the greatest confidence that he understands fully the critical situation in the Pacific and that America will go right out to meet it. For all that America has done, both before and after entering the war, we have the greatest admiration and gratitude.

It is to the people of America I am now speaking; to you who are, or will be, fighting; to you who are sweating in factories and workshops to turn out the vital munitions of war; to all of you who are making sacrifices in one way or another to provide the enormous resources required for our great task.

I speak to you at a time when the loss of Java and the splendid resistance of the gallant Dutch together give us a feeling of both sadness and pride. Japan has moved one step further in her speedy march south; but the fight of the Dutch and Indonese [sic] in Java has shown that a brave, freedom-loving people are more than a match for the yellow aggressor given even a shade below equality in striking and fighting weapons.

But facts are stern things. We, the allied nations, were unready. Japan, behind her wall of secrecy, had prepared for war on a scale of which neither we nor you had knowledge.

We have all made mistakes, we have all been too slow; we have all shown weakness—all the Allied Nations. This is not the time to wrangle about who has been most to blame. Now our eyes are open.

The Australian Government has fought for its people. We never regarded the Pacific as a segment of the great struggle. We did not insist that it was the primary theatre of war, but we did say, and events have so far, unhappily, proved us right, that the loss of the Pacific can be disastrous.

Who, among us, contemplating the future on that day in December last when Japan struck like an assassin at Pearl Harbor, at Manila, at Wake and Guam, would have hazarded a guess that by March the enemy would be astride all the south-west Pacific except General Macarthur's gallant men, and Australia and New Zealand?

But that is the case. And, realising very swiftly that it would be the case, the Australian Government sought a full and proper recognition of the part the Pacific was playing in the general strategic disposition of the world's warring forces.

It was, therefore, but natural that, within 20 days after Japan's first treacherous blow, I said on behalf of the Australian Government that we looked to America as the paramount factor on the democracies' side in the Pacific.

There is no belittling of the Old Country in this outlook. Britain has fought and won in the air the tremendous battle of Britain. Britain has fought, and with your strong help, has won the equally vital battle of the Atlantic. She has a paramount obligation to supply all possible help to Russia. She cannot, at the same time, go all out in the Pacific. We, with New Zealand, represent Great Britain here in the Pacific—we are her sons—and on us the responsibility falls. I pledge you my word we will not fail. You, as I have said, must be our leader. We will pull knee to knee with you for every ounce of our weight.

We looked to America, among other things, for counsel and advice and therefore it was our wish that the Pacific War Council should be located at Washington. It is a matter of some regret to us that, even now, after 95 days of Japan's staggering advance south, ever south, we have not obtained first-hand contact with America.

Therefore, we propose sending to you our Minister for External Affairs (Dr. H. V. Evatt), who is no stranger to your country, so that we may benefit from his discussions with your authorities. Dr. Evatt's wife, who will accompany him, was born in the United States.

Dr. Evatt will not go to you as a mendicant. He will go to you as the representative of a people as firmly determined to hold and hit back at the enemy as courageously as those people from whose loins we spring—those people who withstood the disaster of Dunkirk, the fury of Goering's blitz, the shattering blows of the Battle of the Atlantic. He will go to tell you that we are fighting mad; that our people have a government that is governing with orders and not with weak-kneed suggestions; that we Australians are a people who, while somewhat inexperienced and un-certain as to what war on their soil may mean, are nevertheless ready for anything, and will trade punches, giving odds if needs be, until we rock the enemy back on his heels.

We are then committed, heart and soul, to total warfare. How far, you may ask me, have we progressed along that road?

I may answer you this way. Out of every ten men in Australia, four are now wholly engaged in war as members of the fighting forces or making the munitions and equipment to fight with. The other six, besides feeding and clothing the whole ten and their families, have to produce the food and wool and metals which Britain needs for her very existence.

We are not, of course, stopping at four out of ten. We had over three when Japan challenged our life and liberty. The proportion is now growing every day. On the one hand we are ruthlessly cutting out unessential expenditure so as to free men and women for war work; and on the other, mobilizing woman power to the utmost to supplement the men. From four out of ten devoted to war, we shall pass to five and six out of ten. We have no limits.

We have no qualms here. There is no fifth column in this county. We are all the one race—the English-speaking race. We will not yield easily a yard of our soil. We have great space here and tree by tree, village by village, and town by town we will fall back if we must. That will occur only if we lack the means of meeting the enemy with parity in materials and machines.

For, remember, we are the Anzac breed. Our men stormed Gallipoli; they swept through the Libyan desert; they were the 'rats' of Tobruk; they were the men who fought under 'bitter, sarcastic, pugnacious Gordon Bennett' down Malaya and were still fighting when the surrender of Singapore came.

These men gave of their best in Greece and Crete; they will give more than their best on their own soil, where their hearths and homes lie under enemy threat.

Our air force are in the Kingsford-Smith tradition. You have, no doubt, met quite a lot of them in Canada; the Nazis have come to know them at Hamburg and Berlin and in paratroop landings in France.

Our naval forces silently do their share on the seven seas.

I am not boasting to you. But were I to say less I would not be paying proper due to a band of men who have been tested in the crucible of world wars and hallmarked as pure metal.

Our fighting forces are born attackers; we will hit the enemy wherever we can, as often as we can, and the extent of it will be measured only by the weapons to our hands.

Dr. Evatt will tell you that Australia is a nation stripped for war. Our minds are set on attack rather than defence. We believe in fact that attack is the best defence; here in the Pacific it is the only defence. We know it means risks, but 'safety first' is the devil's catchword today.

Business interests in Australia are submitting with a good grace to iron control and drastic elimination of profits. Our great Labour unions are accepting the suspension of rights and privileges which have been sacred for two generations, and are submitting to an equally iron control of the activities of their members. It is now 'work or fight' for everyone in Australia.

The Australian Government has so shaped its policy that there will be a place for every citizen in the country. There are three means of service —in the fighting forces; in the labor forces; in the essential industries. For the first time in the history of this country a complete call-up, or draft, as you refer to it in America, has been made.

I say to you, as a comfort to our friends and a stiff warning to our enemies, that only the infirm remain outside the compass of our war plans.

We fight with what we have and what we have is our all. We fight for the same free institutions that you enjoy. We fight so that, in the words of Lincoln, 'government of the people, for the people, by the people, shall not perish from the earth.' Our legislature is elected the same as is yours; and we will fight for it, and for the right to have it, just as you will fight to keep the Capital at Washington the meeting place of freely-elected men and women representative of a free people.

But I give you this warning: Australia is the last bastion between the West Coast of America and the Japanese. If Australia goes, the Americas are wide open.

It is said that the Japanese will by-pass Australia and that they can be met and routed in India. I say to you that the saving of Australia is the saving of America's west coast. If you believe anything to the contrary then you delude yourselves.

Be assured of the calibre of our national character. This war may see the end of much that we have painfully and slowly built in our 150 years of existence. But even though all of it go, there will still be Australians fighting on Australian soil until the turning point be reached, and we will advance over blackened ruins, through blasted and fire-swept cities, across scorched plains, until we drive the enemy into the sea.

I give you the pledge of my country. There will always be an Australian Government and there will always be an Australian people. We are too strong in our hearts; our spirit is too high; the justice of our cause throbs too deeply in our being for that high purpose to be overcome.

I may be looking down a vista of weary months; of soul-shaking reverses; of grim struggle; of back-breaking work. But as surely as I sit here talking to you across the war-tossed Pacific Ocean I see our flag; I see Old Glory; I see the proud banner of the heroic Chinese; I see the standard of the valiant Dutch.

And I see them flying high in the wind of liberty over a Pacific from which aggression has been wiped out; over peoples restored to freedom; and flying triumphant as the glorified symbols of united nations strong in will and in power to achieve decency and dignity, unyielding to evil in any form.

Broadcast to Great Britain (27 April)

Men and women of Britain!

I speak to you from Australia, a land that is preparing to meet an invasion. You in Britain know what this means, for it was the courage you showed in the dark days after Dunkirk that has now become a shining symbol to your kindred in this far away continent.

While we watch the enemy approaching ever closer to our shores we remember how the people of Britain used the greatest weapon of all to hold off the invader, the weapon of an indomitable spirit. Like Britain after Dunkirk we find that we have not enough arms; not enough planes. You did not have enough planes nor enough arms, but you did have the will to resist. It was the spirit of the people that saved Britain. And it will be the spirit of the Australian people that will not only save Australia but send us marching forward to victory.

Dangerous days lie ahead of us, but under this threat the Empire is more united than ever before. The people of Australia have no illusions about this struggle. They know that this is not a fight for Australia, nor for the Empire, nor any other section of the world, but a fight for the world itself. One thing this war has demonstrated, and that is the inability of small nations to stand alone and defend themselves.

It is the Empire's unity that has given it the strength to hold on. And it is because the Australian Government believes so earnestly in that unity and the joining of our forces for the common weal, that it so consistently advocated greater collaboration in resisting the Axis countries.

For we are practical Empire patriots, practical democrats. The Australians were the first Empire people to send their men away from their shores to fight for the Empire. They have always fought for the Empire. They have always fought for what is right and always fought against what is wrong, because that is their nature.

Today Australians are serving in every continent in the world. Our sailors can be found on every ocean; our airmen fight in many lands; so too our soldiers. With their blood Australians have written many glorious pages of Empire history.

Australia and Great Britain each belong to that group of countries pledged to the destruction of Axis brutality. We belong to that group of free people known as the United Nations. Each member of a family may have strong individual preferences and views, but on the major issues of life they have a common outlook.

While democracy lives there will always be the British Empire. In that we see a great inspiration for the conduct of this war. Under the system of British unity we have had armed forces of individual nations working under one Commander. And it is an extension of that idea that can be found in Australia today, for we have achieved a degree of unity in this fight for life greater than that previously we have a Commander-in-Chief—a great soldier—General Douglas MacArthur—and in Australia today the fighting men of Australia and America march as one army under one leader.

We have achieved the same unity of command as we did when our soldiers fought under Sir Archibald Wavell, as Commander-in-Chief in the Middle East. For unity is strength and the United Nations will hurl the Japanese back to their island home, will turn Hitler's dream of world conquest into a nightmare of retribution, and release the Italian peoples from their would-be Caesar.

Faced with the threat of an invasion our armies are preparing to take the offensive. That is the Anzac spirit. That is the spirit that is inspiring the Empire and the United Nations today. It is a spirit that knows not defeat.

It is for life itself we strive. Our history is a record of struggle to broaden freedom; not to lessen it and most certainly not to surrender it.

As we see the situation today, Australia is a great bastion of Empire. From a securely held Australia the strategy and forces essential to free the Pacific Ocean, to hold firmly the Indian Ocean and to liberate the enemy occupied places threatening these oceans, can go forward to the offensive.

This purpose abides with us. It keeps the Axis powers in the West separated from their Eastern partner. It is the blow that will prove a turning point in the total conflict. This is Australia's resolve.

On our people and the people of New Zealand now falls the burden of the Empire in the South Pacific. We represent you here. With the aid of the United Nations we shall not fail.

Finally I send to you a message of loyalty and unity to our common cause. Australia is proud of its sonship to the Motherland. In its fealty it accepts the mantle that has come to it. It will inexorably and with all that it has stand side by side with you in upholding what we are, and working and fighting to the end for victory.

Reproduced in full.
Sources: Broadcast by Prime Minister Curtin, Over a Network of United States, Canadian and South American Stations, 14 March 1942, Australian Archives (NSW), ABC Broadcasts Series SP300/1, Box 7; Broadcast by Prime Minister Curtin to Great Britain, 27 April 1942; Australian Archives (NSW), ABC Broadcasts Series SP300/1.

H. C. 'Nugget' Coombs
Seven Million Pairs of Hands, 1942

Herbert Cole 'Nugget' Coombs (1906–1997) was the most prominent economist in Australia's post-war years and an influential supporter of the arts, Aboriginal rights and environmental issues. From an early career as a schoolteacher, Coombs was drawn to the study of the forces of economics in society, completing a PhD thesis on centralized banking at the London School of Economics in 1933. He was employed in the Commonwealth Bank and Federal Treasury before taking up the directorship of the Department of Post-War Reconstruction—the most radical government department ever created in Australia. Under the leadership of the bright, energetic and compassionate Coombs, a team of smart young public servants laid out the philosophical basis for a new peacetime society. This exercise in broad government planning laid the foundation for the great era of immigration, industrial growth, active social welfare and unprecedented prosperity of the immediate post-war decades. In December 1942 Coombs spoke on ABC radio about his vision of a post-war Australia, free of the 'overriding threat of unemployment', and where the government played a major role in the development of Australian industry, communities and social life.

These hands, the hands of the people of Australia, symbolise our greatest economic resource — the resource of human activity. There are of course others. We have our fields, our mines, and our factories, but these are barren and lifeless without the work of our hands. This particular resource has one special quality — it will not keep. We can leave our physical resources in idleness for greater or less periods and in the main they are still there for us to use, but the power and ability to work must be used or it is lost forever.

The failure to realise this was the major weakness of our pre-war world. In Australia during the twenty years before the war there was one pair of hands in seven ready and anxious to work but idle. In 1931/32 the figure was no less than one in three. Idle not in rest or recreation but in the bitter humiliation of unemployment. With the resources cast aside in these years we could, for instance, have cleared our slums and rehoused the greater part of our people. The social cost of this work would have been nothing. We would have been using resources which in fact were wasted forever. And on the positive side of the ledger would have appeared not merely the homes and the happiness [such work] would have brought but pride of craftsmanship and consciousness of achievement instead of frustration and despair.

Mass unemployment must never come again. The power which lies in the hands of the people must be harnessed to social achievement. It can be done. During the war unemployment has disappeared. Every willing pair of hands has found worthwhile work.

It is worthwhile looking at what has been achieved. We have in three years built up a war machine which a few years ago would have appeared impossible. We have built up an economic system capable of maintaining that machine in active operation. At the same time it has been possible to preserve the essential standard of living for the mass of the people. Indeed it has been possible actually to improve the standard of some of those most in need. It is true that we have had to postpone many developmental projects, to delay the expansion of civil industry and forego the improvement of public amenities. It is true that many luxuries and some comforts have disappeared and that some essentials are carefully rationed. But the basic needs of health and efficiency have continued to be available to all. Perhaps most important of all, the overriding threat of unemployment has been removed at least for the time being.

It is significant that the value of goods and services now available for current consumption is as great as it was in [the] depression years, and it is certainly true that those goods and services are now being distributed much more fairly. This is no mean achievement. It has been possible only because the work of all has been used and because that work has been directed towards a common purpose.

The magnitude of our wartime achievements cannot fail to raise the question of whether achievements of equal magnitude are not possible in times of peace, and whether we cannot by full employment and unity of purpose transform the conditions of life in the same way as in these three short years we have transformed our capacity to combat aggression.

There can be no doubt of the answer. If we can use to the full the human resources at our command, if we can know clearly the objectives we seek, and if we can achieve the same unity of purpose which we have found in war, we can build an Australia which will give to its sons and daughters a life at once richer and fuller and more secure than we have known in the past.

The first condition is that we use to the full our human resources—that there should be no idle hands. This raises a problem which has for years worried economists. They have seen that if employment is made a first objective there will inevitably be waste. Men will be employed on one job when perhaps another is really more urgent. We have in our studies and classrooms argued over the ways of achieving the best possible use of resources. This problem is a very real one but its importance has been greatly exaggerated. There can be no waste which comes from using resources for less important purposes anything like so great or so bitter in its consequences as [the] failure to use those resources at all.

Nevertheless the problem must be faced. In the past the use to which resources—human and real—have been put has largely been left to individuals. If we are determined that no resources shall unnecessarily and wastefully be idle, we must accept the fact that the decision as to how at least some of our resources shall be used will be a social decision—made like other social decisions by governments and influenced by public opinion. If these decisions are to be made wisely they must be the subject of careful planning, and full public discussion. It is as well for us, therefore, to think carefully about the nature of the changes we want made. If we can, as I suggest, transform our lives, along what lines do we want them transformed?

The last hundred years have been years of amazing technical and productive development. Every year has added new achievements. It has been characteristic of our way of life that these changes have shown themselves largely in a multiplication of commodities and types of commodities. The range of goods produced and used by the average citizen today would without doubt amaze his great-grandfather with their multiplicity, their technical efficiency and their specialisation. I wonder though whether this multiplication of commodities is the most fruitful way of using the increased productive power which science and discovery have placed in our hands. I want to suggest that there is another and more fruitful way and that the need for social decisions as to the way we use our resources offers us the opportunity to follow that way.

Despite external change the basic elements of human life remain unchanged. It is human relationships which primarily give colour and richness to our lives. It is in love, courtship, and marriage, in the birth and nurture of children, in the excitement of common effort and the triumph of achievement in worthwhile work, in the comradeship of sport and in the fellowship and struggles of political activity that the real quality of our lives resides. In the rush to produce, sell and consume the flood of goods which technical skill has made possible, these human activities have been thrust into the background and our environment has become progressively less adapted to them.

This I conceive to be the task of our hands and the aims of our socially directed activities—to transform the setting in which our lives are lived—to change it from a setting adapted to the production, distribution, and exchange of an increasing flood of goods to one in which these basic human activities can find full opportunity.

What parts of our environment call for change if these objectives are to be gained? Clearly the centre of many of these activities is the home and it is in the home that our reconstruction must begin. We must plan the homes of the future with an eye not merely to beauty but to the activities which are or should be carried on there. In the past many technical improvements on housing have had the result of reducing the effectiveness of the home for its essential purposes. New labour-saving devices, over-elaborate furnishings, the individual garage, and many other 'improvements' have been gained at the expense of spaciousness and quiet. The home of the future should be a place where children can be conscientiously cared for and where there is full opportunity for play. It should be planned so that meals can be easily prepared and served, and so that the processes of hygiene and sanitation can be effectively carried out. It should offer both the opportunity for family group activity and for rest and isolation for its individual members. It should, too, make possible parents' privacy and occasional freedom from parental responsibility.

It is obvious that individual homes for the mass of people cannot provide all of these facilities within themselves. Proper grouping of homes in 'communities', however, will make possible common playgrounds, nurseries and schools, as the supplements to the individual homes which are required if the home is adequately to do its job.

This grouping of homes in communities suggests, too, another change in our environment. Many people fear that the individual will be lost in the group. This fear is false. It is only in a community that the individual can develop. Even the most individualistic people—the artist, the rebel—need the community if only as an audience or an enemy. I believe that the community in this sense will give us the characteristic buildings and institutions of the postwar world. The prototype of the community institution is the school and it is around the school that these institutions may develop. Libraries, theatres, social and political clubs, halls, health centres, sporting facilities. These are, so to speak, the capital equipment of human relationships; it is in them that our friends, our lovers, our comrades, our rivals and our enemies are met and where the essential business of life is carried on.

These communities, however, cannot be built in isolation. The men and women who form them will work in factories, shops, offices and the like. It follows therefore that if we are to build the homes and the communities which a full life demands, we must make changes in our economic organisation. The tendency of the last century, particularly in Australia, has been to centralise industry in the large centres. More than half our population and the major part of our industry are in the six metropolitan areas of the capital cities of our States. These capital cities are, when judged by human standards, failures in social organisation. They are neither beautiful, healthy, nor efficient. We must be prepared to move our industries—to decentralise them—to plan their location so that not merely do we get efficient production but we build up a healthy balanced life for those engaged in industry.

In place of this over-growth of the city and the draining and exploitation of the country, we must plan our development on regional lines. The industrial resources of natural economic regions require to be developed within the region. With the coming of electrical power there is much less need to concentrate industry. Many lines of consumers' goods can be and are produced for relatively small markets. The dispersal of these industries, together with the opportunities offered by local resources, provide the basis for regional development which will break down the barrier between city and country to their mutual advantage and make possible within each region a balanced economic life. In the towns and provincial cities that this regional development will make possible, we have our opportunity to build our communities of homes which are close to the work which the inhabitants have to perform and which fulfil the needs of a healthy communal life.

It is clear from what I have said that if we are to provide for the people the 'capital equipment' for basic human activities, we cannot leave the task to private enterprise. We must in this part of the field at least call a halt to the multiplication of goods, to the wastes of isolated individual effort, and to the anarchy of speculation and jerry-building. To put it on no higher plane it is clear that the vast mass of people cannot afford from their own incomes to pay for the homes and community services which are essential to their lives. We must plan, construct and pay for the equipment of our social life collectively.

This then is the position briefly. The economy of the past has failed in two major respects. It has failed to use to the full the human resources at our disposal. It has failed to organise economic effort so that it facilitates and develops opportunity for those essential activities which are the raw material of the drama of human life. This is then both our task and our opportunity. On the basis of past experience we can assume that on the average private enterprise will leave unwanted some ten per cent of our productive resources. With these resources directed to the regional development of our national estate, to the construction of the capital equipment of social life, and to the building of homes that are not merely shelters but centres of family life and the nucleus of social organisation, we can indeed transform our lives.

In the last four years the seven million pairs of hands of the Australian people have been turned to the tasks of war. Their achievements have been magnificent. Let us plan now so that those hands may be turned against other enemies—the enemies of poverty, unemployment, and the degradation of the human spirit. Let us plan too, for positive aims—to build in Australia a sound environment which the life of our people will take on new colour, new intensity and new dramatic quality.

To this task let us set our hands.

Reproduced in full.
Source: Dr H. C. Coombs, 3AR, 8.45 pm, 4 December 1942, ABC Radio transcript; Australian Archives (NSW), Series SP300/1, Box 7.

———

Enid Lyons
Women in Peacetime, 1943

Dame Enid Lyons (1897–1981) was a seventeen-year-old Methodist girl when she married a 36-year-old Catholic politician in 1915. Her husband was Joseph Lyons, a gentle, reflective man who became in turn Labor premier of Tasmania, federal treasurer, and finally prime minister, leading the anti-Labor United Australia Party from 1932 until his death in 1939. Their life together became a very public Australian love story. Enid Lyons raised twelve children and, at the same time, became a well-loved public figure, supporting her husband's career, advocating women's rights and the dignity of motherhood. In 1943 she entered Federal Parliament as the first female member of the House of Representatives. As the government's kindly matriarch, Lyons managed to impart some of her own sense of compassion and her love for women and children to government policy. Speaking on the ABC's 'Guest of Honour' programme on 19 September 1943, Enid Lyons made her contribution to a widely debated topic: the reproductive responsibilities of Australian women to stem the decline in the national birth rate. She also spoke on the individual duties of women's citizenship in the coming peace.

Let me begin with a platitude. Indeed with two platitudes. We live in a rapidly changing world; and the only thing certain about that world is that in the post-war period it will be in many ways vastly different from the world we know. Just what the role of women will be in that world is a subject upon which many people like to speculate, although a flippant friend of mine assures me that it will be the same old role that it has always been—Hoodwinking the unsuspecting male, as he has it.

The changes that have taken place during the last three or four years are changes due mainly to war conditions but many of them have pointed the way to other forms of living when the war is won; some of them may even linger on in their present form, but only a person very much rasher than I would attempt to predict in detail the conditions that will prevail in five years' time.

That certain spheres of activity and certain forms of occupation will be open to women which formerly were the monopoly of men is obvious. The work of women during the war has proved their capacity and versatility in a most remarkable way. They have done well in administrative work of the greatest importance, in business and industry; even women engineers are no longer a novelty, and it is certain that there will always be women in the future who will claim their right to exploit these fields of labour to the full.

Many people see in this the creation of an enormous problem for post-war solution. I do not share their fears because I believe that the vast majority of women will always find their greatest happiness and the readiest outlet for their talents in their traditional occupation as home-makers, provided the opportunity is given them. Some may wish to combine work in the home with work in the industrial field, and they should have perfect freedom to decide this question for themselves, but I am convinced that the strain involved in the dual role is too great for any but the few to undertake.

This innate love of home and family I believe will provide a large part of the solution to the difficulties arising immediately after the war, when thousands of women as well as men must be re-absorbed into peace-time life. Many are anxiously asking if women who have been earning big wages in wartime industry will be content to go back into housekeeping work. Well, let us take the married ones first. I have talked to many of these young women and they are all agreed that they are going to find it hard to manage on a single income when they have been handling two—their own and that provided by their husbands whether as wage or military allotment. But they feel too that the comfort and happiness of being once more together, free to make a home and to rear a family, will more than compensate for the financial loss. Some, of course, doing highly specialised work, will want to continue, but I believe that they will be so few in number as to have little effect on the general situation.

And what of the unmarried? Well, I haven't the slightest doubt that at least half of them are going to marry and live happily ever after, and they will probably never again be a source of anxiety in industry. Of those still remaining a great many will return to normal peace-time occupation in shops and offices, work now denied them because of the war. Others will demand employment in the new avenues that must be opened out to cope with the general problem of providing work for all. But a necessary condition to any just and lasting solution is equal pay for equal work. No man then will have to compete against cheap female labour. Skill will be the determining factor in any competition that may arise. But, women will see their immediate post-war responsibility, whatever other work they may do, as the task [of contributing to the] reconstruction of the world. Not that their responsibility will end there. Their work even as home-makers will not be completed wholly within the home.

Those people who believe that with the attainment of victory the brave new world will automatically come into existence, are due for a rude awakening. The new order of our dreams will be achieved only by concentrated thought, great effort and a good deal of self-sacrifice. All the efforts of Government to evolve an economic structure based upon social justice will fail of their purpose if the individual fails in justice to his brother. And we whose whole society is founded upon a belief in human dignity, we who are waging war in defence of the God-given rights of the individual man, too often forget that success in any collective undertaking depends upon individual effort. In a highly organised society the fulfilment of many personal obligations to the community is achieved only through government instrumentalities, and the taking of a full share in the shaping of those institutions is the duty of every citizen.

Every public question, of course, is a woman's question: Winning the war, putting our fighting men back into civil life, finding work for all now engaged in war industries; and there are certain things which are women's questions in a peculiar and intimate sense. They are associated for the most part with her greatest and most important function, the passing on of life. They are for that very reason questions of the greatest national importance, and they bear very heavily upon one of the most pressing problems that Australia will have to face after the war, the problem of population.

You will forgive me, I know, for saying that I have good reason to know most of the difficulties that mothers and fathers face these days: the expense connected with their children and the cost of feeding and clothing them, and the anxiety of guiding them through the moral and social evils that they must meet. It takes courage to have a family today; courage and patience and forgetfulness of self, and yet if we are to survive in the world of tomorrow we must have families. Everything, therefore, that eases the burdens upon parents should be a first charge upon the nation's care for the 'foundation of a nation's greatness', to use the words of the late King George, 'is in the homes of its people'. Women, then, will interest themselves first in the provision of homes for all. Every young man home from the war has the right to expect some such provision for his future. Every girl should be able to look forward to turning a house into a home, a home where little children will be welcome.

They will see that mothers themselves have every kind of maternity care, from the pre-natal clinic onwards, and in conjunction with all such care some kind of home help service should be devised. This domestic help scheme will be hard to arrange until the whole status of domestic work has been raised by some form of industrial control, but I believe that if women would apply themselves to the finding of effective means to achieve this end we should soon resolve the difficulty.

For children will demand the utmost in educational facilities, and for the teen-age ones, those that mothers yearn over, there must be rigid control of all those agencies which make for moral degeneration.

None of these things can be achieved except by united effort, and, more and more, women who believe in the possibility of a better society will find themselves engaged in public work.

I have said enough, I know, to show you that in my belief the role of women in the future will be the role of women through all the ages of the past—binding up the family she will do as she has always done, but she will find the opportunity and the means in a larger sphere, the realm of national—and even international affairs.

Reproduced in full.
Source: Dame Enid Lyons, 'Guest of Honour', 3AR, 7.45 pm, 19 September 1943, ABC Radio broadcast transcript; Australian Archives (NSW), Series SP300/1, Box 12.

Miles Franklin
Henry Lawson, 1944

Miles (Stella Maria Sarah) Franklin (1879–1954) was one of Australia's best loved writers and, in later life, a formidable literary figure who promoted the idea of a distinctive Australian literature. She spent her childhood on a succession of increasingly poor grazing properties run by her family in the Monaro district. Aged just nineteen, she completed her famous and partly autobiographical novel, *My Brilliant Career*. But it was not until Henry Lawson—by then an established literary figure—intervened that its publication was secured in London in 1901. Franklin left Australia in 1906, working in Chicago in support of feminist and labour reform causes, later moving to England where she pursued her political and literary interests. Using the pseudonym 'Brent of Bin Bin' she wrote a series of well-received novels; and under her own name she published the acclaimed *All that Swagger* (1936), which charted pioneer life on the Monaro. Franklin returned to Sydney in 1932, where she cared for her elderly mother, kept up a voluminous correspondence and supported many younger writers. She championed Australian writing in talks and broadcasts, most notably for the Commonwealth Literary Fund. In September 1944 Franklin gave a public speech (later broadcast on radio) to commemorate her literary mentor, Henry Lawson. She spoke to a crowd assembled at a sculpture of Lawson by George Lambert, which had been funded through public subscription and erected in 1931 in the Sydney Domain—the site where speechmakers of every ilk would gather to proclaim their views.

We meet here to offer a tribute of gratitude and affection to the life and work of one of our most dearly loved Australians. Academic practitioners of letters concern themselves with the appraisal of Henry Lawson. It has been their preoccupation through the years to measure him by standard yardsticks and to lean heavily on sticks wielded by men overseas who have known literature, but sometimes have not known Australia. That is to have only half the numbers on the slate, for it has been demonstrated that a writer here can attain to accepted or current standards in his work without contributing a little to *Australian* literature. The ablest, the most percipient of Lawson's critics has said: 'his prose is that of a writer who represents a continent.' By that Lawson has earned the right to the silver trumpets of oratory. The oratory and silver trumpets will come with time. Today I attempt nothing beyond a humble personal tribute to Henry Lawson in relation to Australia—a homely and happy privilege. No Australian who has wrestled with the ardors and subtleties of resolving this continent in terms of literature will discount Henry Lawson. Few have equalled him: none has yet excelled him. His achievement remains unique.

This monument, on this lovely site, as well as the other memorial at Eurunderee, and the one at Mudgee, are part of the recognition which time is bringing to Henry Lawson. Such monuments, alas, too often are a saving of face by the living in regard to the neglected dead. We cannot gloze the fact of an element of that in such monuments to Henry Lawson; but with his divine understanding of human frailty, his gentle sympathy for its shortcomings, he would have understood. He would graciously accept our offerings. His spirit would have kindly humor for those imaginary half-crowns contributed by old mates who never saw him. He would chuckle sardonically about them as a touching, if grotesque, outcropping of that mateship which was the Lawson philosophy, and which has become one of this Commonwealth's worthiest traditions.

First among Lawson's achievements was this embodying of the tradition of mateship. Secondly, he was one of the most powerful of that band which in the 'Nineties helped Australians to a realisation of their country. He quickened their instinctive reaction towards it. To remain unrooted in the soil of one's permanent residence is to be forever a prey to nostalgia—a drug so potent, that uncontrolled it can enervate purpose and defer destiny.

The literary artist is an illuminator. Henry Lawson lighted lamps for us in a vast and lonely habitat. I want you to come back to the 'Nineties to recall what Lawson meant to the adolescents of that day.

At concerts and other gatherings, now superannuated by the radio, youthful reciters used to let off steam and thrill to such a stanza as;

'England's sun was slowly setting o'er the hilltops far away, Filling all the land with beauty at the close of one sad day.'

Lawson retracted that nostalgic vision—and the nostalgia too, perhaps, but at least he brought it home. He recalled the far-flung homesickness of the generations which had remained exiled. He made them see Australia's sunsets.

'One day old Trooper Campbell rode out to Blackman's run, his cap peak and his sabre were gleaming in the sun.'

It may have been 'the sad heart-breaking sunset to the new chum worst of all,' or the sunset of the tramp who

'As a bullock drags in the sandy ruts (he) followed the dreary track With never a thought but to reach the huts when the sun went down out back.'

Lawson felt and emphasised drought and hardship, loneliness and failure.

'Desolation where the crow is! Desolation where the eagle flies Paddocks where the luny bullock starts and stares with reddened eyes.'

But adolescence revels in tragedy so long as it is vicarious. Literature translates tragedy into pathos and a channel for emotion. Youth must have nourishment for its emotions and channels for all its glorious capacity for passion and pain and joy and sentimentality. So with Lawson:

'We wondered who would win her as she said her sweet goodbyes But she died at one-and-twenty and was buried on the rise.'

We were thrilled and gooey over the fate of Henry Dale, and 'Someone's heart still bleeds in sorrow for the drover who sleeps amid the reeds.'

It was rapture, it was ecstasy in the grand new discovery of our own sun to see it setting red and real and near at hand among our own trees on the ridge behind the stockyard, or to run to the top of the ridge to see it retreating over the blue-green ranges, where the moke-pokes would soon be calling in the misty moonlight. Henry Lawson gave us this kingdom for our own, wove it so that we could fold it around us with the comfort of a blanket on fire-warmed nights. The warmth and tenderness of his writing made it vital so that he helped to give us a cosy mother country. Noble though that other Motherland had been and remains—Lawson himself has paid the English tradition a poet's homage in 'England Yet!'—noble though that Motherland remains, nevertheless in Lawson's illuminating communication Australia emerged as something nearer and more personal in the way of parent earth. The rich implications of what Lawson and his colleagues articulated remain with cumulative results. Lawson invested the intangibles of atmosphere with reality.

Young imaginations dote on slogans and phrases—slang is mostly the gift of the young to the language. There was magic in finding our own idiom in print. There it was, dressed in the authority of book covers which before had sheltered only forests and woods, brooks and meadows. Like Henry Lawson in *The Old Bark School* we too had undergone expatriate information:

> 'And Ireland—that *was known from the coast-line to Athlone*
> *But little of the land that gave us birth,*
> *Save that Capt Cook was killed, (and very likely grilled)*
> *And our blacks are just the lowest race on earth.'*

Due to Lawson and his colleagues, now enjoying their literary rights were the gums, the bush, the creek; gully and spur and sideling; the paddock the stockyard, the sliprails. We were on the track, and burning off down in the gully; hobble chains and camp ware were jingling to a tune.

The lingo of everyday was endearingly setting-out familiar properties —a heady feast that could not be spoiled by any spectres at the board. The spectres were conquered by this-releasing expression. School girls and boys in the bush copied into exercise books the Lawson poems that came their way and chanted and droned them by heart. We didn't elide and suppress the rhymed words as if they were illegitimate children to be shamefully denied. We stressed them and revelled in them honestly and got the full worth of them as one of the most seductive and arduously cultivated of linguistic devices.

When I was in my tens and teens, Henry Lawson was a hero glamorous with success. He had all of sympathy, all of glory that youthful adoration could bestow. In that wonderland that was opening to us we were unaware of the struggles of literary geniuses. We could judge only by the literary product, and that enchanted us. We were sure that if we could see Henry Lawson he would understand our every delight, our every aspiration, our every growing pain of discontent. He was a superman—the perfect big brother of our dreams.

With this conception of Henry Lawson it was inevitable that I should reach him with my literary growing pains. The result is part of the Lawson legend. With your indulgence I should like to add my recollection of Henry Lawson in the flesh.

What is so rare to critical, exacting, over-sensitive youth, he fulfilled my expectations of him, and more. I remember my first sight of him. He was beautifully dressed. His linen was irreproachable. He was tall and slim, with exceptional physical beauty. The beauty of his eyes is also part of his legend. His manner—it had that sensitive warmth, that winning gentleness, that understanding—well, Lawson was as Lawson wrote. You had not to work up to friendliness with him: he was spontaneously a mate. He called on me, alone, he said with a humorous smile skimming across his features, to find out what sort of an animal I was—whether a mate or a mere miss. He would come next day to take me to his wife. The Lawsons were then living in a most delightful cottage with—garden paths embowered in shrubs. Mrs Lawson was equally up to expectation in her friendliness, her youthfulness, her beauty.

Henry Lawson was then at the height of his powers. He was preparing for the inevitable hegira to London. This lent additional romance to his doings. He was rising to increasing renown and surely it must be accompanied by prosperity.

He went to London.

I came down from the bush and saw him again on his return.

I recall the last time I saw him. He and his family were waving goodbye to me from the wharf as I boarded a ferry. No family group could have excelled it in charm; the beauty of the parents was repeated in the two children.

No other portrait of Henry Lawson has for me ever overlaid my own. Nothing blurs it nor detracts from it. It was etched indelibly by the clearcutting mind of youth.

I never saw Henry Lawson again. I too left Australia. When I returned, the earth—that Australian earth cleansed of history by an oblivion of fallowhood, lay kind upon him who had helped to imbue it with national significance.

I had no more than settled in the house after the bustle of arrival before my mother said, 'You must see where they have laid your friend Henry Lawson. I'll take you tomorrow.'

No one can estimate what Henry Lawson may mean to the future of this country: what will be the fate of small national groups in the postwar order no prophet can say. But having succeeded in our military struggle, if we shall be able to retain here in this isolated paradise of the Pacific our continuing Australian identity then Lawson's fame will be sure with the years.

Our indebtedness to him will increase because he has rendered this continent. He has helped to make Australia ours in a way that no system of land exploitation nor even droughts and floods and pests can take it from us—a great gift from a greatly gifted man—Henry Lawson!

Reproduced in full.
Source: Mitchell Library, State Library of New South Wales, Miles Franklin Papers, MSS 364/76–77 (Microfilm CY Reel 3586).[44]

Jessie Street

New Horizons: The United Nations, 1945

Jessie Mary Grey Street (1889–1970) was one of Australia's greatest social re-
formers, with interests that spanned women's rights, international feminism, peace,
socialism and Aboriginal equality. After a happy childhood spent in India, on a New
South Wales pastoral station and in England, Street graduated in Arts from the
University of Sydney, where she met her husband-to-be, law student (and future
chief justice of New South Wales) Kenneth Street. The family's relative economic
security gave Street the opportunity to campaign on behalf of all women for financial independence via equal pay, child endowment and the end of discrimination.
She was involved in various women's organizations, becoming the president of the
United Associations of Women in 1929, a position she held intermittently for the next
two decades. During the 1930s, Street's interests turned to the role of the League
of Nations in promoting opportunities for women. She visited the USSR, and was
later to be involved in the Australia–Soviet Friendship Society. Street joined the
Labor Party in 1939, and during World War II was instrumental in organizing a
national Women's Charter, which laid out a blueprint for improving the position of
women within the policy planning for peacetime reconstruction. An idealist who was
also a pragmatic and effective lobbyist and assured public speaker, Street was a
public figure of considerable influence. In 1945 she was the only Australian female
advisor sent to the founding United Nations Conference on International Organization, held in San Francisco. There, she worked with other women to ensure that the
United Nations Charter enshrined gender equality, and that a commission on the
status of women was established. Street was to represent Australia at this commission in 1946–48 and to be its vice-president. On 2 October 1945 Street—who
was in London en route to Moscow—recorded a radio broadcast for listeners in
Australia. This conveyed her sense of the historic importance of the new United
Nations and its potential as a solid basis for world co-operation: it is a speech of
hope for the 'new horizons' of the post-war world.

So many world-shaking events have occurred since the San Francisco
Conference started that it has not yet taken its rightful place in the public
mind. The achievement of the Conference in forming an all-embracing
organization of the peace-loving nations of the world qualifies it to be
considered as one of the most important events in modern history.

The Conference was called for the purpose of setting up a machinery
for the maintenance of world peace and security, and I believe these aims
can be achieved by the opportunities provided in the Charter of the
United Nations Organisation.

But the successful working of the Organisation depends upon two
factors; first, upon the continued friendship, confidence and unity in
action of the British Commonwealth, the United States and the Soviet
Union; and second, upon the intelligent and sympathetic co-operation of
the people and people's organizations in all countries. I believe these two
conditions to be essential. In the United Nations Organisation, Trades
Unions, religious bodies, women's organizations, trades, financiers, those

working for sex equality, racial equality, health, education, in fact, everyone concerned with economic or social problems of any kind is afforded
an opportunity of tackling those problems on an international basis. The
fact that the United Nations Organisation is formed and is in existence
will not, of course, solve any problem. You can build a motor car with
every modern accessory but it will not take you anywhere unless you get
in and drive it. And so it is with the United Nations Organisation. Let us
realise this and let all of us who are genuinely anxious for peace and security make it our business to understand and take advantage of possibilities
offered by these Commissions. They can be developed into channels,—
through which the non-governmental and voluntary bodies throughout
the world can bring their influence to bear on the United Nations
Organisation. They can be an important factor in the growth of democratic inter-nation co-operation between groups with common interests.
Their possibilities are limitless. The development of their possibilities is a
challenge to the peoples and organizations of the democratic nations.

It can be said by those that wish to damp down enthusiasm for inter-
nation co-operation, that the recommendations of these Commissions
and of the Economic and Social Council are little else than pious aspirations, since they have no power to enforce them. But we must not over-
look the force of moral suasion. Every country wishes to create a good
impression on world opinion. The opinion of the world will be considerably influenced by the reports made by member countries at the Annual
Assemblies of the United Nations. Recommendations made by responsible bodies of the Organisation and disregarded will not create good
impressions. The moral force of public opinion can be utilised in the
international sphere as affectively as it is in national or family life.

Of course, nothing can be done until the United Nations Organisation
holds its first Assembly. When this takes place, the countries to be represented are the Economic and Social Council and other principal organs
of the United Nations Organisation will be elected. The Governments
of the countries elected will then have to make their appointment to
the principal organs. When this has been done, the Economic and Social
Council will be able to commence its work.

At the final meetings of the Commission of the Conference which
decided the functions and powers of the Social and Economic Council,
various recommendations were made by delegations, and supported or
opposed by others. One of the recommendations I was particularly interested in was that a Commission on the 'Status of Women' should be
appointed. This recommendation was supported by every delegation
present. It was gratifying to hear the tributes of the men delegates to the
part women had played in the Services in industry and in the Resistance
Movements. There was a world-wide acknowledgement of the substantial
contribution made by women to the victory and successful functioning
of the economy of their countries. Many speakers pledged themselves to
initiate measures in their own country to improve the status and opportunity of their women. We must sincerely hope that the recognition of

the contribution of women to the victory of the United Nations will not be confined to flattering words and empty phrases. Women had to share equally in the trials and tribulations of war, invasion, occupation, liberation, they now want equal status and opportunity, and there is no reason why they should not get them. The subjection of women is part of Fascism. We remember that among the first things the Nazis did were to take the vote away from the women and to dismiss them from all positions of authority and importance. Until discrimination against women is eradicated, we cannot claim to have eradicated Fascism.

Another very important Commission—the setting up of which should be considered by those interested, is a Commission on 'Unemployment'. Such a Commission would provide effective machinery for the co-operation of the Trade Union Movement and the United Nations Organisation, and would also assist in putting into effect the policy of full employment and rising standards of living to which all members of the United Nations Organisation are pledged.

After the Conference ended I had an extremely interesting two months in the United States and Canada. I met a number of Senators, members of Congress, judges and leading men and women in the Trade Union and social welfare circles. I addressed meetings in various cities and did a number broadcasts.

In the United States, the Trade Union Movement is split into two competing bodies, the American Confederation of Labour and the Congress of Industrial Organisations. Neither body has any political affiliations. There is no Labour Party in the United States, and the Trade Union Leaders do not encourage the formation of one. They believe their most effective weapon to obtain better conditions and protect their members to lie in their bargaining strength. There is a considerable amount of good feeling and co-operation between the rank and file of these two bodies, but the leadership is often in opposition. However, on a number of recent occasions, they have made joint recommendations to the Labour Department so there is hope in some quarters that these two important branches of the Trade Union Movement will reach a permanent basis of friendly co-operation.

I attended the State Quarterly Conferences of these Trade Union bodies. Considerable attention was paid to the need for development of post-war plans for employment. Apparently the Government had not faced this question at all, leaving it entirely to private enterprise. There were 2 million unemployed within a fortnight after VJ Day, and according to the newspaper reports last week they anticipate 10 1/2 unemployed by Christmas. I believe the plans of the Australian and New Zealand governments for the demobilisation, training and absorption of Service personnel and munitions workers are an example to the world. I have found nothing like them either in the United States or in England.

I flew to England in a flying boat via Newfoundland and Ireland. When you get here, well, you just feel proud to belong. There are streets full of gaping, bombed housed, great masses of rubble piled higher than the surrounding terraces every hundred yards or so where the fragments of the destroyed buildings have been heaped, and you are told that 25% of the houses in England have been damaged. But the people are well and cheerful, the children look splendid, the food has very little variety and the authorities must have achieved a veritable triumph of organization to keep the hilt of the nation in the good state that it is.

At meetings I have addressed, both in the United States and over here, there is the same lack of interest and knowledge about the United Nations Organisation. Some League of Nations enthusiasts are inclined to regard it as a usurper, and protagonists of a world Parliament are disappointed at its limitations. I would say that United Nations organization is a product of, and successor to the League of Nations, and is an indispensable fore-runner of a world Parliament. To have a world Parliament nations will have to surrender some of their sovereignty. No nation is prepared to do so yet, and there is no war other than by war to force them to do so. If the United Nations Organisation succeeds in achieving a solid basis for world co-operation, the nations will be more inclined to surrender powers which will make a world Parliament possible. So we can say that upon the success of the United Nations Organisation depends the ultimate formation of a world Parliament.

One word more. I believe that what took place at San Francisco makes it necessary for the governments of nations and all organizations in-terested in social and economic affairs to overhaul their policies. New horizons have been revealed. New methods and machinery are available. We must discard a pre-San Francisco approach to problems in a post-San Francisco world.

Reproduced in full.
Source: Transcript 'Calling Australia' broadcast, Pacific Service, 2 October 1945. National Library of Australia, MS 2683, Jessie Street Papers, Series 5, No. 206. By permission of the National Library of Australia.

Katharine Susannah Prichard

Tasmanian Memories, 1945

Katharine Susannah Prichard (1883–1969) maintained her commitments to political action and literature throughout a long career and was a noted public speaker on both. Born in Fiji, Prichard grew up in Melbourne and Tasmania. Her journalist father suffered from depressive illness and the family finances were strained. After a stint as a governess, Prichard left Australia in 1908 to work as a journalist overseas and achieved literary fame with her first novel *The Pioneers*. In London she met military hero Jim Throssell; they were married in 1919 and set up their home in Perth. Prichard was drawn to the ideology of the Communist Party, and her political activities included authoring polemical pamphlets, giving public lectures against war and fascism and campaigning during elections. Success in the late 1920s with the novels *Working Bullocks* and *Coonardoo*—a controversial tragedy highlighting the exploitation of Aboriginal women in the cattle industry—established Prichard's literary reputation. After a visit to Russia in the 1930s, her writing reflected a new interest in social-realist literature. As an eminent writer, Prichard was invited to deliver morale-boosting talks on national radio during World War II. In these broadcasts, she drew upon years of public speaking and political rallying to great effect. On a visit to Tasmania in late 1945 Prichard spoke warmly of her childhood, although listeners familiar with her semi-autobiographical novel *The Wild Oats of Han* would be aware how family poverty haunted those memories. She also pondered on the need for young writers to seek recognition overseas, and linked her literary work with her political belief in 'human progress'. A handwritten directive on the typescript of Pritchard's radio speech, delivered on station 7ZR on 19 October, reads: 'Publicise this as much as possible. She is Australia's No. 1 writer, and her association with Tasmania will be of interest to a very wide audience.'

It has been pleasant to visit Tasmania after so many years. Some of the happiest years of my childhood were spent in an old house on the top of a hill, overlooking Launceston. There was a Kentish cherry orchard on one side of it, and apples and apricot trees on the other, as well as rows of gooseberry bushes and currants and raspberry canes. Whenever I have smelt syringa in other parts of the world, in France, or Russia, or America, my thoughts have drifted back to the big bush which used to stand at the gate of that house in Trevallyn.

And it was there I first broke the news to my father that I intended to be a writer. I can still see him as he used to stand on the verandah, in the evening, smoking his peace pipe as he called it, and looking out over the shining river, or away to the mountains in the distance. Before that, the family had been disturbed by my ambitions to be a circus rider, or a missionary. So father took my announcement about becoming a writer with an indulgent smile.

'Oh, well', he said, 'you'll need plenty of patience and plenty of postage stamps.'

Patience, I thought would be easy to acquire. One had to be patient fishing from a rock at the Basin beyond Cataract Gorge when we went there for a picnic. But postage stamps! To a harum-scarum little girl of nine, plenty of postage stamps meant more money than I was likely to possess.

Life on the Hill, at that time, was full of delightful adventures anyhow, and I and my two brothers spent most of our days—when we weren't at school—running wild in the bush which crept up almost to our back fences.

These memories of my childhood, some of you may have read in *The Wild Oats of Han*. The story is very biographical, really. And although one critic suggested, in the quaint way critics have, that the incidents are improbable, they mostly happened as I have described.

We did run away from school to see the circus parade, and I did nearly break my neck practising to be a circus rider on the willows in the garden. And we did find that underground cave on the hillside over the Cataract Gorge. I have heard, years afterwards, that it had aroused considerable interest and was thought to have been a native burying ground.

And Commander Crawford Pascoe R.N. did come to see us when were living on Trevallyn. He was my mother's godfather, and used to tell my brothers and me how his father, who was Nelson's flag lieutenant, had hoisted the famous signal: 'England expects that every man this day will do his duty.' Cap'n Pascoe, as we called him, had made surveys of the Tasmanian and Australian coasts in the early days, too, and had wonderful stories to tell of hair-raising experiences by land and sea. Somewhere in the Cataract Gorge, there is a rock on which his initials are carved, with an anchor entwined. He carved them on day when I was with him, and I promised to see that they did not become overgrown with moss. Until we left Tasmania, I used to go, now and then, and scrape away at my old friend's initials to keep them clearly defined; but I suppose lichens and moss have hidden them by now.

Father was editor of the 'The Daily Telegraph' in Launceston. When it ceased publication, we went back to Victoria; but my first story was written before we left Tasmania. It appears on the children's page on a Melbourne weekly called 'The Sun'. Of course, I was very pleased with myself, and took it out to show father when he was smoking on the verandah, just as he had been when I told him I was going to be a writer.

He was quite proud of that first effort too; but how he laughed when I said: 'It only cost one postage stamp!'

Years afterwards, working as a journalist in London, I understood how right father had been about the need for patience and postage stamps. If I hadn't had plenty of both, by that time, I never would have overcome the disinclination of the English press, and publishers, to be interested in the work of a young, unknown Australian writer.

Before I went abroad, however, my first journalistic experiences were associated with Hobart. It was this way. I had been writing short stories and receiving small cheques for them. But father was ill and worried that he did not feel able to write his weekly letter for 'The Mercury'.

'I'll do it,' I said, in order to reassure him.

I was about twenty at the time, but didn't know anything about politics, I'm ashamed to say. Most young people understand how important it is to be politically wide-awake, these days. But I had to sit up nearly all night, studying the newspapers in order to write the neat, lively sort of paragraphs about parliamentary news my father used to write. Father wasn't well enough to read the result, so I posted it, and for several months wrestled with his Melbourne letter for 'The Hobart Mercury.' After father's death [in 1907], I wrote explaining why I had substituted for him, and received a very kindly and courteous reply. It invited me also to continue writing the Melbourne letter.

Some success with short stories and other journalistic work made it possible for me to go to London soon afterwards. At that time, it seemed necessary for a writer to win recognition overseas before people in Australia would realise that our writers had as high as standard as many in other countries. When my first novel [*The Pioneers*] won the Hodder and Stoughton prize, and messenger boys from some of the big English newspapers were sitting on my doorstep waiting for copy, I felt that I could come home and devote myself to interpretation of Australia and the Australian people. First of all because I love them, and then, too, because every part of our country seems to me to hold the stuff of great literature, in poetry, prose and the drama.

Through literature, I believe, we are able to reach all sorts and conditions of people, and stimulate their awareness of why so many lives go awry, and what we must do if we are to know the real values of living, and that inner joy and serenity which come of being in accord with great ideals of humanity, and of serving the cause of human progress.

While I have been reviving these memories of my childhood in Tasmania, it has occurred to me how much rather I would be talking of some of the splendid things you people have done to improve your way of living: giving the next generation a better chance to be sturdy, intelligent, socially conscious citizens, than ours had. Your Area Schools, for instance have created interest all over Australia, and I feel sure, will have an important effect on educational plans for the future. Your wonderful Child Welfare Centre at Sandy Bay, built by community effort, and other centres in Launceston and Burnie, indicate the progressive thought that is stirring in Tasmania, and will inevitably safeguard the well-being of all who live here.

What a repudiation of the Past these movements represent! That Past which abused this beautiful island by planting on it a system of brutal tyranny and oppression. The people of Tasmania, today, have thrown aside the shadow of the time and are facing the future with courage and enthusiasm. Already, they have made strides towards the unity and organisation which will make all our dreams of a better world come true.

Abridged.
Source: Transcript, 'Tasmanian Memories', 1945. National Library of Australia, Katharine Susannah Prichard Papers, MS 6201, Series 7, Box 12, Folder 5. By permission of the National Library of Australia.

Doris Blackburn

Woomera Rocket Range, 1947

Doris Amelia Blackburn (1889–1970) was a campaigner for peace and human rights and a practical and compassionate politician. Her early interest in feminism drew her to the Women's Political Association, but in partnership with her husband, the left-wing lawyer Maurice Blackburn, her interests extended to the labour movement, anti-conscription agitation and the Council for Civil Liberties. In 1946, as an Independent Labor candidate, she was elected to Federal Parliament for the seat of Bourke—formerly held by her husband who had died in 1944. She soon established herself as an active and principled voice on welfare, women's and family issues. In 1947 British defence needs resulted in a joint project with Australia to establish the Woomera Rocket Range for the testing of long-range ballistic missiles. Blackburn was appalled, and presented two impassioned speeches to her colleagues on 6 March and 1 May. Her arguments invoked the rights of Aboriginal communities living in the remote stretches of inland Australia and drew upon her general opposition to weapons of destruction. The first missile was launched in March 1949. Blackburn was later to visit Woomera, in South Australia, and in the 1950s was a co-founder of the Aboriginal Advancement League.

6 March:

I wish it to be quite clear that I am concerned on behalf of the Australian aborigines and also because I believe that the whole of the people of Australia must suffer because of a departure from standards of justice of which we have become accustomed to boast, the betrayal of our responsibilities, and the denial of certain principles of peace for which we have declared ourselves before the whole world.

A proposal to establish a guided weapons range has been made in that part of Central Australia which has at one of its extremes Mt. Eba and, as its terminal at the other end the Ninety Mile Beach in Western Australia. The proposal for the construction of the range has been announced as a joint venture with the United Kingdom Government. There are in the area concerned from 1,000 to 2,000 natives. We may assume as a fair estimate that there are about 1,500 natives there. That may be regarded as but a few natives; but it is worth bearing in mind that that number, although it seems small, represents nearly 5 per cent. of the total number of Australian aborigines alive to-day after 150 years of contact with the white race.

The range is intended to be 2,000 miles long and 200 miles wide. Presumably, the white people living within the limits of the range will be removed from their homes, but we must remember that the area is recognized principally as an aboriginal reserve, as the last home of the nomadic tribes who wander about in the reserve and at times go away from it only to return to it again as their natural home. We cannot but question the usefulness of a report relative to measures proposed to be taken to ensure the safety and welfare of these tribes. The range is to go through the reserves and accordingly there can be no measure of protection for the tribes who regard the land as their own, for whom it holds certain hallowed places, sacred to them even as our churches are sacred to us, their hunting grounds, and the area in which their water-holes are situated. In what way can it be possible to safeguard from 1,500 to 2,000 nomadic people from contact with the personnel of the so-called guided weapons range? How will it be possible to prevent the encroachment of military and other personnel into areas of special significance to the aborigines? How will it be possible to protect the water-holes if a projectile, even without a warhead, falls in that particular area? This land is as sacred to the aborigines as are the war memorials and cemeteries of the white man.

It has been pointed out that in the past our ignorance, indifference, and sometimes hostility, in respect of the aborigines has led to their degradation and to a decline in their numbers. Humanitarians everywhere have been appalled at the effect that European civilization has had upon native populations, not only in Australia but also in other countries. We know now that the native populations flourish only in those areas where the white man has not penetrated, and because we realize this, in an attempt to prevent further wrongs being inflicted upon them, we have made reserves available for their sole use.

The chance of natives being struck by missiles fired from the range is perhaps remote, and the serious aspect of the proposal is the effect of permitting military and other personnel to enter the areas reserved for the aborigines, the danger of interference with the native women, the possibility of lives being ruined and the desecration of tribal lands. If the range is completed no measures can be taken to ensure the safety and welfare of the women who will come into the area if a road is constructed or observation posts built. The tribes, as was found in the establishment of the Trans-Australian railway, flock in, and immediately there is a danger to them from interference. We might just as well bomb them out of existence at once. That would be kinder than disintegration of the moral and physical lives of primitive people by white men who have the habit of forgetting they are civilized.

1 May:
Today is a most appropriate occasion on which to discuss this subject. This is May Day—a day of celebration and review for labour peoples all over the world. It is also a day when we decide on what we should do and should have for greater freedom, liberty, and justice for the people. On May Day throughout the world plans for the future are made. In the past, many honorable members on this side of the House have taken part in May Day processions, celebrations and demonstrations for the liberty and freedom of the individual. Therefore, this is an appropriate day on which to remind honorable members that there are still oppressions and injustices to be overcome, that here in Australia we have a voiceless

minority, and that so far we have failed to achieve any measure of justice for those who comprise it. We should remember this when we take part in our May Day rejoicings.

Whenever this House assembles we profess to deliberate for the true welfare of the people of Australia. The means, I assume, for the whole of the people of Australia. The question has been asked: What is the attitude of the people of Australia to the proposal to establish a testing range for guided weapons in Central Australia? The people have not been consulted, and I do not believe that they would be in favour of the project if they were consulted.

Recently, a meeting was held in the Melbourne Town Hall for the purpose of discussing this proposal, I have no hesitation in saying that the people of Australia do not approve of the establishment of this range, either because of the danger that it constitutes to aboriginals, or because of the danger to Australia itself of proceeding with military measures on this enlarged scale.

[Earlier] the Leader of the Opposition (Mr. Menzies) spoke of defence secrets which could not be revealed to the Australian people. What are these secrets? Is it a secret that the objective at the western end of the range is to be Christmas Island? Is that a defence secret? If so, it is only a secret to the people of Australia, for details of the whole of this project, including the objective at Christmas Island, were published many months ago in the newspapers of the United States of America. Why should information be freely given to the people of the United States of America about an Australian project and kept secret from the people of Australia?

I say that if we are to be involved in another war the weapons with which it is proposed to experiment will be absolutely worthless. In the next war the first nation to strike with an atomic weapon will presumably be the victor; and unless we propose to use an atomic warhead on these projectiles and make them a weapon of aggression the proposal is meaningless. We have been assured that there is no intention to use atomic warheads on these projectiles. Well, that may be so, but the point is that while we may perfect the projectile without using an atomic warhead some other country may use the weapon which we perfect to carry an atomic warhead. Scientists, not only in Australia, but in other countries, are not anxious to allow the results of their experiments to be used for purposes of destruction, and there is great agitation amongst them because they fear that their efforts may be used for this very purpose.

We are not discussing the future of atomic energy; we are discussing guided weapons. Those weapons are intended for mass destruction, and I am opposed to their development in Australia in time of peace. The real issue is: Must the welfare of the individual be swamped in that of the mass? Must the wishes of the minority always be subordinated to those of the majority? And in regard to the subject under discussion, namely, the welfare of subject peoples, must they be swamped by the will of the dominant nations?

The whole issue may be stated in the question: Is preparation for war the best means of preserving peace? We appear to be dominated by the military machine—and that is a hideous admission to make after we have fought two great wars to end war. I maintain that we have committed, or propose to commit, an offence on a weaker people who cannot speak for themselves, and I maintain that in the spending of millions of pounds for war in time of peace we are doing a great disservice to the Australian people.

Abridged.
Source: *Commonwealth Parliamentary Debates*, vol. 190, 6 March 1947, pp. 435–7; 1 May 1947, pp. 1826–45.

———

Ben Chifley
The Light on the Hill, 1949

Joseph Benedict 'Ben' Chifley (1885–1951) was a former engine driver who became Labor prime minister in 1945. His predecessor, John Curtin, had died in office, weighed down by the burdens of leading his country through the Pacific War. Between them, the two leaders laid the basis for Australia's post-war Keynesian economy, with its emphasis on manufacturing, migration, social welfare and full employment led by a strong government sector. At the same time, the Communist Party was attacking the Labor Party as the stooge of the capitalists. In June 1949 communists supported a coal miners' strike, paralysing New South Wales railways and gas supplies. Both Chifley and Labor premier McGirr confronted the strikers. Eight union leaders were jailed and Chifley ordered troops onto the coalfields to reactivate the open-cut mines. To many radicals, this use of military strike breakers still stands as a signal example of Labor's betrayal of working-class rights. Ironically, this conflict was on the horizon when Chifley coined Labor's most memorable ideal, 'the light on the hill'. The phrase evoked Chifley's rejection of all-encompassing ideologies such as Marxism and avowed a kind of compassionate pragmatism, investing Labor with an almost biblical mission. The occasion was the Prime Minister's speech to the annual conference of the New South Wales ALP on 12 June 1949. 'Chiff' began by telling delegates that, while the rest of the world struggled with economic difficulties, Australia was entering a 'Golden Age' of unbounded opportunities.

In Australia, today you have what I have probably said before—the Golden Age. I am one who has had enormous faith in the potentialities of this country and, allied with that, an enormous faith in the intelligence and ability of the Australian people who work in the various industries. When

I look over the period since the war concluded, I do not think that even the Australian people realize the enormous expansion that is taking place in secondary industries and other industries, nor are they able to contemplate the confidence and faith which not only producers and manufacturers of this country but of other countries have in the potentialities of this country. That is true of American industrialists who want to bring factories or branches here. Indeed only last week we reached an agreement which will bring a new type of manufacture here. Similar arrangements in conjunction with American holders of patents and licences are being made which should be of considerable benefit.

The Commonwealth government has a programme in co-ordination with the New South Wales government, of needed public works—not scenic roads or shifting sands—but schemes absolutely desirable for the potentialities of this country to be realized. That programme of public works—schools, hospitals, hydro-electric schemes, conservation of water and a hundred and one other things—totals about £700 million. It does not include the planned expansion by private industry. Besides all that, we have a programme ready to pick up any slack which may occur in other forms of production in this country. The great difficulty is to get the technical men to draw up the plans right down to the last detail to enable the work to be gone on with. Further work is held up not for want of money, but because of lack of bricks and steel and manpower.

I make this challenge here this morning. No government in the history of Australia has ever given to private industry so much assistance and advice and help as has been given by the Commonwealth Labour government. Whether it is a matter of increased steel production at Port Kembla or Broken Hill or Newcastle, or whether it is in any other industry, no matter how small is the man or how large is the company, the doors of the government have always been open to these persons, provided that it is some desirable form of increased manufacture or new manufacture. No matter what may be said by newspapers in regard to private enterprise, I do not think that at any time in the history of Australia have people in all sections of the community been given a greater helping hand than by this government. If it be capital equipment from overseas we have tried to get it.

One of the things that has held us up is our inability to produce basic materials in this country. Again I get back to bricks, coal, steel and all things necessary, not only for increased manufacture, but for housing which is so badly needed. We have an enormous leeway to make up. A new problem is our embarkation on the policy of bringing to this country a great number of migrants. I knew when we started that programme that we would have many difficulties. Some trade unionists thought we were trying to undercut them in some way in their employment or that migrants would get jobs, when work became scarcer, which Australians should have. I give an undertaking to the trade unions and to the Labour movement that that was never intended and will not be done. If this country is to go ahead, it must have labour to produce the things we want and the population must be increased to meet the great needs of development. I ask the Labour movement to help the government in making these people feel as much at home as possible. They have come from war-torn countries. The sufferings that many of them had to bear are almost impossible to believe. When you realize that the Potsdam Agreement meant that eleven million people in Europe had to be turned from their homes and displaced and transferred to some other country; when you realize that millions in Europe today are in grievous and serious want with no future and no hope while they remain in that position; when you realize that one million children in Europe have no future; then we owe a debt to humanity to do something for them. I ask you to join with the government to help in this matter.

I mention the shortage of basic materials. It is perfectly true there may be at the moment enough toasters and electric irons, but not enough coal and steel are being produced. These are some of the basic things that are necessary not only to make things we need now but for the future development of this country. I only want to say, if representatives of the miners' organizations are here today, that I read that yesterday they made a decision to recommend a stop-work meeting. I say this to the miners: It is complete ingratitude on their part if, as a result of any decision they make, they hold up the coal production of this country at a time when their fellow-citizens—their fellow-unionists—need the thing they can produce most urgently.

Our men and women who fought and who pioneered the Labour movement back in the nineties and built it up as it is today do not need advice and assistance and policies brought from other countries. They can create their own policies, having regard to their own needs and their own necessities. I say this to the miners, realizing their desire to get improved conditions and improved facilities and amenities in the mines: Both governments have done all they could, having regard to physical limitations. It has not been a matter of financial limitations in that respect. We ask them to show some return for what has been done and what it is proposed to do by producing to the limit of their capacity because it is necessary to the lives and convenience and comfort, not of the rich, but of their fellow-workers in this community.

I have had the privilege of leading the Labour Party for nearly four years. They have not been easy times and it has not been an easy job. It is a man-killing job and would be impossible if it were not for the help of my colleagues and members of the movement. No Labour Minister or leader ever has an easy job. The urgency that rests behind the Labour movement, pushing it on to do things, to create new conditions, to reorganize the economy of the country, always means that the people who work within the Labour movement, people who lead, can never have an easy job. The job of the evangelist is never easy. Because of the turn of fortune's wheel your Premier (Mr McGirr) and I have gained some prominence in the

Labour movement. But the strength of the movement cannot come from us. We may make plans and pass legislation to help and direct the economy of the country. But the job of getting the things the people of the country want comes from the roots of the Labour movement—the people who support it. When I sat at a Labour meeting in the country with only ten or fifteen men there, I found a man sitting beside me who had been working in the Labour movement for fifty-four years. I have no doubt that many of you have been doing the same, not hoping for any advantage from the movement, not hoping for any personal gain, but because you believe in a movement that has been built up to bring better conditions to the people. Therefore the success of the Labour Party at the next elections depends entirely, as it always has done, on the people who work.

I try to think of the Labour movement, not as putting an extra sixpence into somebody's pocket, or making somebody Prime Minister or Premier, but as a movement bringing something better to the people, better standards of living, greater happiness to the mass of the people. We have a great objective—the light on the hill—which we aim to reach by working for the betterment of mankind not only here but anywhere we may give a helping hand. If it were not for that, the Labour movement would not be worth fighting for. If the movement can make someone more comfortable, give to some father or mother a greater feeling of security for their children, a feeling that if a depression comes there will be work, that the government is striving its hardest to do its best, then the Labour movement will be completely justified. It does not matter about persons like me who have our limitations. I only hope that the generosity, kindliness and friendliness shown to me by thousands of my colleagues in the Labour movement will continue to be given to the movement and add zest to its work.

Abridged.
Source: J. B. Chifley, 'For the Betterment of Mankind—Anywhere', speech delivered 12 June 1949.[45]

———◆———

Robert Menzies
Socialism Without Limit, 1949, & The Forgotten People, 1942

Robert Gordon Menzies (1894–1978) dominated Australian conservative politics and public life throughout the middle of the twentieth century. He was born in Jeparit, Victoria, and after completing law degrees at the University of Melbourne embarked on a career as a talented barrister. By 1928 he had entered State Parliament, where he enjoyed a rapid rise through the ranks of conservative politics, becoming prime minister in 1939—and that September dramatically telling the nation 'It is my melancholy duty to inform you' that Australia had entered World War II.[46] But the spell was broken in 1941 when the silver-tongued Menzies lost government to Labor's plain-speaking leader, John Curtin. Curtin put the country on a war footing by introducing government control of agriculture, industry, the workforce and the economy. Labor also laid the ground for post-war reconstruction by planning a partnership between private enterprise and a strong state sector, underpinned by a broad system of welfare. When the banks moved to block these reforms, Labor retaliated by attempting to nationalise the banks.

Menzies responded to Labor's program of dynamic socialism by forming a new Liberal Party in 1944. Five years later he regained government, primarily by using his modulated and powerful oratory to convince voters that Labor was mounting an attack on social vigour and individual freedom. He delivered his campaign launch for the 1949 election at Canterbury in Melbourne's eastern suburbs, arguing that in Australia socialism was 'an alien and deadly growth'.

When we speak of Socialism, we no longer speak of a theoretical or far distant goal. Our opponents mean business. To the limits that the Constitutional divisions of power will permit, indeed without limit if their platform plank of giving all power to the Commonwealth Parliament obtains public approval, they have determined upon 'Socialism in our time'.

Since the general election, without mandate, in defiance (in the case of banking) of the most overwhelming indications of public opinion, they have moved further along the road to the all-powerful State than all the previous Australian Labour Governments added together.

Since 1946 we have had the Bank Nationalisation Act, the taking over of more airways, Government shipping, broadcasting control, a television and frequency modulation monopoly, the announcement of nationalised medicine, advances of interest of something over £4 million to Trans-Australia Airlines. You will realize how much as been done in so short a time.

This is our great year of decision. Are we for the Socialist State, with its subordination of the individual to the universal officialdom of government, or are we for the ancient British faith that governments are the servants of the people, a faith which has given fire and quality and direction for the whole of our history for the 600 years?

This question cannot be avoided. In 1946 you could vote Labour, reasonably supposing that it was a party of reform and not of socialization. In 1949 it is clear that a Labour vote is for the Socialist objective, and nothing else.

The Canberra Socialists have recently begun to claim that their objective—'The Socialisation of industry, production, distribution and exchange'—does not mean what it says.

As, in all their literature, the objective has been printed as the *sole* objective of the Labour Party, for 28 years—ever since 1921, when it was adopted and hailed by Labour leaders as the splendid product of the teachings of Karl Marx—this recent claim is a singular confession of deceit. 'For 21 years you thought we meant what we said! We now tell you we did not'.

Menzies was also a brilliant radio performer. In 1942, while he was still in Opposition, he had given a series of thirty-eight radio talks. In the best-known of these addresses, he championed Australia's middle class as 'the forgotten people', but nonetheless the real creators of innovation and wealth. They were also the great makers of homes—a powerful moral force in the Liberal view of society. Menzies began his broadcast by ridiculing the very idea of a class war waged between the idle rich and the exploited poor. He went on:

But if we are to talk of classes, then the time has come to say something of the forgotten class—the middle class—those people who are constantly in danger of being ground between the upper and the nether millstones of the false class war; the middle class who, properly regarded, represent the backbone of this country.

We do not have classes here as in England, and therefore the terms do not mean the same; so I must define what I mean when I use the expression 'middle class'.

Let me first define it by exclusion. I exclude at the one end of the scale the rich and powerful: those who control great funds and enterprises, and are as a rule able to protect themselves—though it must be said that in a political sense they have as a rule shown neither comprehension or competence. But I exclude them because in most material difficulties, the rich can look after themselves.

I exclude at the other end of the scale the mass of unskilled people, almost invariably well-organised, and with their wages and conditions safeguarded by popular law. What I am excluding them from is my definition of the middle class. We cannot exclude them from the problem of social progress, for one of the prime objects of modern social and political policy is to give to them a proper measure of security, and provide the conditions which will enable them to acquire skill and knowledge and individuality. These exclusions being made I include the intervening range —the kind of people I myself represent in Parliament—salary earners, shopkeepers, skilled artisans, professional men and women, farmers, and so on. These are, in the political and economic sense, the middle class. They are for the most part unorganised and unselfconscious. They are envied by those whose social benefits are largely obtained by taxing them. They are not rich enough to have individual power. They are taken for granted by each political party in turn. They are not sufficiently lacking in individualism to be organised for what in these days we call 'pressure politics'. And yet, as I have said, they are the backbone of the nation.

Now, what is the value of this middle class, so defined and described? First, it has 'a stake in the country'. It has responsibilities for homes.

Second, the middle class, more than any other, provides the intelligent ambition which is the motive power of human progress. The idea entertained by many people that, in a well-constituted world, we shall all live on the State is the quintessence of madness, for what is the State but us? We collectively must provide what we individually receive.

Third, the middle class provides more than perhaps any other the intellectual life which marks us off from the beast; the life which finds room for literature, for the arts, for science, for medicine and the law.

Consider the case of literature and art. Could these survive as a department of State? Are we to publish our poets according to their political colour? Is the State to decree surrealism because surrealism gets a heavy vote in a key electorate? The truth is that no great book was ever written and no great picture ever painted by the clock or according to civil service rules. These things are done by man, not men. You cannot regiment them. They require opportunity, and sometimes leisure. The artist, if he is to live, must have a buyer; the writer an audience. He finds them among frugal people to whom the margin above bare living means a chance to reach out a little towards that heaven which is just beyond our grasp. It has always seemed to me, for example, that an artist is better helped by the man who sacrifices something to buy a picture he loves than by a rich patron who follows the fashion.

Fourth, this middle class maintains and fills the higher schools and universities, and so feeds the lamp of learning.

What are schools for? To train people for examinations, to enable people to comply with the law, or to produce developed men and women?

Are the universities mere technical schools, or have they as one of their functions the preservation of pure learning, bringing in its train not merely riches for the imagination but a comparative sense for the mind, and leading to what we need so badly—the recognition of values which are other than pecuniary?

One of the great blots on our modern living is the cult of false values, a repeated application of the test of money, notoriety, applause. A world in which a comedian or a beautiful half-wit on the screen can be paid fabulous sums, whilst scientific researchers and discoverers can suffer neglect and starvation, is a world which needs to have its sense of values violently set right.

Now, have we realised and recognised these things, or is most of our policy designed to discourage or penalise thrift, to encourage dependence on the State, to bring about a dull equality on the fantastic idea that all men are equal in mind and needs and deserts: to level down by taking the mountains out of the landscape, to weigh men according to their political organisations and power—as votes and not as human beings? These are formidable questions, and we cannot escape from answering them if there is really to be a new order for the world.

The case for the middle class is the case for a dynamic democracy as against a stagnant one. Stagnant waters are level, and in them the scum rises. Active waters are never level: they toss and tumble and have crests and troughs; but the scientists tell us that they purify themselves in a few hundred yards.

That we are all, as human souls, of like value cannot be denied. That each of us should have his chance is and must be the great objective of political and social policy. But to say that the industrious and intelligent son of self-sacrificing and saving and forward-looking parents has the same social deserts and even material needs as the dull offspring of stupid and improvident parents is absurd.

If the motto is to be, 'Eat, drink and be merry, for tomorrow you will die, and if it chances you don't die, the State will look after you: but if you don't eat, drink and be merry, and save, we shall take your savings from you', then the whole business of life will become foundationless.

Are you looking forward to a breed of men after the war who will have become boneless wonders? Leaners grow flabby; lifters grow muscles. Men without ambition readily become slaves. Indeed, there is much more slavery in Australia than most people imagine. How many hundreds of thousands of us are slaves to greed, to fear, to newspapers, to public opinion —represented by the accumulated views of our neighbours! Landless men smell the vapours of the street corner. Landed men smell the brown earth, and plant their feet upon it and know that it is good.

If the new world is to be a world of men, we must be not pallid and bloodless ghosts, but a community of people whose motto shall be, 'To strive, to seek, to find, and not to yield'. Individual enterprise must drive us forward. That does not mean that we are to return to the old and selfish notions of laissez-faire. The functions of the State will be much more than merely keeping the ring within which the competitors will fight. Our social and industrial obligations will be increased. There will be more law, not less; more control, not less. But what really happens to us will depend on how many people we have who are of the great and sober and dynamic middle-class—the strivers, the planners, the ambitious ones. We shall destroy them at our peril.

Sources (in order)
Abridged.
R. G. Menzies, 'Joint Opposition Policy—1949', 10 November 1949.[47]

Abridged.
'The Forgotten People', commercial stations 2UE in Sydney and associated stations in Victoria and Queensland, 22 May 1942, radio broadcast transcript; reprinted in R. G. Menzies, *The Forgotten People*.[48]

PART THREE

Part Three: 1950–2002

One winter's night in 1953 hundreds of Australian boys were lying awake twiddling their crystal sets. In the darkness, they were listening to a cricket commentary from faraway Lord's—and hearing the pock of the ball on willow, followed by a rattle of English applause. Australia's Keith Miller had scored his century. As those boys lost themselves in that radio signal crackling across the oceans, many of them sensed 'the tyranny of distance'. True, their Australia was linked to the world by ships, mail, aeroplanes, telegraph, radio, telephone, newsreels and films. And television was just three years away. But this barrage of communications often made Australia seem remote. The world of action, celebrity, news and power was some-where else—an enticing and frightening place known as Overseas.

In their isolation, middle Australians ached for security. Security against invasion, security against communists, security of income. And the security of a loving family home. As Prime Minister from 1949 until 1966, Robert Menzies persuaded the majority of Australian voters that these were securities that he could provide.

To wage earners, he offered the security of knowing that wages and entitlements were fixed by law and the security of knowing that, in this age of full employment, Australians could afford to buy a home—and raise a brood of kids. For the post-war world was dominated by the ideas of the English economist John Maynard Keynes. He argued that the inevitable booms and busts of capitalism could be ironed out by government control. By influencing wage levels, by spending money on large public projects at the right time and by manipulating other economic factors (such as interest rates, exchange rates and tariffs), a skilful government could orchestrate stable, economic growth—ensuring security for all. This appealing new orthodoxy committed Menzies to a level of state enterprise and social welfare that earlier conservatives—including the young Menzies himself —had vilified as socialism.

For all his anti-socialist rhetoric, Menzies adopted many of Labor's grandest plans. He oversaw the great Snowy Mountains Hydroelectric Scheme, the expansion of the welfare system and the increasing use of a system of arbitration to fix the wages and conditions of Australian wage-earners and resolve disputes. He also expanded the regime of tariffs insu-lating Australia from cheap Asian imports. At the same time, the world market was clamouring for the kind of primary resources produced by Australians, particularly minerals, wheat and wool. It was the start of the 'Long Boom'.

This was also the great era of immigration. For a fee of just £10, young Britons were encouraged to make a new life in Australia. The country also gave sanctuary to European refugees of World War II. Ship-loads of migrants from northern Europe followed. In the 1950s and 60s more ships arrived, carrying Italians, Greeks, Yugoslavs and people from the Middle East. Many were subsidized by the Australian Government. And almost all of them were white.

The official policy declared that this flood of newcomers would assimi- late into 'the Australian way of life'. The trouble was that no one was sure exactly what that meant. For all their bravado, Australians were chronically insecure about their place in the world. In 1950 the critic A. A. Phillips struck a chord of recognition when he wrote that Australians, particularly the writers, suffered from a 'cultural cringe'. Anything from overseas — especially anything from 'the Mother Country'—was bound to be superior to the nation's own efforts. This, after all, was still an overwhelmingly British Australia: 'God Save the Queen' was the national anthem; the British Privy Council was the highest court of appeal; and some Australians who had never even been abroad referred to Britain as 'home'.

In the face of this mixture of strut and cultural insecurity, many of the European migrants learnt the manners of Australia—but also stuck to their traditional ways. Migrant children took strange food to school in their lunchboxes; Mediterranean people planted olive trees and grape vines in their back yards; and new churches, synagogues and mosques were built. Some Anglo-Australians reviled the strangers as 'wogs', 'Balts' and 'reffos'. But others welcomed them, with kindly condescension, as 'new Australians'. In time, most urban Australians would come to believe that these new arrivals were enriching the culture of their cities and giving Australia the confidence to be a nation.

Anglo-Australians had greater faith in their cultural supremacy when they compared themselves with the Aborigines, many of whom lived in terrible poverty. It was argued by welfare authorities that so-called 'half- caste' children were better off living in white foster homes, away from their black families. Today, many Aborigines of the Stolen Generations, as they have come to be so tellingly termed, have painful stories of how they were forcibly removed from their families. In 1967 just over 90 per cent of white Australians supported a referendum declaring that Aborigines were full citizens. Many were expressing their faith in 'assimilation'—their con- viction that Aborigines were capable of living as whites. The reality proved to be more complex.

Menzies was often a genial fellow, but he was also a hard-faced warrior of the Cold War. He used the police and the Secret Service to persecute suspected communists and told the electorate—again and again—that the Labor Party was riddled with communist sympathizers. In fact, Labor was in turmoil. Many dyed-in-the-wool Catholics in the labour movement shared Menzies' alarm at the growing power of communists in militant trade unions. In 1955 these Catholics split from the party, forming the Democratic Labor Party. In elections, the DLP supported Menzies. And in sectarian Australia, the unthinkable was happening: Irish Catholics were backing this same man—the country's greatest Anglophile and monarchist.

Menzies shared the conviction of the United States that poverty and social inequality were the breeding grounds for unrest and revolution. He supported the United States policy to resist the spread of communism in South-East Asia and the Pacific with a combination of foreign aid and military might. In 1951 Australia, New Zealand and the United States of America signed the ANZUS security pact, under which they agreed to act together if any of the three was attacked. In their isolation, Australians had found another kind of security, to be provided by the nuclear weapons of the United States.

In 1965 the United States hurled all their fury into a civil war in Vietnam, supporting the anti-communist junta in the south. Menzies heartily approved, and he announced that Australian troops would join the fighting. Better to resist communism in the rice paddies of Asia than on the beaches of Australia—so went the thinking. So committed was Menzies to this war that he ignored a great lesson of Australian political history: he introduced conscription for military service overseas. A year later, before the pictures of misery and death in Vietnam started to appear on the TV news, old Bob Menzies bowed, and winked, and retired from public life.

This was The Sixties. Many Aussie teenagers were out of sympathy with the old men who ran the country. They were impatient with all the talk of war and the hunger for security. They scorned the old racial fears and animosities. And they turned their backs on the 'rat race' of the 9-to-5 job. These kids were riding a global wave of youth rebellion promising a new age of peace and love and rock 'n' roll. They generated a new enthusiasm for Australian culture that was to be expressed in the 1970s 'new wave' of Australian drama and the renaissance of the Australian film industry.

At the same time, a new generation of women was asserting its sexual freedom and demanding the right to control one's own body. Feminists, such as Germaine Greer, denounced the culture of 'patriarchy'. They spoke about the loneliness of suburban motherhood, about women's right to a career and, as the decades rolled on, about the need for adequate child-care and the mounting tensions between work and family life that characterised modern society.

Greer was also, as it happened, a leader of another kind of movement —the movement of talented people away from Australia. Like Barry Humphries, Robert Hughes and Clive James before her, she found the isolation and the fixation on security intolerable. Life really did need to be lived somewhere else.

Meanwhile, Labor had found Gough Whitlam—a man who could talk as persuasively as Menzies; who was as patrician as Menzies; who was a QC, like Menzies. But Whitlam spoke of the future. In 1972 he told the electors that it was time for a change. A slender majority of the electorate agreed. And, in four tempestuous years, Whitlam transformed Australia with innovations including a state-funded health system, no fees for universities, no-fault divorce, equal pay for women, government support for Aboriginal land rights, and the end of most constitutional ties to Britain.

Then the escapade collapsed in a welter of runaway inflation, grandiose miscalculations and a ruling-class determination to win back power at any cost. On 11 November 1975 the Governor-General, Sir John Kerr, sacked Mr Whitlam, appointed his Liberal opponent Malcolm Fraser as prime minister and ordered an election. The Liberals won in a landslide.

But the era of reform was not over. The former Labor Attorney-General Lionel Murphy survived for a decade as a Justice of the High Court; the federally funded Australia Council continued to nurture Australian arts; and many white Australians began to confront their own racism. The Whitlam Government had declared that multiculturalism—not assimilation—was the new ethos of immigration. What's more, the White Australia Policy was dead: migrants were no longer selected according to race. Now, with Fraser's support, this ethos of multiculturalism became a new orthodoxy in Australia. In the rapidly expanding cities of Sydney and Melbourne especially, most people seemed delighted that 'cultural diversity'—which now encompassed more recent immigrant populations from Vietnam and China—had become the hallmark of their cities.

To the astonishment of many of his supporters, Malcolm Fraser was also a stern critic of South African apartheid and a leading advocate of a world-wide boycott of that country. In the same vein, Fraser passed Aboriginal land rights legislation for the Northern Territory and the Australian Capital Territory.

But the security of the 1950s had slipped away. Britain was now largely closed to Australian exporters, with around sixty per cent of Australian exports going to the Asian region. World commodity prices were unstable. And many of Australia's subsidized industries had grown inefficient. In 1983 Australians turned back to the Labor Party, led by the charismatic larrikin Bob Hawke and then (from 1991) by his Treasurer, the suave Paul Keating. Together they ended Australia's dependency on tariffs. With the support of the trade union movement, they opened Australia to global competition, they lowered wages and they weakened the power of the centralized wage system. As Keating liked to say, Australia was now really part of Asia. Its economic and military security now depended not on insulation from its immediate geographical region but on embracing it.

Meanwhile, Indigenous activists won a major victory in 1992 when the High Court used a land claim by a Torres Strait Islander named Eddie Mabo to rule that both Islanders and Aborigines had ancient land rights, which, in some circumstances, were still valid in white law. Paul Keating welcomed the decision. He passed the Native Title Act by which Aboriginal communities living on crown land might have their traditional titles recognized. A national movement for cross-racial reconciliation was indicative of a new recognition within mainstream Australia of the disastrous legacies of colonialism on Indigenous communities, and many Australians pondered how these inequalities might be addressed.

But Keating's commitment to Asia and to Aboriginal rights roused conservative Australians to a fury. The conflict between the champions of diversity and the defenders of cultural cohesion is one of the shaping forces of Australian history. And once more, the balance between the two was about to change. In 1996 the ultra-conservative John Howard was elected Liberal Prime Minister in a landslide win. In the same election, Queenslanders elected independent candidate Pauline Hanson to the House of Representatives. Hanson spoke stridently for those Australians who wanted to distance themselves from Asia and who believed that government aid had made Aborigines a privileged minority. Hanson's glory was brief. But she gave conservative Australians the courage to speak out loud. The advance of the Aboriginal cause stalled. Asia was once again a foreign zone. And a new wave of refugees, who had entered Australia in contravention of its migration laws, were confined behind barbed wire.

On the morning of 12 September 2001 millions of Australians turned on their televisions to see a ghastly and surreal sight. A jet aircraft had plunged into one tower of the World Trade Center in New York and been swallowed up. Then a second plane had hit the other tower. In retaliation, US President Bush proclaimed a 'war on terror'. A year later, terrorists bombed a nightclub in Bali, where many young Australians were partying. In such a world, the voice of tolerance suddenly sounded very small.

Percy Spender

Australia's Centre of Gravity: Asia and the Pacific, 1950

Percy Claude Spender (1897–1985) became Minister for External Affairs following the election of the Menzies Liberal Government in 1949. Believing that Australia's 'centre of gravity' in world affairs had shifted to the Pacific and to Asia, Spender was a strong supporter of the Colombo Plan for regional co-operative economic development. He was also an early proponent of the 'domino principle'—the view that the recent communist victory in China was likely to trigger communist insurgency throughout South-East Asia. Concerned to resist this threat, Spender argued for closer defence ties with the United States. Indeed, he was instrumental in Australia's decision to sign the regional defence ANZUS Treaty with New Zealand and the USA in 1951, signalling the shift away from Australia's alliance with Britain. Spender delivered his first major speech to Parliament on 9 March 1950, staking out the key elements of Australian foreign policy for the next two decades.

The aims of Australian foreign policy are self-evident and unchanging. They are essentially the preservation of peace and our way of life. Inseparable from these aims is the closest possible co-operation within the British Commonwealth and with the United States of America and other nations friendly to the Commonwealth. Our purpose must be to determine in what ways we can co-operate in achieving our objectives, and in supporting the United Nations in its pursuit of world peace. Broad aims or objectives are, however, one thing; the ways or means employed by a nation to secure these aims or objectives are entirely different. These ways and means may change, sometimes frequently, and reflect a varying emphasis or point of view. It is this ever-fluid situation in world affairs which is the subject-matter of foreign policy.

Situated as we are in the south-west corner of the Pacific, with the outlying islands of the Asian continent almost touching our own territories of New Guinea and Papua, our first and constant interest must be the security of our own homeland and the maintenance of peace in the area in which our country is geographically placed. We could many years ago reasonably regard ourselves as isolated from the main threats to our national security. Our security, however, has become an immediate and vital issue because changes since the war have resulted in a shifting of potential aggression from the European to the Asian area, and our traditional British Commonwealth and United States of America friends have not yet completed their adjustments to the new situation.

The birth of new members of the Commonwealth, Pakistan and Ceylon and the Republic of India, the creation of new national entities in the form of the Republic of Indonesia, and the States of Vietnam, Laos and Cambodia in what was previously known as French Indo-China, are developments which have helped to shift the centre of gravity of world affairs more and more to this area. Our policy must be to ensure, to the full extent we can, that these new States co-operate with each other and with us in meeting positively and actively the new problems created in this area by the emergence of a Communist China, and by the ever increasing thrust of communism, which endeavours to ally itself, in the pursuit of its ends, with the national aspirations of the millions of people of South-East Asia. In other words, we should work with the new States, economically, commercially, and in the technical as well as the political fields, in order to maintain newly won independence. But it should at all times be stressed that here, in this part of the world, we are faced with special problems, and it is to a solution of these problems that our attention should primarily be directed.

It is essential to have at the back of all our thinking—indeed unless it is constantly kept before us any conduct of foreign policy will be utterly unreal—the broad global picture and the struggle which has developed since actual hostilities ceased, between the western democracies and other nations that follow the democratic tradition on the one hand, and on the other the Soviet Union and the eastern European and other countries over whose foreign policies the Soviet Union appears to exercise effective control. That struggle has divided Europe and Asia in such a way as to impede, if not make impossible, the achievement of conditions of peace and stability throughout the world. It has prevented the normal flow of communication and information between different areas of the world. It has precluded those personal contacts which can help to overcome suspicion and mistrust. It has stemmed the regular course of trade and so directly and adversely affected the living standards of the peoples of Europe and Asia. It has held the world in a trance of uncertainty, doubt and fear.

Up to the present the main focus of the conflict between democracy and communism has been Europe. But a situation that is in essence no different from that in Europe is now developing throughout Asia and the Pacific. There are, in fact, good grounds for thinking that the success of the western democracies in presenting and holding a firm front against communism in Europe has been partly responsible for the increased interest shown by the Soviet Union in fostering the spread of communism in Asia. The dominating fact is that China, with the largest population of any country in the world, has come, in recent months, almost completely under the control of a government which is Communist in form. This has fundamentally changed the whole picture in Asia. The task of restoring, after the Japanese invasion, political and economic stability in areas that are of most direct importance to the future welfare of Australia, has increased immeasurably. To the south of China lies a group of States, all of them endeavouring to improve their material well-being. Many, if not most of them, are anxious to work in co-operation with those western countries from which they have inherited a tradition of modern democratic government. Up to the present the efforts of international communism to control and direct the new spirit of nationalism in these countries have met with very limited success. But each of these countries has its own internal Communist problem, and Communist groups throughout the whole of South and South-East Asia can be expected to take fresh heart from the success of their brethren in the vast neighbouring country to the north.

Above all, we shall watch closely for evidence of China's interference in the affairs of the neighbouring state of Vietnam. Honorable members will know something of the bitter conflict that has raged in Vietnam, since the end of the war, between the French authorities and the Communist-dominated Vietminh, and that has gravely disrupted the life of the territory. There are supporters of the Vietminh who claim that many of its leaders are not Communists but genuine nationalists who desire nothing more than an independent Vietnam. It is possible that they may wish to follow the lead of Tito in resisting domination by Moscow or Peking. Whether this is so or not, it is an incontrovertible fact that their unchallenged leader, Ho Chi-minh, received his political training in Moscow. It is certain that if the Vietminh were to overrun the whole country the present Government of Vietnam would be replaced by a régime scarcely distinguishable from other Communist satellite governments. This is the great present danger point in the South-East Asian area. Should the forces of communism prevail and Vietnam come under the heel of Communist China, Malaya is in danger of being outflanked and it, together with Thailand, Burma and Indonesia, will become the next direct object of further Communist activities.

We are indeed a Pacific power. But it must never be forgotten that only our eastern coastline faces the Pacific Ocean. We have deep and far-reaching interests in the Pacific. We have similar interests, strategic and otherwise, in the South and South-East Asian area. No nation can escape its geography. That is an axiom which should be written deep into the mind of every Australian. Even though our cultural ties have been and will remain preponderantly with Europe, there is nothing we can do to alter our geographical position. We live side by side with the countries of South and South-East Asia, and we desire to be on good-neighbour terms with them. Above all, it is in our interest to foster commercial and other contacts with them and give them what help we can in maintaining stable and democratic governments in power, and increasing the material welfare of their peoples. In doing so we take the long view. We will be helping to provide them and ourselves with the best defence against the effective penetration of Communist imperialism.

As regards Australian New Guinea it is our duty to ensure that it is administered and developed in a way best calculated to protect the welfare of the native inhabitants and at the same time to serve Australia's security interests. New Guinea happens to be the largest and most important of these island areas that are of direct concern to us. But in the same way we cannot be passive observers of any developments in Timor, the New Hebrides and New Caledonia that might have unwelcome consequences to Australia. But that is negative. We are prepared positively to join with the governments of these countries in arrangements of mutual economic and security benefit. There is no question of interference in the affairs of others; it is simply a matter of common prudence and mutual co-operation.

There is no simple and magic cure for the grave ills which have developed in the post-war world. All of us, however, must proceed to live our lives and to carry out our responsibilities in the faith that, if we honestly pursue those objectives which we believe have lasting value, we shall succeed in the task of maintaining them and spreading their influence. The experience of two world wars has shown that authority which depends on force alone rests upon hollow foundations if it is not sustained by honesty of purpose, and a recognition of the value of individual human beings. If from time to time the task ahead of us may seem almost insuperable, we should do well to remember that the empire of a dictator, whose authority depends, not upon persuasion and sympathetic popular support, but solely upon force, rests in the last resort upon such insecure foundations that it may fall to the ground and be shattered with the same speed with which it was established.

One part Australia, along with other countries similarly placed, can play is to emphasize that countries and peoples are too dissimilar to expect harmony and easy agreement on all, or even the more important, questions. This is frequently forgotten in the constant recriminations and counter-recriminations which characterize present international relations. It cannot too often be emphasized that there are very great technical, apart from other, difficulties in working out ways in which two different economic and political systems can live side by side. So far, we have not come face to face to work out these difficulties. What contact there was during the war has been severed. We grow day by day further apart, and further, therefore, from a solution of the problems of living together. This drift must be arrested. I believe that if we are steadfast, it will be. Man, a civilized, rational being, is bound to seek means to escape his own destruction.

Abridged.
Source: *Commonwealth Parliamentary Debates*, vol. 206, 9 March 1950, pp. 621–40.

———◆———

William McKell

Citizenship: The Australian Way of Life, 1951

William John McKell (1891–1985) was a boilermaker and a union activist who became Labor Premier of New South Wales in 1941. He developed into a pragmatic and seasoned politician, notable for winning support among rural voters and for his commitment to water and soil conservation, and to national parks. In 1947 Prime

Minister Ben Chifley appointed McKell to the position of Governor-General, provoking a storm of controversy: after all, McKell was Australian, working-class and a Labor premier! McKell rode out the storm with his customary political acumen. Australia had launched an ambitious immigration scheme, opening its borders to migrants from Britain and Europe. On 22 January 1951 McKell opened the Jubilee Citizenship Convention in Canberra. His speech reinforced the view that migrants, especially 'new Australians' of non-British origin, should assimilate to a distinctively Australian way of life. But he also called on 'old Australians' to show understanding to the new arrivals, foreseeing that they brought with them cultures that would one day enrich the nation.

The great immigration project upon which we are now firmly embarked is undoubtedly one of the most constructive and notable events in the history of Australia. Immigration means the development of our resources, the strengthening of our security and defences and the rapid expansion of our population, while to hundreds of thousands of people in the United Kingdom and Europe, it means the opportunity to live a new life in Australia.

Australia, in her immigration programme, is not only benefiting herself; she is helping in a real way to relieve acute population problems in Europe. Australia is today offering a haven to many of the victims of the war. In her reception of displaced persons she has played a leading if not the leading role amongst all nations of the world.

One hundred years ago, in 1851, the discovery of rich gold fields in Australia led to an inrush of hundreds of thousands of people in search of that precious metal. It has been said that the gold rush 'precipitated Australia into nationhood.' At that time our total population was considerably less than one million, our economy was dominantly a pastoral one, and Australia was a land of separate British colonies.

Only fifty years later, in 1901, the Commonwealth of Australia was formed, self-government prevailed in all the States, our economy was gradually developing a range of diverse industries, our population was approaching the four million mark, and a national culture was developing in distinctive form.

This great change in the Australian scene was very largely the result of large scale immigration, and the natural increase of the newcomers. In the thirty years 1860–1890, our population was increasing at an average rate of rather more than 3 per cent per year.

Although we have had bursts of immigration at intervals since, they have been somewhat sporadic. During the twenty years up to the resumption of immigration in 1947, our total annual population growth was only about 1 per cent. including natural increase. So the population gain by immigration was comparatively small.

Today we are once more on the march, with immigration playing the same vital role as it did during the gold-rush period. Our rate of population growth is once more exceeding 3 per cent. a year, and we are in all gaining from immigration and natural increase about a quarter of a million people a year. We can look forward with confidence to an Australian population of nine millions by 1954 and ten millions in 1958.

We are now receiving close on 200,000 migrants a year, compared with the 20,000 or 30,000 a year we were happy to obtain several decades ago. Our new settlers, both British and foreign, are coming here, not in search of gold as in earlier days, but in search of that happiness, prosperity and security which a developing Australia can offer them.

It is evidence of our progress that we are today able to accept newcomers, not only in larger numbers than ever before, but with the widest range and diversity of skills. Science, inventive genius and the industry of Australians has made us a mature society. Australia is today a highly industrialised nation as well as one of the world's principal primary producers. This growth in manufacturing capacity coupled with the demands of the great public development projects now under way, gives abundant scope for the absorption of migrants for many years to come.

The problems involved in population building are many. In the nineteenth century they were solved in a rather rough and haphazard individual way. Housing was a matter of canvas and corrugated iron, and the newcomers had, in large measure, to look after their own transport, welfare and employment.

In the present circumstances, immigration must, in a large degree, be a planned enterprise, in the interests both of the migrants and Australia. We cannot carry through successfully a project of the size of the one we are engaged upon without careful selection of assisted migrants, and the planning of their transport, accommodation, employment, education, assimilation and welfare.

It is with the assimilation of the newcomers into Australia that you and the organisations you represent at this Convention are principally concerned, and it is an indication of the change from haphazard to planned migration that for the first time in Australia's history, citizenship conventions have been called which bring together all the organisations concerned with the welfare, employment and spiritual care of the migrant.

It is true that the problems of assimilation are greater than ever before in Australia, as we are now receiving larger numbers of both British and non-British migrants than in any previous period. I have complete confidence, however, in the ability of the Australian people to solve these problems.

Concurrently with its growth in national status, Australia has been working out during the last hundred years a distinctive culture and way of life, which, while sharing fully the traditions and way of life of the great British family of nations, has its own characteristics. In the nineteenth century period of rapid growth, a sense of 'mateship,' fair play, independence of spirit and self-reliance was engendered which forms a vital part of our tradition of nationhood.

It is these qualities, which are amongst the best in the Australian character, that we must seek to pass on to the newcomers. By a wise handling of assimilation our migrants will not only conform to our standards of citizenship, but will add their own contribution. There will be give and take; assimilation will be a two-way process, demanding much of both the migrants and ourselves, and the result will be mutual enrichment. For the migrants are bringing to Australia not only the benefits of their knowledge and skills, but of their age-old cultures. The old and new should blend into a better and more varied community of people.

These will not be easy tasks, however; they demand great qualities of tolerance and imagination on the part of both native-born and new Australians. We have to extend this understanding particularly to those of the newcomers who settle here with backgrounds of upheaval, war and distress, so different from our own.

I commend these problems to your earnest consideration, and in formally declaring this Convention open wish you every success in your deliberations.

I would ask you now to stand with me for a few moments in silence whilst we seek Divine guidance on your important work.

Reproduced in full.
Source: Commonwealth Jubilee Citizenship Convention, *Report of Proceedings*, Department of Immigration, Canberra, 1951, p. 8.

H. V. Evatt

Banning the Communist Party, 1951

Herbert Vere 'Doc' Evatt (1894–1965) was at the end of a brilliant legal career when he became leader of the federal Labor Party in 1951. A barrister who specialised in civil liberty cases, in 1930 Evatt became the youngest judge ever appointed to the High Court, where he gained a reputation for his sharp intellect and compassion. In 1940 he entered federal politics, serving as attorney-general and Minister for External Affairs in the wartime government of John Curtin. During 1948–49 he was president of the United Nations General Assembly. When Labor was toppled from power in the 1949 federal election, Liberal Prime Minister Robert Menzies assumed sweeping powers to outlaw communist organizations, confiscate their property and exclude communists from key jobs. Civil libertarians were alarmed. The new law was retrospective; it placed the burden of proof on the people it targeted; and it gave the government the power to punish people not for what they did but for what they believed. Menzies justified these tough measures on the grounds that Australia was literally 'at war' with communists who owed their allegiance to the Soviet Union. But when his Communist Party Dissolution Act was challenged, the High Court ruled that there was no war and that the government had exceeded its powers. The law was invalid. Menzies retaliated by announcing that he would hold a referendum to alter the Constitution. Doc Evatt was to head a very lively public campaign against the referendum, which was held in September 1951. By a slender majority, the people refused to give Menzies the new powers he demanded. On 10 July, Evatt, who had led the original challenge in the High Court, detailed his objections to the proposed law in parliament.

Once this matter is fully explained to the people of Australia I believe that they will not support such a proposal. The tragedy is that this measure is being put forward by a Government part of which at least calls itself liberal. But the bill authorizes action which is the very antithesis of liberalism. None of the great Liberals of Britain would consider such a measure for one moment. Even to-day no party in the House of Commons, and I do not believe a single member, would endorse such a proposal. Liberalism stands for the proceedings of justice and the due processes of law. The great framers of the American Constitution had in mind the struggles of the British people towards freedom, and their various constitutional victories, when they framed their own Constitution. They therefore included safeguards in the American Constitution against such attacks upon the freedom of the people. It is a sad and tragic thing that a Liberal Government should sponsor such a measure in this century. It is being done despite the fact that the existing laws of Australia provide fully for the prosecution and punishment of every form of sedition including seditious activities, enterprises and conspiracies. If the Government believes that it should proceed against the Communist party and have it declared unlawful, there is a provision in the Crimes Act to deal with the matter.

The Government could take proceedings to-morrow in a Supreme Court or in the High Court of Australia for a declaration that the Communist party or any of its auxiliaries is an unlawful association because it advocates the overthrow of the Constitution by force or violence. It may well be asked why the Government has not used that power. Why does it want the Parliament and the Executive to do what a court is already empowered to do? One reason may be that when proceedings are taken under the Crimes Act the facts must be brought before the court. It must be proved by evidence that the people in question advocate the overthrow of the Constitution by force or violence.

The *Oxford English Dictionary* defines communism as—

> *A theory which advocates a state of society in which there should be no private ownership, all property being vested in the community and labour organized for the common benefit of all members; the professed principle being that each should work according to his capacity and receive according to his wants.*

'Communist' would have a similar meaning. Therefore, it is possible that members of many political and economic groups might be caught up in the definition of 'Communist'. It would be a matter for the court to interpret, and the court would not be bound by any definition given by the Parliament on another occasion. That raises the question whether there is not a far more sinister purpose lying behind these proposals of the Government. Why does the Government need these powers now that the act has been rejected by the court? I say that any person who believes in socialism could be brought within the scope of this definition. The Prime Minister, in his 1949 policy speech, referred to the Labour party, and said that he was going to make war on socialism. By that he meant that he would make war on the Labour party.

[Government Supporters.—Hear, hear!]

My point is proved by the 'Hear, hears!' which have come from Government supporters. Apparently they do not dissociate the Australian Labour party from socialism. Therefore, this definition would be broad enough to cover the activities or membership of the Australian Labour party. If these powers are granted to the Parliament there will be no barrier in the way of those who wish to extend the reach of measures such as the one that the court rejected, to ensure that organizations like trade unions, labour groups and the like, will be caught up by them. As a matter of fact no reference has been made by the Prime Minister to the necessity for this measure, and not a single argument has been adduced in support of it.

When one turns to the objectives of the Australian Labour party one sees that it proposes socialization or social control to the extent necessary to eliminate exploitation. There is enough in that to justify the Parliament or the Government, if it were so minded, to attack trade union activities and the political activities of the Labour party. The Government or the Parliament will be the judge of what is necessary or expedient. That would be an extraordinary provision to find in a constitution. Usually an act of parliament contains principles and sometimes a regulation-making power.

Here there is a provision that the power to make laws shall be determined by what the Parliament considers to be necessary or expedient for the defence or security of the Commonwealth. That is completely opposed to, and overrides, the High Court. Therefore, it overrides the Constitution, because the basis of the federal constitution is an independent court which may determine whether the acts of the Australian Parliament fall within its power under the Constitution. Now, it is proposed that instead of the High Court being the arbiter, the Parliament should place itself in the position of the court. The High Court will not make the decision on the matter dealt with in this measure; the decision will be made by the Parliament. Moreover, there is no provision for appeal, and no constitutional challenge to the dragnet powers of the Government. Without using any legal process, the Government could take action against any persons who belonged to the group mentioned or who subscribed to the theory mentioned. It would be subject to no restraint whatever.

This bill bears no semblance of liberalism. It is extreme reactionary conservatism. Indeed, it is more than that. It is totalitarianism. It is fascist in spirit and a definite step towards the police State. It will cut a link between this country and the basic features of British law and jurisprudence. When we are considering amending the Constitution, we must remember that any alteration that may be agreed to will not die with the life of one parliament but will become a permanent alteration, unless a further change be made after a referendum. It is most important to consider a proposed alteration of the Constitution as something enduring, and intended not to deal with a momentary problem of a government, but to be enshrined permanently in the Constitution. This alteration, if made, will be regarded as a blot upon our Constitution and upon the records of all who sponsored it.

We believe that if a Communist commits acts of sabotage or engages in seditious enterprises, he should be dealt with under the ordinary criminal law. That is the principle upon which Labour governments have acted. When Communist threats were made to hold up work on the guided missiles testing range [at Woomera], a Labour government secured the passage of the Approved Defence Projects Protection Act, which prescribed criminal penalties for any boycott of defence projects. No attempt was made to give the Executive special powers to deal with those threats, and the matter was left to the courts of justice. The Approved Defence Projects Protection Act was 100 per cent effective, and no further similar threats were made.

When some Communists attempted to sabotage production in this country by fomenting a general coal strike in 1949, a Labour government secured the passage of the National Emergency (Coal Strike) Act. Offenders against that measure were convicted according to the ordinary processes of law, not for being Communists but for disobeying court orders. Offending trade unions were also dealt with on the same principle. When a Communist leader in Australia talked about welcoming a foreign army that might land on these shores, a Labour government invoked the existing Crimes Act against him, and he was tried before a jury. In other similar cases, some men were convicted and others were acquitted.

The Government has in its hands, in the shape of the Crimes Act, a weapon that it can use against such a person, but it appears not to be worried whether crimes have been committed. It wants to proceed against certain individuals because they hold particular political ideas, either alone or in common with others. We say that mere ideas or beliefs do not enter into the picture, and that what matters is what a man does or attempts to do. We say that no man should be convicted, or deprived of civil rights, merely because he holds certain beliefs, any more than that he should be allowed to justify the commission of some crime on the ground that he held such beliefs. It is not the beliefs but the crime that matters.

In this great democracy the people are being asked to adopt totalitarian methods in order to defeat the totalitarian doctrine of communism. For those reasons we shall urge the people of Australia to reject these proposals. We believe that they are retrograde. The Government, apparently, believes that it can establish a dictatorship over ideas. It is not content, as it should be, with dealing with specific criminal acts of sedition or conspiracy. To ban political groups or to disqualify their members from civil rights on mere government declaration without proof of overt acts, or of specific crimes, without a hearing or without a charge, would in all instances be tyrannical and unjust. Such action can never be justified under the conditions that exist in this country. To support an alteration of the Constitution as we are now asked to do would be to become a party to tyranny and injustice. The Australian people should therefore be asked to reject the measure and to refuse to put a fascist and totalitarian blot on their Constitution.

Abridged.
Source: *Commonwealth Parliamentary Debates*, vol. 2313, 10 July 1951, pp. 1216–23.

———

Bill Harney
The Dreamtime and the Modern World, 1951

William 'Bill' Edward Harney (1895–1962) was an experienced Queensland bushman who joined the Native Affairs Department as a patrol officer in 1940. Over the next twenty years he established a national reputation as a storyteller, a home-spun philosopher and an expert on Aboriginal culture. During this time, many white Australians began to see Aborigines no longer as the doomed relics of 'the stone age' but as a deeply spiritual people, with powerful connections to 'the Dreamtime'. Harney's published writings, including his collections of Aboriginal stories, contributed to this new appreciation. This sympathy for Aborigines tended to feed a belief in assimilation—the view that, since Aborigines were intelligent and creative, they were destined to abandon their primitivism and take their place in white civilization, particularly as stockmen and rural domestics. In a talk on ABC radio in June 1951 Harney gave his view of what Aborigines in the remote Northern Territory were losing and gaining in this time of change.

When the white people first met the aborigines of Australia, they didn't realise that before them were a people who had evolved a system of living in perfect harmony with their surroundings. Every water and landmark had been discovered and named. The seas, swamps, jungles, mountains, deserts and plain lands had been prospected for foods. And around the camp fires at night, the black mothers chanted to their children those myths that recorded the story of how these things came to be formed in the Dreamtime.

Each year the elders of the tribe held their sacred rituals, and by these they taught the youth of the tribe that age and knowledge are greater than force.

A perfect pattern of life in a backwash of time, but helpless against the solid wave of civilisation that crept relentlessly through them, until today we find them a shattered helpless people struggling to adapt themselves to their changed environment. And as they struggled, there arose a hundred organisations to show them the way to a better life.

The missionaries preached, societies passed resolutions and government departments directed the aborigines, who, for their part, just drifted along and held council around their camps devising various means of dodging Aboriginal Protectors and their laws. Centuries of adaptation to a hunting life had developed within the aborigines a cunning brain and an ability to hunt game by studying the weakness of the animals they needed. Useless to run down the fleet-footed emu, they poisoned the waters with the leaves from a desert tree, and the birds became easy game, as they staggered about in a drugged condition after drinking the water.

There is an old saying in the Northern Territory that 'any white man who takes the blackfellow for a fool is a bigger fool himself', and few whites will deny that the aboriginal is an important economic factor in the development and management of cattle properties in the north.

Today, two thousand black stockmen, with their wives as domestics, muster the vast herds of cattle in the Northern Territory and aboriginal drovers help their white masters drove the mobs to the markets. In every walk of life in the Northern Territory, the black man has moulded his life to our own. In the tin mines of Maranboy, the Ngulpun miners chant their ritual songs as their drills bite into the tough pegmatite dykes of that field. Over the desert lands Walpri and Arunta camel men trail their camel strings to distant destinations. On Melville Island and Coburg Peninsula the Tiwi and Uwadja axemen fell cypress pine trees for the houses of Darwin. A change of ideas meant new conditions for the aborigines, and very few of the fifty tribes in the Northern Territory live today in their original tribal areas. The towns and cattle stations attract them, and as one tribe dies away, new migrant tribes displace them. This is the tragedy of culture contact and Darwin is the greatest graveyard in the Northern Territory.

Such then is the story. But what does the blackfellow think about all this change? To them it is just 'white-fella business' as an old aboriginal friend of mine remarked to me as we sat on the beach and looked over the Timor Sea. 'We Melville Island blackfellow got name for white fellow—we call him 'Worry'. All day him worry—worry for nothing. No rain him worry —plenty rain him worry all the same. Must worry, that him business.'

And once when a superintendent of an aboriginal settlement became ill from constant worry about the blacks under his care, the aboriginals laughingly commented on the foolishness of a white man who became a nervous wreck worrying over a people who themselves rarely worry and don't care.

And this mental make-up of the aboriginal in the past was the very factor that hindered his forward movement. He simply did not care, and such sentiment about their worrying over the tribal decline was something outside his line of reasoning. For them life was real and death was, as an old dying blackfellow explained to me, 'All a same—nothing!'

Aboriginals believe in their ritual that has evolved within their pattern of life and a tribal blackman that does not believe, cannot exist. Well do I remember an old blackman of the Larrakia tribe who was a great stickler for the tribal ritual, but every Sunday he washed off his tribal marking to go to the whiteman's church. I questioned him about this and he replied, 'Blackfellow law right but I go to white man's church to make white man happy—that nothing.' Old Berber was polite but not religious.

Yet within the last ten years in the Northern Territory I have seen a change come over its black people. To them has come a realisation of their ignorance to the white man's learning and a keen desire to have their children educated as a black mother said to me 'All a same white fella fashion'. And around their camp fires at night, the white man's knowledge is discussed, and out of this talking and living in towns has arisen a new understanding.

Held to their tribal land in the past by ritual ties, and depending on white masters whose cattle grazed on their hunting area, the aborigines were helpless, but travel to towns and an interchange of ideas has broken down their fear of things outside the tribal lands. So everywhere the low murmurings of the aborigines has grown louder as courageous men of their tribes demand a new deal in this post war world. Amidst these factors, good or bad, according to one's viewpoint, arise certain facts that should be known. In the past some missions, and I emphasise *some* have maintained the kinship ties, and on these [missions] the aborigines are multiplying. The Northern Territory Medical administration maintains a flying doctor service and on every outlying station the radio station's call for help brings medical aid to black and white alike, and this year a medical patrol with doctor well versed in tropical ills will inspect natives in the Northern Territory. A difficult job for one man when one realises the superstition he must encounter, but it is the beginning, for superstition is the one factor the white doctor must overcome. By medical treatment he must combat the medicine men of the tribe who forever preach that sickness and death come from magic which only they can cure.

In the past that news of a white Doctor meant sick black people fleeing to the hills and bush before his arrival. But gradually under native welfare this ancient order of things is slowly dying away, and the black Doctors have gone off to new fields. The learning and lore of the Elders of the tribe are being helped by white teachers, who before taking up posts at native schools are now taught the rudiments of the aborigines' way of life before they go north to educate over 600 black children at eight Government controlled aboriginal settlements in the Northern Territory.

Organised education, medical assistance and child welfare are on the way and above these is the increasing demand by the union movement and organised labour that the blackworkers shall be paid according to their worth.

These are the things that are making our black people feel that at long last we Australians are helping them in their struggle to survive.

Reproduced in full.
Source: W. E. Harney, 'Black people of the Northern Territory', talk for broadcast 1 June 1951, 10 p.m., 2BL (ABC Radio); Australian Archives (NSW), Series SP36911.

Owen Dixon
Strict and Complete Legalism, 1952

Owen Dixon (1886–1972) was a wealthy son of the Melbourne Establishment whose brilliant legal career led him to the High Court bench in 1929. He was a dominant force in the Court's decisions to disallow the Chifley Government's nationalization of the banks and airlines as contravening the free trade guarantees in the Constitution. As a result, Labor politicians saw him as their judicial enemy. But in 1951 he showed his independence of mind by ruling against Prime Minister Robert Menzies' attempt to outlaw the Communist Party. Dixon had a mighty reputation among other lawyers and was considered by many contemporaries to be the greatest jurist in the English-speaking world. In 1952 Menzies appointed Dixon the sixth chief justice of the High Court. On the day of his swearing in, various luminaries gave their words of congratulation. Dixon responded with the following speech, where he referred to the 'strict and complete legalism' with which his view on legal processes had become associated. Dixon believed that it was the role of judges to interpret rather than make laws, following the legal system of precedent and avoiding any suggestion of political influence on judgments. The Rule of Law, then, upheld fairness and stability, providing certainty of social principles when it came to resolving disputes as well as supporting the individual liberty of Australia's citizens.

I am, and of course it is needless to say, deeply moved by the very generous and over-kind statements you have made about my judicial work. It is only too true that I came to the Bar a long time ago and I came to the Bench a long time ago. I have spent a little under nineteen years at the Bar and I have spent a little over twenty-three years on the Bench.

I think it is hardly useful to refer to the past except to explain the present. But my work at the Bar covered a period when I was younger and when perhaps according to the ordinary nature of man he derives greater pleasure and excitement from his activities. The activities at the Bar are greater than those on the Bench, and the responsibilities are no less. The Bar has traditionally been, over the centuries, one of the four original learned professions. It occupied that position in tradition because it formed part of the use and the service of the Crown in the administration of justice. But because it is the duty of the barrister to stand between the subject and the Crown, and between the rich and the poor, the powerful and the weak, it is necessary that, while the Bar occupies an essential part in the administration of justice, the barrister should be completely independent and work entirely as an individual, drawing on his own resources of learning, ability and intelligence, and owing allegiance to none.

The work of solicitors in the administration of justice has the greatest possible importance, but their allegiance is perhaps more to their clients who have a more permanent or at all events a longer relation with them than the transitory relations between client and counsel when the full enthusiasms and force of the advocate are attached to the individual for a short space of time.

I would like to say that from long experience on the Bench and a not much shorter experience at the Bar there is no more important contribution to the doing of justice than the elucidation of the facts and the ascertainment of what a case is really about, which is done before it comes to counsel's hands. Counsel, who brings his learning, ability, character and firmness of mind to the conduct of causes and maintains the very high tradition of honour and independence of English advocacy, in my opinion makes a greater contribution to justice than the judge himself.

The court is a co-operative institution; the position of the man who presides differs very little from that of any other judge. Perhaps he receives a little more attention from the Bar than he deserves because he announces the conclusions of the court first, but all my judicial experience tells me that a man's influence on the court does not depend on where he sits.

In saying that this represents simply the appellate tribunal and the tribunal for Federal questions in the judicial system of the Commonwealth, I do not overlook the distinction which we unfortunately maintain between State and Federal jurisdiction. That is an eighteenth century conception which we derived from the United States of America in the faithful copy which was made of their judicial institutions. It is to be hoped that at some future time it will be recognised that under the English system of law, the British system of law which we inherited, the whole body of law is antecedent to the work of any Legislature and that the courts as a whole must interpret and apply the whole body of law, so that there should be one judicial system in Australia which is neither State nor Commonwealth but a system of Australian Courts administering the total body of the law.

The High Court's jurisdiction is divided in its exercise between constitutional and federal cases which loom so largely in the public eye, and the great body of litigation between man and man, or even man and government, which has nothing to do with the Constitution, and which is the principal preoccupation of the court. Federalism means a demarcation of powers and this casts upon the court a responsibility of deciding whether legislation is within the boundaries of allotted powers. Unfortunately that responsibility is very widely misunderstood, largely by the popular use and misuse of terms which are not applicable, and it is not sufficiently recognised that the court's sole function is to interpret a constitutional description of power or restraint upon power and say whether a given measure falls on one side of a line consequently drawn or on the other, and that it has nothing whatever to do with the merits or demerits of the measure.

Such a function has led us all I think to believe that close adherence to legal reasoning is the only way to maintain the confidence of all parties in Federal conflicts. It may be that the court is thought to be excessively legalistic. I should be sorry to think that it is anything else. There is no other safe guide to judicial decisions in great conflicts than a strict and complete legalism.

The court and the legal profession stand as the necessary foundation of any community. Indeed it may be said that the courts and the system of law are both the foundation and the steel framework, but neither a foundation nor a steel framework is ever able to do more than support a structure with stability and at rest.

Lawyers are often criticised because their work is not constructive. It is not their business to contribute to the constructive activities of the community, but to keep the foundations and framework steady. Those who believe in a planned society should perceive that the rule of law administered by the courts offers a reconciliation of ordered liberty with planned control. Those who, on the contrary, believe that society is best served by giving rein to the competitive exertion of the energies of everyone in his calling or pursuit must also see that the courts must preserve the rights of each from the encroachment of the others. Between those two views there are gradations in which the court must serve the like function.

The authority of the courts of law administering justice according to law is a product of British tradition and it is for us to maintain it. There is I believe a general respect for the Queen's courts of justice which administer justice according to law, and I believe that there is a trust in them. But it is because they administer justice according to law.

It is important to maintain the prestige of the legal profession and it is important to maintain the status of the judiciary. The status of the judiciary is perhaps first and foremost the responsibility of the judges themselves. The respect for the courts must depend upon the wisdom and discretion, the learning and ability, the dignity and restraint which the judges exhibit. But there are other factors which are not within the control of the judges. We are not accustomed in Australia to administer justice in the stately edifices of other countries. We are not accustomed to accord judges the same high precedence as they are accorded in other countries.

There is in Australia a large number of jurisdictions and a confusion in the public mind as to the functions the jurisdictions possess. The character of the functions is misunderstood and the public do not maintain the distinction between the administration of justice according to law and the very important functions of industrial tribunals.

I have devoted the greater part of my life to the study and practice of the law. I come to this responsible office with an undiminished belief in the fundamental importance of the courts of justice in sustaining the whole edifice of society, and all I can say in conclusion is that I will do my best to maintain and protect their reputation and status.

Abridged.
Source: Swearing in of Sir Owen Dixon as Chief Justice, 21 April 1952; *Commonwealth Law Reports*, vol. 85, pp. xi–xvi.

A. R. Downer

An East–West Pot-Pourri?, 1960

Alexander 'Alick' Russell Downer (1910–1981), scion of a prominent South Australian political dynasty, spent over three years as a prisoner-of-war of the Japanese at the Changi camp in Singapore. In 1949 'Digger' Downer entered Federal Parliament. As Liberal Minister for Immigration between 1958 and 1963, he presided over an easing of the White Australia Policy. The notorious dictation test was abolished, and the number of non-Europeans in Australia increased. The patrician and well-mannered Downer was a skilled public speaker who could be both frank and diplomatic. On 28 July 1960 he delivered the following public lecture at Stawell Hall in Sydney, challenging the claim that Australia was culturally part of Asia. Downer was deeply loyal to Britain and the Commonwealth, and he declared that Australia's enduring European heritage was essential to its social coherence. Any sizeable influx of Asian immigrants would provoke destabilizing tensions. Rather, he argued, it was Australia's unique role to assist an interchange of values between East and West.

Today it is fashionable to say that Australia is part of Asia. Geographically, millions of years ago the two continents may have been joined, but there the nexus ends. Our population, with the exception of a fractional percentage, is European. Our racial origins are European. Our religion and ideas are European. In a more particular sense, of course, this is still a British country with many of the virtues and faults of our northern ancestors. One of the merits of the infusion of three-quarters of a million settlers from the European Continent, as distinct from the United

Kingdom, in the last fourteen years, is the possible eradication of some of our inherited, and locally acquired, defects which we exhibit in good measure.

But those who would classify Australia with Asia confuse a state of being with an object of policy. Part of our destiny may well be with Asia; if so, we must fulfil it spiritually, unselfishly, with shining enlightenment. There is some evidence that we possess personal characteristics which will enable us to serve as a more acceptable interpreter of European ideas than Europeans themselves; there is a mutuality of interest in many of our aims; there are features of our respective economies which make them complementary. These things may enable Australia to act as a bridge between East and West. This I believe we can do, and if we can construct it, it will stand as the most glorious achievement, so far, in our history. But the essence of our role will be that of a rather novel interpreter of Anglo-European ideas, institutions, and a manner of life, and likewise in reverse between Asia and Europe. The measure of our success will be the influence, through our Australian idiom, that our contacts will bring.

How far would this role of go-between be advanced by abandoning our immigration policy of the past sixty years in favour of an intermixture of Asian and European peoples within our own continent? I do not propose to discuss this controversial matter at any length tonight, for it is a subject in itself; but in this particular context I think the disadvantages would outweigh whatever good might flow from such a revolutionary change of attitude. The experience of countries where racial intermixtures have been tried is not encouraging. The United States has still not solved her Negro problem; the story of South Africa has stilled to be played out, but meanwhile there is a warning to us in the predicament of the unhappy country which elementary state-craft demands that we heed here.

I do not believe that Australians, certainly at this stage of their development, either desire or are ready for, an East-West pot-pourri. Indeed, on the basis of other nations' experience, and from my knowledge of the temperament of our own people, there is strong possibility that an inflow of Asians would defeat the very object of our foreign policy towards our Asian friends. Instead of relieving misunderstanding it would provoke tensions. It would create internal social problems which fortunately we have hitherto escaped. These in time would engender animosities which would ripple sensationally throughout every country from Arabia to Japan. Instead of enabling us to fulfil our mission, it could prevent us from carrying it out. The growing interest and understanding of our Asian neighbours might well become stunted by intolerance and bitterness.

Despite the intellectual attraction of some of their arguments, the advocates of either partial or radical change in our Asian migration policy never appear to me to make out a convincing case. Without wishing to appear complacent I believe that both Australia's national growth and our international relations will best be served by continuing our present policies. For they observe well-tried principles of homogeneity, readiness of absorption, familiarity of religion, the same fundamental attitudes to living. Above all, the thought processes of the people we seek to attract are, if not the same, at least in tune with ours. This is a characteristic which I would stress, for in our contemporary world perhaps the highest barrier between people of other nationalities and races is mental understanding.

Abridged.
Source: The Roy Milne Lecture for 1960, Stawell Hall, Sydney, 28 July 1960, reproduced in Kenneth Rivett (ed.), *Immigration Control or Colour Bar?*[49]

———◆———

Bernard Smith
The Myth of Isolation, 1961

Bernard William Smith (1916–) is Australia's most influential art historian whose criticism has probed into issues of Australian culture and identity. In 1961 Smith's left-wing nationalism was provoked by the landmark 'Exhibition of Recent Australian Paintings' held at the Whitechapel Gallery, London. Several London critics declared that the show demonstrated the cultural 'isolation' of Australian painters—sometimes with pleasing results. They lifted this idea from a catalogue essay, written by the precocious young Australian critic Robert Hughes. Hughes had asserted that Australian painters worked in 'complete isolation from the Renaissance tradition, and, parallel with that, a similar isolation from most of what happens now in world art'. But Smith denounced this notion as a ridiculous if commonplace myth. When Australian artists neglected European practice, he argued, they were not acting out of provincial ignorance. They were committing a conscious act of rejection. In fact, he said, in the high summer of Australian nationalist painting Australian artists were in frequent contact with the European centres. Smith was a polished public speaker, with a distinctively learned and lively style, and expounded his ideas in the John Murtagh Macrossan public lecture given at the University of Queensland.

Between 1885 and 1900 there was a constant coming and going of artists between Sydney, Melbourne, Paris and London. Artists overseas maintained links with their friends here by correspondence. Roberts, for example, continued to write to John Russell, the Sydney artist who became a close friend of Vincent Van Gogh when they were fellow students together in Fernand Cormon's studio. Russell discussed painting techniques, among other things, in his letters. I suspect that other Australian artists in Paris during the 'eighties did likewise: Bertram MacKennal, G. Douglas Richardson, Phillips Fox, Walter Withers. It would be surprising, surely, if none of these artists saw French impressionist paintings during their years in Paris. Nonetheless the Heidelberg painters did not embrace that interest in colour science and divisionist techniques adopted by the French impressionists. This is sometimes used to prove that the Heidelberg school was ignorant of French impressionism. I doubt this. I think it more likely that they adopted one half of the impressionist programme and rejected the other. How many French painters resident in Paris had adopted divisionism before 1890? Only a small minority. And the reason? Not isolation but rejection: the impressionists were avant-garde. Indeed I would suggest that if one is endeavouring to assess just what is individual, what distinguishes the work of the Heidelberg school from work being done in England and France at this time, the key is to be found in the acceptance of some aspects of the impressionist programme and not others. Acceptance without question is the essence of provincial-ism: the colonial painters accepted picturesque and romantic conventions without question. An indigenous tradition, on the other hand, not only assimilates, it also rejects. Indeed it must exercise choice if it is going to be more than a pale imitation of the metropolitan culture to which it is affiliated.

Even so, by 1900 most of the founders of the Heidelberg School found the claims of Europe and tradition greater than the claims of Australia and nationalism. 'After the Genesis', wrote William Moore in 1905, 'came the Exodus'. For Australian art the first decade of the twentieth century was the time of the Edwardian expatriates. Most of them remained overseas in London or Paris for twenty years; some, like Rupert Bunny, were away for over forty. They all became closely associated with the academic and conservative tradition of the time embodied in the Royal Academy and the Paris Salons: and they rejected the modern movement to a man. The myth of isolation is frequently invoked here too, in order to explain what occurred. It has been claimed that they had little knowledge of the *École de Paris*. But in the case of the Edwardian expatriates it was not isolation but a wholesale rejection of the modern movement that occurred. We know, for example, that Roberts, Lambert, George Bell and others saw the first Post-Impressionists exhibition in London, organized by Roger Fry at the Grafton Galleries in 1910. They thought it a joke. 'I think it's a real gag and very amusing', wrote Roberts to Alfred Deakin. Indeed they held, George Bell has informed me, a little comic post-impressionist show of their own at the Chelsea Arts Club. In Paris, likewise, Australians such as Rupert Bunny and Max Meldrum had ample opportunity to witness the growth of fauvism, cubism and the beginnings of abstract painting. Again it was not isolation but rejection that occurred. Even Bunny, who enjoyed Van Gogh and Gauguin and was the least antagonistic to the modern movement was very cautious. 'I cannot', he remarked when he visited Australia in 1911, 'consider Matisse anything but a humbug'.

After the First World War the Edwardian expatriates all came back; howling reactionaries almost to a man. Of that generation only George Bell in his mid-forties experienced a change of heart and came to understand Cézanne, and what sprang from Cézanne; and in the 1930s, through his teaching, his press criticism and the art societies he founded, Bell became the leader of modern art in Australia. But, if the rest of Bell's generation were reactionary we cannot in truth assert, at the same time, that they were isolated from Renaissance tradition. Indeed, they saw the modern movement as an attack upon that tradition. And who will say they were wrong? Certainly, the modern movement in art springs from one of the deepest qualities in European art, an abiding interest in experiment and change, a quality that goes back to the Greeks. But the champions of the modern movement in Europe attacked Renaissance tradition. They attacked, for example, the search for an ideal harmony in pictorial composition, which Renaissance artists had inherited from Platonic thought, in favour of personal expression. True, something of these ideals lingered on in geometric abstraction, but the individualism at the heart of modern art has been against it; and in recent years the Renaissance heritage lingering on in geometric abstraction has been overwhelmed by the more expressive and romantic forms of abstraction: tachisme, abstract expressionism, action painting, and so forth.

Furthermore, the modern movement attacked that central achievement of Renaissance art, the creation of an illusory world by linear perspective, and the manipulation of tone and colour. With cubism the picture became autonomous, possessing its own construction, its own space and colour, like a building or a jewel. Again, the Renaissance painters were responsible for inventing and perfecting two of the basic categories of European painting: the portrait and the landscape, and that important mixed category, the landscape with figures. Modern art has blurred these categories, because they have become of less importance to its central doctrine, the work of art as a thing in itself. For both portraiture and landscape are, of course, essentially mimetic; categories developed for the purpose of representing man and nature.

Following their return to Australia, the Edwardian expatriates dominated art and art criticism in Australia during the period between the wars. The expatriates became patriots, became trustees, directors of galleries, art critics, and received official honours; became, in short, the Establishment in painting. During this period Australia was indeed isolated, not from Renaissance tradition, but from contemporary art and thought in Europe. It was not so much isolation however but *isolationism* which operated, a conscious endeavour on the part of the Establishment to cut Australian art off from the influence of the contemporary movement. Exhibitions from Europe virtually ceased. Indeed between 1923 and 1932 I do not know of any significant exhibition, academic or modern, to reach Australia, whereas during the 1880s and 1890s they had been fairly frequent.

But the isolationist attitude of the 1920s is not, in itself, a sufficient reason for our lack of contact with the contemporary movement. The First World War is probably more important. Sixty thousand dead and 226 000 casualties was not a small proportion of the young men of a nation of less than 5 million people. For those who survived the war and wished to turn to art, training was not so easy to come by as after the Second World War. And those of the war generation who did complete an art training were in no position to influence taste in art until the 1930s. This becomes clear if one studies the biographies of artists like Sir Daryl Lindsay and Rah Fizelle who were in service during what in normal times might well have been their student years. It is, I believe, no accident that during the 1920s and much of the 1930s women artists played a greater part in forming contemporary taste in Australia than they have before or since: Norah Simpson, Grace Cossington Smith, Margaret Preston, Thea Proctor, Daphne Mayo, Grace Crowley, Vida Lahey, Dorrit Black—the list is a long one. It is at least a reasonable speculation, surely, that had there been no war a student body who had made direct contact with fauvism, cubism and abstract art, would have come back from their art studies in Paris and London and that this generation would have produced leaders able enough to challenge the ideals and authority of the Edwardian generation. But in the event that authority was not seriously challenged until 1939, the year the Second World War began, and the first large exhibition of contemporary and British modern art was shown in Australia.

But if we accuse the established artists of the 1920s of isolating Australian art from the revitalizing effects of the modern movement, we cannot in truth also accuse them of isolating us from Renaissance tradition. Rather the reverse. The artists and critics who fought the crucial battle for the recognition of contemporary art here inherited a situation in which Renaissance tradition was strongly entrenched. You may call it a debased and degraded tradition or a fine one according to your taste, but it was certainly there: perspective and tonal illusionism taught by Hall and Meldrum in their influential schools in Melbourne; and the Renaissance categories, portraiture, landscape, and landscape with figures remained intact. Now it was within these very categories that the most significant achievements of Australian painting during the 1940s and most of the 1950s were to be realized. Indeed it was not until the years 1956–57 that the last vestiges of Renaissance tradition began to disappear in the experimental work of a group of Sydney painters influenced by the more informal types of postwar abstraction.

If my reading of the record is correct then the history of Australian painting since 1880 is precisely opposite to that which the Whitechapel Catalogue and many London critics are today confidently asserting. Australian art has always been highly conservative in its movement and growth, and testifies to a survival of Renaissance tradition. The waves flow outwards. Astronomers tell us that if we are only far enough away from them it is possible to see the light of the dead stars.

It is clear at least that today, in London, Australian art is being interpreted as if it were an exotic art, as an art standing outside Renaissance tradition. But it is not. And that to my mind is the most interesting thing about its reception. The hands are the hands of Esau but the voice is Jacob's voice. Has the wave begun to flow back? It is impossible to say and foolish to prophesy. But I could not agree more with Mr Hughes when he writes: 'To think of Australia as a *jardin exotique* is a fashionable way of missing the point, for to its painters it is not an exotic garden. It is the place where we live.' But it is also a place where Renaissance tradition has lived.

Abridged.
Source: 'The Myth of Isolation', the first of two John Murtagh Macrossan Lectures, University of Queensland, 1961; first published in Bernard Smith, *Australian Painting Today, The John Murtagh Macrossan Lectures*, University of Queensland, St Lucia, 1962.[50]

Robert Menzies
The Royal Tour, 1963

Robert Menzies led the Liberal Party to a triumphant victory in 1949. While the Labor Party fragmented in ideological disarray, Menzies held the prime ministership in magisterial style until he resigned in 1966. His anti-socialist rhetoric proved an effective weapon against Labor. Nevertheless, Menzies maintained Labor's welfare state, expanded education and built national prosperity behind a massive wall of tariff protection. He not only won votes with his ruthless prosecution of the Cold War; he also appealed to a popular sentimentalism for an Empire that was swiftly fading into the past. When Menzies welcomed the young Queen Elizabeth to Australia during her Royal Tour in 1963, he could scarcely contain his ardour, although his sentiments were by now out of step with the Australian public. The closing quotation of this impromptu speech caused a deal of embarrassment in Australia—in film footage it appears that even the Queen and Prince Philip were embarrassed.

Ma'am, there are a lot of interesting people in the world who would like to attack the monarchy. There are clever people in the world, at least so I understand, who have suggested all sorts of things ought to be done to democratise the monarchy. I am proud to say that ours is the most democratic monarchy in the whole, wide world.

We pay no attention to that. When we see you, we see you as our Queen. We see you as our Sovereign Lady. We see you as the successor of monarchs who, in this very century have by their own standards and their own conscience have helped to preserve our monarchy in a world in which crowns have been tumbling and disasters have best mankind.

We are proud to think that so far from abrogating any of our liberties, because we are your subjects, we know that we add to our liberty.

It is a proud thought for us to have you here to remind ourselves that in this great structure of government which has evolved, you, if I may use the expression, are the living and lovely centre of our enduring allegiance.

You have today begun a journey around Australia. It is a journey you have made before. You will be seen in the next few weeks by hundreds of thousands, and I hope by millions, of your Australian subjects.

This must be to you now something that is almost a task. All I ask you to remember in this country of yours is that every man, woman and child who even sees you with a passing glimpse as you go by will remember it— remember it with joy—remember it in the words of the old seventeenth-century poet who wrote those famous words, 'I did but see her passing by and yet I love her till I die.'[51]

Abridged.
Source: *Sydney Morning Herald*, 19 February 1963, p. 6, corrected by reference to ABC film footage.

Arthur Calwell
Vietnam, 1965

Arthur Calwell (1896–1973) had a long involvement in labour politics, and became federal leader of the Australian Labor Party in 1960. On 29 April 1965 Liberal Prime Minister Robert Menzies announced that an Australian battalion of regular and con-scripted soldiers would join US forces fighting in Vietnam. For Menzies, the enemy was Chinese communism. If Vietnam fell, then countries throughout South-East Asia, perhaps even Australia itself, would tumble like dominoes before the communist hordes. Five days later, Calwell rose in Parliament to deliver his condemnation of Menzies' decision. Over the next eighteen months, as police and demonstrators battled in the streets, the stoical veteran stumped the country, campaigning against the war. But when Labor was thrashed in the 1966 federal election, Calwell resigned from Parliament. In hindsight, his retort to Menzies is one of the prophetic speeches of the anti-war struggle.

The Government's decision to send the First Battalion of the Australian Regular Army to Vietnam is, without question, one of the most significant events in the history of this Commonwealth.

On behalf of all my colleagues of Her Majesty's Opposition, I say that we oppose the Government's decision to send 800 men to fight in Vietnam. We oppose it firmly and completely.

We do not think it is a wise decision. We do not think it is a timely decision. We do not think it is a right decision. We do not think it will help the fight against Communism. On the contrary, we believe it will harm that fight in the long term. We do not believe it will promote the welfare of the people of Vietnam. On the contrary, we believe it will prolong and deepen the suffering of that unhappy people so that Australia's very name may become a term of reproach among them. We do not believe that it represents a wise or even intelligent response to the challenge of Chinese power. On the contrary, we believe it mistakes entirely the nature of that power, and that it materially assists China in her subversive aims.

Let us examine the case of South Vietnam itself. It is a gross and misleading over-simplification to depict this war in simple terms of military aggression from the North. That there has long been, and still is, aggression from the North and subversion inspired from the North, I do not for one moment deny. But the war in South Vietnam, the war to which we are sending this one battalion as a beginning in our commitment, is also a civil war and it is a guerrilla war. The great majority of the Vietcong are South Vietnamese. The object of the Vietcong in the war—this guerrilla war—is to avoid as far as possible direct entanglement with massed troops in order that by infiltration, subversion and terrorism, they may control villages, hamlets, outposts and small communities wherever these are most vulnerable. This, like all civil wars and all guerrilla wars, has been accompanied by unusual savagery. This war has a savagery and a record of atrocities, with savage inhumanity daily perpetrated by both sides, all of its own. We cannot condemn the atrocities of the one without condemning those of the other. We of the Labour Party abhor and condemn both, as we condemn all atrocities. I repeat: The war in South Vietnam is a civil war, aided and abetted by the North Vietnamese Government, but neither created nor principally maintained by it. To call it simply 'foreign aggression' as the Prime Minister does, and as his colleagues do, is to misrepresent the facts, and, thereby, confuse the issue with which we must ultimately come to terms.

The people of Vietnam may, therefore, be divided into three kinds: Those who support the present Government and are actively anti-Communist; those who are Communist and of whom the Vietcong are actively and openly engaged in subversion; and those who are indifferent. I have not the slightest doubt that the overwhelming majority of the ordinary people of Vietnam fall into the last category. They watch uncomprehendingly the ebb and flow of this frightful war around them, and as each day threatens some new horror, they become even more uncomprehending. And because this is so, our policy of creating a democratic anti-Communist South Vietnam has failed. That failure can possibly be reversed, but it cannot be reversed by military means alone.

The Americans have supported four of the governments of South Vietnam and have opposed the other four. There is not one jot or tittle of evidence to support the belief that is being sedulously fostered in this country that the local population cares one iota whether it happens again eight or nine times in the coming 18 months. The Government of South Vietnam does not base itself on popular support. Yet this is the Government at whose request, and in whose support, we are to commit a battalion of Australian fighting men. And we are told we are doing this in the name of the free and independent Government and people of South Vietnam. I do not believe it, and neither does anybody else who considers the matter with any degree of intelligence.

The Government will try, indeed it has already tried, to project a picture in which once the aggressive invaders from the North are halted, our men will be engaged in the exercise of picking off the Vietcong, themselves invaders from the North and stranded from their bases and isolated from their supplies. But it will not be like that at all. Our men will be fighting the largely indigenous Vietcong in their own home territory. They will be fighting in the midst of a largely indifferent, if not resentful, and frightened population. They will be fighting at the request of, and in support, and presumably, under the direction of an unstable, inefficient, partially corrupt military regime which lacks even the semblance of being, or becoming, democratically based.

But, it will be said, even if this is true, that there are far larger considerations—China must be stopped, the United States must not be humiliated in Asia. I agree wholeheartedly with both those propositions.

But this also I must say: Our present course is playing right into China's hands, and our present policy will, if not changed, surely and inexorably lead to American humiliation in Asia.

Humiliation for America could come in one of two ways—either by outright defeat, which is unlikely, or by her becoming interminably bogged down in the awful morass of this war, as France was for ten years. That situation would in turn lead to one of two things—withdrawal through despair, or all out war, through despair. Both these would be equally disastrous. What would be the objective of an all out war? It could only be the destruction of the North Vietnamese regime. And what would that create? It would create a vacuum. America can destroy the regime, but it cannot conquer and hold North Vietnam, and into that vacuum China would undoubtedly move. Thus, if that happened, we would have replaced a nationalistic communist regime—in a country with a thousand years history of hostility towards China—with actual Chinese occupation, and either we would have to accept this disaster or face the even greater disaster of all out war with China.

By its decision, the Australian Government has withdrawn unilaterally from the ranks of the negotiators, if indeed it was ever concerned about them. Our contribution will be negligible, militarily. But we have reduced ourselves to impotence in the field of diplomacy.

Australia's aim should have been to help end the war, not to extend it. We have now lost all power to help end it. Instead, we have declared our intention to extend it, insofar as lies in our power. We have committed ourselves to the propositions that Communism can be defeated by military means alone and that it is the function of European troops to impose the will of the West upon Asia.

The despatch of a battalion of Australian troops to South Vietnam is the outcome of that thinking. By this decision, we set our face towards war as the correct means of opposing Communism, and declare against the social, economic and political revolution that alone can effectively combat Communism.

How long will it be before we are drawing upon our conscript youth to service these growing and endless requirements? Does the Government now say that conscripts will not be sent? If so, has it completely forgotten what it said about conscription last year? The basis of that decision was that the new conscripts would be completely integrated in the Regular Army. The voluntary system was brought abruptly to an end. If the Government now says that conscripts will not be sent, this means that the 1st Battalion is never to be reinforced, replaced or replenished. If this is not so, then the Government must have a new policy on the use of conscripts—a policy not yet announced. Or, if it has not changed its policy, the Government means that the 1st Battalion is not to be reinforced, replaced or replenished from the resources of the existing Regular Army. Which is it to be? There is now a commitment so 800. As the war drags on, who is to say that this will not rise to 8,000, and that these will not be drawn from our voteless, conscripted 20 year olds? And where are the troops from America's other allies? It is plain that Britain, Canada, France, Germany and Japan, for example, do not see things with the clear-cut precision of the Australian Government.

I cannot close without addressing a word directly to our fighting men who are now by this decision, committed to the chances of war: Our hearts and prayers are with you. Our minds and reason cannot support those who have made the decision to send you to this war, and we shall do our best to have that decision reversed. But we shall do our duty to the utmost in supporting you to do your duty. In terms of everything that an army in the field requires, we shall never deny you the aid and support that it is your right to expect in the service of your country. To the members of the Government, I say only this: if, by the process of misrepresentation of our motives, in which you are so expert, you try to further divide this nation for political purposes, yours will be a dreadful responsibility, and you will have taken a course which you will live to regret.

And may I, through you, Mr. Speaker, address this message to the members of my own Party—my colleagues here in this Parliament, and that vast band of Labour men and women outside: The course we have agreed to take today is fraught with difficulty. I cannot promise you that easy popularity can be bought in times like these; nor are we looking for it. We are doing our duty as we see it. When the drums beat and the trumpets sound, the voice of reason and right can be heard in the land only with difficulty. But if we are to have the courage of our convictions, then we must do our best to make that voice heard. I offer you the probability that you will be traduced, that your motives will be misrepresented, that your patriotism will be impugned, that your courage will be called into question. But I also offer you the sure and certain knowledge that we will be vindicated; that generations to come will record with gratitude that when a reckless Government wilfully endangered the security of this nation, the voice of the Australian Labour Party was heard, strong and clear, on the side of sanity and in the cause of humanity, and in the interests of Australia's security.

Abridged.
Source: *Commonwealth Parliamentary Debates*, vol. 46, 4 May 1965, pp. 1102–7.

Faith Bandler

Equal in the True Sense of the Word, 1969

Faith Ida Lessing Bandler (c. 1918–) is a charismatic political activist and author who was born on a banana farm in Tumbiulgum in northern New South Wales. Her father was a Hebridean Islander who had been brought by 'blackbirders', or slave traders, to Australia in 1883 to work on the sugar plantations; her mother was of Indian–Scottish ancestry. Bandler's schooling was interrupted by the Great Depression, and she later joined the wartime Women's Land Army. In 1956, now married and a mother, Bandler became a full-time political activist. With Pearl Gibbs, she founded the Aboriginal Australian Fellowship, and later served on the executive of the Federal Council for the Advancement of Aborigines and Torres Strait Islanders. A persuasive and memorable speaker, Bandler championed the cause of Aboriginal citizenship at public meetings and media interviews in the lead-up to the successful federal referendum in May 1967, which altered the Constitution to recognize Indigenous rights. By now she was a prominent public figure. In 1969 she presented a speech at the annual general meeting of Kirinari, the Aboriginal Children's Advancement Society which provided hostels and educational opportunities for Aboriginal teenagers. Bandler mounted the podium after federal politician and Aboriginal rights activist Gordon Bryant. She spoke informally—displaying her customary personal warmth—in recognition of the importance of maternal health and education for Aboriginal people but at the same time expressed her concern that any perpetuation of welfare dependency denied Indigenous communities the right of true equality and dignity within Australian society.

Gordon Bryant has spoken, Mr Chairman, about the need for political action to further the advancement of Aborigines, and of course being on the Federal Executive Council for so many years I am convinced that political action is absolutely vital. I thought that you might think for a short time this afternoon about what education has to do with Aboriginal advancement.

In the first place, I find it hard to accept the word 'advancement'. I am rather sorry that it has been used in various committees established to assist the Aboriginal people. I am not convinced that it is advancement for the indigenous Australians to become like the European Australians.

When one thinks of the murder, rape, and theft and all the crookery under the sun that has been introduced into this country since the invasion of the white man, I am not sure that this word advancement is used advisedly in connection with a better deal for the indigenous Australians. I don't think there is any doubt at all that there is tremendous emphasis on education and this is one particular field that I have never bought into myself, mainly because I have concerned myself with legislative changes and employment.

No doubt, education has very real part to play. But when you sit down and talk about the kids who are ready to go into secondary school or the kids who need a scholarship to go on to university I think it is a serious mistake not to think about the mothers of these children.

Now Gordon over there is probably thinking 'There's Faith on her hobby horse again'. When one has a house to run as well as help run *his* Federal Council one thinks of the needs of the people on this earth who give birth to the population—the mothers. It is my belief that tremendous thought should be given to the mothers of Aboriginal children not only in NSW but throughout the whole of Australia today.

I am not necessarily thinking about nursing mothers, once the baby is born. I am thinking about the pre-natal period, because it seems to me that if you are going to have children grow up and have the powers to concentrate, to do the work that is set before them, and at the same time to work in a school curriculum set out for middle-class white people, then you have got to have relatively healthy kids to stand up to it.

I have yet to find a family, be they black, white or brindle, where the mother has been undernourished or underfed in the pre-natal period where [subsequently] a child of very high I.Q. has been produced. I would ask you to give some very special thought to this and when you are going to your State or Federal member, you might ask that they consider providing a little extra finance for the mothers of Aboriginal families in order that milk may be bought and that bread and butter and other day-to-day necessities may be there in the house. If you don't give some thought to the mother and the infants, it is silly to start at the top of the tree. To my way of thinking it is merely mowing the lawn without getting to the grass roots. I would like to point out I have come to this conclusion over a period of 8 or 9 years, in consultation with some of our Sydney medical people who have given this tremendous thought, particularly two who spent some considerable time in Walgett and Broken Hill.

I would say 'So much for education', and you must think about this new aspect which I have just briefly mentioned. To me this question of advancement has to do with dignity. How can anyone have any dignity at all if they are permanently living on the receiving end? Now Alan Duncan told me just before this session started, about 'Grant in Aid'. It seems to me that if such a thing as this were introduced we are going back to 1930. Dignity is a very important aspect of Aboriginal advancement. I hope the time is not too far off when you can close up shop.

It is still necessary to seek public money, but I have to confess that on the days of door-knock appeals for assistance of Aborigines, be it for Hostels or be it for whatever you like, these are the days in the year that I put a sari on, because this appeal has to do with my dignity. You are not going from door to door for the crippled, or the deaf or blind, you are knocking on people's doors asking for financial assistance for a particular group of people whose skin happens to the wrong colour for a fair chance of education. While I do see that necessity in the next few years for this particular type of work—the building of hostels, and the special assistance being given to children for education—I only hope that you can see the end of it. An end to this help can only occur if something is done about employment. I have said this before and I shall say it again.

I was born in poverty myself. The other day when we were looking at a plan for the re-development of La Perouse, and I made a suggestion about the right of those people out there to own the seven acres, someone said, 'Well that's all right for you Faith, you live up there.' Well I didn't always live up there. I lived in conditions far worse than the people living at La Perouse. Deep down within, we have dignity. It so happened that I was born into a family that understood what trade unions meant. Because of this we didn't work for lower wages than the chap with the white skin. We became very independent people. If I thought that were it not for good well-meaning European people who are prepared to get up and—do something, [that] my children would have no chance of a higher education, then I would almost despair with deep regret and shame. I would want to know that my kids would be educated out of the money that came into my home each week, and I believe that this is the sincere hope of every dark Australian, right throughout the country. They have got to be independent, they have to have equal pay for equal work to begin with, they must be able to build their own houses wherever they wish, they want to be able to pay for their own houses.

In essence, I am saying that we must work towards the time when this special assistance must surely end, and the Aborigines will be equal in the true sense of the word. I don't want you to feel for one minute that I don't appreciate and value the magnificent [work] that you are doing here at Kirinari. But I remember when we set about forming the Aboriginal-Australian Fellowship, that one night on the verge of tears and desperation, and not knowing which way to turn, I hopped in the car and went down to Narrabeen to see [Reverend] Alf Clint, and he said to me 'Don't worry girl, you know if we don't work ourselves out of a job in the end, then we aren't working in the proper way'.

I think this should be your goal—to eventually work yourselves out of a job by bringing Aboriginal people in this country to where they no longer need any special help. They will merely get their ordinary wages and get the concessions in Social Services as all other Australians do. They will also contribute as far as taxes are concerned.

I'm afraid I am a very poor substitute for Kath Walker, and I must confess that I didn't have sufficient time to prepare all the other things I wanted to say to you. Forgive me for having rambled, but I want to say first of all that I look on the Federal Council (this is not another commercial by the way) for the Advancement of Aborigines and Torres Strait Islanders, as an organization that has worked for and given tremendous confidence to Aboriginal people not only in one state but throughout all states. It is true that at first nobody would stand up and have a say, but recently one of the teachers from the Teachers' Federation who was at the last conference said to me, 'You know Faith, I don't know that I'll go to another of your Conferences,' so I said 'Why not?' 'Well I've got to paint myself black if I want a chance to say anything.'

I think this is a fair indication of an organization that has worked in a very sincere and genuine way, truly providing a platform for the Aboriginal and Islanders voice.

Reproduced in full.
Source: *Kirinari*, vol. 1, no. 4, March 1969, pp. 23–4.[52]

Jim Cairns
The Vietnam Moratorium, 1970

James Ford 'Jim' Cairns (1914–2003) was a gentle, idealistic Labor politician who began his working life as a policeman before completing a PhD at the University of Melbourne in Economic History. He entered federal politics in 1955, serving both as a minister and as deputy prime minister in the Whitlam Government. In opposition, Cairns was influential in his critique of Australian foreign policy and became the inspirational head of the Moratorium movement which opposed the Vietnam War. Its first great march took place on 8 May 1970, when Cairns led a hundred thousand people through the streets of Melbourne in a peaceful and resolute protest. The police, the conservative press and the Liberal Party expected a communist riot. But Cairns famously addressed the vast crowd that day in words of peace:

> When you leave here today, realize a sacred trust.
> You have the trust to stand for peace and for the qualities of the human spirit to which we must dedicate ourselves ...
> Our spirit is the spirit of peace and understanding.

> Our spirit is opposed to violence, opposed to hate, opposed to every motive that has produced this terrible war.
>
> And in developing our own spirit, we will change the spirit of other people.
>
> We can overcome ... and I have never seen a more convincing sight than I see here now to give me confidence that we shall overcome.[53]

Supporters of the war insisted that the protesters were not genuine. They were ridiculed as 'rent-a-crowd', or as naïve youngsters who were being manipulated by communist agitators sympathetic to the North Vietnamese. A month earlier in Parliament, Liberal Attorney-General Tom Hughes had expressed criticisms of the broadly-based Moratorium movement. Cairns rose to defend those who opposed war in Vietnam, and the democratic right of individuals to express their views through peaceful protest. He spoke in the measured and gentle voice which, as his comrade Tom Uren later said, 'people of all political persuasions and from all walks of life found disarming.'[54]

There is no need for any conspiracy theory to explain the opposition to what is being done in Vietnam. It exists all round the world. It is only in Australia that this Communist conspiracy theory is ever put forward by responsible people. In most other countries a person is given credit for his views on any matter at all and these views are examined on their merits. But that does not happen here. The favourite manoeuvre of practically everyone on the Government benches who speaks of the opposition on these matters is to divert it to a question of Communist influence and Communist association. Hardly ever is the argument put forward treated on its merits. If this Communist conspiracy is not the explanation for it, as I believe it is not, what then is the explanation for opposition to this war? It can be found in what is happening in Vietnam.

Is it surprising that there is intense opposition to what has happened in Vietnam from students, workers and all sorts of people all around Australia and in every country of the world? There is surely a limit to the number of human beings anyone will kill—even if they are coloured, foreign and Communist—to achieve any particular purpose. What is the limit in Vietnam? Is there any limit? It is not those who oppose the war who are in such a strange position that they should have to explain their conduct. It is not those who oppose the war who need some international system of obedience and orders, or rewards and benefits to explain their conduct. It is the supporters of the war in Vietnam who need to explain what they do. It is not they who are responding to orders from abroad.

It is not those who act as they do because they feel that what is happening in Vietnam is wrong who should explain their conduct. It is not those who resist conscription for military service who need to explain their conduct. It is for those to explain their conduct who conscript others whilst they avoid any cost, inconvenience or embarrassment for themselves, and who as well gain votes, profit and promotion from their militaristic attitudes and policies. Opposition to the war in Vietnam and to conscription for it is a normal and natural way of feeling about a situation which is possessed by tens of thousands of normal human beings who need no conspiracies from overseas or anywhere else to explain their conduct.

A question now arises: What is such a person expected to do if he feels this way? Is he expected to retire into apathy and disinterest? The answer to this question requires an understanding of what democracy is. Some people seem to think that democracy is just Parliament alone. They seem to think that all the ordinary citizen has to do is to vote once every 2 or 3 years and then leave everything to the Constitution and to those who happen to be elected to Parliament. But times are changing. A whole generation is not prepared to accept this complacent, conservative theory. Parliament is not democracy. It is one of the manifestations of democracy and it can become a most important manifestation of democracy if people are prepared to come out of their apathy and do something about it. What has to be done is not merely to refuse to talk politics or religion, as is almost the general custom, to vote once very 2 or 3 years and leave everything to those who win seats in Parliament. This is the way to make Parliament a hollow ritual and a fraud, which it has recently been called by leading journalists who observe its proceedings. This is the way to make it a fossilised institution and into a talking shop–or, even worse, into a talking shop which is hamstrung by rules and gagged by men who seek to run it as if it were a government department, a factory or a departmental store.

The weaknesses of Parliament have been widely recognised. They will not be cured by accusations of anarchy and mob rule whenever anyone decides to do something about it. Democracy is government by the people, and government by the people demands action by the people. It demands effective ways of showing what the interests and needs of the people really are. It demands action in public places all around the land. The authorities of today are not accustomed to that. The laws restrict this action, and governments panic and even stimulate fear and insecurity.

I believe that in normal circumstances action by the people should be peaceful, inoffensive and dignified. We can guarantee that only if fair and reasonable outlets are available for protest and dissent. They are not available today, and so no-one can guarantee that result in those circumstances. I deplore violence and repudiate anyone who initiates it or deliberately uses it. I think I may be able to claim to have more power to modify it in political affairs than perhaps anyone else in Australia. But I live also in the radical tradition and I have learnt more of that tradition in the United States of America than anywhere else. Recently Professor Staughton Lynd wrote about the principles of 200 years of American radicalism in these words:

> *The proper foundation for government is a universal law of right and wrong self-evident to the intuitive commonsense of every man; that freedom is a power of personal self-direction which no man can delegate to another; that the purpose of society is not the protection of property but fulfilment of the needs of living human beings; that good citizens have the right and duty, not only to over-*

throw incurably oppressive governments, but before that point is
reached to break particular oppressive laws; and that we owe our
ultimate allegiance, not to this or that nation, but to the whole
family of man.

[Mr James—Who wrote that?]

Professor Staughton Lynd wrote that as a summary of the great American tradition of radicalism, which is my political philosophy. This radical tradition is the very opposite of authoritarianism and centralism and, being that, is the very antithesis of Communism. But this radical tradition has no room for witch hunting or the creation of political pariahs. In a given situation Communists can be right. If they are right I will never say that they are wrong. If a Communist stands for something that is right and if that thing concerns me I will stand with him for that thing. Communists believe that it is right to oppose the war in Vietnam. I believe that it is right to oppose the war in Vietnam. I will oppose the war in Vietnam [along] with anyone who opposes it. I will not be deterred from doing so by threats or pressures or intimidation. I sincerely hope that no-one else will be deterred. Communists can be a threat to democracy, but threats to democracy in Australia come from a different direction. They come from some of those who can draw upon all the traditional and conventional values and who, because of their status and authority, can make people look over their shoulder, lapse into silence in the presence of injustice and sneak off out of sight. It is not Communists in Australia who can silence people, who can sack and fail to promote. It is not, in Australia, Communists who can set up a system described a long time ago by Ben Chifley as a system of 'spies, pimps and perjurers'. It is the people who have prestige and authority who can do that: they do so far more than is necessary in this country. The police state in Australia will ride on the back of anti-Communism, if it ever rides at all.

I will not be deterred from reasonable public political actions by fears that something might go wrong. I will do everything in my power to prevent it from going wrong–but I am not going to work within the limits imposed by my political opponents. I am not going to be driven into a corner away from action that is even in the slightest bit radical just because if I come out of that corner I might find myself standing near some Communist. I have no intention of doing this. As I said, I stand on this matter where J. B. Chifley stood a long time ago. On 1st June 1951 J. B. Chifley said:

> *I can only hope that you will be inspired by the same things which*
> *inspired the pioneers of this movement, and that you will not be*
> *frightened ... over to the 'right' because of the whispered word*
> *'Communist'. I could not be called a young radical. But if a thing it*
> *worth fighting for, no matter what the penalty is I will fight for*
> *the right, and truth and justice will prevail.*

Ben Chifley had no intention of being frightened over to the right because of the whispered word 'Communist'. He took the occasion of his last speech to make that clear. I think it is not any longer possible to solve political problems in this country in terms of hanging a Communist label on them and thinking that you have solved the problems and dismissed the issues. I do not think that anyone must be deterred from working against the immoral and unjust military invasion of Vietnam by the Australian Government and its allies. I hope that every Australian citizen will realise that if he is to govern himself he cannot perform that task by leaving it to others. He must perform that task himself.

Democracy begins on the farms, in the factories and in the streets, and if people will not, often at risk to themselves, stand up for their rights in those places there will be no democracy. I do not think the generation over 35 years of age realises the significance of how thoroughly this think- ing has gripped the younger generation. The younger generation is not going to be satisfied with all the trappings of the past. It is going to endeavour to determine effective ways of governing itself. The important thing for the authorities to realise is that unless reasonable opportunities are given to those people who hold these views who feel strongly about issues such as Vietnam and conscription and many other issues then the authorities will be failing in their responsibilities in government and will be forcing the very circumstances to develop that they appear not to want. Today in Australia we need an understanding that the old methods are not going to be adequate for the solution of new problems. All round the world there is an inability by people to be fooled as easily as they once were. All round the world there is a determination to do something about the issues that people feel strongly about and to find ways of expressing those issues in the making of decisions, not only in Parliament but in every other part of the community that determines and influences the lives of the people concerned.

I think it is a tragedy that so few people on the other side of the House are capable even to be aware of this situation. They never seem to express any sympathy or understanding of it at all and constantly take the attitude that everyone who expresses dissent or protest is either an idiot or a Communist and should not be taken seriously. I think it is a tragedy that the generation that has acquired powers of government and powers of authority has today, in Australia, so many in it who take that view. Of course, unless there is a change there will be difficulties in the future in the development and extension of democracy, because democracy is government by the people. What is being done in the Vietnam Mora- torium Campaign is an example of government by the people; it is an example of people taking action about issues that are important to them, actions which they believe will be influential in the making of national decisions in the ways that are open to them and in the ways in which they can make their decisions effective. The important thing for us, to my mind, is to work for a proper, peaceful and dignified expression of that activity and not endeavour to blackguard it, as the Minister did by his statement this evening, or to drive it into corners so that it would become the problem that the Minister seems to think it is already.

Abridged.
Source: *Commonwealth Parliamentary Debates*, vol. 66, 14 April 1970, pp. 1065–8.

Germaine Greer
Woman's Body: Woman's Choice, 1972

Germaine Greer (1939–) became an international celebrity upon the publication of her feminist classic *The Female Eunuch* (1970). She had grown up in a Catholic middle-class family in Melbourne, attending university there and in Sydney before departing for London in 1964 to pursue academic studies and journalism. Greer's book appeared at a time when many young women were asserting the right to control their own fertility—a revolution aided by the new contraceptive pill and by the possibility of increasingly safe medical abortions. Criminal prosecutions of abortionists were not uncommon. But recent reforms in Victoria, New South Wales and South Australia allowed abortion where a pregnancy threatened the life or the mental health of the woman (so-called 'therapeutic abortions'). However, as feminists pointed out, this change still placed (usually male) professionals in control of women's bodies. In March 1972 the expatriate Dr Greer was on a controversial tour of Australia when she joined a public debate on abortion at the Sydney Town Hall. She opened by reflecting on the misery that accompanied the birth of unwanted children and argued that the 'sanctity of life' was a principle that needed to be applied to all of the lives involved—not just the life of the foetus. In any case, she argued, the present situation was filled with misery and hypocrisy.

I do not propose to talk to you about the potpourri of fashionable questions that appear on the advertisements for tonight's debate, but rather on the basic question which is the title of the whole debate, that is, 'Abortion—right or wrong?' In other words, I want to discuss morality. Morality is something my name is not usually associated with. There seems to be an abiding conviction among people who have never read a word I wrote, and who are not really interested in the question anyway, that I am some sort of intellectual super-whore who is just zooming around Australia stirring as much of the sacred element as she possibly can. I think I may claim more seriousness than that. I do not, however, claim to be religious. *The Female Eunuch* has been claimed by certain avant-garde Catholics as the newest thing in radical theology since Aquinas, but I repudiate this suggestion, and I'm going to re-read it very carefully.

But I do flatter myself that I'm concerned about morality. About the quality of human life, not only in terms of whether you get three meals a day; learn to read by the time you're seven, and can be relied upon to be able to breathe without obstruction or see without infectious trachoma, or whatever else may be required to lead a life of something like the standard we expect. I'm also concerned with the spiritual resonance of our lives, with just how much responsibility we are permitted to take for our own actions. It seems to me that the history of civilisation is the history of people learning more and more about reality and about the ways of dealing with it, and escaping from the ritual stranglehold of virtually unconscious behaviour. The story of civilisation is the story of increasing consciousness and deliberateness about the ways in which one lives one's life.

It seems to me that the discussion tonight has been conducted on a frivolous level, even by the most serious speakers, because they have assumed that morality was somehow rule-following; that if you had the right rule and you followed it you grew in spiritual grace. I think this is quite improper; that the old rules do not apply to new situations, that they have never been properly formulated. They are ambiguous in themselves; and the first question anyone asks when he faces a moral act or the possibility of an immoral act is, which rule applies, and what does it mean?

The same is true of the law, which goes to some pains not to be ambiguous and ends up being inscrutable. The same is certainly true of the Bible when it says, 'Thou shalt not kill'. It doesn't say whom thou shalt not kill. It simply says you shall not do it—ever—at all. But we assume they didn't mean abattoirs, whoever they were who wrote the Bible, because we do an awful lot of killing in them, and they didn't mean flies, and they didn't mean war, and they didn't mean this and they didn't mean that.

The way I learnt that rule, when I was at school, was that it applied not only to my killing other people, but also to the possibility of my killing myself. I had no rights whatever, according to the nuns who taught me, over life and death in any of its forms, except presumably those accounted lower on the evolutionary scale. Now, this means that if I'm to consider questions of contraception and abortion, I must consider not only the life of the unborn child, but my own life, and the other lives that impinge on mine.

Now I am no longer a Catholic, but for the purposes of this discussion, we might as well stick to that very idea, the Christian tenet 'Thou shalt not kill', and see where it gets us when examining the intricacies of the issue of abortion.

We hear a good deal about rights in our society, even though we know in our cynical hearts that rights do not exist where they cannot be defended. We speak of the right to control one's own body. Some of us may be naive enough to suppose that in some metaphysical arena it actually exists. But it doesn't exist. It doesn't exist for the imprisoned man, it doesn't exist for the convicted man, it doesn't exist for the patient in hospital, it doesn't exist for the soldier, it doesn't exist for the child, it doesn't exist for a man declared mad. And under all those headings you may include women. Women in all those categories have no control over their own bodies, and indeed women in general have no control over their own bodies, and will not have, until they have the political power to enforce some such right, and to enact their own punishment on those who infringe it.

This leads us to the problem of the right of someone who will never have the power to defend it, the right of the unborn child. Now it's very ironic that this right is so tenderly regarded when the rights of women are not regarded in the same way at all. I would argue that any attempt to rationalise abortion law, which pretended that the right of the unborn did not exist or need not be considered at all, was simply skirting the issue, which most people find painful, and that is the one we must contemplate. And in the strength and clarity of our contemplation of these questions will come our spiritual growth. It's too late now to hive it all off on God! We've simply got to face these issues for ourselves.

Supposing we agree that the unborn has a right. Certainly in law he does have, and the right may be defended in specific instances. We then have to consider that right in conjunction with other rights. We cannot assume because it is a right, it takes precedence over all other rights. Our moral decisions in this century are not as easy as that. We are no longer faced with simple questions of right and wrong, black and white. Every single decision we make involves a consideration of consequences that stretch beyond our power to understand them. And my contention is that the essence of moral existence is in the continuing struggle to confront all the ambiguities of experience; that morality derives from a creative confrontation of reality as we understand it, and cannot be separated from exercise of the intelligence.

A woman who has an abortion may or may not suffer guilt. I know of no woman who has ever contemplated an abortion, who has not considered it very carefully, and quite painfully. I know of many women who perhaps would have had children if they thought the society would have allowed them to do so. For some of us do cry for the right to bear as well as the right not to bear. But if such a woman has confronted the problem and has come to the decision that, in justice to herself and to the other people with whose lives her own life entangles, this pregnancy must be terminated, then it is the sheerest hypocrisy to abrogate her right of decision and confer it on a board of psychiatrists or doctors or hospital counsellors or whatever they are. Footballers, plumbers, bishops. It is the sheerest hypocrisy to pre-empt her decision, because the board—the doctors, the two psychiatrists, whoever they are—do not really take responsibility for the action. They take symbolic responsibility. They say, 'No, no, we don't think this abortion is necessary. Go ahead and have the child. We are doing the right thing for you on your behalf.' But they never have actually to go through with the consequences of that moral decision. And so it is not their moral decision at all. It's a game. It's a drama, a ritual assumption of the right to decide an issue which doesn't concern them.

Now make no mistake. I think it may very well be that in some cases to decide to have an abortion might be a mistake. But the essence of moral action is also being prepared to do the wrong thing, and to admit it. This may seem a very strange thing for me to say, but there's no point in assuming that because you've decided to do something, it is therefore right. You might as well consider the possibility that it was not, that perhaps you do consider that there was someone else to be consulted. If you feel that, it's enough to change the character of your decision. I personally feel, for example, that I have no right to steal a child from a man of my choice, against his will. Other women in this room would not feel that way. But I would feel it was improper to steal a child from a man, and bring up offspring of whose existence he was unaware. That seems like a crazy, far-out sort of question. But these are the questions which we have to face. They're not as simple as: 'I'll go mad if I have this baby, or I won't be able to keep it or it'll be brought up in a slum or it's going to be deformed.' All these issues are peripheral to the main issue of the amount of responsibility one is prepared to take for one's own actions.

Now if one does bear an unwanted child, sin is compounded every day—if you accept that there is such a thing as 'sin'. I mean evils like resentment, inadequacy, inability to cope, petty sins of ego-destruction or bitchery, withdrawal of affection, game-playing and all the rest of the multifarious sins that corrupt our communication with each other. Such sins are committed every day. And whereas we might say yes, abortion is not an entirely right act, it does crush the rights of one small person, we then have to say, but the woman who is forced by the decision that other people make for her, to struggle to accept a child she doesn't want is hopelessly, helplessly sinning herself into a state of moral apathy every day of her life.

And that sin will go on. It will go on in the resentment the child bears to her and the twisted, warped, peculiar ways it relates to other people. You all know I'm not in favour of the gluttonous maternal relationship as our society extols it. But I'm not in favour either of forcing a reluctant woman into this eye-to-eye confrontation with her child, so that she has to struggle to keep that from warping into a kind of extraordinary, inverted hatred. The difference is not between maternal love and lack of it, the difference is in maternal love as deformed in one way, and deformed in another. And I would willingly see both deformations disappear, and the relationship between children and their society be more collective and spontaneous and less fearful than the one we seem to think is right.

Abridged.

Source: 'Transcript of the address given by Dr Germaine Greer at the Abortion Debate at Sydney Town Hall on Thursday 2nd March, 1972, and broadcast by the ABC in "Fact and Opinion" on Wednesday, 22nd March, 1972'; Australian Archives (NSW), AuC1989T1, Australian Broadcasting Commission, Head Office, Radio Scripts Files, Alphabetical Series C, Box 12.

Don Dunstan

Legalisation of Homosexuality, 1972

Donald Allan Dunstan (1926–1999) put South Australia at the forefront of civil rights reform during his two periods as Labor premier in the late 1960s and throughout the 1970s. In 1972 Don Dunstan introduced a Bill to legalise homosexuality, overriding opposition pleas for a delay and resisting the outrage of such pressure groups as the Moral Standards Committee. The emotive issue of gay rights was gaining momentum overseas: Britain had decriminalized homosexuality five years before on the advice of the Wolfenden Report. It was not uncommon for the advocates of reform to argue that homosexuality, rather than being a crime, was an unfortunate condition—perhaps even a disease—which gays themselves 'could not help'. Furthermore, homosexuals were vulnerable to being bashed—even by police, who sometimes hung around public toilets in order to entrap unwary men. Indeed, as an opposition member pointed out immediately before Dunstan rose to speak, the issue had been inflamed in South Australia by the recent death of Dr George Duncan, a homosexual who was drowned in the Torrens River by a group of men, widely believed to have been police. Here are the highlights of Premier Dunstan's speech on the second reading of the Bill.

The honourable member who has just resumed his seat has suggested that we are debating this Bill in an atmosphere of emotion following the death of Dr. Duncan. I do not think that the emotions that have been aroused following the death of Dr. Duncan are anything but salutary to the community. That this community should contemplate a law allowing people to do, as was shown at the inquest, assault and murder under what they believed was the protection of the law, in that their victims would be frightened of going to claim the normal protection of citizens from assault and murder, is surely something that should cause us grave alarm. If we suggest that the community should say, 'Oh, well, that has happened. Let us not be emotional about it; let us wait the 10 years it took Britain to move after the Wolfenden committee's report', how many more assaults, murders and blackmails in that intervening period will this community have to suffer?

The honourable member is correct: I had a Bill drawn on this matter when I was Attorney-General but I did not proceed with it then because the climate of public opinion was not such that I believed we could obtain a sufficient consensus of opinion to support an amendment to the law—not that I did not believe it is right to make a change now, for my experience in the criminal law had been such that I had seen the misery, the harm, the hurt and the injustice that have occurred in this area of the law. In practice, I saw what happened to clients whom I had had to represent. As Attorney-General, I saw two cases of people who hanged themselves as a result of accusations under the law, although what they had done had been done in private with consenting males and had actually done no harm to anyone except perhaps themselves. In all humanity, I could not believe that the law should remain as it was then or it is now.

As Secretary of my Union, since there is a larger proportion of people who are homosexually inclined in the acting profession than almost anywhere else, naturally enough I came into contact with cases of people who were obviously homosexual; and those people who were obviously so caused my hackles to rise, as they would most people in the community. The vulgarity and unpleasantness of the behaviour in which they indulged was something that would obviously offend most people. I had the traditional prejudices of the community about this, and there were some cases which frankly astonished me, concerning people whom I had considered obviously masculine and apparently normal. When I discovered, since it happened in the course of my union activities, that matters occurred in front of my eyes that astonished me, that those people were homosexuals, I simply could not understand it. I poured all this out to a prominent producer in Australia who, with his wife, was having dinner with my wife and me on one occasion, and he bitterly attacked me, as did his wife, and said that I was utterly lacking in understanding. I was hopelessly prejudiced and did not know what I was talking about. He proceeded to assail all my previous assumptions. I think that that was a salutary lesson for me, as a matter of fact. I think everyone of us, in life and in politics, needs constantly to question his own assumptions.

I came to realize that, in fact, from my own observations (and later this also became obvious in the course of my practice in the law from the numbers of cases with which I had to deal) there were people in the community who were apparently, from all observations and any other conceivable criterion, completely normal in their activities, attitudes, modes of living and the like, but who nevertheless were homosexuals. They were able to live normally, but the problem for them was that, although they were socially useful (they related satisfactorily to other people in the community; they were able to carry out their jobs, and they were often charming, pleasant, intelligent and sensitive people) they lived subject to the constant threat that, since their motives were different from the norm and from the outlooks and tastes of the majority of the community, they were liable to prosecution, persecution and blackmail.

Having seen the kind of misery that was caused by the community, I came to question whether in fact, this was right. What were we doing by this kind of law? What they were involved in was a departure from a sexual norm, or at least a departure from what society lays down as acceptable sexual behaviour, according to the Christian ethic. However, that Christian ethic is widely departed from in other respects (fornication, adultery and Lesbianism, which is not proscribed by the law at all). In those circumstances, why should this departure from the norm be proscribed? Was it specifically and uniquely harmful to the community? There was no evidence that I could find that this was so. In fact, the majority of people with whom I dealt in my practice who had been charged in relation to these matters were quiet and discreet, and, as I said, were causing no harm to anyone but perhaps themselves.

Why should this area of the law differentiate, and why should it produce the sort of situation that occurred in relation to Dr. Duncan or the other people who at the inquest gave evidence of assault and persecution? I could see no reason for that. The view which I then came to adopt was fortified by my reading of the Wolfenden report.

What are the excuses for maintaining a law which interferes in this area alone with what might be called deviant or sinful sexual behaviour? One excuse is that it is an affront to public decency that this should occur. It is certainly contrary to the majority public taste but surely that is not sufficient for us to say that, because most of us do not regard this as something that is in any way attractive but rather, repulsive, other people who view the matter differently should have our views imposed on them privately. The second suggestion is that there is a necessity to help the people involved. The law as it stands does not help the people involved: it does not assist people to seek help. As the honourable member for Bragg has said, it prevents people from seeking help.

What is more, of course, one must face the fact that the majority of people who are homosexual do not regard homosexuality as a disease at all, not do they regard it as a condition to be cured. They regard it as normal and natural. They may be unhappy about it. As the honourable member will recall from a play that he once acted as censor for, there was a passage in it, 'Show me a happy homosexual, and I will show you a gay corpse.' Undoubtedly, the condition of the minority involved in this is a condition, in many cases (not always, but often) of unhappiness. At the same time, while it is often a condition of unhappiness, it is not a condition that the unhappy people regard as, for themselves, abnormal or avoidable.

In those circumstances, I do not believe that society has any right whatever to trespass in this area. The purpose of the criminal law is to protect persons from physical harm and from active affront, and their property from harm, also. Outside of that area, I believe the criminal law has no place at all, and it is for the social influences of the community to impose or induce or persuade the moral standards which various sections of the community advocate, to establish the moral standards which will be accepted by the majority of the community. The law is not a means of enforcing morality. It is a means of protection of persons and property from harm.

Finally, I agree that since the Wolfenden report advocated that the law should be changed to allow homosexual acts between consenting adult males in private to be free of the intrusion of the law, then it should be the adulthood which is the matter in question. Since adulthood here, following the Latey report in Great Britain, is now at the age of 18 years, we should provide that that is the age at which consent could occur. Some honourable members may argue that there is an anomaly in that we allow the age of consent for females to be 17 years of age and that there is a discrepancy of a year. However, at any rate at this stage, the age of 18 years seems to conform to the general provisions of the recommendations of the Wolfenden report, so that it is a sensible move to make and I believe should be supported in the Committee stage.

Abridged.
Source: *South Australian Parliamentary Debates*, 1972, vol. 2, 18 October 1972, pp. 2204–8.

———◆———

Gough Whitlam
'It's Time', 1972, The ABC, 1974, Handback to the Gurindji & The Dismissal, 1975

(Edward) Gough Whitlam (1916–) was Australia's most ambitious reformist prime minister, despite being in power for a relatively short period (1972–75). He entered Federal Parliament in 1952 and was federal leader of the Labor Party from 1967 to 1977. Whitlam was a towering individual and an eloquent and sometimes imperious speech maker. He was also the first Australian political leader to make open use of speech writers, notably Graham Freudenberg. Whitlam's epic 'It's Time For Leadership' election speech outlined a score of reforms in areas ranging from defence to urban sewerage. As he outlined his policy initiatives at the Blacktown Civic Centre on 13 November 1972, Whitlam opened with the grand claim that Australians had reached a decisive moment in their history.

The decision we will make for our country on 2 December is a choice between the past and the future, between the habits and fears of the past, and the demands and opportunities of the future. There are moments in history when the whole fate and future of nations can be decided by a single decision. For Australia, this is such a time. It's time for a new team, a new program, a new drive for equality of opportunities: it's time to create new opportunities for Australians, time for a new vision of what we can achieve in this generation for our nation and the region in which we live. It's time for a new government—a Labor Government.

During his term as Prime Minister, Whitlam was a prolific speech-maker. The following speech about the Australian Broadcasting Commission nicely demonstrates Whitlam's habit of arguing from a position of high principle, with appeal to historical precedents. By quoting his predecessor John Curtin, Whitlam conveys the strong sense that he is advancing a long-term Labor project, while his emphasis on modernization and transparency points to the capacity of his government to be a responsible and responsive agent of change. The occasion was the opening of a grand new ABC building (now sadly neglected) at Collinswood, Adelaide, on 29 March 1974.

It is almost 42 years since the Australian Broadcasting Commission was founded with the requirement that it 'shall broadcast from the national broadcasting stations adequate and comprehensive programs, and shall take in the interests of the community all such measures as in the opinion of the Commission are conducive to the full development of suitable broadcasting programs'.

At this time the Commission began its operations in South Australia from an old stone building in Hindmarsh Square—the first freehold property 'acquired' by the A.B.C. in Australia. Today the Commission is able finally to house itself in Adelaide in up-to-date adequate accommodation. The new ten-storey administration, radio and orchestral studio complex here at Collinswood is spacious and, among other things, fully air conditioned. The building will provide vastly improved accommodation for all administrative and program departments, News, Technical Services, Publicity, 'TV Times', Staff Association and Credit Union Offices. Large studios for the South Australian Symphony Orchestra and for light entertainment programs and two smaller studios for drama and general production are already fully operative. Hindmarsh Square will be completely vacated by late this year when the last A.B.C. units have moved into this new building.

It is appropriate that such a long-needed development is taking place in 1974. For it appears that this year will be one of great modernisation for the A.B.C. It is only about two weeks since the Minister for the Media, Senator Doug McClelland, tabled in the Federal Parliament the document which provides for modernisation. I refer, of course, to the report prepared by the management consultants, McKinsey & Company. The report suggests a number of important recommendations for the future development of the A.B.C. These range from management organisation to program output.

By the nature of its charter, the Commission itself will take the final decision on acceptance or otherwise of the McKinsey Report recommendations, although inevitably the Government will be involved if these proposals require amendments to existing legislation. There is, however, one simple decision, involving both the Commission and the Government which has already been made and the importance of which can easily be overlooked. This is the decision to make the McKinsey Report public. When the company made a similar study of the B.B.C., its report there was not published. Both the A.B.C. and the Government decided that the British precedent should not be followed in the handling of what is after all a report for Australians about their national broadcasting system.

Looking beyond the needs of Australians generally, the Government and the Commission decided that it was important for the staff of the

A.B.C.—6,700 people—that they should have ready access to the report. It is too important a document about too important an institution involving too many people for it to remain the subject of rumour and speculation. In as much as morale problems may exist within the A.B.C., I trust that our action in publishing the report indicates a desire and a willingness for the staff to participate in the debate that flows from it. Indeed, it is interesting that the first thorough discussion, including an interview with the A.B.C. Chairman, took place on an A.B.C. program, 'This Day Tonight'. It was especially appropriate for this program to open the debate fully and, dare I say it, even with some relish.

While there may be a need for modernising the A.B.C., 'This Day Tonight' and its sister program 'Four Corners', symbolise the need for the durability of certain basic principles in the operation of the organisation. They, more than any other programs, have been the subject of controversy arising out of these principles. Simply stated, they have been central to the debate about the independence and freedom from political interference of the organisation. They have involved men and women whose determination to maintain independence and to resist interference deserves high praise.

There will, of course, be some argument about the extent to which the independence and freedom of the A.B.C. have been threatened. I know that previous Chairmen of the A.B.C. have stated that such trends have always been exaggerated. I will say now, however, that those trends have at times been real, although some of them have been implicit rather than stated. I have only to mention what happened in the 1960s when an interview of a former French Premier, M. Bidault, was banned to establish my point. I have only to mention what happened to 'The Quiet Mutiny', a program about Vietnam produced by an Australian, John Pilger, and what happened about 'End of Dialogue', a program on apartheid in South Africa, to support my point.

I would mention in this context the disquiet I expressed in a speech in 1971 about what I saw as a new means of potential unilateral censorship. I spoke then about the dangers of applying too rigidly a policy of not allowing a point of view to be put on the A.B.C. if the opposing point of view was not presented more or less at the same time. I pointed out that it would be absurd for the one point of view not to be put simply because its opponent chose to remain silent. By all means, they should be given the opportunity to speak but, by no means, should their decision to remain silent enable the stifling of the viewpoint which they oppose. 'It is wrong that politicians of either Party should in effect be able to censor a debate by refusal to appear,' I said then.

Pressure against the A.B.C. has always involved means other than direct approach or intervention. A public statement, even if unaccompanied by action, can in itself be a source of pressure, designed to frighten men and women engaged in the delicate task of presenting information about matters of public controversy. I have no reason to revise my suspicious views of the motives of a former Postmaster-General who could say: 'I think in some programs there is not what I would call a proper balance, which gets very close to leading to bias on the program and I don't merely say political bias.'

I see no reason to revise my suspicions of the motives of the same man who said in the same statement that the Australian Broadcasting Commissioners should preview controversial programs or programs that were likely to be controversial. I certainly see no reason to revise my suspicions about one Reverend parliamentarian who thought the answer to the problem was to come up with his own set of guidelines for the A.B.C.

I have never made any secret of my great admiration for a former Labor Prime Minister, John Curtin. In talking about the A.B.C., I find again that on this, as on so many other subjects, what he had to say made profound sense. It is worth quoting at some length a statement he made on 12 April 1945. He said then:

> *The Government recognises that the intent of the Australian Broadcasting Act is to create a position of special independence of judgment and action for the national broadcasting instrumentality. This is inevitably the case because of its highly delicate function in broadcasting at public expense news statements and discussions which are potent influences on public opinion and attitudes. As the legislation provides, this peculiar function calls for an undoubted measure of independence for the controlling body of the national broadcasting instrumentality which cannot be measured by the constitution of other semi-governmental boards or agencies which do not impinge on the tender and dangerous realms of moral, religious, aesthetic and political values.*
>
> *In the last resort, the healthy and beneficent functions of national broadcasting and the maintenance of public confidence in the system must rest, in all matters touching these values, solely on the integrity and independent judgement of the persons chosen to determine and administer its policy, and not on either review by, or pressure from, any sources outside it, political or non-political. This principle holds good in spite of the necessary responsibility of the Commission to Parliament through the Minister, for the legitimate use of its funds under the terms of the Act, and all the sections of the Act should be read in the light of the above general intent of Parliament to the establishment of the Commission.*

Those principles hold good today. Those principles, after a period of questionable activity, are being applied again today. I can affirm from this platform that, since it came into office sixteen months ago, the present Government has not sought to interfere with A.B.C. programs. I can affirm that, in that time, we have not sought to suppress any program or determine its contents. Indeed, I can point to one major instance where the present Government has created the opportunity for fuller debate of public issues. It has been the practice of Prime Ministers to make occasional broadcasts to the nation about major matters of public interest. Inevitably those broadcasts have involved at times statements which the Parties opposed to those Prime Ministers would dispute vigorously. When I was Leader of the Opposition, I never had the opportunity to gain a similar forum for the statement of contrary views. The present Leader of the Opposition has such a forum. In the last sixteen months the A.B.C. has acceded to every request he has made for the right to reply to any Report to the Nation which I have delivered.

I talked earlier about the need for durability of basic principles, even at a time of modernisation. My Government is firmly committed to those principles of independence and freedom from political interference. We have sought to maintain and enhance them for the A.B.C. since we came into office. It is our hope that we will establish such a strong precedent in this way that no future government will dare to deny them, that no future government will dare to belittle the competence and judgment of honest men or worse, to seek to drive them from the organisation.

Whitlam had come to power on a platform that included an acknowledgement of the need to legislate for Aboriginal land rights. In 1966 Vincent Lingiari and members of the Gurindji people walked off Wave Hill Station in the Northern Territory in an industrial dispute because Aboriginal workers were paid less than white stockmen. After the Gurindji established a camp at Wattie Creek, traditionally known as Daguragu, the strike action escalated into a land claim. Following lengthy negotiations, in 1975 part of the Wave Hill lease was relinquished to Aboriginal control. On 16 August Whitlam flew to Daguragu, and in a speech suggested by H. C. Coombs, Whitlam formally transferred the Crown lease of the Gurindji ancestral lands to Lingiari. After the speech, in a symbolic gesture, Whitlam poured a handful of earth into Lingiari's hands. Lingiari then stated: 'We are all mates now ... They took our country away from us, now they have brought it back ceremonially'.

On this great day, I, Prime Minister of Australia, speak to you on behalf of the people of Australia—all Australians who honour the land that we live in.

For them I want:

First, to congratulate you and those who have shared your struggle on the victory you have won in that fight for justice begun nine years ago when in protest you walked off Wave Hill Station;

Secondly, to acknowledge that we Australians have still much to do to redress the injustice and oppression that has for so long been the lot of black Australians;

Thirdly, to promise you that this act of restitution which we perform today will not stand alone—your fight was not for yourselves alone and we are determined that Aboriginal Australians everywhere will be helped by it;

Fourthly, to promise that, through their government, the people of Australia will help you in your plans to use this land for the Gurindji;

Finally, to give back to you formally in Aboriginal and Australian law ownership of this land of your fathers.

Vincent Lingiari, I solemnly hand to you these deeds as proof, in Australian law, that these lands belong to the Gurindji people and I put into your hands this piece of earth itself as a sign that we restore them to you and your children forever.

In late 1975 Whitlam faced a constitutional crisis when the Senate refused to pass his government's budget. On 11 November 1975, the Governor-General Sir John Kerr broke the deadlock by sacking Whitlam, ordering a federal election, and appointing Liberal leader Malcolm Fraser as caretaker Prime Minister. A proclamation to this effect was read by the Governor-General's secretary to an angry crowd of Labor supporters, who had gathered at the steps of Parliament House in Canberra. The proclamation ended with the words 'God Save the Queen.' Whitlam stepped to the microphone and gave what is arguably Australia's most famous short speech of the late twentieth century.

Well may we say 'God Save the Queen', because nothing will save the Governor-General! The proclamation which you have just heard read by the Governor-General's official secretary was countersigned 'Malcolm Fraser' who will undoubtedly go down in Australian history from Remembrance Day 1975 as Kerr's cur. They won't silence the outskirts of Parliament House, even if the inside has been silenced for the next few weeks. The Governor-General's proclamation was signed after he already made an appointment to meet the Speaker at a quarter to five. The House of Representatives had requested the Speaker to give the Governor-General its decision that Mr Fraser did not have the confidence of the House and that the Governor-General should call me to form the Government.

Maintain your rage and enthusiasm through the campaign for the election now to be held and until polling day.

Speech sources, in order:
Abridged.
Source: 'It's Time For Leadership', 1972 Labor Party Policy Speech, Blacktown Civic Centre, 13 November 1972, Whitlam Institute Archives.

Reproduced in full.
Source: 'Speech at the Opening Ceremony of new A.B.C. Building complex, Collinswood, Adelaide, 29 March 1974', Whitlam Institute Archives.

Reproduced in full.
Source: Gough Whitlam, *The Whitlam Government 1972–1975*.[55]

Reproduced in full.
Source: Gough Whitlam, *The Truth of the Matter*.[56]

Al Grassby

A Multi-Cultural Society in 2000, 1973

Albert (Al) Jaime Grassby (1926–) is a writer and commentator, and a former poli-tician in the New South Wales and federal parliaments. During 1972–74, he was Minister for Immigration in the Labor reformist government of Gough Whitlam. Grassby's flamboyant personal style—he sported continental sideburns and favoured wide colourful ties—was accompanied by a robust vision of a modern Australia where a pluralist society offered equal opportunities to all regardless of their 'origins, beliefs, wealth or ability'. He was responsible for the swift introduction of a host of reforms in the areas of immigration, citizenship and social services to Australians from non-English-speaking backgrounds. On 11 August 1973 Grassby delivered a lively land-mark speech at a public symposium organized in Melbourne and entitled 'Strategy 2000: Australia for Tomorrow'. Here, Grassby officially launched the influential idea of a multicultural Australia, where migrants would be supported by the state in the maintenance of their ethnic diversity, rather than expected to adopt previous policies of assimilation or integration with Anglo–Australian social and cultural norms. In the decades that followed, the effectiveness of the policy and philosophy of multi-culturalism to provide social equality and promote national unity has been variously debated in academic, governmental and populist forums.

I wish to record at the outset my conviction that the future of our society is essentially hopeful. When we consider the achievements of the suc-cessors to that non-descript band of 'assisted passage' migrants who landed at Sydney Cove on the first Australia Day 1788, we must be pardoned for some small sense of national pride. This pride derives as much from the creation of a stable and relatively just society as from any material success.

Again, I am hopeful because there has come about in our community in recent years a greater self-awareness and a new self-criticism which are indicative of our greater maturity. The 'lucky country' syndrome is losing something of its cynical ring. The desire to do something with our herit-age rather than simply live off it is becoming commoner, as seen in the ecology movement. Today there seems to be more of a desire to see things re-ordered as they could be or should be, rather than simply retained as they have always been. These stirrings are triggered by, and in turn con-tribute to, the growth of a 'new nationalism', as it is already being called. Who are we in Australia? What are our social origins? How should these origins influence us today? How should we build upon them in shaping a better and more just future? Is the process to be one of steady evolution or noisy revolution?

We may justly claim that to have woven our present national fabric from originally rather ill-assorted strands, but without suffering the major upheavals marking the histories of other societies, is no small achieve-ment. Again, to have built up hitherto a sort of national expertise in absorbing people from many different backgrounds lends us confidence as migration continues to strengthen and enrich the character of our society. In itself, however, this does not permit us to assume that solutions to yesterday's problems will provide answers to today's—or tomorrow's—challenges. For, as the very composition of our society changes, every problem takes on a new twist. The complexity of the issues now calls for a new flexibility of mind in approaching them and grappling with them. In the face of such change and the increasing ethnic diversification which has provided the impetus for much of it, young Australians seem to exercise an admirable openness and tolerance.

Unfortunately, this cannot be said of all other groups in the community. Despite the diversity that has always been present in Australian society—and today is the very hallmark of it—many intellectual circles in the community show scant evidence of recognizing its importance, or even its existence. A widespread ignorance seems to prevail about what is actually happening to the fabric of Australian society under the continuous impact of a migration which, in terms of proportionate numbers of newcomers to the base population, is virtually without parallel in modern times.

Something of a conspiracy of silence persists in many quarters about the social impact of other than Anglo-Saxon influences on our national life. To take a homely illustration, how often do our television screens reflect anything like the variety of migrant groups encountered in a real-life stroll through our city streets, or particularly our near-city suburbs?

The image we manage to convey of ourselves still seems to range from the bushwhacker to the sportsman to the slick city businessman. Where is the Maltese process worker, the Finnish carpenter, the Italian concrete layer, the Yugoslav miner or—dare I say it—the Indian scientist? Where do these people belong, in all honesty, if not in today's composite Australian image? Are they to be non-people—despite their economic contribution to our well-being—because they do not happen to fit the largely American-oriented stereotypes of our entertainment industry? It would seem a mark of national maturity to be able to identify firstly what is essential and distinctive about one's own land and its people, and then to portray it consistently with insight and sympathy.

If it is a fact that Australia is now one of the most cosmopolitan societies on earth—and the evidence confirms that it is—it is time that all Australians were encouraged to develop a better understanding of what this implies.

To the average Australian, whether 'old' or 'new', terms like 'assimilation', 'integration', 'homogeneous' or 'pluralistic' society are probably meaningless. The concept I prefer, the 'family of the nation', is one that ought to convey an immediate and concrete image to all. In a family the overall attachment to the common good need not impose a sameness on the outlook or activity of each member, nor need these members deny their individuality and distinctiveness in order to seek a superficial and unnatural conformity.

Today, irrespective of what labels we use, the fact is that the increasing diversity of Australian society has gradually eroded and finally rendered untenable any prospects there might have been twenty years ago of fully assimilating newcomers to the 'Australian way of life', to use a phrase common at that time.

We might well ask ourselves: what is the Australian way of life? The life styles and values of the suburban housewife in Moonee Ponds, the Italian travel agent in Carlton, the Turkish car factory worker, the Slavic Orthodox priest, or the Aboriginal at Lake Tyers? It is all too easy to over-look the pre-existence in this land of the original Australians, millennia before the advent of us 'white ethnics'. Any theory that fails to accord these people an equal place in the family of our nation is out of the ques-tion today and in the future. Likewise other ethnic groups introduced to this land by our migration programs may not be denied an equal place in our future society.

My vision of our society in the year 2000 foreshadows a greatly in-creasing social complexity, in which the dynamic interaction between the diverse ethnic components will be producing new national initiatives, stimulating new artistic endeavours, and ensuring great strength in diver-sity. In foreshadowing the future character of this interaction, we do little service to our history to imagine that Australia could ever have become a pale reproduction of Britain, a pseudo-America, or a make–believe Asia. In this respect we have always diverged from the ethnically static societies of the Old World and share the potential dynamism of the developing societies of the New World.

The dynamism in an ethnically diverse society seems somehow related to the group life within that society. It is not simply the product of the individual differences between its citizens. These may indeed become blurred through interaction over a period of time, but the life of an ethnic group is more resilient and retains its identity. Thus a social philosophy that presupposes the submergence of all ethnic diversity in a melting pot—at a time when current migrant is continuing to infuse new members —also seems out of touch with the realities. The corporate life of ethnic groups represents a great deal more than the simple totality of their members' lives and activity. To an extent, they have created their own national image. They have brought with them a common history and cul-ture, an ideology different from the Anglo-Saxon. They perceive different goals and pursue them in their own traditional ways. In short, they lead a way of life which, while in living touch with its ancient forms and impulses, is imperceptibly coming to terms with—or at least learning to co-exist with—that of many other ethnic groups in our society and of course with the 'old Australians'. Such pluralism is not operating within a time scale, but looks far ahead into the future.

There have been critics of the pluralist approach who have seen it as leading to a fragmented society, lacking in cohesion and threatening to produce a complete, permanent and hostile segregation of one part of our population. I believe this is postulating an unreal threat—a sort of com-munal apartheid—which is not founded on fact. The situation in Australia today is that concentrations of multiple ethnic groups do exist in our major cities, and that these show signs of considerable durability. However, economically they are already integrated with our society by virtue of their involvement in the Australian work-force. Further, because of the co-existence in these localities of many different ethnic groups in close proximity, there can be no question of one part of the population permanently living in hostile segregation from the majority.

In this situation, there is nothing threatening to Australia's future in the year 2000. We need to bear in mind that time is on our side. In terms of world history, we are still a young country, and our achievements thus far promise for an even brighter future.

Our prime task at this time in our history must be to encourage practical forms of social interaction in our community. This implies the creation of a truly just society in which all components can enjoy freedom to make their own distinctive contribution to the family of the nation. In the interests of Australians of the year 2000, we need to appreciate, embrace and preserve all those diverse elements which find a place in the nation today. This involves the most fundamental issues of human rights such as those enshrined in the United Nations International Covenant on Civil and Political Rights, which the Government has expressed its intention of ratifying. The Covenant guarantees freedom of social and cultural expression for all residents of countries ratifying it.

The social and cultural rights of migrant Australians are just as compelling as the rights of other Australians. The full realisation of these would lead to reduced conflicts and tensions between the groups which are weaving an ever more complex fabric for Australian society as we hurry towards the turn of the century.

My personal ambition is that Australians of all backgrounds will always be proud before the world to say in whatever accents, 'I am an Australian', just as the proudest boast in the days of the Roman imperium was contained in the words, 'Civis Romanus sum'.

Abridged.
Source: A. J. Grassby, *A Multi-Cultural Society For the Future*, paper delivered at the Cairnmillar Institute's Symposium 'Strategy 2000: Australia for Tomorrow', Melbourne, 11 August 1973.[57]

Manning Clark
The 'Cleansing Fire' Speech, 1978

Charles Manning Hope Clark (1915–1991) is the author of the six-volume epic *A History of Australia* and undoubtedly Australia's most famous historian. He was professor of History at the Australian National University during 1949 to 1972, but moved beyond the confines of academia in the scope and literary approach of his writings and in his engagement with public life. In 1972 Clark came under the spell of Gough Whitlam, elected that year as the first Labor prime minister for a generation. Whitlam was an intellectual, a lover of high culture, a reformer and a champion of working people. To Clark, Whitlam held out the hope that Australians might at last claim their true independence and celebrate their own culture. But in November 1975, a Governor-General wearing an English top hat dismissed Whitlam from office. When the electorate ratified that dismissal, Clark was filled with rage and despair; perhaps peaceful social reform in Australia was impossible. In this dark fury, Clark delivered his 'Cleansing Fire' speech at a graduation ceremony at the Australian National University on 21 April 1978. The speech was both a fiery call to insurrection and a bleak warning that the scourge of political violence was about to sweep the land.

I would like to thank the ANU for giving me the chance to speak to the graduands, though I am somewhat at a loss to know what persuaded you that a man who was well past the throbbings of noontide could have anything to say. When a man is young, we have been told, he walks where he wants to walk, and when he is old he stretches forth his hands, only to be led where he no longer wants to go.

I am a historian. I like to believe that a knowledge of the past can make both our living and our dying easier, can make life both more intelligible and more bearable, and clothe it with majesty. And as a historian I can only speak to you by creating a scene.

My scene is in Melbourne of the late 1920s or early 1930s. I was at that time of life when all things are great darkness to us, and we are so to ourselves, watching with astonishment of heart adults sing 'Land of Hope and Glory', especially the words:

Wider still and wider may thy bounds be set, God, who made thee mighty, make thee mightier yet!

I am thinking not just of the absurdity of a group of human beings who, having sung the first line loudly, tried to sing the next line so much more loudly that all sorts of curious octave leaps and cracking of voices and dissonances occurred as they shouted, 'make thee mightier yet'. But I am thinking of the greater absurdity of these men and women who saw themselves as guardians of human behaviour being carried away by such words: of matronly bosoms showing unmistakable signs of what we now call heavy breathing; and a look of exaltation, sometimes of wild ecstasy, in the eyes of men not given to wearing their hearts on their sleeves; the absurdity of these men and women assuming that their benevolent God was on their side, rather than, say, with the Irish, or the Germans, or the Chinese; or, for that matter, perhaps indifferent to the wilder hopes and silly dreams of human beings.

I mention this scene because, of course, 'Land of Hope and Glory' belongs now in the dustbin of human history. It is a song about, or a hymn of praise to and approval of, domination—in this case the domination of one people over the rest of the world. Now, like me, you have had the misfortune in your years here to be educated in a system which is still affected by the days of domination. Like me, you sampled this system when domination was on the way out, and the education system which had been designed to serve the interests of the British governing class was still with us—with all its absurdities.

Now, all forms of domination are thought of as evil—of man over nature, class over class, man over woman, father over children, teacher over students. Hence, one of the exciting things for you to take part in is to write the books and select the literature which will prepare humanity for a future without domination, because it looks as though at long last men and women are about to be freed from their gaolers and oppressors. That is my first point. My second point is that we do not know what human life is going to be like once the last stains of domination have been washed from the human heart—of both the dominator and the dominated. We have been given prophecies—a time will come when the distinction between brain and manual labour will disappear, when the freedom of each will be the condition of the freedom of all. But these are as vague as that great earlier comforter of mankind. All those millions of people down the ages have professed a belief in the life of the world to come, without saying what that would be like. We can be sure only of one thing: that when posterity looks at us, they too will find much that will appear foolish, because the story of mankind is partly the record of human folly, a record of the passions of mankind, and all the madness in our hearts.

Now it looks as though we here in Australia are in for a period of upheaval, of turbulence, as domination disappears. At the moment there is a lull: a great dullness so deep that no one can fathom it has descended on us. But it looks as though this might be the calm before a great storm. A tempest or, to change the image, a cleansing fire, or a destructive fire may sweep over our ancient continent, stirring up the madness in men's and women's hearts—maybe a fratricidal war. We might all be tried in a fiery furnace.

The land, we know, will recover. That is the miracle we Australians know, that after a great dry, or a fire, the bush has its own resurrection. The great question will be whether we humans can also, as it were, rise again out of the ashes. That is where your membership of what I will poetically call 'the eternal city' becomes relevant. Those who have thought about the things that matter, those who care (happily a much wider community than just the community of graduates, and I like to believe in a coming alliance between the intellectuals, the artists, writers and the people—there being wisdom in the people who know old Australia) must address themselves to the central questions: the ownership of wealth, who is going to exercise power, why there is evil in the world. They will note the great divisions of humanity, especially perhaps between the followers of the Enlightenment and those who hold a religious view of the world. These people will be standing on entrenched ground; they will not be distracted or seduced by the trivialisers, or the muddiers of the waters. Above all, those who care, including you, will be watching to see the direction of the great river of life.

I suppose the great chance for a person who *cares* (including you) is that they won't find themselves in a billabong. Even if horrible things happen again in our country, such people will still hear the music of the spheres, and not allow the muddy vesture of civil strife to darken the picture in their minds and their hearts of what it is all about—what it has all been for. All of us are, in that sense, believers. Don't let anyone kill that faith.

Reproduced in full.
Source: Manning Clark, *Speaking Out of Turn.*[58]

———◆———

Malcolm Fraser

Opposing Apartheid in South Africa, 1982

(John) Malcolm Fraser (1930–) speaks in a style that is both hesitant and curt—his haughty accent betraying his origins as heir to a wealthy pastoral dynasty. Fraser achieved the dismissal of the Whitlam Labor Government in 1975 and was endorsed by a record majority at the polls. As a result, Labor supporters loathed him as a stony-hearted conservative who had perverted the Constitution. But, with the passing of time, Fraser has been recast as a rock-solid defender of human rights—and one of the last of the Menzian liberals. Fraser was to win two further elections, in 1977 and 1980, and his most famous one-liner, 'Life was not meant to be easy', summed up his wariness of the welfare state. He was a vigorous proponent of an official policy of multiculturalism and, under his leadership, Australia's immigration intake increased—most notably with the arrival of migrants from Vietnam. In the international arena Fraser had declared opposition to ideas of racial superiority at a meeting of Commonwealth heads in 1977, and he worked through the Commonwealth for the independence of Zimbabwe. Following his predecessor Whitlam, Fraser was critical of South Africa's apartheid government and imposed cultural sanctions on South African products. This move found sympathy within the wider community, where protests had been directed towards South African sporting teams, boycotts had targeted South African goods, and Australian trade unions and churches had expressed support for the anti-apartheid activities of their South African counterparts. During parliamentary Question Time in March 1982, Fraser's decision to ban Australia's national airline, Qantas, from flying to South Africa was challenged. His speech in reply was characteristically brief and decisive, inviting no debate. In 1985 Fraser was to continue his opposition to South Africa when he was invited by Bob Hawke, the Labor prime minister who ousted him from power, to join an eminent persons' panel on the issue.

Qantas is operating to Mauritius and it is hoped that it will extend such operation to routes in southern Africa and further on. I know that Qantas has been examining the matter. The Government was concerned that Qantas should not re-establish its direct link with South Africa. I think the reasons for that are well known. We do not wish to, and do not, encourage trade with South Africa. Although there is no prohibition of it, there is no active promotion of trade with South Africa. We believe that maximum pressure should be exerted against South Africa, to seek to break down the system of apartheid. I think we all know that there is a degree of racial intolerance amongst all countries, but most countries around the world, by law, practice or custom, seek to diminish and eradicate racial intolerance. That is certainly the approach of the States and the Commonwealth of Australia. It is certainly the approach of the overwhelming majority of Australian citizens of all political complexions. The difference in South Africa is simply that racial intolerance, bigotry and discrimination are enshrined in the law in a multitude of ways. People cannot move without a police pass. People of the wrong colour cannot live in certain areas. People of the wrong colour might be allowed to get a job in an area, but their wives and families have to stay 300 miles behind, in the hills. The honourable gentleman may know people who work in South Africa. An engineer, the son of some people with whom I am on friendly terms, does in fact work in South Africa, and the letters that are sent back describe, whether it be on the playing field or whatever, kinds of discrimination which Australians would certainly find abhorrent.

Sir Robert Menzies indicated in earlier discussions, going back I suppose 20 or 30 years, that he believed that the whole system of apartheid was abhorrent and doomed to the most ghastly failure because, in all its simplicity, the South Africans were saying that they would give black Africans educational and economic equality but never, of course, political equality. Therein is the certainty that apartheid must one day fail, because the more people have educational or economic equality, the less will they be prepared to accept or tolerate political inequality. Whatever view one might have of the immorality of apartheid, logically, and on a straight analysis of what apartheid is about, it is doomed to failure. Therefore, successive Australian governments over time have sought, with many other nations, to exert pressure in relation to South Africa so that there may be a modification and change of policy; so that something that is abhorrent to the very nature of people and of human relationships can be modified and changed by evolution rather than by much rougher and more difficult means if there should be no change on the part of the South African Government. It is based on our attitude to the South African regime, to its nature, to the fact that apartheid and discrimination are enshrined in law, that we take certain actions that we otherwise would not. As I have said on a number of occasions, it is not South Africa that is a bulwark against communism in Southern Africa. Rather, it presents an invitation to communism because the nature of the system that it has established invites communism to overthrow something that is repugnant to the whole human race.

Reproduced in full.
Source: *Commonwealth Parliamentary Debates*, vol. 127, 25 March 1982, p. 1396.

———◆———

Lionel Murphy
Mr Neal is Entitled to be an Agitator, 1982

Lionel Keith Murphy (1922–1986) was the reforming Attorney General in the Whitlam Government, until he became a progressive High Court judge in 1975. He often disagreed with his fellow judges and he remained outspoken on the great issues of the day. Unlike conservative judges, Murphy drew on a wide range of scholarly sources to examine questions of social justice and human rights. This free-ranging style is well demonstrated in the famous case of Mr Neal. Percy Alfred Neal chaired the Council of the Yarrabah Aboriginal reserve in northern Queensland. One evening, he and another man confronted Mr Collins, the white manager of the Yarrabah store, and accused him of selling substandard products to the Aborigines, including rotten meat. The men began arguing angrily at the front door of Collins' house, until Neal spat in Collins' face. Neal ended up in the Magistrate's Court, where he was fined $75 for unlawful entry and was given a hefty two months with hard labour for spitting. The Queensland Court of Criminal Appeal not only refused to hear Neal's appeal, it increased his sentence to six months hard labour. Neal then appealed to the High Court, where all four judges agreed the case had been seriously mishandled and quashed the Supreme Court's ruling. But two of the High Court judges refused to interfere with the original two-month sentence. Justices Murphy and Gerard Brennan dissented. Murphy was appalled by the racism in the case and by the magistrate's revelation that he was punishing Neal not simply for spitting but because he was a political troublemaker. In this context, argued Murphy, Mr Neal was entitled to be an agitator.

The appellant [Mr Neal] is an Aborigine, as was the person with him. The complainant [Collins] is a white officer of the Department of Aboriginal and Torres Strait Islanders Affairs. All other officers employed by the Department at the reserve are white, with the exception of a 'liaison officer'. The magistrate said the population on the communities, of which Yarrabah is one, 'is usually made up of hundreds of Aboriginals compared with forty to fifty white staff including families'. The magistrate told Mr Neal: 'Your actions in taking unto yourself the task of removing all whites from Yarrabah cannot be condoned from any angle from which you may view community affairs'.

And further: 'Violence is something in recent times which has crept into Aboriginal communities. I blame your type for this growing hatred of black against white. You are not giving true representation as a leader to the people who voted you their leader. As a magistrate I visit four to five communities, and I can say unequivocally that the majority of genuine Aboriginals do not condone this behaviour and are not desirous in any shape or form of having changes made. They live a happy life, and it is only the likes of yourself who push this attitude of the hatred of white authority, that upset the harmonious running of these communities.'

These remarks disclosed, if it were not already apparent, that this was a race relations case, intimately related to the politics of Aboriginal communities and the system under which Aboriginals live in the communities. The remarks assume more importance because they were advanced in this court as a justification for sentences by the magistrate and by the Court of Criminal Appeal. The Crown claimed that they showed that the magistrate had properly taken into account the special circumstances of the Aborigines. Rather the magistrate's remarks show that he had put himself in opposition to the political stance of the defendant that conditions need changing on the reserves. Although Mr Collins had told Mr Neal he should 'go through the channels' if he desired change, the magistrate told him it was wrong to seek to change anything. The Court of Criminal Appeal did not disapprove or comment on these remarks. The magistrate took into account political views and actions against the appellant. This is rarely, if ever, justified, whether it be on trial or sentence. Those remarks were not only patronising and insulting; they also made clear that anyone who agitated for change, 'in any shape or form', in the Aboriginal communities, would be under a disadvantage in that Magistrate's Court. In its supervision of the criminal justice system of the State, the Court of Criminal Appeal has a duty to see that racism is not allowed to operate within the judicial system. It should have disapproved of the unjudicial manner in which the magistrate dealt with sentence.

That Mr Neal was an 'agitator' or stirrer in the magistrate's view obviously contributed to the severe penalty. If he is an agitator, he is in good company. Many of the great religious and political figures of history have been agitators, and human progress owes much to the efforts of these and the many who are unknown. As [Oscar] Wilde aptly pointed out in *The Soul of Man under Socialism*, 'Agitators are a set of interfering, meddling people, who come down to some perfectly contented class of the community and sow the seeds of discontent amongst them. That is the reason why agitators are so absolutely necessary. Without them, in our incomplete state, there would be no advance towards civilisation.' Mr Neal is entitled to be an agitator.

The evidence showed that Mr Neal and his fellow Aborigines at the Yarrabah Community have a deep sense of grievance at their paternalistic treatment by the white authorities in charge of the Reserve, including Mr Collins. The Council and Aboriginal members of the Community had no control over what was sold at the store under management of Mr Collins. The evidence at the hearing was that although Mr Neal complained that Mr Collins sold rotten meat, Mr Neal and the Aboriginal Council were powerless to do anything about it, apart from making representations to departmental officers. Mr Collins gave evidence before the magistrate that the management would consider Council representations and make a determination independent of the Yarrabah Council and the Aboriginal Community. Affidavit evidence before the Court of Criminal Appeal showed Mr Neal had been elected to the Aboriginal Council on a platform of self-management; he had made continuing representations to the Federal and State Governments in an endeavour to obtain self-management for his community, without success; and the Yarrabah Council, chaired by Mr Neal, had made application to the Federal Government to have the Yarrabah Community declared a self-managing community under the Aboriginal and Torres Strait Islanders (Queensland Reserves and Communities Self-Management) Act 1978.

Aboriginal sense of grievance has developed over the two hundred years of white settlement in Australia. Early in the nineteenth century Aborigines were 'being treated with arrogant superiority, often accompanied by considerable brutality'. The plight of the Aborigines was compounded by the introduction of European diseases and alcohol which, in addition to white colonization, 'contributed to the fragmentation of Aboriginal society and helped to promote the apathetic attitudes erroneously attributed by the Europeans to inferior intellectual capacity'. Aborigines have complained bitterly about white paternalism robbing them of their dignity and right to direct their own lives. In 1938 the New South Wales Aborigines' Progress Association protested, [according to Lilla Watson]: 'You took our land by force ... you have almost exterminated our people, but there (are) enough of us remaining to expose the humbug of your claim... We do not wish to be regarded with sentimental sympathy like koala bears as exhibits ... (nor) studied as scientific or anthropological curiosities... Why do you deliberately keep us backward? Is it merely to give yourselves the pleasure of feeling superior? ... that we are naturally a backward and low race is a scientific lie... At worst we are no more dirty, lazy, stupid, criminal or immoral, than white people. Also your slanders against our race are moral lies, told to throw all the blame for our troubles on to us.'

That Aborigines have a right to participate in and direct their own policies has been reiterated by Aboriginal representatives speaking for themselves and for their people. The United States' experience has shown that persons frustrated by powerlessness through the exercise of racist policies and practices, and the expression of racist ideals, feel their grievances deeply and sometimes express them in the only way possible—by protest or violence. The complaints enumerated in that report are well replicated in Australian society in every State of the Commonwealth.

The Director of the Australian Institute of Criminology [William Clifford] has said: 'At the cutting edge of the contact between black and white communities in this country is the law and particularly the manner of its enforcement. Its gross injustice to the Aboriginal, in its present form ... [is an issue] ... paraded by scholars, agencies and departments again and again ... Whether the criminal justice system is a discriminating instrument of power or a social scapegoat for problems which society cannot solve, we might regard it as a useful barometer of the state of balance between law and order on the one hand and human rights on the other ...'.

Although Aborigines comprise only 1% of the total population they make up nearly 30% of the prison population, and at times exceed that level. Comparing the disproportionate numbers of arrests of Indians in Canada, Maoris and Islanders in New Zealand, and Malays in Sri Lanka, Australia's rate according to the 1976 Census of 726.5 Aborigines in prison per 100,000 (there are about 140,000 Aborigines in this country) can reasonably be speculated to be 'the highest rate of imprisonment in the world'. Elizabeth Eggleston in her pioneering work on Aborigines and the criminal justice system concluded that there is 'discrimination against Aborigines in sentencing and this discrimination chiefly occurs in the choice of imprisonment as a suitable sentence in a higher proportion of Aboriginal cases, instead of the imposition of a lighter penalty'. A disproportionate number of Aborigines in South Australia are charged with minor offences, and they are also more likely than other persons appearing on minor offences to receive gaol sentences. This disparity also occurs in NSW and in other States.

Spitting is humiliating and degrading. It is a typical response of children and others without power, attempting to humiliate and degrade those who are seen as oppressors. The sentence of imprisonment imposed upon Mr Neal will not improve race relations but will tend to embitter them. Taking into account the racial relations aspect of this case, the fact that Mr Neal was placed in a position of inferiority to the whites managing the reserve should have been a special mitigating factor in determining sentence.

In sentencing the court should consider the offence, the character and record of the defendant and all mitigating and aggravating circumstances. Where there is no specific justification for withholding credit for mitigating factors the sentencer will be expected to make an appropriate reduction. Not to do so is an exceptional course limited to those cases where a particular emphasis on deterrence is justified, or where there are other considerations such as the prevention of further offences, which are compelling. A sentence which fails to reflect the presence of recognized mitigating factors will, in the general run of cases, be reduced on appeal.

Because of these considerations leave to appeal against the magistrate's sentence should be granted and the appeal allowed. Taking into account the fact that Mr Neal has already served over a week's imprisonment, and that his movements during his time on bail were severely curtailed, an appropriate sentence for the assault is a fine of $130, that is, one week's wages.

Abridged; bibliographical references and reference to other cases have been removed.
Source: Neal v The Queen 149 *Commonwealth Law Report* 305, at 314–20, 24 September 1982.

———▶———

Geoffrey Blainey

The Warrnambool Speech: 'Too Many Asians', 1984

Geoffrey Norman Blainey (1930–) has transformed Australians' sense of their past with inventive histories such as *The Tyranny of Distance* (1966) and *The Triumph of the Nomads* (1975). After graduating from the University of Melbourne with an Arts degree, majoring in History, Blainey worked for some years as a successful freelance historian, returning to the university where he held professorships first in Economic History and then in History. He is a public speaker of seamless eloquence, with a compelling use of language and metaphor. By the mid-1970s Blainey had established a unique public profile, serving on national arts and advisory bodies, chairing the Australia–China Council and advancing his view of Australian history in a television series. In March 1984 he attracted national attention, and was criticised by many of his academic colleagues, after he gave a widely reported speech to a Rotary Club conference in the Capitol Theatre in the Victorian town of Warrnambool. Blainey's offence was that he attacked the principle of a 'multicultural Australia'. For over a decade, multiculturalism had been so widely promoted that most urban liberals imagined it enjoyed broad community support. But Blainey warned that, under the Hawke Labor Government, Asian migrants had reached numbers which threatened Australia's European traditions and its social cohesion. In the furious public debate that followed, Blainey hardened his position, warning that Australia was fragmenting into 'a nation of tribes'. In retrospect, the seismic impact of this speech signalled that patriotic conservatism was regaining a level of public authority within Australian politics and the community that it had not exercised since the late 1960s.

In the last few years—especially in the last year—we have given powerful preference to Asian migrants. It is almost as if we have turned the White Australia Policy inside out. More than half our immigrants are now from Asia, and many come from a peasant background, which is very different to the educated background of the typical Asian immigrant of recent years. Rarely in the history of the modern world has a nation given such preference to a tiny ethnic minority in its population as the Australian government has done in the last few years. They have made that minority the favoured majority in its immigration policy.

The pace of Asian immigration is now far ahead of public opinion, especially the public opinion in those suburbs and workplaces to which many of these Vietnamese and Kampuchean refugees will go.

In the last resort it is not the politicians, it is not Canberra, which determines whether an immigration program will succeed. It is public opinion which decides.

In a time of large unemployment, any immigration program has to be managed with skill and care. Is our immigration program being run with sufficient skill and care? An increasing proportion of Australians seem to be resentful of the large numbers of Vietnamese and other south-east Asians who are being brought in, have little chance of gaining work, and are living—through no fault of their own—at the taxpayers' expense. The present government is jeopardizing the remarkable gains in tolerance and understanding slowly built up in Australia in the last third of a century.

The flaw in the old White Australia Policy was its arrogance, its insensitivity, its lack of proportion. The flaw in this new immigration policy is its arrogance, its insensitivity to a large section of Australian opinion.

Mr Hawke's government has deservedly won praise for its attempt to heal old wounds, for what is called consensus. The present immigration program, if it is not looked at more carefully, could do more than anything in the last thirty years to weaken or explode that consensus.

Abridged.
Sources: Blainey spoke largely off the cuff that day. A local journalist taped the speech and reported key sentences. These form the first paragraph of this reconstruction (*Standard*, Warrnambool) 19 March 1984, p. 1. The final paragraphs printed here are quoted from the only part of the speech Blainey wrote out in advance, reproduced in Geoffrey Blainey, *All for Australia*.[59]

Galarrwuy Yunupingu
Land Rights and Uranium, 1984

Galarrwuy Yunupingu (1948–) is a Gumadj elder of the Yolngu people and a prominent land rights activist and statesman. He was born at Melville Bay near Yirrkala in East Arnhem Land, on the Gove Peninsula in the Northern Territory. As a young man, Yunupingu acted as an interpreter when his people mounted a pioneering legal case in the Supreme Court of the Northern Territory. This was the famous *Gove Land Rights* case (1971), in which the Aborigines asserted their right to expel a mining company from their traditional territory. The court acknowledged that Aboriginal land law existed but ruled that it had no force under Australian law. Legally, the entire continent was unoccupied when whites arrived: it was *terra nullius*. This stark judgment gave new energy to the land rights struggle, and in 1976 the Fraser Government passed the Land Rights Act, allowing Aboriginal communities in the Northern Territory to claim their traditional territories. In the midst of these reforms, Yunupingu became chairman of the new Northern Lands Council. To the dismay of many environmentalists and anti-nuclear campaigners, he promptly negotiated an agreement allowing the Ranger uranium mine to proceed on his people's land. Yunupingu was not opposed to mining in principle, as long as Indigenous people retained control of their lands and benefited economically from mining wealth. He became Australian of the Year in 1978 in recognition of his negotiation with mining companies and government. In June 1984 Yunupingu explained his position to the National Press Club in Canberra. An exceptional linguist and powerful speaker, he began his speech with a message in his own language to Aboriginal people in the Northern Territory, especially in Arnhem Land.

Let me explain why we need land rights. It is not to get back at white people for taking our land from us, or to take the richest land we can. Our relationship with the land is part of our religion and our beliefs. Aboriginal religion is not some mumbo-jumbo that started when white men came to this country. Our relationship with the land is part of our religion and our belief. Aboriginal culture is as rich, as deep, as varied as any in the world. Our heritage can help make Australia culturally rich and one of the most diverse and satisfying nations of the world. Our past is as alive as the present, and directs our future. It is our responsibility and obligation to care for and look after the traditional countries, to sing life into the land so that the land will continue to give us life itself.

Our Creation Time created the blueprint for Aboriginal social life. Good and bad things happened during this time and we will learn and solve our problems by using these events as our permanent guidelines. Guidelines we know to be right because our culture has lived and flourished under their protection for thousands of years. We will not throw our blueprint for life away and take your laws when even you have to keep changing your laws because they don't work for your own culture. Our past is real and this cannot be manipulated to fit into the last two hundred years. You can only talk about it. Our past cannot be chopped off with new laws like yours. Our past is our system of life. Then, now and for the future. It cannot be changed and we cannot tell lies about it.

This leads me to talk about the attack made by mining companies and the Northern Territory Government that Aboriginal sacred sites were invented and dreamed up by white missionaries and anthropologists and are not part of our past. Every time mining companies or governments say sacred sites are made up it tells us they don't understand any of our ways. They don't have any knowledge of our laws which bind tribal country and give those people the right to claim their land. We cannot lie about sacred sites. Our past cannot be killed. We do not advertise our religion like the white man does. To us it is something very deep. That is why we keep our sacred sites secret. They are not something we want everyone to know about, to advertise so people can walk over them and photograph them. It is our life-force, not a tourist attraction we are talking about. Aboriginal people are very reluctant to reveal where their sacred sites are. We only do that when mining looks like threatening them. We only define a general area of sacred sites when there is no other alternative. When will people listen and think reasonably about who Aboriginal people really are? Aboriginal people have culture, and cultural systems and a relationship to land and the land has a relationship with the people. We own the land and the land owns us. We belong to each other. This is the reason I point out very strongly that the land we claim is really ours and the sacred sites are real.

What is true is that some Aboriginal people want mining to go ahead on their land and others don't want it. Where my people want mining I will help them get it. Where they do not want mining I will help them stop the mining company from entering their land. Our right under the Land Rights Act is to be able to say no to mining if we don't want it.

We know we can only begin to gain true economic independence through mining royalties and, in the case of my people, that means allowing uranium mining on our land. We would be happy if the mines were not uranium but they are. This is a fact of life that cannot be changed. The position of the Northern Land Council on uranium mining is quite clear. Our attitude is the attitude of our people, the traditional owners of these lands. If they say they want to mine uranium then that is what I will fight for. I carry out their decisions.

Let me make our positions clear about Kuinda and Jabaluka mines. The traditional owners of those areas want uranium mining to proceed but the Federal Government is stopping the new mines. We want the Government to change its policy. That is something everyone needs to know. We do not want to make life difficult for anyone, we merely want to exercise our power of ownership over our own land. Land ownership is power. Decision-making about land is power. Management of land is the symbol of ownership of power, determining what happens on land is carrying out the power of ownership.

We are not being manipulated by anyone. We have our own brains that make our own decisions. Before I can commit the Northern Land Council to anything, I must consult with every one of the traditional owners in the area whose land is affected. Then they have to discuss things among themselves and tell me what they want to do at the full Land Council meetings. It is not easy to get together eighty people from remote areas. It takes time but mining companies do not have time. The ore has been there in the ground for millions of years. We have managed the land for forty thousand years. On these scales the delay the miner speaks of are only the blink of an eye.

When the land rights were born in Australia twenty years ago Aboriginal people began speaking out for themselves and saying things that the white man had not heard us say before. Now we make our own decisions and people listen to us and that worries some mining companies. They are scared of us and because of their fear and ignorance they have run campaigns against us, against land rights and against the Government's Aboriginal Heritage legislation. Some of them have made disgraceful attacks on us as a race of people. Since I have been representing my people I have met many people in high places including Prime Ministers and Premiers, leaders of big companies and all sorts of people. I have learnt one thing—we Aboriginal people really can't trust anyone. They all want to use us for their own reasons. Politicians see us as votes whether they are for us or against us because Aboriginal people are good electoral issues. The mining companies use us as their whipping post and other people see us as the next trendy cause to fight for. But the politicians are worse. I say this here at the National Press Club, because I know some of you must agree with me.

In less than two weeks the ALP will hold its National Conference here in Canberra and I am very interested in what happens to the policy on uranium. But it is all a big act. Most of the delegates will be debating issues which have been decided. Everything me and my people have been doing over the past few months supporting our claims to be able to do as we like with out land, hinges on that conference. Unfortunately a very small group within the ALP is determined to stop uranium mining in this country at whatever cost. The left-wing has decided that it will impose on you and me and on the whole country its own views on uranium mining. It is dictating to the Labor Party and therefore the Government of this country.

But does it have the right to do that? Sixty-five percent of Australians are in favour of uranium mining but the left-wing ignores that figure. They also ignore the fact that many of them claim to support us in our land rights. They are hypocrites when they say that. If they support us they would respect our rights to make our own decisions on our land. They have dumped us, the Aboriginal people. By its action the left-wing of the ALP is threatening the future independence of Aboriginal people. They are also threatening the leadership of their own party leader, Australia's most popular Prime Minister [Bob Hawke]. I believe that if the left-wing succeeds on uranium mining issues then the Prime Minister and his Government will lose the support of many people. If that happens the Hawke Government stands a good chance of losing the next election, all because of this very small, very active group of people. I would like to think that the uranium policy will be changed because it will mean so much to my people and to our country. But I am not an expert on these things. I am not a politician but I speak from my heart.

Three weeks ago the Northern and Central Land Council held talks here with the Prime Minister, the Minister for Energy and Mines and the Minister for Aboriginal Affairs but they could not say to us, 'Yes, the government will support you. Yes, you will be able to do as you want on your land.' So, as I say, uranium is not the issue. The real issue is what I have been talking about, land rights for Aboriginals. That is what is important. If the Government recognises and endorses that then it must override everything else. If it doesn't then the land rights we have been given are worthless, they are just token, something to keep the Aboriginal people happy for a while. If that is the case then I am sorry for my people and my fellow Australians because my country, our country that we all love will go bankrupt. I appeal to the Prime Minister to say, from his heart, that he will support us and honour his party's promises to my people.

Abridged.
Source: Galarrwuy Yunupingu, 28 June 1984, Speech to the National Press Club, Canberra, reproduced in Tony Maniaty (ed.), *The Power of Speech: 25 Years of the National Press Club*.[60]

Patrick White
Hiroshima Day, 1984

Patrick White (1912–1990) won the Nobel Prize for Literature in 1973 and is best known for his novels set in Australia, including *The Tree of Man* (1955), *Voss* (1957) and *Riders in the Chariot* (1961). By the 1980s, nuclear disarmament became an urgent issue for radicals in Europe and Australia, and White became convinced that it was 'the most important moral issue in history'. In 1983 he was invited to speak on this issue to a gathering of scientists in Canberra. White was always apprehensive about public speaking—and this occasion filled him with dread. His speech was called 'Australians in a Nuclear War' and it had an astonishing impact, being broadcast by ABC radio on several occasions, sold on cassette and published in a number of anthologies. Dismayed that the Hawke Labor Government had failed to distance Australia from the nuclear defence policies of the United States of America, White became a generous financial supporter of Australia's Nuclear Disarmament Party. He received extensive news coverage for the following speech on their behalf in Sydney Town Hall on Hiroshima Day, 9 August 1984.

Fellow citizens—this is about WAR—the ferocious death's head that has been grinning at us down the decades—never more blatantly than in 1984—when, if the arms race reaches a climax, the grin may well be wiped off the death's head itself—along with the faces of innocent, frivolous, unthinking humanity and this radiant earth on which it has been our privilege to live.

This, of course, is a frivolous statement on my part when so many people in this hall—in Australia—and throughout the world have been giving so much thought and time to averting the disaster of a nuclear war. Not yet enough of us, however—even though the evidence *against* war, both before and after Hiroshima, would *seem* to be enough.

Take World War II in Europe: Stalin admitted 20 million Russians were killed. It is believed the figure was higher, but the Russian dictator did not want to admit it because it would have reflected on his leadership.

Back in the 1950s [Albert] Einstein, and Bertrand Russell the British philosopher, mathematician, and peace activist, foresaw the danger of nuclear war escalating into a universal holocaust. They issued a declaration which warned, 'Remember your humanity and forget all other things. Man's continued existence is in doubt.' Could you think of two nobler apostles of peace than Einstein and Russell? At the time when the declaration was made it was signed by Communists and non-Communists alike. The famous Russian physicist Markov still speaks with passion of the declaration. *I* urge all Australians, even the holy joggers and extrovert footballers, if a few syllables of this declaration should reach their ears, 'Remember your humanity. Forget all other things. Man's continued existence is in doubt ...' These are the voices of Einstein and Bertrand Russell from out of the universe—not just that silly old bastard Patrick ranting his head off about something at a meeting.

To return to War, before it developed into the super-consumer—Helmuth von Moltke the elder, an architect of the modern German army, wrote in 1890, 'Woe to him who first sets fire to Europe.' In the 1914–18 trench warfare, millions were killed. The Battle of the Somme which began in 1916 and lasted from July to November, saw about 1,300,000 soldiers killed or wounded on both sides. There are Australians still alive who experienced this nightmare.

How right von Moltke was. What did World War I settle? Nothing. It was only a stage in the development of war. After Europe was set on fire it continued to smoulder. How did it start? Lloyd George, British Prime Minister towards the end of World War I, admitted, 'We all muddled into war ...' It would be less alarming if we could say today we are still muddling, but the leaders of the superpowers seem heading towards it with the fixed grin of the death's head itself. The clash could occur at any moment.

The horrors of World War I did not prevent us getting into it again in 1939. This time certainly Hitler was responsible. There followed the devastation of London, Coventry, Hamburg, Dresden, Berlin. In the Pacific sphere, the climax came with Hiroshima and Nagasaki. Our gathering together tonight commemorates their destruction.

Alas, the habit of war will not let go. Our leaders are hooked on it. At the time it seemed to the more thoughtful that what happened at Hiroshima and Nagasaki was the peak of human bestiality. But here we are, set for it again. The results could be infinitely more horrendous, thanks to the perverted ingenuity of certain scientific 'geniuses'.

Michael Howard, one of the more objective historians of war, recently wrote:

'I am an Englishman whose youth was passed in watching the dreadful onslaught of totalitarianism in Europe, and whose young manhood was passed in fighting it. I am a professional historian who has spent the last thirty years studying the phenomena of military power. I have noted the appetite of powerful states for more power to protect themselves, and the edge ideology can give to the appetite. I do not think I have any illusions about the Soviet Union. But when I hear some of my American friends speak of the country, when I note how their eyes glaze over, their voices drop an octave and they grind out the word *the Soviets* in tones of gravelly hatred, I become really frightened ...'

That perceptive American journalist and political analyst Thomas Powers has remarked, 'Statesmen thrive as long as war only threatens.' Looking back, I find that extraordinarily true. Like politicians when in opposition, they thump the drum, then so often shrink to pygmy size when in power and faced with reality.

What is reality? we may ask. Something different for everyone. Look at Reagan, the straw cowboy, and his buddy, Bush, flexing their muscles on the election trail, in their Texas hats, flanked by a couple of busty starlets. Such a set-up must mean reality for many American electors or it couldn't be practised so successfully. War, I feel, must be a celluloid adventure, a series of clips from *Gone with the Wind* or *Apocalypse Now*, for those who have not experienced it on their own soil, or anyway since away back in history.

For that matter, Australians haven't known war at home. True, there are the lists of friends and relatives who didn't come back from overseas and who, in many cases, remained a long-lasting source of grief, but our experience of war in Australia has only been peripheral, the bombing of Darwin in World War II, a pearling fleet sunk off Broome, and those Jap subs which entered Sydney Harbour, when in the alarm which ensued, one of my great aunts fell off her bed and broke a leg. Fringe events, with a dash of bathos.

Like so many Australians, Americans probably can't believe in war because *they* haven't been its target. War hasn't rolled through their back yards, crushing, disembowelling. They haven't seen their homes crumble, or neighbours and loved ones turned to corpses suppurating in familiar streets. *Unlike* the Russians—millions killed, frozen, starved.

The British found out about it on their home ground in World War II—surviving only if they were lucky under the rubble created by bombs. Friends you had shared a joke with that evening, often could not be found next morning—after one of those rumbling nights of fug and farts, in the underground or your own cellar.

I experienced something of the Blitz on London. I know something of the starvation and humiliations of a country like Greece under occupation by a foreign power.

The pain, the horrors, the devastation, the hunger, the corruption, the rape, the adulteries of War ... Alas, we are all to some extent to blame! That is one of the terrible truths. Germany can hardly deny that most Germans knew the Jews were being rounded up and carted off somewhere it was best not to think about. If any of us are to survive a nuclear holocaust, those survivors will know it happened because a majority of the world's population was too inert, too hedonistic, too ignorant, too complacently wealthy to organise timely resistance to the leaders who devised it.

I should have thought Hiroshima, back in the horse-and-buggy days of nuclear weapons, would be warning enough. For me the icon of Hiroshima I shall always remember is the figure of a man they saw standing naked amongst the ash and the tatters of human flesh in the black wastes of what had been his native city staring dazed at one of his eyeballs on the open palm of his extended hand. This could be the fate of any of us if we don't unite—you, or your father, uncle, son, standing in the wastes of what had been Sydney—at Lidcombe, say—or Maroubra—the Cross—Double Bay—Mosman—or wherever.

The extraordinary part is that President Reagan, his backroom scientists, and our own piddling politicians, of broken promises and immoral uranium policies, have never caught sight of this Hiroshima man. Or is it that they are so shocked by the sight and thought of the sacrificial figure that they are metaphorically blinded by his reality? It is easier to turn to the theories of deterrence and safeguards, and generally lick the arse of an imperious, materialistic ally who will continue manipulating his puppets for whatever purpose *he* sees fit.

None of this will *deter*. If we achieve anything it will be through the peoples of the world and more and more of us are marshalling our forces in the cause of nuclear disarmament and peace.

All power in particular to the New Zealander[61] This now needs to be no 33 in withstanding the pressures put on him by the United States and faithless members of our own Government. May he and his peace supporters continue to resist. (Since I wrote this, I must say, one of our ministers seems to have seen the light.)

I don't know how many of you are aware of the Nuclear Disarmament Party which is being formed in Australia, and which aims to provide candidates for the next Federal Elections to the Senate and House of Representatives. It is a single issue party and its platform is as follows:

To close all foreign military bases in Australia.

To prohibit the stationing of nuclear weapons through Australian waters or airspace.

To terminate immediately all mining and export of Australian uranium, and to repudiate all commitments by previous Australian governments to mining, processing and export of uranium.

In this way Australia could set an example which those of like mind in other countries might follow, to share in the joys of LIFE instead of its extinction by nuclear war.

Reproduced in full.
Source: Patrick White, *Patrick White Speaks*, Primavera, Sydney, 1989, pp. 161–5.[62]

Anne Summers

'God's Police' in the 1980s, 1984

Anne Fairhurst Summers (1945–) was a high-profile feminist based in Sydney when she wrote a key text of women's history, *Damned Whores and God's Police*, published in 1975. After working for many years as a senior journalist and editor, she was appointed to the Office for the Status of Women in 1983. Summers introduced a program across government departments to examine how public spending affected women. By the early 1980s, women comprised almost forty per cent of the labour market. Despite a series of anti-discrimination laws passed in the 1970s and 1980s, culminating in the 1986 Affirmative Action (Equal Employment for Women) Act, these women still endured wages and working conditions inferior to men's. In December 1984 Summers delivered the Caroline Chisholm Lecture to a packed audience at La Trobe University in Melbourne. Her speech turned an historical spotlight on the social and economic status of women as she outlined the need for 'new codes of conduct' in Australia's gender relations.

There is a noticeable thread connecting the efforts of [Caroline] Chisholm and those of many women's groups today. Despite differences in the framework of values under which they operate, much of their energy is directed, still, towards remarkably similar activities: providing shelter and protection for destitute women and girls, seeking jobs for unemployed women, recognising that homelessness leaves women vulnerable to unwanted predatory attentions. It is fruitless to speculate whether Chisholm would have adopted a more radical position on the question of women's independence were she carrying out her work today: although it is worthy of note that her views *were* radical when it came to questions of land ownership and of allowing Asian immigration into Australia.

What *is* worth examining, however, particularly in the light of the legacy of her brilliant 'God's Police' aphorism, is the extent to which it is still realistic, in the terms she herself employed, to characterise women in Australia as having a special moral role to play.

The issue is a complex, and even confusing, one. Many women who would argue, for instance, that they want no such responsibility if it is portrayed in terms of family responsibilities would nevertheless contend that women have a special—and surely moral—duty to preserve the world from nuclear extinction. The vast involvement of women in the contemporary peace movement rests on an often unstated view that women, because of their child-bearing role, have a special stake in the future and a responsibility to ensure human survival. It is not a matter they are able to leave to the Masters of War who are (almost always) men. Many feminists today adopt this position. A great many, indeed, demonstrated their belief in colourful fashion at the US base at Pine Gap [near Alice Springs] in December 1983.

The crux of Chisholm's argument was that women, by virtue of their innate characteristics including their capacity to bear children, were a moderating and civilising influence on society. This influence was to be exercised through their roles as wives and mothers, through the family. It hardly needs to be pointed out that this view of the role of women is still a potent one today. It is manifest in the world of politics, where variations of Chisholm's views form the basis of the policies of many pro-family groups. It has been a constant theme in our literature, and in other facets of our social existence. It surfaces, for instance, in the reasons advanced by some of the mining company participants in the Government's Affirmative Action Pilot Program as to why they are anxious to employ women in remote area mining sites. Whereas in the past, such places of employment might have been thought of as 'too rough for a woman', today the mining companies are keen to employ women because they have a marked civilising effect on site life: the men are likely to drink, fight and swear less, and to take more care of their personal appearance and physical surroundings, if women are present.

Despite some surface similarities, however, much has changed in Australia in the past 130 years. These changes have had a profound effect on women. Perhaps the greatest change has been in the past ten.

No longer a beleaguered minority, women today have choices which were unimaginable to their great-great-grandmothers. Women today are, less and less, the full-time mothers and housewives Chisholm wanted them to be. A combination of economic circumstances, a demand for labour in the tertiary sector, fewer numbers of children and personal choice have propelled large numbers of women into the workforce.

By seeking to participate fully in society, women are rejecting the notion of differentiated and fixed roles based on gender; they are defining a universe for themselves which extends well beyond the domestic sphere. They have called for 'equality', for 'liberation', for 'equal opportunity' and, now, for 'affirmative action'. Each is an expression of want. It is a repudiation of what was expected of women in the past, that they be subservient, docile, selfless. What used to be seen as the exclusive domain of men, those areas of work and study which are now called, from women's perspective 'non-traditional', are attracting more and more women and girls. This is no longer criticised. Instead, the criticism is made that there are insufficient women with training and experience in areas such as engineering, metallurgy, operation of heavy equipment and so on, to take advantage of the opportunities many employers (and educators) are now prepared to offer.

This is perhaps a paradox, but it exemplifies the point that women can no longer do it all alone. They require the active assistance of a society which is now agreeing to their participation in virtually all spheres of activity. A woman cannot easily study a non-traditional course if she is the only woman engaged in that course and is subject to jeers and jibes from fellow students, parents or peers. A woman cannot easily take on a demanding job requiring long hours of work if her child-care centre insists she pick up her children at 5 pm and the local shops close at six. The full and free participation of women in all areas of society requires new codes of conduct governing relations between women and men. It is now no longer expected that women require sexual protection from father or husband—the patriarchal notion of a woman as property is rejected—but it is still not acknowledged sufficiently widely that women need to be free to work or to study without verbal or sexual harassment from colleagues or teachers or bosses.

I suppose Caroline Chisholm would agree with the way in which this issue has been taken up by women and, now, by Governments. But she might also argue that women ought not be in situations where such harassment could occur; she might will reject the notion of women's workforce participation were she to view today's world through 19th century eyes. I am sure she would *not* do so were she alive today because she was a practical and realistic woman. Which is more than we can say for some of today's people of both sexes who would claim to be perpetuating her views.

Those views are expressed in several forms today. They include the notion that married women are taking jobs from youth. (This ill-informed and inaccurate idea is currently being refined into the notion that older women are taking jobs from teenage girls.) The idea that women work only for pin-money, or to acquire luxuries such as swimming pools and second cars is another variation of the same theme, as is the idea that women are 'selfish' to want to work. Interestingly, the SRG Survey queried its sample of women on these questions and found that 80 per cent disagreed that working women were selfish, and majority also disagreed with the proposition that working women deprived young people of jobs.[63]

Against assertions and prejudices which fly in the face of what the majority of women want, women are increasingly assertive about their entitlements in the workforce and in the home. At home, women—especially young women—seek no reason why family work such as cooking, cleaning and shopping, should not be shared by husband, partner and children. At work, women see no reason why they should work for 80 per cent the average male weekly wage.

Governments (as policy makers and employers) educational institutions and trade unions are increasingly being required to rise to the challenge laid down by women. These challenges pose difficult, often complex, issues many of which have sometimes expensive implications. Perhaps the biggest single challenge women themselves face is to address the economic argument that their demands, while just and reasonable, simply cannot be afforded during periods of budgetary restrictions. Or is this only a problem for women?

Isn't the case women are making essentially one that argues that the massive shift of women into the work-place and the world outside the home requires a corresponding shift in policy responses? Women are at the forefront of urging this shift through offices such as the Office of the Status of Women, the Women's Affairs Offices most State Premiers now have, and the Women's Units which are currently being established in all Commonwealth Departments. Their success will be judged by the extent to which the views they express on behalf of women—and the necessary policy responses—become integrated in the general policies of government, employers, trade unions and other relevant decision-making bodies. Only when such decision-makers consciously, and without the need for constant prodding from women, recognise and take into account the new diversity of a world in which women are active participants and respond recognising these issues and needs, will women have truly thrown off the role Caroline Chisholm defined for us.

Abridged.

Source: Anne Summers, *God's Police in the 1980s*, The Caroline Chisholm Lecture, La Trobe University, Melbourne, 1984, pp. 1–8 (pamphlet).

Reproduced with permission of the author.

—•—

Donald Horne

Funding the Arts, 1985

Donald Richmond Horne (1921–) is a feisty public intellectual best known for his half-sardonic, half-despairing account of Menzies' Australia, *The Lucky Country* (1964). As a journalist, an academic and a prolific writer, he has commentated on Australian society and political culture for several decades. In 1985 Horne was appointed chairperson of the federal government's arts funding body, the Australia Council. This was a time when neo-liberals (better known as economic rationalists) were beginning to reshape social policy. These champions of the free market saw little reason to subsidise social activities which could not survive as profitable businesses. Horne, on the other hand, was a champion of 'high culture', which he saw as imperilled precisely because it was no longer the culture of the country's rulers. In fact it was 'likely to uphold the disinterest, even the subversiveness, of artistic and general intellectual creation'.[64] Forget sport. For Horne, it is the arts that offer Australia vigour, dimension and a sense of national identity. His inaugural speech in his Australia Council role, received enthusiastically by a crowd of several hundred people at the Art Gallery of New South Wales, outlined his views on the importance of the arts, and adequate arts funding, for both the 'human' and economic future of the nation.

Why subsidise art? Why not leave it to the market place? A first answer might be that in managed capitalist societies there are not many activities that *are* left completely to the market place. The second might be that, on the whole, individual artists *do* exist in the market place. An actor or a musician looking for a job, for example, or an author or a painter looking for sales are operating in a market much tougher than most. And they don't make much of a living out of it. And ultimately even highly subsidised theatre companies are still market-related, in that they must maintain indications of audience support. But the real answer is that—at least so far as museum culture is concerned (the museums themselves, the libraries, the theatres, the orchestras, etc)—we are maintaining the basic human heritage. We are preserving repertoires from the past (reinterpretable into modern circumstances) of what it might be to be human. We are storing past human experience, so that it can continue to be available to us as critics or as celebrants of existence.

Perhaps at this stage one might start the counter attack against the imagined questioner, and ask questions in reply. What is *not* to be subsidised? The humanities and social science faculties at the universities, for instance? Shall we shut them down? The libraries? Shall we shut them down? The art museums and the museums? Should they be shut down? So far, very few people are likely to answer 'yes'. The question then comes that, if all *these* institutions are to survive, is there the same case for the survival of orchestras, opera companies, dance companies, drama companies and others. Are they also not preserving part of the human repertoire?

Perhaps our imaginary questioners might now change course and modify their question to something like this: Well then, let us preserve the human experience, if you insist, but why should we subsidise new art? To that our first answer might be: do you want the making of art to stop? If they say 'yes' we might then argue the case for art as an organizer, as it were, of new experience, or new perspectives, of new perceptions of the world and human vision. Without new art, even the re-interpretability of old art would cease. If they say no, they don't want to stop the production of new art, but why subsidise it, then our next answer would be that if we want new art we must concern ourselves with the material circumstances of its production. The romantic view that new art is best made by people who live precariously can perhaps be answered by evidence that most of the old art was not made by people living precariously. The truth of the precariousness theory is not self evident. Experience might suggest the opposite. To base a whole policy on the theory of the need for artists' material suffering seems quite reckless. One might also ask: why should artists—compared with professors, say, or librarians, or scientists or museum curators—subsidise the rest of the community?

I shall make only two more arguments for arts-support programs—although there are many others.

The first is simple, but to my mind, one of the most significant of all: This is the argument of what you might call the ripple-effect. It has already been demonstrated how the Australian film industry came out of a culture wider than itself. One might regard support for new art as the 'research program', as it were, of the whole arts and entertainment industry (and here one is speaking of a multi-million dollar industry) and, for that matter, of the whole 'information' industry (an industry of even greater proportion). That 'research program' is developing new perspectives and styles that even if they do not reach the mass of the people directly can reach them indirectly, by influencing other works. The industries we are speaking of here are much larger than the sports industry—yet, in proportionate terms, the seeding money is less.

The other argument is a relatively new one. What is we have now seen the end of the Keynesian era of economic management in which full employment could combine as a matter of course with low inflation? What is we are now witnessing a re-ordering of modern societies in which the 'growth and jobs' ethos no longer works as it did in the early 1970s? If so, then one might argue that the time for the arts has come. For those who are still part of the carnival of the consumer society, there are increased chances for leisure. For those who have no longer been invited to the carnival (that is to say, the unemployed), to put it mildly, there are also increased chances for 'leisure'.

The idea of 'economic growth' is, we should remember, only one way among others of arranging national statistics. It seems to me that both for those who still accept the idea of 'growth' as the main basis for policy-making and those who do not there is now an important place in economic policy-making for arts-support programs and general leisure programs. For those who are now skeptical about 'growth' as the prime basis for social policy, the case is obvious. But for those who still see 'growth' as the principal social dynamic, the case should also be obvious. Many of the old forms of 'growth' no longer work as effectively as they used to: the old dynamics have lost their strength. Here are new areas of 'growth', measurable in economic terms, labour-intensive and important in the pursuit of human fulfilment.

As to the future? There is a need for strong arts organizations, able to plan for the future, with a degree of stability (subject to continuing tests of artistic, and also financial competence and of response to changes within a field). I believe that those organizations, however, as one of the conditions of their stability, should be expected to assist in the cultivation of Australian creativity and that as another of the conditions of their stability they should be expected to play a part in access programs, as, for example, in extension programs in the electronic media. But there is also a need for innovation and experiment, and for the nurturing of new organizations. And there is, I think, a basic need for the increase in support for the work of creative individuals in Australia.

In contemplating these various needs, is it not possible that the Australia Council, while still providing some support for the large organizations, should be somewhat in the van, especially concerned with encouraging the risky and the innovative, with providing support for the creative individuals and innovative institutions, with experimenting with appreciation, access and participation programs—and that perhaps in its support for the large established organizations there might also be a special concern with assisting them in *their* more innovatory programs, in *their* support for Australian creativity and in *their* access programs? The experimental and innovative work is the work that is least likely to attract private sector or market support. Yet it is, as I suggested, the 'research program' of a field much wider than its own.

What seems to be needed, perhaps, is a marginal shift in funding for the large arts organisations so that they can find the security they need, but find it in new revenue sources in their own areas. The tourist industry, for example, should make some contribution—in many United States cities, the tourist industry helps subsidise art through a hotel/motel tax.

In 1988 Australia will be holding a national festival whose theme will be 'living together'. It will, I hope, be more than a dedication to the future than a celebration of the past and, I hope, an occasion in which many of us can commit ourselves to the politically bi-partisan national idea of a multicultural Australia. But this is an ideal that can go beyond the acceptance of ethnic difference within an overall social unity. There is another form of multiculturalism—a recognition that the seeking of meaning and the enlargement of the human imagination in art are one of the main forms of human liberation and the very basis of cultural diversity.

Once, at the great period of Australian liberal expansion at the end of the last century and the beginning of this, Australian politicians were able to see Australia as setting an example to the world. In those days it was the politicians who provided much of the vision. Perhaps we should now support our politicians in seeing again, with the eyes of vision.

But, just as ordinary Australians have proved, in effect, to be more tolerant than their leaders ever imagined they would be in the great changes that have come in immigration since the second world war, so there might also be potential for popular support for a great program of expansion for the arts. When I came back to Sydney a couple of weeks ago, the first thing Professor Yerbury showed me was a survey report that showed a support for the arts among the ordinary people of Australia that may be close to unique among modern industrial nations. It is, I believe, a great challenge for our leaders to gain confidence so that they can live up to aspirations that, this survey suggested, are already in the minds of the Australian people.

Abridged.
Source: Donald Horne, 'Supporting the Arts in Australia', *Artforce*, no. 47, 1985, pp. 6–10.

Gary Foley and Charles Harris

The Bicentennial: We Have Survived, 1988

Gary Edward Foley (1950–) and the Reverend Charles Harris were among Aboriginal activists who spoke to a gathering of up to thirty thousand people gathered in protest on 26 January 1988, the Bicentenary of white invasion—or 'settlement' as it was officially called—of the Australian continent. A decade earlier Prime Minister Malcolm Fraser had established the Australian Bicentennial Authority to oversee a large budget and an extensive schedule of anniversary activities extended throughout 1988, promoted under the slogan 'Celebration of the Nation'. Commemoration of the arrival of the First Fleet in Sydney Cove in 1788 had aroused opposition for several decades from Australians seeking the end of racial discrimination against Indigenous peoples. At the sesquicentenary in 1938, Aboriginal activist William Cooper had led the Day of Mourning campaign, which pointed out the injustices Aboriginal people had experienced since European invasion. Aboriginal activists dubbed 1988 the Year of Mourning and called for a Treaty. On 26 January perhaps as many as two million people gathered in Sydney Harbour to see two hundred boats from around the world and eleven ships that had sailed from England in a re-enactment of the voyage of the original First Fleet. At the same time, in protest, a March for Freedom, Justice and Hope was organized by Aborigines and their sympathizers. At the end of the march, the crowd gathered for an afternoon of speeches. Foley, who had previously been involved in political activity, including a prominent role at the Aboriginal Tent Embassy in Canberra in 1972, was a strong presence on the podium, introducing the speakers. Harris opened the proceedings with a prayer. This was an historic moment and attracted considerable coverage from national and international media.

Gary Foley:

Confusion, chaos, happiness and joy, and solemnity and dignity—we're about to begin.

I'd like to start off by welcoming everybody here today. It's so magnificent to see black and white Australia together in harmony. It's what we've always said could happen. This is what Australia could be like and what better, what better occasion for us to come together in this sort of spirit than on the two-hundredth anniversary of the invasion. What we're saying here today, and what's very clear, and what will be very clear to Bob Hawke and to people all over the world when they see their television screens tonight and tomorrow, is that *we have survived*. We have survived, and we are here today to call on the Australian Government to give us justice, to give us the opportunity to attain our economic independence so we can be free and dignified as people in our own land, and decide for ourselves our own future in this country. And then all of us in this country for the future and, perhaps, in another hundred years, we can all come together and have a good party together.

Reverend Charles Harris:

First of all I would want you to join me in prayer. Let us pray.

God of the Dreamtime, you who are with us for these 40,000 years or more before 1788, you who gave us our ceremonies, and the law and our stories, and our sacred sites. You who gave us our Dreaming, you who gave us this land. You were with us through the last 200 years of onslaught, of terrorism, and of apartheid that has been administered to our people in this land. And you have helped us and enabled us to survive through the odds that were great against us. We pray that you will avenge your people, the Aboriginal and the Islander people. Show to the world, today, the evil deeds of those who came and robbed us, raped our land and our people, murdered and lied to our people. Expose them to the world today. Look and see the chains of oppression that keep your people, the Aboriginal and Islander people, in bondage. Hear the cry, and the call, and the plea for justice to be done in this land. Show the people that you are a God of justice, and bring hope.

It's a great feeling to have marched today with the Aboriginal nation in the streets of Sydney. You young people out there can tell your children and your grandchildren about this because this week has been an historic week in this country. It has been a week where Aboriginal and Islander people have come together to lay their claim for freedom, justice and hope for their people. It has been this march that has caused the Aboriginal and Islander people to plead to the nation that exists here that we want justice to be done. In justice we call for land rights, for equality, for sovereignty, and for a treaty and for compensation. We call for these things that are included in the justice package and we want this nation to know that, we want the Government of this nation to know that, and we want the world to know that.

For too long the Aboriginal people and the Islander people have been victims of gross injustice. For too long the Aboriginal people and the Islander people have been manipulated and oppressed. For too long our children have been victims of racism in schools and in the public places of this country. For too long the Government has set the agenda for our lives and for the lives of our children. For too long we have been treated less than migrants and immigrants and foreigners in our own land. This is the time when we, as the original owners of this land, will begin to assert and begin to exercise our sovereign rights and our sovereign powers. We are the sovereign people of this land. We are the original owners of this land. And we want the Government of this nation, we say to this nation, that we want to be part of the negotiating body that negotiates the affairs of this country and particularly the affairs of the Aboriginal people.

The thing that motivated me to become involved in the struggle was a guy who I pay deep respect to at this time of mourning, and we marched a few moments ago in a march of mourning, and I would like to here take time out to pay my respects to one of the greatest leaders of the

Aboriginal community. I refer to him as the Dr. Martin Luther King of the Aboriginal people and that is Pastor Don Brady. He has died now but I'd like to show my respect to him at this point of time. If it wasn't for him I would not be here today. He was the one that taught me, he was the one that led me into the struggle back there in Brisbane. As I sat with the people in Musgrave Park and saw the people drinking themselves to death out of sheer hopelessness, it was out that feeling of sense of hopelessness, and it was out of that fear, the fear of death so to speak, that the fire of radicalism burned in my being. I am sometimes termed the 'Radical Pastor' or the 'Radical Minister', but I say that you can't be a Christian today and be a conservative because nobody is going to listen to you.

We want the Government to take a stand and see that the original owners of this land should be given the ownership that is entitled to them and the compensation that is due to them for dispossession of their land, of their tribal land, and of their culture, a culture that was here in existence for 40,000 years and was almost eradicated and almost totally destroyed in the short period of 200 years. That, to me, is crime. That, to me, is a shame on this nation, and on the government of this nation. We here today are gathered to show solidarity across the board.

You white people that are here, you white supporters, we are wanting you to sign a pledge of continuing support to the Aboriginal struggle, to be genuine about your support, and to stand alongside the Aboriginal people, because you know as well as I do that the thing that is happening only about two kilometres away from here, the 'celebration', is a farce. It's hypocrisy. We call you, we call upon you to be upright and standing alongside the Aboriginal people in your support for them. We thank them. We thank you for your support today and we are so happy to have you here.

One of the things that we should be looking at as the Aboriginal people, we should be looking at setting up our own democratic processes where we begin to get the grass roots people involved and begin to empower them at grass roots level. Empowering the powerless, because the people at the grass roots seem so powerless as to what happens in Aboriginal affairs across this nation. There needs to be power imparted to the people at the bottom rung of the ladder and the people at the grass roots are those people. They feel so powerless and if we can empower them then we will be a force to be reckoned with in the world. We have to get them to elect their leaders and the leaders must be responsible totally and fully to those people at the grass roots. *Not* to the Government as many of our leaders are today. They are responsible to the Government and they have neglected their own people, the people at the grass roots. And so we need to set up our own democratic process where the people at the grass roots are involved in the struggle and involved in the decision-making processes in Aboriginal affairs.

The second thing I would like to propose is the revitalising of our Aboriginal spirituality. We, as a people, are a spiritual people, we come from a spiritual culture, we have a spiritual background and that is the very basis of our existence—our spirituality. As we can develop that we can have a firm foundation on which to carry our struggle forward in this land of Australia. The Government's method has been to make us fight and struggle against their odds on their terms. Now we can never win on their terms, in their way, because the odds are so great against us and they have the machinery and the equipment to defeat us all the way down the line. We've fought for 200 years and if we can establish our spiritual base as a people and let the elders be part of the establishing of this spiritual base, then we will have a strong foundation to launch our attack, to launch our struggle, and to launch our fight against oppression and against racism and against all those things that destroy us a people.

Abridged.
Source: Reproduced from a verbatim transcript in Jack Davis, Stephen Muecke, Mudrooroo Narogin and Adam Shoemaker (eds), *Paperbark: A Collection of Black Australian Writings*.[65]

William Deane and Mary Gaudron
Mabo Judgment, 1992

William Patrick Deane (1931–) and Mary Genevieve Gaudron (1943–) were justices of the High Court (Gaudron as the only woman ever appointed) when the momentous *Mabo and Others v State of Queensland* case was heard. In 1982, Eddie Koiki Mabo (1936–1993) and other Torres Strait Islanders from Mer Island had brought a case for land rights before the Supreme Court of Queensland. Evidence was brought before the High Court in May 1992. On 3 June the seven judges of the High Court delivered four distinct judgments, including a joint judgment from justices Deane and Gaudron, extracted here. The High Court's decision overturned the doctrine of *terra nullius*, finding that at the time of European settlement Indigenous people did have a claim to their land, and acknowledged that the cultural ties of the people of Mer Island—and by extension, mainland Aborigines—with their land were ongoing. Deane and Gaudron acknowledged that in the sections of their judgment that examined Aboriginal dispossession, they had 'used language and expressed conclusions which some may think to be unusually emotive for a judgment in this court'. This was not to 'attribute moral guilt', but because the 'full facts' pertaining to Aboriginal dispossession were necessary in order to assess the legitimacy of any claim to *terra nullius*. But their language did attract the criticism that it strayed from the expected 'impartiality' of legal rulings. And the High Court's landmark decision was followed by intense public—and political—debate about the issues of Indigenous land rights, the role of the High Court and whether the *Mabo* decision was a 'judicial revolution'.[66] One of the responses to the *Mabo* case was the Native Title Act, passed in 1993, which transferred the High Court's decision to the mainland. The High Court's *Wik* decision in 1996 found that the native titles and pastoral leases could co-exist.

Nobody accurately knows the numbers of the Aboriginal inhabitants of the Australian continent in 1788. Nor do we accurately know the relationship between them and the lands on which they lived, and the content of their traditional laws and customs. But the following broad generalisations can be accepted as least as regards significant areas of the territory which became New South Wales.

The numbers of Aboriginal inhabitants far exceeded the settlers' expectations. Current estimates for the whole continent range from between 300,000 and a million or more. Under the laws or customs of the relevant locality, particular tribes or clans—either on their own or with others—were custodians of the land from which they derived their sustenance and from which they took their tribal names. Their laws or customs were elaborate and obligatory. The boundaries of their traditional lands were likely to be long-standing and defined. The special relationship between a particular tribe or clan and its land was recognised by other tribes or groups within the local native system, and was reflected in differences in dialect over relatively short distances. In different ways and in varying degrees of intensity, they used their homelands for all the purposes of their lives: social, ritual, economic. They identified with their land in a way that transcended the common law's notions of property and possession. Their claim to the land was ordinarily that of the tribe or other group, not of an individual in his or her own right.

From these generalisations we must conclude that when New South Wales was established in 1788 there existed, under the traditional laws or customs of the Aboriginal peoples, widespread special entitlements to use and occupy defined lands. These gave rise to a native title, recognised under the law of the new colony.

Was native title extinguished on the establishment of the colony of New South Wales? The answer is no. If we examine the act of state leading to the establishment of the colony of New South Wales, the most that can be said is that it envisaged: (1) that some land within the colony would be available for establishing the penal settlement and for making land grants to emancipated convicts and new settlers; and (2) that the native inhabitants would be protected and not subjected to unnecessary interference. The expectations that some land would be available for the Crown's own use and some for future grants to others was an expectation that probably would have existed in all British colonies in the 18th and 19th centuries. It may be possible to argue (although we think not) that the formal instructions given to Captain Arthur Phillip authorised the extinguishment of any existing native interests in land where that was necessary to establish the convict settlement. Otherwise, though, nothing in the act of the state establishing the colony expropriated or extinguished any existing native interests in the vast land areas in the new colony, or negated the presumption of the common law that native interests were respected or protected under the law of the new colony.

Sometimes, events occurring after an act of state can resolve uncertainty or ambiguity about what was involved in the act of state itself. But in the case of New South Wales there is no ambiguity. It is plain that nothing done after the settlement was established constituted an expropriation of pre-existing native interests in land, or negated the firm assumption of the common law that pre-existing native interests were respected and protected. It is true that later activities became increasingly inconsistent with the existence of Aboriginal claims to land; but they cannot be properly seen as indicating an intention to extinguish Aboriginal interests of a kind that the common law was presumed to recognise. When post-settlement activities were later rationalised and justified, it was on the basis that there were no pre-existing Aboriginal interests of the kind the law could respect and protect. Thus it came to be asserted that all the lands of the colony were unoccupied and, being unoccupied, that the Crown had acquired not merely the radical title but had become the complete and unqualified owner of the land.

In the early days of the colony, the disregard of Aboriginal claims and their resulting dispossession may be explained by the settlers' ignorance of the rights of particular tribes or clans under pre-existing local law and custom to occupy and use particular areas of land. But that does not plausibly explain later events. Increasingly, it came to be known that particular tribes or clans enjoyed traditional rights to occupy and use traditional lands for ritual, economic, and social purposes. Increasingly so, that fact was acknowledged by government authorities and in formal despatches. Indeed, Imperial and local authorities came to realise that dispossessing the Aboriginal occupants could involve infringing the rights recognised by the common law. This is clear, for example, in the story of the development of South Australia, where Letters Patent in 1836 expressly protected the rights of Aborigines to occupy or enjoy their land.

Inevitably, we must acknowledge two propositions that lay behind the dispossession and oppression of the Aborigines. One was the view that in 1788 the territory of New South Wales was unoccupied for legal purposes. The other was that the Crown was the full legal and beneficial owner of all the lands in the colony, unaffected by any claims of the Aboriginal inhabitants. These propositions provided the legal basis and justification for the dispossession. They also meant that Aboriginal attempts to protect their traditional occupation or use were unlawful. Their endorsement by the administrative practice and court judgments provided the environment in which the Aborigines came to be treated as a different and inferior people, whose very existence could be ignored in determining the legal right to occupy and use their traditional homelands.

The full facts of the dispossession are critically important in assessing the legitimacy of the two propositions. Long acceptance of legal propositions, particularly relating to land, can give legitimacy and preclude change. But these two propositions have been associated with dispossessing the Aboriginal peoples; and that prevents them from acquiring the legitimacy which more than 150 years would give them.

The content of native title which the law recognizes and protects varies according to the extent of the pre-existing interest of the relevant individual, group or community. It may be an entitlement to an individual, through his or her family, band or tribe, to a limited special use of the land in a society that does not know notions of property in land and does not distinguish between ownership, possession or use. Or it may be a community title that is practically equivalent to full ownership in accordance with English notions of property or law. But even where native title approaches full ownership, it is subject to important limitations.

The first limitation relates to the right to dispose of the land (the right of 'alienation'). Native title cannot be disposed of outside the local native system, except by surrender to the Crown. Some scholars have questioned this rule, but to our view it is fully established. However, the rule does not preclude changes to the rights and enjoyment within the local native system itself.

The second limitation is that the title (whether of an individual, family, band or community) is only a 'personal' right. Even so, in some situations, rights under native title are similar to rights that flow from full ownership of land at common law [under the common law].

The third limitation is that native title is liable to be extinguished if the Crown makes an unqualified grant of an interest in the land that is inconsistent with the rights under the native title. For example, native title is extinguished if the Crown makes a freehold grant (unless the grant in invalid). It is also extinguished if the Crown deals with the land in circumstances where the rights of someone else intervene , or where the native title holders' actual use or occupation is terminated.

This is not to say that native title is merely a 'permissive occupancy' which the Crown can cancel at any time regardless of the wishes of those who live on the land or use it for their traditional purposes. That would be to deprive the traditional inhabitants of any genuine security, since they could be dispossessed at the whim of the Government, however unjust.

Like other legal rights, native title rights (and the title itself) can be dealt with or extinguished by valid Commonwealth, State or Territory legislation. These rights are not entrenched; they are not beyond the reach of legislative power. However, legislation must contain clear and unambiguous words before Parliament will be assumed to have intended to extinguish valuable property rights without fair compensation.

There are some important limitations on the legislative power of the Commonwealth, State or Territory Parliaments to extinguish or diminish the native titles that survive in this country. With regard to the Commonwealth, section 51 (xxxi) of the Constitution requires any acquisition of property to be on 'just terms'. Because rights under native title are true legal rights, recognised and protected by the law, any Commonwealth legislation extinguishing those rights is an expropriation of property within that section.

Also important is the Commonwealth *Racial Discrimination Act* 1975. Being a Commonwealth Act, the *Racial Discrimination Act* prevails over any inconsistent State or Territory legislative powers to extinguish or diminish native title.

Native title preserves rights to use or enjoyment under the traditional law or custom of the relevant territory or locality. The content of the rights and who may enjoy them must be ascertained by reference to that traditional law or custom. However, the traditional law or custom is not frozen at the moment the colony was established. As long as the changes do not diminish or extinguish the relationship between a particular tribe or group and a particular area of land, later developments or variations do not extinguish the title.

The rights of an Aboriginal tribe or clan entitled to the benefit of native title are personal only. The enjoyment of the rights can be varied and dealt with under the traditional law or custom. The rights cannot be disposed of outside the overall native system, though they can be voluntarily extinguished by surrender to the Crown. They can also be lost by abandoning the connection with the land or by the tribe or group becoming extinct. It is not necessary in this case to consider whether the rights are lost if the traditional customs and ways are abandoned—though our present view is that they are not, at least where the tribe continues to occupy or use the land.

Abridged.
Source: Peter Butt, Robert Eagleson and Patricia Lane, *Mabo, Wik & Native Title*.[67] This is an edited series of extracts based on the actual words of Justices Deane and Gaudron in the Mabo case and has omitted technical language, bibliographical references, and quotations from other court cases.[68] The *Commonwealth Law Reports* contain a full transcript of the judgment.

———◄►———

Paul Keating
The Redfern Address, 1992

Paul Keating (1944–) was prime minister (1991–96) when he launched the International Year for Indigenous People on 10 December 1992. Thousands of people packed into a park in Redfern, the inner Sydney suburb that is home to many of that city's Aborigines. It was a cheerful, sunny day and the festive crowd carried balloons and flags. They were clearly surprised and delighted by the expression of empathy for Indigenous experiences of dispossession conveyed powerfully in Keating's speech. From the leader of the Australian people, this was a remarkable acknowledgement of responsibility for the devastating effects of colonialism on Indigenous lives. Earlier that same year, the High Court of Australia had handed down the radical Mabo judgment which defined circumstances in which the traditional land rights of Indigenous Australians still operated on crown land. Keating responded to the decision by setting up procedures by which traditional owners could claim such estates. In 1996 Keating's Labor Government was savaged at the polls by the Howard Liberal Government. Howard supporters denounced this speech and the spirit of reconciliation that it represented. And in early 2004, tension in Redfern would escalate into violent and tragic confrontations between Aborigines and the police.

Ladies and gentlemen

I am very pleased to be here today at the launch of Australia's celebration of the 1993 International Year of the World's Indigenous People. It will be a year of great significance for Australia. It comes at a time when we have committed ourselves to succeeding in the test which so far we have always failed. Because, in truth, we cannot confidently say that we have succeeded as we would like to have succeeded if we have not managed to extend opportunity and care, dignity and hope to the indigenous people of Australia—the Aboriginal and Torres Strait Island people.

This is a *fundamental* test of our social goals and our national will: our ability to say to ourselves and the rest of the world that Australia *is* a first rate social democracy, that we are what we should be—*truly* the land of the fair go and the better chance.

There is no more basic test of how seriously we mean these things. It is a test of our self-knowledge. Of how well we know the land we live in. How well we know our history. How well we recognise the fact that, complex as our contemporary identity is, it cannot be separated from Aboriginal Australia. How well we know what Aboriginal Australians know about Australia.

Redfern is a good place to contemplate these things. Just a mile or two from the place where the first European settlers landed, in too many ways it tells us that their failure to bring much more than devastation and demoralisation to Aboriginal Australia continues to be our failure. More I think than most Australians recognise, the plight of Aboriginal Australians affects us all. In Redfern it might be tempting to think that the reality Aboriginal Australians face is somehow contained here, and that the rest of us are insulated from it. But of course, while all the dilemmas may exist here, they are far from contained. We know the same dilemmas and more are faced all over Australia.

That is perhaps the point of this Year of the World's Indigenous People: to bring the dispossessed out of the shadows, to recognise that they are part of us, and that we cannot give indigenous Australians up without giving up many of our own most deeply held values, much of our own identity–and our own humanity. Nowhere in the world, I would venture, is the message more stark than it is in Australia.

We simply cannot sweep injustice aside. Even if our own conscience allowed us to, I am sure, that in due course, the world and the people of our region would not. There should be no mistake about this — our success in resolving these issues will have a significant bearing on our standing in the world. However intractable the problems seem, we cannot resign ourselves to failure-any more than we can hide behind the contemporary version of Social Darwinism which says that to reach back for the poor and dispossessed is to risk being dragged down. That seems to me not only morally indefensible, but bad history.

We non-Aboriginal Australians should perhaps remind ourselves that Australia once reached out for us. Didn't Australia provide opportunity and care for the dispossessed Irish? The poor of Britain? The refugees from war and famine and persecution in the countries of Europe and Asia? Isn't it reasonable to say that if we can build a prosperous and remarkably harmonious multicultural society in Australia, surely we can find just solutions to the problems which beset the first Australians-the people to whom the most injustice has been done.

And, as I say, the starting point might be to recognise that the problem starts with us non-Aboriginal Australians.

It *begins*, I think, with that act of recognition. Recognition that it was we who did the dispossessing.

We took the traditional lands and smashed the traditional way of life.

We brought the diseases. The alcohol.

We committed the murders.

We took the children from their mothers.

We practised discrimination and exclusion.

It was *our* ignorance and *our* prejudice.

And *our* failure to imagine these things being done to us.

With some noble exceptions, we failed to make the most basic human response and enter into their hearts and minds.

We failed to ask—how would I feel if this were done to me?

As a consequence, we failed to see that what we were doing degraded all of us.

If we needed a reminder of this, we received it this year. The Report of the Royal Commission into Aboriginal Deaths in Custody showed with devastating clarity that the past lives on in inequality, racism and injustice. In the prejudice and ignorance of non-Aboriginal Australians, and in the demoralisation and desperation, the fractured identity, of so many Aborigines and Torres Strait Islanders.

For all this, I do not believe that the Report should fill us with guilt. Down the years, there has been no shortage of guilt, but it has not produced the responses we need. Guilt is not a very constructive emotion. I think what we need to do is open our hearts a bit. All of us. Perhaps when we recognise what we have in common we will see the things which must be done—the practical things.

There is something of this in the creation of the Council for Aboriginal Reconciliation. The Council's mission is to forge a new partnership built on justice and equity and an appreciation of the heritage of Australia's indigenous people. In the abstract those terms are meaningless. We have to give meaning to 'justice' and 'equity'—and, as I have said several times this year, we will only give them meaning when we commit ourselves to achieving concrete results.

If we improve the living conditions in one town, they will improve in another. And another. If we raise the standard of health by twenty per cent one year, it will be raised more the next. If we open one door others will follow.

When we see improvement, when we see more dignity, more confidence, more happiness—we will know we are going to win. We need these practical building blocks of change.

The Mabo Judgment should be seen as one of these. By doing away with the bizarre conceit that this continent had no owners prior to the settlement of Europeans, Mabo establishes a fundamental truth and lays the basis for justice. It will be much easier to work from that basis than has ever been the case in the past. For that reason alone we should ignore the isolated outbreaks of hysteria and hostility of the past few months. Mabo is an historic decision—we can make it an historic *turning point*, the basis of a new relationship between indigenous and non-Aboriginal Australians.

The message should be that there is nothing to fear or to lose in the recognition of historical truth, or the extension of social justice, or the deepening of Australian social democracy to include indigenous Australians. There is everything to gain. Even the unhappy past speaks for this.

Where Aboriginal Australians have been included in the life of Australia they have made remarkable contributions. Economic contributions, particularly in the pastoral and agricultural industry. They are there in the frontier and exploration history of Australia. They are there in the wars. In sport to an extraordinary degree. In literature and art and music.

In all these things they have shaped our knowledge of this continent and of ourselves. They have shaped our identity. They are there in the Australian legend. We should never forget—they have helped build this nation. And if we have a sense of justice, as well as common sense, we will forge a new partnership.

As I said, it might help us if we non-Aboriginal Australians imagined *ourselves* dispossessed of land we had lived on for fifty thousand years—and then imagined ourselves told that it had never been ours.

Imagine if *ours* was the oldest culture in the world and we were told that it was worthless.

Imagine if *we* had resisted this settlement, suffered and died in the defence of our land, and then were told in history books that we had given up without a fight.

Imagine if non-Aboriginal Australians had served their country in peace and war and were then ignored in history books.

Imagine if *our* feats on sporting fields had inspired admiration and patriotism and yet did nothing to diminish prejudice.

Imagine if *our* spiritual life was denied and ridiculed.

Imagine if we had suffered the injustice and then were blamed for it.

It seems to me that if we can imagine the injustice we can imagine its opposite. And we can *have* justice.

I say that for two reasons: I say it because I believe that the great things about Australian social democracy reflect a fundamental belief in justice. And I say it because in so many other areas we have proved our capacity over the years to go on extending the realms of participation, opportunity and care.

Just as Australians living in the relatively narrow and insular Australia of the 1960s imagined a culturally diverse, worldly and open Australia, and in a generation turned the idea into reality, so we can turn the goals of reconciliation into reality.

There are very good signs that the process has begun. The creation of the Reconciliation Council is evidence itself. The establishment of the ATSIC—the Aboriginal and Torres Strait Islander Commission—is also evidence. The Council is the product of imagination and good will.

ATSIC emerges from the vision of indigenous self-determination and self-management. The vision has already become the reality of almost 800 elected Aboriginal Regional Councillors and Commissioners determining priorities and developing their own programs. All over Australia, Aboriginal and Torres Strait Islander communities are taking charge of their own lives. And assistance with the problems which chronically beset them is at last being made available in ways developed by the communities themselves.

If these things offer hope, so does the fact that this generation of Australians is better informed about Aboriginal culture and achievement, and about the injustice that has been done, than any generation before. We are beginning to more generally appreciate the depth and the diversity of Aboriginal and Torres Strait Islander cultures. From their music and art and dance we are beginning to recognise how much richer our national life and identity will be for the participation of Aboriginals and Torres Strait Islanders. We are beginning to learn what the indigenous people have known for many thousands of years—how to live with our physical environment. Ever so gradually we are learning how to see Australia through Aboriginal eyes, beginning to recognise the wisdom contained in their epic story.

I think we are beginning to see how much we owe the indigenous Australians and how much we have lost by living so apart.

I said we non-indigenous Australians should try to imagine the Aboriginal view. It can't be too hard. Someone imagined this event today, and it is now a marvellous reality and a great reason for hope.

There is one thing today we *cannot* imagine.

We cannot imagine that the descendants of people whose genius and resilience maintained a culture here through fifty thousand years or more, through cataclysmic changes to the climate and environment, and who then survived two, centuries of dispossession and abuse, will be denied their place in the modern Australian nation.

We cannot imagine that.

We cannot imagine that we will fail.

And with the spirit that is here today I am confident that we won't.

I am confident that we *will* succeed in this decade.

Thank you

Reproduced in full; original italics.

Source: Speech by the Hon. Prime Minister, P. J. Keating MP, Australian Launch of the International Year for the World's Indigenous People, Redfern, 10 December 1992, Prime Minister's Department.

———◆———

Pauline Hanson

Maiden Speech to Parliament, 1996

Pauline Hanson (1954–) was born in Brisbane. Although she likes to represent herself as a poor working-class 'battler', Hanson's parents were successful shopkeepers —and she was comfortably off when she was elected to the nearby Ipswich Council in 1994. As a councillor, she soon discovered that many local whites shared her hostility to Aboriginal causes. The following year she won the federal Queensland seat of Oxley as an independent with a 19 per cent swing. On 10 September 1996 she gave her maiden speech in the House of Representatives, substantially written by her advisor, John Pasquarelli. The speech poured scorn on multiculturalism, the United Nations, Asian immigration and Aboriginal advancement—key issues which many progressive Australians blithely believed were safely enshrined in a national consensus. Pauline Hanson's own One Nation Party rose and fell over the next decade, but by then many of her divisive, hard-line attitudes had become commonplace in conservative attitudes and policies.

Mr Acting Speaker, in making my first speech in this place, I congratulate you on your election and wish to say how proud I am to be here as the Independent member for Oxley. I come here not as a polished politician but as a woman who has had her fair share of life's knocks.

My view on issues is based on commonsense, and my experience as a mother of four children, as a sole parent, and as a businesswoman running a fish and chip shop. I won the seat of Oxley largely on an issue that has resulted in me being called a racist. That issue related to my comment that Aboriginals received more benefits than non-Aboriginals.

We now have a situation where a type of reverse racism is applied to mainstream Australians by those who promote political correctness and those who control the various taxpayer funded 'industries' that flourish in our society servicing Aboriginals, multiculturalists and a host of other minority groups. In response to my call for equality for all Australians, the most noisy criticism came from the fat cats, bureaucrats and the do-gooders. They screamed the loudest because they stand to lose the most — their power, money and position, all funded by ordinary Australian taxpayers.

Present governments are encouraging separatism in Australia by providing opportunities, land, moneys and facilities available only to Aboriginals ... This nation is being divided into black and white, and the present system encourages this. I am fed up with being told, 'This is our land.' Well, where the hell do I go? I was born here, and so were my parents and children. I will work beside anyone and they will be my equal but I draw the line when told I must pay and continue paying for something that happened over 200 years ago. Like most Australians, I worked for my land; no-one gave it to me.

Apart from the $40 million spent so far since Mabo on native title claims, the government has made available $1 billion for Aboriginals and Torres Strait Islanders as compensation for land they cannot claim under native title. Bear in mind that the $40 million spent so far on native title has gone into the pockets of grateful lawyers and consultants. Not one native title has been granted as I speak ...

Reconciliation is everyone recognising and treating each other as equals, and everyone must be responsible for their own actions. This is why I am calling for ATSIC to be abolished. It is a failed, hypocritical and discriminatory organisation that has failed dismally the people it was meant to serve. It will take more than Senator Herron's surgical skills to correct the terminal mess it is in. Anyone with a criminal record can, and does, hold a position with ATSIC. I cannot hold my position as a politician if I have a criminal record — once again, two sets of rules.

If politicians continue to promote separatism in Australia, they should not continue to hold their seats in this parliament. They are not truly representing all Australians, and I call on the people to throw them out. To survive in peace and harmony, united and strong, we must have one people, one nation, one flag.

The greatest cause of family breakdown is unemployment. This country of ours has the richest mineral deposits in the world and vast rich lands for agriculture and is surrounded by oceans that provide a wealth of seafood, and yet we are $190 billion in debt with an interest bill that is strangling us.

Youth unemployment between the ages of 15 to 24 runs at 25 per cent and is even higher in my electorate of Oxley. Statistics, by cooking the books, say that Australia's unemployment is at 8.6 per cent, or just under one million people. If we disregard that one hour's work a week classifies a person as employed, then the figure is really between 1.5 million and

1.9 million unemployed. This is a crisis that recent governments have ignored because of a lack of will. We are regarded as a Third World country with First World living conditions. We have one of the highest interest rates in the world, and we owe more money per capita than any other country. All we need is a nail hole in the bottom of the boat and we're sunk.

In real dollar terms, our standard of living has dropped over the past 10 years. In the 1960s, our wages increase ran at three per cent and unemployment at two per cent. Today, not only is there no wage increase, we have gone backwards and unemployment is officially 8.6 per cent. The real figure must be close to 12 or 13 per cent ...

We have lost all our big Australian industries and icons, including Qantas when it sold 25 per cent of its shares and a controlling interest to British Airways. Now this government wants to sell Telstra, a company that made a $1.2 billion profit last year and will make a $2 billion profit this year. But, first, they want to sack 54,000 employees to show better profits and share prices. Anyone with business sense knows that you do not sell off your assets especially when they are making money. I may be only 'a fish and chip shop lady', but some of these economists need to get their heads out of the textbooks and get a job in the real world. I would not even let one of them handle my grocery shopping.

Immigration and multiculturalism are issues that this government is trying to address, but for far too long ordinary Australians have been kept out of any debate by the major parties. I and most Australians want our immigration policy radically reviewed and that of multiculturalism abolished. I believe we are in danger of being swamped by Asians. Between 1984 and 1995, 40 per cent of all migrants coming into this country were of Asian origin. They have their own culture and religion, form ghettos and do not assimilate. Of course, I will be called racist but, if I can invite whom I want into my home, then I should have the right to have a say in who comes into my country. A truly multicultural country can never be strong or united. The world is full of failed and tragic examples, ranging from Ireland to Bosnia to Africa and, closer to home, Papua New Guinea. America and Great Britain are currently paying the price.

Arthur Calwell was a great Australian and Labor leader, and it is a pity that there are not men of his stature sitting on the opposition benches today. Arthur Calwell said: 'Japan, India, Burma, Ceylon and every new African nation are fiercely anti-white and anti one another. Do we want or need any of these people here? I am one red-blooded Australian who says no and who speaks for 90% of Australians.'

I have no hesitation in echoing the words of Arthur Calwell.

There is light at the end of the tunnel and there are solutions. If this government wants to be fair dinkum, then it must stop kowtowing to financial markets, international organisations, world bankers, investment companies and big business people.

Abolishing the policy of multiculturalism will save billions of dollars and allow those from ethnic backgrounds to join mainstream Australia, paving the way to a strong, united country. Immigration must be halted in the short-term so that our dole queues are not added to by, in many cases, unskilled migrants not fluent in the English language. This would be one positive step to rescue many young and older Australians from a predicament which has become a national disgrace and crisis. I must stress at this stage that I do not consider those people from ethnic backgrounds currently living in Australia anything but first-class citizens, provided of course that they give this country their full, undivided loyalty.

Abridged.
Source: *Commonwealth Parliamentary Debates*, vol. 208, 10 September, 1996, pp. 3860–63.

Peter Doherty

Science and Australian Discovery, 1998

Peter C. Doherty (1940–) was awarded the Nobel Prize for Physiology and Medicine in 1996 for research discoveries on 'the nature of the cellular immune defence'. Educated at the University of Queensland, and the University of Edinburgh, Doherty conducted his Nobel work while at the John Curtin School of Medical Research in Canberra. He now works both in the United States and at the University of Melbourne. Doherty is a leading advocate of science education and the funding of biomedical research in Australia. He is a popular—and accessible—commentator on scientific matters, giving public lectures and speaking to the media. On 27 August 1997, Doherty delivered a public lecture on behalf of the Sydney Institute at the Regent Hotel, Sydney. In reflecting on Australia's scientific heritage, and the sheer excitement of 'discovery', he outlined the importance of scientific research for the future prosperity and freedom of the nation.

When I came to write the Larry Adler lecture I realized that I had spent a lot of time in Australia over the past two years campaigning for increased research funding. Unfortunately, any lobbying effort can sometimes come across as carping and negative. After a few false starts, I realised that what I wanted to do here is give a positive sense of how this nation has been formed by, and contributed to, scientific culture. Both contemporary Australia and modern science have their roots in the 18th century, and have evolved over the past 200 years. It also seemed to me that people have any real idea of what science is, though we are all aware of the impact of technology on society. Weaving these threads together in such a brief format may well be beyond the scope of my limited skills, but the Australian ethos requires that we should be prepared to 'have a go, mate!'.

What I want to convey to you more than any other single point is the excitement of science, the excitement of discovery. The excitement of finding something that no human being has ever seen before, of opening a door that we did not even know existed. This is what real science is about. Without discovery we are at best innovative technologists, and even that capacity is slowly lost in the absence of intellectual drive and curiosity. I will try to persuade you that science and discovery are central to the Australian experience. The need to deal rationally and effectively with an unfamiliar reality has given a sharp and critical edge to the national character.

Think of the excitement that must have built slowly during 1770 in naval Lieutenant James Cook and his crew as they realised that they were surveying hundreds of miles of virgin coastline, seeing strange animals, different plants and new people. The voyage of the *Endeavour* resulted primarily from a commission by the Royal Society of London to observe the transit of Venus from the southern skies. The *Endeavour* arrived in Tahiti in 1769, the measurements were made and the converted coal carrier then ploughed westwards, carrying her crew and a supercargo of 10 scientists. That is what scientists are supposed to do, sail into the unknown, though most of us no longer do so at the risk of our lives!

Australia thus has the peculiar distinction of being the only nation state established as a direct consequence of a scientific expedition, Cook's first voyage, and the lobbying efforts of a senior scientist, [Joseph] Banks.

Cook, Banks and [Daniel] Solander were Australia's first scientists. Hold on, you say, what about the people who were here for 60,000 years or more before the time that any European sighted the place? They must have done experiments to discover, for example, which plants were edible and what pigments could be used to create the magnificent legacy of the cave and rock paintings that we all can see in Kakadu. The Aborigines recognized six seasons and lived in harmony with their environment though some of their practices, like burning to drive large animals towards hunters, forever changed the ecology of Australia. What we would be arguing about is not their achievements but the definition of the term 'science'. The reason that it is inappropriate to describe the indigenous people of Australia as scientists is that they did not record their actions. Their tradition is the stuff of tribal lore and established practice, not science. First and foremost, science must be written. This point is made very strongly by the eminent philosopher of science Karl Popper, who died last year.

Science can be a game, and many of the best scientists feel that they are uniquely privileged because society rewards them for playing. However, the science game has very firm rules and we get paid because we also achieve something of social value. The first and foremost rule is that we must make careful observations and do controlled experiments. The second rule that most, but not all, scientists accept is Popper's sanction that we should make every effort to falsify our hypothesis. The really big ideas, like Charles Darwin's theory of natural selection, have stood the test of time because they are just not readily falsified. Falsification means that we must try to detect the flaw in our reasoning, the worm in the apple. Biting into the worm can be a nasty surprise, but the worm hole can sometimes lead somewhere new and intriguing.

Most good scientists think this way, and delight in demolishing rigid intellectual edifices. In the broad sense, science can be deeply subversive and very unlike, for example, the world of precedent that comes naturally to many of the lawyers who dominate most political systems. Curiosity driven science thrives in open societies and will always, in the end, be perceived as dangerous by authoritarian religious, academic and political systems. Such regimes lead inevitably to repression, brutality and to intellectual and economic poverty. It takes a substantial level of sophistication for politicians to understand that they must support the creative process. Interestingly, most members of the US Congress seem to have embraced this message, at least for the sciences. Maybe this reflects that American politicians have generally been exposed to four years of undergraduate life that includes a good measure of science. The key to the American university system is a belief in liberal education. Future scientists must also study literature and a foreign language!

The great experiment of nature that is there for all to see in Australia's biological heritage also influenced the momentous 19th century debate that changed forever the way that we understand ourselves and our world. The survey ship *HMS Beagle*, carrying the unpaid naturalist Charles Darwin, made port in both Sydney and Hobart after mapping and exploring islands off the coast of South America. Darwin was able to observe for himself the different characteristics of the plants and animals that had been preserved and had evolved in this physically isolated continent. What he saw in the Sydney hinterland helped him to formulate the arguments that were published in his classic work of 1859, *On the Origin of Species*. Darwin's arguments resonated with Thomas Huxley, who had visited as assistant surgeon aboard *HMS Rattlesnake*, which was given the job of charting passages to the north of Australia. Huxley married an Australian woman, Henrietta Heathorn, and made his initial scientific reputation for a study of Australian jelly fish. He wanted to stay here, but his application for a Chair in Natural Sciences at the University of Sydney was turned down. Perhaps this was just as well, for it was Huxley as a lecturer at London University who defended natural selection successfully against the then powerful established church, personified in the unfortunate and pompous Bishop Wilberforce.

It was London University with its size, diversity and substantial focus on the natural sciences that was to form the model for the foundation of our oldest universities in Sydney, Melbourne and Adelaide. Oxford and Cambridge were at that stage strong in religion and poetry, and probably provided the motivation for the neo-gothic and the ivy, but they were not to modernize until the late 19th century / early 20th century. The isolation of the Australian of that era forced William Bragg, a professor of mathematics and physics at the new University of Adelaide, to build his own equipment for practical classes, an experience that sparked his interest in doing research. Publication of his incisive work on alpha particles, then beta and gamma rays led rapidly to a substantial reputation and recruitment 'home' to Leeds University after 18 years in the City of Light. Working with his son Lawrence, who provided some of the key theoretical insights, he developed the basics technology for X-ray crystallography. The Braggs were awarded the 1915 Nobel Prize for physics. Lawrence Bragg was only 25 years of age, the youngest Nobel Prize winner to this date and the first to be born in Australia.

Adelaide University also provided our next Nobel Laureate, Howard Florey, who graduated from the medical school and was recognized for his contributions at Oxford University to the production and evaluation of penicillin. During the first 20–30 years of this century it was difficult to develop a substantial profile in basic medical research in this country, tough the situation changed gradually with the work of major scientists like the virologist/immunologist Sir Macfarlane Burnet at the Walter and Eliza Hall Institute (Nobel Prize 1960) and the neurophysiologist Sir Jack Eccles at the Kanematsu Institute in Sydney and later at the Australian National University (Nobel Prize 1963). Eccles spent an interim period in New Zealand after the good doctors that controlled the Kanematsu effectively shut him down because they thought his research on the transmission of impulses in the brain was too esoteric, a good example of the need for external peer review and the damage that can be done by authoritarians. Burnet and Eccles were both graduates of Melbourne University medical school. Research themes that they pioneered accounted for a significant proportion of the first class work done in this country through the 1950s to the 1980s.

Sir Lawrence Bragg was still Director of the prestigious Cavendish laboratory in Cambridge when his very junior colleagues, James Watson and Francis Crick, worked out the nature of DNA in 1953, thereby triggering the molecular biology revolution that we are living through today. Their sense of excitement is brilliantly conveyed in the BBC movie based on Jim Watson's refreshingly open account in his book, 'The Double Helix'. The Watson/Crick model was based on X-ray crystallographic data generated by Rosalind Franklin and Maurice Wilkins obtained, in turn, using the technology pioneered by Braggs. Poor Franklin died young, while Watson, Crick and Wilkins won the 1962 Nobel Prize for Medicine. Watson has, in turn, played a major role in promoting the massive international effort to map the human genome, an enterprise that will impact the lives of us all. Application of a combination of molecular biology and X-ray crystallography has led to the recent development in Australian of a specific inhibitor for the influenza A viruses, pathogens that were also a major focus of Mac Burnet's research fifty years ago. The contemporary influenza team included scientists from the CSIRO and the Australian National University, working with Australian expatriates in the USA.

The preceding tells us a lot about the nature of science. Basic science is open, it is for the long run and it does not recognize national boundaries. Lineages can be traced over decades and even from century to century. Though we may divide science into categories, like medicine, physics and chemistry, discoveries often depend on technologies and insights that come from a spectrum of disciplines. The final message is that Australia is a serious player, and has been for some considerable time. The main problem for Australia now is whether this country can afford to up the ante as other advanced nations increase their relative level of research spending. There is only so much money to go around in any political system. It takes real policy leadership to abandon precedent and reallocate resources.

The wealth of the nations through the 21st century will derive from the enthusiasm, ability and commitment of a perceptive and energetic citizenry. The perils of relying largely on a natural resource-based economy must be obvious to all of us. The coming decades will be driven by rapid advances in science and the speedy application of novel technologies. Thoughtful citizens need to make certain that this society builds for the future and that the Australian political process does not fall down on the job of providing real opportunities for the practitioners of both basic and applied science in our universities, research institutes and industries. Ensuring that every high school student has some understanding of the strength and limitations of science may also be our best hope for maintaining a critical and thoughtful body politic that does not sink into mysticism and the contemporary equivalent of Luddism, fear and reaction. On the other hand, a new dark age controlled by technology would be at least as bad as any other form of repression. Liberal education, open discussion and creativity are what drives a culture of innovation and real economic achievement. There can be no better way of guaranteeing the maintenance of freedom and prosperity in this country.

Abridged.
Source: Peter Doherty, 'A Scientist Looks at the Australian Experience', *The Sydney Papers*, Spring, 1998, vol. 10, no. 4, pp. 101–12.

William Deane

The Swiss Canyoning Tragedy, 1999

William Patrick Deane (1931–) joined the High Court of Australia in 1982, after a distinguished career as a barrister and judge in lower courts. He was appointed Governor-General in 1996 by Labor prime minister Paul Keating, but within months the political wind changed when the conservative John Howard was elected prime minister. Bill Deane soon established a reputation as a thoughtful and articulate man, who used—or as critics would claim, politicised—his position to speak out for people who were suffering, disadvantaged or the victims of intolerance. On 31 July 1999, fourteen Australians were among a group of young people killed by a flash flood when they were abseiling in a canyon near Interlaken in Switzerland. Deane picked sprigs of wattle from his garden at his official residence Yarralumla, and flew to Switzerland for the service of commemoration. Around the country, there was a feeling that his speech—and his gesture of tossing the wattle into the river where the tragedy occurred—was a dignified and moving tribute on behalf of the nation to the victims of the accident.

We are gathered in great sadness to mourn the deaths of the 21 young people who were killed in the canyoning accident near here, last week. They came from five nations—Switzerland, the United Kingdom, South Africa, New Zealand and Australia. Their loss is a profound tragedy for their families and friends who are in the thoughts and the prayers of all of us at this service today. We pray with them for their loved ones who have died. And we also pray that, in the words of our Lord (Matthew Ch.5, v.4), they will truly be comforted.

Fourteen of the victims of the tragedy came from Australia. Collectively, their deaths represent probably the greatest single peacetime loss of young Australians outside our own country. That loss affects not only their families and friends, dreadful though that is. It also deeply affects our nation as a whole and all of its people.

I have, as Governor-General of Australia, with Senator John Herron of our Government, come here on behalf of Australia and of all Australians, to mourn them, to be with and to sympathise with their family members and friends who are here, and to demonstrate how important they were to their homeland. For us, the tragedy is somehow made worse by the fact that they died so far away from the homes, the families, the friends and the land they loved so well.

Australia and Switzerland are on opposite sides of the globe. Yet, in this age of modern telecommunications, one effect of the disaster has been to bring our two countries closer together. On every night since the accident, Switzerland has been in every Australian home that has been tuned into the television news, as well as on the radio, in all our newspapers and other media outlets. Conversely, the fact that two-thirds of those who died came from Australia has given rise to an increased awareness here in Switzerland of my country and its people.

Switzerland has, of course, itself experienced the shock and sorrow of overseas tragedy in the past. Perhaps that has heightened the sympathy and understanding which it has shown in recent days. I have already had the privilege of meeting with you, Madam President, and with Vice-President Ogi and exchanging condolences. I would, on this solemn occasion, like to express to the Swiss authorities and to the people of

Switzerland, particularly the people of the Wilderswil and Interlaken regions, our abiding gratitude for all the help and assistance they have provided in the aftermath of the tragedy. In particular, I pay tribute to the bravery of all those who worked in the rescue efforts. We thank them for their skill and dedication. I also particularly mention the competence, the compassion and the kindness of all who have helped to look after the survivors and the relatives who have come here.

The young people—certainly the young Australians—who have been killed all shared the spirit of adventure, the joy of living, the exuberance and the delight of youth. That spirit inspired their lives, and lit the lives of all who knew them, until the end. We remember that and so many other wonderful things about them as we mourn them and grieve for young lives cut so tragically short. And all of us feel and share in their collective loss. For these 21 young men and women were part—a shining part—of our humanity. As John Donne wrote, 'No man is an island'. Anyone's 'death diminishes' us all because we are all 'involved in mankind'.

Yesterday, my wife and I, together with family members and friends of the Australian victims, visited the canyon where the accident occurred. There, in memory of each of the 14 young people who came from our homeland, we cast into the Saxetenbach 14 sprigs of wattle, our national floral emblem, which we had brought with us from Government House in Canberra. Somehow, we felt that was bringing a little of Australia to them.

It was also, in a symbolic way, helping to bring them home to our country. That is not to suggest that their spirit and their memory will not linger forever, here in Switzerland, at the place where they died. Rather, it is to suggest that a little part of Switzerland has become, and will always be, to some extent, part of Australia. As it will also be part of the other countries outside Switzerland—New Zealand, South Africa and the United Kingdom—from whence they came.

It is still winter at home. But the golden wattles are coming into bloom. Just as these young men and women were in the flower of their youth. And when we are back in Australia we will remember how the flowers and the perfume and the pollen of their and our homeland were carried down the river where they died to Lake Brienz in this beautiful country on the far side of the world.

May they all rest with God.

Reproduced in full.
Source: Address by Sir William Deane, Governor-General of the Commonwealth of Australia, on the occasion of an ecumenical service for the victims of the canyoning tragedy at Interlaken, Switzerland, Thursday, 5 August 1999. The website of the Governor General of Australia, www.gg.gov.au

David Malouf

Australia's Heritage, 2000

David (George Joseph) Malouf (1934–) is a Brisbane-born award-winning writer of poetry, fiction and prose. He is best known for his highly acclaimed and widely read novels, many of which deal with the moments and mythologies of Australian history, including *The Great World* (1990), *Remembering Babylon* (1993) and *Conversations at Curlow Creek* (1996). Malouf's literary vision often explores the ways in which the past, however obscure or personal, is contained in the present. In this National Trust Heritage Lecture, presented to a public audience in Sydney in 2000–the year that city hosted the Olympic Games–Malouf reflected on the notion of 'heritage'. The concept of 'heritage' was popularized in the 1970s to assert the value—even the sanctity—of buildings and places that somehow put people in touch with their history and culture. Malouf celebrated contemporary projects in which the past was acknowledged—the site of the Olympic Stadium at Sydney's Homebush Bay was one example. And he mourned the loss of memory in places decimated by vandalism or neglect. In the following part of the speech, Malouf reflected on the way white Australians were learning from the Aborigines.

A few years back, when the notion of a sacred site first came into general awareness, non-indigenous Australians were puzzled, and sometimes downright suspicious, when some sites that were claimed as sacred turned out to be places, as far as they could see, that had no distinguishing features, offered nothing, even to the sympathetic eye, that was in any way remarkable, let alone touched with the necessary glow of the sacred.

It seems to me that what we now understand of how a site is constructed by Aboriginal people, how it is read, how all the levels of it are preserved, has helped us understand how places might come to exist vividly in our own consciousness; how heritage might work to deepen our lives and anchor us more firmly—I mean through feelings rather than rights of law—in the places that we are attached to.

Of course it is easy to say that in forty thousand years a place might well become dense in this way. All we have behind us is a couple of centuries. But forty thousand years are just forty thousand years, time itself means nothing. What makes the difference is the remembering, the keeping alive in the memory, of lives lived, stories told; the not allowing the sort of erasures to occur that obliterate lived life and reduce to silence and emptiness a place once noisy with the energy of human activity. A great deal might accrue to a place in a hundred years, even in twenty. What we need to do is learn how better to mark and remember.

But remember what? Preserve what? What are the grounds on which we are to decide, among so many choices, what is worth remembering and what we will allow to be erased or demolished, given over to the developers or to oblivion?

Malouf went on to remember the south bank of Brisbane, where he grew up—a place and time he evoked in his autobiographical novel *Johnno* (1975).

It was always an area of play, some of it not quite reputable. The Cremorne Theatre was for fifty years or more Brisbane's chief vaudeville house. Part of the Tivoli circuit, it was where I first saw Roy Rene and Bob Dyer and Will and Nancy Hayes, and my favourite of all comedians Sid Beck. The Trocadero, close by in Melbourne Street, was Brisbane's main palais de dance till Cloudland was built in the early 40s, and its great Big Band centre. There was also the Blue Moon Skating Rink, and a dozen old-fashioned verandahed pubs, the liveliest of which after the war was Manhattan Gardens. Later, when the whole area was levelled for the Brisbane Expo, a good many of the pubs were preserved and incorporated into the site and have survived into the new one.

The present precinct makes a real attempt to establish a continuity with the previous life of the place. A maritime museum recalls the wharves to the west of the bridge. Some of the Expo site and its pavilions have been transformed into pleasure gardens and greenhouses. Theatres, one of them called the Cremorne, and an opera and concert hall, establish a link with earlier playhouses. The previous mix of high and low culture has been kept, as if high and low were actually—as they are, of course—continuous and can be set side by side so that people can shift, as we all like to do, between them.

This is an extraordinarily rich site both in what it offers visitors in the way of mixed entertainment—a swimming strand, arenas for pop music, a library, art gallery, several museums, a theatre complex, restaurants, pubs, garden walks—and what it tempts us to discover of a continuing history. It is a place where citizens are encouraged to pursue their own interests but also to respect the interests of others. Its diversity encourages us to recognise and value diversity. It is a place where the past, very lightly, lives through into the present and new forms of play remember the old ones. It says a good deal for our growing sophistication in these matters that the designers and planners of the site have left room for history, for traces of a century and a half of previous use to shape the site and to be themselves either preserved in the fabric or in other ways recorded and commemorated. In doing all this it deliberately avoids making judgements about what kind of activity in the past, high or low, deserves to be recalled, deliberately mixes the two, allowing one sort of entertainment to exist, freely, in the same space as another. In this way it is gently educative, a place that in its very form inspires neighbourliness and tolerance, an easy mixing, and in a light way deepens our awareness of the city's past by establishing a clear line of continuity within change. In all of these ways it seems to me to be exemplary.

Malouf concluded:

The remembering of previous lives, the recreation, in all its density and detail of the previous life of places—that, as much as the rescue of endangered monuments, outstanding examples, or what is unique or representative—is the sort of work we must do here. That, in our wider understanding of the term, the one that will have relevance in our sort of place, must be the deeper work of heritage; to pay as much attention to what is ordinary and specific as to what is exemplary and rare. We may need other terms than the ones used in Britain, say, or by that vigilant and sometimes over-zealous organisation the Belle Arti in Italy, for evaluating what needs to be saved from the process of erasure. The danger here may be less from change and development than from the natural process of forgetting. We may need a more open and active form of marking, of remembering and documenting: the small and specific, all that dense and sometimes muddled and muddling activity that makes up the lived life of a place: the affections, conflicts, forms of industry and forms of play that fill a space with life, even with the life of ghosts. But ghosts whose presence, and hunger for living we can still feel, and whose energy, if we can sense it, will make rich and crowded a place that might otherwise seem empty, whose felt presence will fill with voices a place where otherwise our own might seem brittle and without resonance, and our own lives detached, with no grounding in time or the great continuity of human warmth and presence that is the one true gift of heritage anywhere.

Abridged.
Source: David Malouf, National Trust of Australia (NSW) Heritage Lecture 2000, National Trust of Australia (NSW), Sydney, www.nsw.nationaltrust.org.au/ Reproduced with permission of the author.

Noel Pearson
'The Light on the Hill' Revisited, 2000

Noel Pearson (1965–) was born on an impoverished Aboriginal mission in Cape York, Queensland. He won a scholarship to St Peter's College in Brisbane, and graduated in Law and History from the University of Sydney, a member of a rising generation of Indigenous Australian leaders who have had access to greater educational opportunities than their parents did. He became prominent in the fight for land rights and later as a critic of the impact of the social welfare system on Aboriginal communities. Pearson is an orator of great power and with a capacity to reach wide audiences. In his 2000 Ben Chifley Memorial Lecture, 'The Light on the Hill', presented at the Bathurst Panthers Leagues Club on 12 August 2000, Pearson acknowledges that the welfare state has 'civilized' white Australia. But he says that, for his mob, it has created a culture of dependency. This has given rise to alcoholism, drug addiction and violence, which are destroying traditional communities. What Aborigines need, Pearson argues, is fewer handouts, fewer excuses, and a greater spirit of entrepreneurialism and responsibility. This appeal to self-reliance has won Pearson considerable conservative approval. But Pearson also holds quite left-wing views: he argues that modern materialism functions to keep the salary-earning class compliant, unreflective and uncritical. How else, he asks, can we explain the failure of white Australia to comprehend and react to the historical legacies and contemporary forces that are destroying Aboriginal societies?

The predicament of my mob is that not only do we face the same uncertainty as all lower class Australians, but we haven't even benefited from the existence of the Welfare State. The Welfare State has meant security and an opportunity for development for many of your mob. It has been enabling. The problem of my people in Cape York Peninsula is that we have only experienced the income support that is payable to the permanently unemployed and marginalised. I call this 'passive welfare' to distinguish it from the welfare proper, that is, when the working taxpayers collectively finance systems aimed at the their own and their families' security and development. The immersion of a whole region like Aboriginal Cape York Peninsula into dependence on passive welfare is different from the mainstream experience of welfare. What is the exception among white fellas—almost complete dependence on cash handouts from the government—is the rule for us. Rather than the income support safety net being a temporary solution for our people (as it was for the whitefellas who were moving between jobs when unemployment support was first devised) this safety net became a permanent destination for our people once we joined the passive welfare rolls.

The irony of our newly won citizenship in 1967 was that after we became citizens with equal rights and the theoretical right to equal pay, we lost the meagre foothold that we had in the real economy and we became almost comprehensively dependent upon passive welfare for our livelihood. So in one sense we gained citizenship and in another sense we lost it at the same time. Because we find thirty years later that life in the safety net for three decades and two generations has produced a social disaster.

And we should not be surprised that this catastrophe was the consequence of our enrolment at the dependent bottom end of the Australian welfare state. You put any group of people in a condition of overwhelming reliance upon passive welfare support—that is support without reciprocation—and within three decades you will get the same social results that my people in Cape York Peninsula currently endure. Our social problems do not emanate from an innate incapacity on the part of our people. Our social problems are not endemic, they have not always been with us. We are not a hopeless or imbecile people.

Resilience and the strength of our values and relationships were not just features of our pre-colonial classical society (which we understandably hearken back to)—our ancestors actually managed to retain these values and relationships despite all of the hardships and assaults of our colonial history. Indeed it is a testament to the achievements of our grandparents that these values and relationships secured our survival as a people and indeed our grandparents had struggled heroically to keep us alive as a people, and to rebuild and defend our families in the teeth of a sustained and vicious maltreatment by white Australian society.

So when I say that the indigenous experience of the Australian welfare state has been disastrous I do not thereby mean that the Australian welfare state is a bad thing. It is just that my people have experienced a marginal aspect of that welfare state: income provisioning for people dispossessed from the real economy.

Aboriginal Policy is weighed down by mixed-up confusion. Many of the conventional ideas and policies in Aboriginal Affairs—ideas and policies which are considered to be 'progressive'—in fact are destructive. In thinking about the range of problems we face and talking with my people about what we might be able to do to move forward, the conviction grows in me that the so-called progressive thinking is compounding our predicament. In fact when you really analyse the nostrums of progressive policy, you find that the pursuit of these policies has never helped us to resolve our problems—indeed they have only made our situation worse.

Take for example the problem of indigenous imprisonment. Like a broken record over the past couple of decades we have been told that 2% of the population comprise more than 30% of the prison population. The situation with juvenile institutions across the country is worse. Of course these are incredible statistics. The progressive response to these ridiculous levels of interaction with the criminal justice system has been to provide legal aid to indigenous peoples charged with offences. The hope is to provide access to proper legal defence and to perhaps reduce unnecessary imprisonment. To this day however, Aboriginal victims of crime—particularly women—have no support: so whilst the needs of offenders are addressed, the situation of victims and the families remains vulnerable. Furthermore, it is apparent that this progressive response—providing legal aid support services—has not worked to reduce our rate of imprisonment. In fact Aboriginal legal aid is part of the criminal justice industry which processes Aboriginal people routinely through its systems. It is like a sausage machine and human lives are processed through it with no real belief that the outrageous statistics will ever be overcome.

The truth is that, at least in the communities that I know in Cape York Peninsula, the real need is for the restoration of social order and the enforcement of law. That is what is needed. You ask the grandmothers and the wives. What happens in communities when the only thing that happens when crimes are committed is the offenders are defended as victims? Is it any wonder that there will soon develop a sense that people should not take responsibility for their actions and social order must take second place to an apparent right to dissolution. Why is all of our progressive thinking ignoring these basic social requirements when it comes to black people? Is it any wonder the statistics have never improved? Would the number of people in prison decrease if we restored social order in our communities in Cape York Peninsula? What societies prosper in the absence of social order?

Take another example of progressive thinking compounding misery. The predominant analysis of the huge problem of indigenous alcoholism is the symptom theory. The symptom theory holds that substance abuse is only a symptom of underlying social and psychological problems. But addiction is a condition in its own right, not a symptom. It must therefore be addressed as a problem in itself. Of course miserable circumstances make people in a community susceptible to begin using addictive substances, but once an epidemic of substance abuse is established in a community it becomes independent of the original causes of the outbreak and the epidemic of substance abuse becomes in itself the main reason for why addiction and abuse becomes more and more widespread. The symptom theory absolves people from their personal responsibility to confront and deal with addiction. Worse, it leaves communities to think that nothing can be done to confront substance abuse because its purported causes: dispossession, racism, trauma and poverty, are beyond reach of social resolution in the present.

But again, the solution to substance abuse lies in restriction and the treatment of addiction as a problem in itself. When I talk to people from Cape York Peninsula about what is to be done about our ridiculous levels of grog consumption (and the violence, stress, poor diet, heart disease, diabetes and mental disturbance that results) no one actually believes that the progressive prescriptions about 'harm reduction' and 'normalising drinking' will ever work.

A rule of thumb in relation to most of the programs and policies that pose as progressive thinking in indigenous affairs, is that if we did the opposite we would have a chance of making progress. This is because the subservience of our intellectual culture to the cause of class prejudice and stratification is so profound and universal. What we believe is forward progress is in fact standing still or actually moving backwards.

Much of my thinking will seem to many to indicate that I have merely become conservative. But I propose the reform of welfare, not its abolition. Like all of you here tonight I am also concerned for the long-term preservation of our commitment to welfare as a nation. If we do not confront the need for the reform of welfare and to seize its definition, then we will lose it in the longer term.

This country needs to develop a new consensus around our commitment to welfare. This consensus needs to be built on the principles of personal and family empowerment and investment and the utilisation of resources to achieve lasting change. In other words our motivation to reform welfare must be based on the principle that dependency and passivity are a scourge and must be avoided at all costs. Dependency and passivity kills people and is the surest road to social decline. Australians do not have an inalienable right to dependency, they have an inalienable right to a fair place in the real economy.

Abridged.
Speech: Noel Pearson. 'The Light on the Hill', Ben Chifley Memorial Lecture, delivered at Bathurst Panthers Leagues Club, 12 August 2000, www.capeyorkpartnerships.com/noelpearson/

———◆———

Tim Flannery
Sons and Daughters of Australian Soil, 2002

Timothy Fridtjof Flannery (1956–) is Director of the South Australian Museum, and is best known as the author of an award-winning history of Australian ecology, *The Future Eaters* (1994). Delivered at a time when population policy was a lively topic of debate, Flannery's 2002 Australia Day Address—given in Sydney—attracted controversy when the anti-immigration lobby used it to support their claims. This largely right-wing group was building on the momentum created by in the 1980s by Geoffrey Blainey's attack on Asian immigration, and in the 1990s by the support for Queensland independent Pauline Hanson and the Howard Government's unsympathetic policy towards refugees. Flannery himself took a moderate position on immigration—as the speech makes clear. It emphasises concepts which have become central to environmentalists. These include the idea that the climate determines how we live (an idea pioneered in Australia by the geographer Griffith Taylor in 1920s), and the insistence that Australian survival depends on adopting methods of farming, business and everyday living which are ecologically sustainable.

For Australians, the land has a special significance. That's because our country is so very different from any other. The Europeans that migrated to North America found a land not so very different from that which they had left, but those that came to Australia sometimes felt that they had arrived on another planet. Our European heritage left us appallingly equipped to survive, long-term, in this country. For a start it left many colonial Australians unable to see the subtle beauty and biological richness of the land, and what they could not understand they strove to destroy as alien and useless. For most of the last two centuries we have believed that we could remake the continent in the image of Europe—turn the rivers inland and force the truculent soils to yield. We even knowingly introduced pests—from starlings to foxes and rabbits—in our efforts to transform this vast Austral realm into a second England. Much of this terrible history reads as a rush towards 'development', which was then—and often still is—just a soft word for the destruction of Australia's resource base.

That arrogant colonial vision left a fearful legacy, for it actually made people feel virtuous while they dealt the land the most terrible blows. Already one of every 10 of Australia's unique mammals is extinct, and almost everywhere—even in our national parks—biodiversity is declining. Australia's soils are still being mined—salination will destroy the majority of Western Australia's wheat belt in our lifetime if nothing is done—while our rivers are in great peril and sustainable fisheries everywhere have collapsed. It is the bitter harvest of all of this that we reaping so abundantly today. The last fifty years have been marked by a retreat of Australians from the countryside towards the cities, partly because the resource base they relied on had been destroyed by earlier generations.

Yet despite all this, there are signs that things are changing for the better. Today, as the Australian environment subtly teaches those who listen to it, Australians are undergoing a radical reassessment of their relationship with the land, particularly when it comes to the basics like food, water and fire. After 200 years of destruction, revolutionary changes are taking place in the countryside as farmers and graziers strive to make primary production sustainable in Australia's unique conditions. Leading the way are people like the Bell family, who run cattle sustainably in the ultra-dry Lake Eyre Basin, or the many involved in the development of sustainable aquaculture. These people are my national heroes. They mean far more to me than Ned Kelly or the Man from Snowy River, because they're not just acting out European dramas on an Australian stage; instead they are throwing out old, inappropriate European-based practices and inventing their own, distinctively Australian futures in a bid to create sustainability in this land.

I have no doubt that today many farmers are very far ahead of the majority of Australians in most aspects of environmental thinking. What's needed now is a change in consumption patterns by city-dwellers to provide a market for sustainably produced products. As the 'buy Australian' campaigns and the advertising of many products as 'environmentally friendly' shows, there is a great desire among Australians to preserve their environment. Yet still much damage continues, in part because urban-dwellers need to become well informed about what environmental sustainability really means, and how they need to alter their patterns of consumption in order to achieve it.

The way we use water is also slowly changing in response to Australia's unique environment. Because of our continent's great rainfall variability, Sydneysiders need eight to ten times the water storage of the inhabitants of New York or London—that's around three Olympic-sized swimming pools' worth per person. The economic and environmental costs of this are stupendous, and they are forcing us into new ways of thinking about water, as plans for more dams are shelved and water is re-priced. This shift has the power to alter our urban landscapes—for the beloved Europe-green lawn, English rose and London plane tree are all thirsty drinkers.

Nothing seems to rouse the passions of some Australians so much as disparaging roses, lawns, plane trees and the like. Yet I really do think that they are a blot on the landscape. I used to joke that I'd shout beer all round at my local pub the day someone brought me a plane tree leaf that an insect had actually taken a bite out of. The fact is, that as far as Australian wildlife goes, plane trees are so useless that they might as well be made of concrete. Australia is home to 25,000 species of plants, as opposed to Europe's 6,000 or 7,000. Surely amongst that lot we can find suitable species that will provide shade, and food for butterflies and native birds as well. To be honest, there is another reason I dislike many introduced plants. If gardens are a kind of window on the mind, I see in our public spaces a passion for the European environment that indicates that we are still, at heart, uncomfortable in our own land. If we can see no beauty in Australian natives, but instead need to be cosseted in pockets of European greenery, can we really count ourselves as having a truly sustainable, future adapted to Australian conditions?

While we cannot know what some future nation that has adapted to Australian conditions would be like, we will know when the transformation is complete, because then we will be living sustainably, and for the first time our children and their children will have a long-term future here. Such a culture will almost certainly still contain elements brought from elsewhere, but in all of its truly important aspects—those that touch on our interaction with our land—it will have been transformed by the dictates of the unique Australian environment ... Australia still has so much to offer, and so much can be done to ensure that the country provides the very best of life to its people. This, however, cannot happen while we imagine that we are people from another place. A series of changes needs to occur both in government policy and in the hearts and minds of all Australians, before we can think of ourselves as having a secure future here.

As I indicated earlier, the single most important change is the need for all Australians to achieve true environmental sustainability. An extraordinary start has already been made in the area of primary production, but much more remains to be done. The development of a population policy is central to this process. Such a policy, I believe, would result in better environmental and humanitarian outcomes. Australia's population policy should be based on recognition of the environmental constraints of our land, our economic needs, and the social desires of its people. The only way that such a policy can be achieved is for the nation to engage in a broad, vigorous and truthful debate, accompanied by a Government inquiry that is charged with setting an optimum population target. Once the target has been decided we should redesign our immigration program in light of it, with an eye to more flexibility and greater fairness. Before the inquiry has done its work it is not possible to say how large the immigration intake could be, but almost any imaginable scenario would allow for a reasonable level of immigration.

The development of such a policy would take much of the hysteria and negativity out of the immigration debate, for an immigration program firmly embedded in a population policy will transparently serve the national interest, and thus have the support of most people. It would also result in a better humanitarian outcome for those involved, because the intake could be framed over a longer period than the current annual intake, allowing us to accommodate those caught up in international emergencies.

In the very first Australia Day address, [the novelist] Thomas Kenneally discussed how central the concept of a 'fair go' is to Australians, and how precious our accepting, relatively equal society is. We are fortunate that our experience in this land has encouraged the development of such a society. Yet now globalisation has brought other social models, developed in other, more competitive places, and these are beginning to influence us. How can we engage with the world while keeping our society equitable, generous and cohesive? We each of us can think of some things that will help, but I'm afraid that all signs are that we are losing this vital battle to preserve the defining values of Australian society. Perhaps if we all gave some thought to the issue each Australia Day, we would stand a better chance.

The darkest horror lurking in the imaginings of 19th century Australians was that this wild continent might somehow claim them, or their children, to itself. As the currency lads and lasses grew up, tall, barefooted and at ease in the bush, those dark fears increased, for their parents saw degeneration in every deviation from standard European cultural practice. The continent, they feared, somehow forced all of its inhabitants—from its seemingly half-formed marsupials and egg-laying platypus to its naked, black savages—into a base and primitive form. Right up to the time of Sir Robert Menzies and beyond, their worst fear was to return 'home' only to find that they had become degraded 'colonials'.

Today that dark, lurking fear—that this wide brown land might somehow claim us as its own—is, I suspect, our best hope for a sustainable, long-term future. For we have realised that we have no other home but this one, and that we cannot remake it to suit ourselves. Instead we must somehow come to terms with its conditions, to surrender our 'otherness' and thereby find our own distinctively Australian way in a very different, large and sometimes threatening world.

Abridged.
Source: Tim Flannery, Australia Day Address, 'The day, the land, the people', for the Australia Day Council of New South Wales, Sydney, 26 January 2002, www.australiaday.com.au/australia_day_address.html

Julian Burnside

Refugees: Australia's Moral Failure, 2002

Julian Burnside QC (1949–) is a gracious Melbourne barrister who has campaigned for the rights of asylum seekers. By 2001 the Liberal Howard Government had become alarmed by the numbers of people sailing for Australia in search of asylum. In August that year, the Norwegian container ship *Tampa* rescued 438 such people, mainly Afghans, from a derelict fishing boat sinking in the Indian Ocean. The Howard Government refused to allow the *Tampa* to land the people in Australian territory. Instead, many were imprisoned on the island nation of Nauru, which had negotiated a $1.2 million fee for acting as Australia's jailer. Howard's so-called Pacific Solution was popular with many voters, especially following the terrorist attacks in the United States of America on 11 September 2001. At a fund-raising dinner to aid asylum seekers held in Sydney on 11 June 2002, Burnside's stirring speech began by denouncing the Pacific Solution as 'state-sponsored piracy and kidnap'—a system that had reduced Nauru to a state of 'prostitution'. Then he addressed what this Australian system of 'indefinite mandatory detention' (especially in remote centres at Port Hedland, Woomera and Curtin) meant to the asylum seekers themselves.

It is a startling thing to think that, at the beginning of the twenty first century, we have a system which, by legislative mandate, involves people being locked up without any judicial order in what, on any view, is a prison. They have no recourse to the courts to review the question of whether they should be locked up. They are being locked up for a period that no one can predict: it is indefinite. When they go inside, unlike any common criminal, they cannot count the days before they will be free again.

Furthermore, unlike the orthodox prison system, eighty per cent of asylum seekers are kept in facilities that are so remote from any centre of civilisation that, if they had the prospect of anyone coming to visit them, that prospect is lost. Broadly, this is because to visit Woomera, or Port Hedland or Curtin involves literally days away from your ordinary activities. I said that the conditions in the detention centres are worse than would be tolerated in the prison system. It is a little surprising at first because they are for the most part run by the same people who run the prisons, but the fact is that conditions in the centres are appalling.

I was interested recently to come across some observations of Professor Richard Harding who is Western Australia's Inspector of Custodial Services, and a person familiar with the prison system. He visited Curtin in June last year, and he said this:

'The so called education program was largely a charade—bear in mind how many children are kept in these places, bear in mind that the DIMIA [Department of Immigration, Multicultural and Indigenous Affairs] contract with A.C.M. [Australian Correctional Management] requires that education be provided appropriately to all people who need it.'

'That insight,' he said, 'really set the tone for the whole place. The huts in which the people lived were grossly overcrowded, many of the toilets were broken, some of the washing machines were also broken, and the so-called shop was abominably stocked and rather inaccessible. The system for sending mail breached all standards of privacy and confidentiality, and above all, medical and dental facilities were inadequate. In summary, the conditions that exist in the Curtin centre are almost intolerable. Such evidence as exists indicates things are little better at the other centres, yet these things are also largely invisible except when riots occur.'

It is easy to be thought to be exaggerating when you talk about conditions in detention centres. This is a letter written to us in February [2002] by one of the Afghani people from the *Tampa*. He is currently in Nauru. He mentions the water supply:

'I mean that we do not have enough water for going to toilet, taking bath, or washing our clothes. For example in one corner of the camp there is one water store, in which most often only one water tank is delivered everyday and here are almost 500 people consuming water from the same tank.

'An interesting story is that when Mr Phillip Ruddock came here our water stores were all full. And we tried to utilise it to our best. Most of us bath when it rains heavily, however our water is spent very soonly and then for the rest of the day and night our toilets are awfully smelling and there are thousands of flies and mosquitoes in each toilet'.

This is a person who has been writing to us now for a few months and who has been extraordinarily restrained in his comments about conditions, but whose personality is gradually deteriorating. Things are intolerable there. And those words are matched perfectly by reports that you get from Curtin, and from Port Hedland, and from Woomera, and to a lesser extent from Villawood [in Sydney] and Maribyrnong [in Melbourne].

It is not easy to choose the things that illustrate most economically the problems of conditions inside of the detention centres. They have to queue for soap. It is common to be subjected to the minor, but irritating torment of queuing for half an hour for soap at Woomera and to reach the head of the queue, only to be told to come back half an hour later, for no reason at all. All you want is a piece of soap but they send you away and have you come back later. The people who are in charge of these places develop very rapidly, it seems, the mentality of guard versus prisoner.

I had an interesting experience myself a few weeks ago in Maribyrnong [Detention Centre in Melbourne]. Kate Durham and I went out to Maribyrnong to visit a couple of people there, and it happened that I was due to represent one of them in court the next day.

When you go to Maribyrnong you get a piece of paper at the security entrance. You write your name, you write your address and phone number, the names for the people you want to visit and your connection to them, and then you show them a passport to prove who you are. Kate wrote the same two names as I did because we wanted to see the same people. She wrote that her connection to them was 'friend'. I wrote that my connection was 'barrister'. This was in the 7–9pm social visiting spot. Kate sailed through the double security lock, but I was told that there was a problem with my form.

I said: 'What's the problem, Chris?'

'You're a barrister, aren't you?'

'That is true.'

'Lawyers' visiting hours are between 9 and 5.'

He clearly took pleasure in saying that.

I said: 'Oh, but surely it can't mean that lawyers aren't allowed to visit in the evening visiting slot?'

And he said: 'Well that's the rule: visiting hours for lawyers are between 9 and 5.'

'Surely the rule can't mean that.'

'Well it's the rule.'

'Can we have a look at the rule and check whether that's what it really means?'

'No.'

'Why not?'

'It's confidential.'

It was all very good humoured. He was obviously enjoying himself. Having stepped through the looking glass, I was quite amused by it all. I had another run at him, but it was to no avail.

I said to him: 'Look, I'm a friend to one and a lawyer for the other, what am I meant to do?'

'You'd need two forms.'

'Perfect, can I have a second form please?'

'No.'

'Why not?'

'You're not allowed two forms.'

Now I'm sure there is a luxurious pleasure in jerking around a lawyer who doesn't represent your own view of the world. But if he was prepared to do this to me, with the reasonable expectation that I might make a fuss about it (although I didn't), what is he likely to do to people who are hopelessly dependent on the ACM guards? If detainees get on the wrong side of any of the ACM people they can expect to be treated badly. The potential for torment is appalling, and torment of course there is.

In the desert camps, when a woman has her period, she must fill in a form requesting sanitary pads. She must then queue to see the nurse and hand in the form. She will be given a packet of 10. If she needs more, she will have to fill in another form and explain why she needs more.

A few weeks ago when a friend of mine was in Woomera. She saw a couple of teenage Afghani girls wandering around wearing nappies. When she asked why that was, she was told that the stress had made them incontinent. These are teenagers, reduced to wearing nappies. Perhaps that is the best reflection of what the conditions are like: just look and see what it does to the people.

Kate and I have organized a campaign of writing letters to detainees. We have received hundreds of replies. They give a powerful and terrible picture of what we are doing to people.

This is from a letter written by someone at Maribyrnong. He wrote:

'I don't must be sensitive and I don't must cry, because the cry make happy the enemy. But finally I will write for you the difference between detention centre and zoo: in the zoo the humans care for animals but in detention centres the animals care for humans.'

From Port Hedland: 'My hope really is finished for make life in your country. I don't know what happen to me in Iran, but I know death in my land is better than dying in this detention or in this hell. I lost everything. I lost my life, my love, my family and now I think maybe if I stay here I lose my mind.'

From Woomera: 'I really appreciate your paying attention to Woomera detention and especially to me. You had just watched, read about what happened, but the fact is bigger than that. The ACM officers had changed to monsters, they couldn't see anything except how to hit the people. They entered the compound with the blue uniform so that you couldn't see any part of their bodies. They were like an army. They used the sticks and hurt the people without any mercy or thinking about women or children.

'After that they used the teargas against the families and they were avoided to film when they used that gas. Then at 2 o'clock in the morning they came to the buildings and pushed all the people to go to the mess for head account without paying attention to the pregnant women or the children when the weather was too cold. They hit and hurt anyone refused to move. Then they had chosen 40 men and they had put handcuffs on their hands and ordered them to sit on the ground till morning like criminals. They did not allow us to smoke or go to toilets or even pray. I wondered at that moment if this is where we had chosen and asking for protection. What the difference between this and our countries, and why we escaped from there.'

Contrary to the government's alarmist rhetoric, there are very few refugees in Australia at present. They are people who have been accepted into the country after months or years of detention. By comparison with other countries, the total number of refugees we have accepted is pathetically small. Asia has 8 million; Africa has 5.5 million; Europe has 5.6 million; North America has 1 million. Australian and New Zealand together have only 76,000.

We have about 2,500 in detention presently seeking to be accepted as refugees. They have committed no crime, unless it be a crime to flee persecution in a pitiable attempt to give their children and themselves a chance of a life worth living. They are not 'illegals': they are human beings. There are about 4000 informal arrivals each year. It is a tiny number. These people do not pose a risk to our national sovereignty.

They are being held in gaol. It is hypocrisy to call it detention. Their human rights are ignored, their conditions are kept secret. When ultimately they are released from detention each refugee is indebted to the Commonwealth for the cost of their accommodation, at the rate of about $120 per day. Thus, a person who suffers the misery of Woomera for 24 months is asked to pay more than $100,000 for the privilege. So, even at the end of the torment, we add insult to injury.

We have a choice: imprison asylum seekers, in defiance of international law, or let them into the community after initial screening, whilst their claims for asylum are assessed. There should be a maximum of 3 weeks initial detention, to be extended only if a judge rules that the circumstances justify continued detention. Community release after initial health and security checks could be secured by bail conditions. Bail works very well in the criminal justice system. There is no evidence that it would not work for innocent people seeking asylum. Since more than 80% of asylum seekers turn out to have good claims to our help, it seems barbarous to lock them up for years while we consider whether they are entitled to our protection.

Extract.
Source: http://members.westnet.com.au/jackhsmit/burnside2.htm; This speech was previously published on Julian Burnside's website and an extract in the *Sydney Morning Herald*, 12 June 2002, p. 15.

Pru Goward

How to be a Working Mother, 2002

Prudence Jane Goward (1952–) was a political commentator and journalist before being appointed by Prime Minister John Howard to head the Office of the Status of Women in 1997. She became Federal Sex Discrimination Commissioner in July 2001. Most Australian girls were now entering adulthood with the expectation that they would have a career or at least a paid job. It was a legal requirement that women receive the same pay as men doing the same work, and employers who discriminated against women were penalized. At the same time, the pressures of globalization, the weakening of trade unions and increased materialism had made the culture of work far more demanding. The forty-hour week, for so long the pride of Australia, now increasingly seemed a luxury, especially for the middle class. As the working day lengthened, the new complaint from parents was that they could no longer 'juggle work and family'—and, as a consequence, family life was suffering. Pru Goward focussed on this dilemma. One of her solutions was a well-publicized campaign to introduce paid maternity leave. In this 2002 speech which outlined her proposed policy, she began by identifying two facts as central.

Fact one—Women are in the workforce to stay. They have a right to work. We taught them to read and write, we encouraged them to become educated, learn a trade and pursue careers. And so here we are—an integral, necessary and crucial part of Australia's workforce today.

Fact two—If work isn't working for women, then it isn't working for the family. Why? Because in addition to being integral members of the workforce, women are the bearers of, and remain the primary carers for, children. So if it isn't working for her then it isn't working for her family, her partner, her children and babies.

What do these facts mean? They mean that if we want to reverse the increasing trend of women having fewer children later in life, if at all; if we want to ensure ourselves a future generation; if we want to address community concerns about the health and welfare of children we need to do so by creating an environment that supports women as they work and have children. Because, like men, women have a right to do both. And most women want to do both, although some want to do only one or the other.

Let's look for a moment at the very simple model proposed by researcher Catherine Hakim. Hakim argues that you can divide women into three groups based on their attitude towards work and family: 15–20 per cent are overwhelmingly home centred; 15–20 per cent are overwhelmingly career centred; and the remaining 60–70 per cent fall in the middle. This middle group wants both a career and a family and seeks different ways to balance both work and family responsibilities.

What is relevant here is not whether we agree with the categorisation of women into these three particular groups—the consultations bear out that there are a number of ways women's life patterns can be grouped—but the acknowledgement that women are not a homogenous group. Some work, some have children and some do both—either together, or serially, moving in and out of the workforce, or start with part time work and seek full time work when the kids are older. There are varying attachments and focuses. The majority of women work and have children.

Because of this, we need to formulate an entire suite of measures that will make it possible for work and family to be combined in a way that works for women. Because if it works for women it will work for families. This is clearly the direction in which we need to move.

Our declining fertility rate tells us that women are having fewer babies every year. Our fertility rate currently sits at 1.7. A year ago it was 1.75. A decade ago it was 1.9. A fertility rate falling below the necessary replacement rate of 2.1 is the symptom of something going very wrong.

But it is only a symptom. It is not the disease itself. We are wary of this turning into a 'womb gazing' debate when it is about women's lives. It is about making work work for women—and therefore work for families. It is about reducing the motherhood disadvantage gap that contributes to our declining birth rate.

And there are ideas around as to how we can do this—ideas that are plausible, sound and well thought out. They have emerged in the debates on this issue over a decade. They are represented in a number of the submissions we have received in response to our interim report, which now number over 200; we have heard them in the nationwide consultations we have been holding on paid maternity leave with employer groups, unions, and women's and community groups across Australia; and are now appealing in the media—in editorials, expert opinions, op-ed pieces, letters to the editor and on talk-back radio.

At this point, I would like to say that part of HREOC's [Human Rights and Equal Opportunity Commission's] job is to raise issues and bring them to the public domain for debate. It has been fantastic to see the debate on paid maternity leave unfold. There have been so many views expressed. We as a nation have embraced this opportunity to have a healthy debate on these issues of national significance.

The broader national debate we are having today on work and family began with a debate on paid maternity leave—because paid maternity leave is a crucial component in any suite of measures that successfully addresses the work and family balance for women. Of course it is only a component, but as so many of you told us during the consultations, you don't get much balance, if you can't first recover from the birth of your child.

Just ask the rest of the world. Along with the US we remain the only OECD country without a national scheme of paid maternity leave in place. But why is paid maternity leave so important if we are going to make work and family work for women? What can a national scheme of paid maternity leave do for us? Let's briefly consider some of the possible objectives of a national scheme of paid maternity leave.

First, the health and welfare objectives. Paid maternity leave will allow women the time needed directly after the birth of a child to recover physically from childbirth and establish a feeding routine without being forced to return to work due to financial necessity. Many we consulted related accounts of returning to work as early as two weeks after the birth of a child, driven by the need to earn.

Second, while nobody suggests that paid maternity leave alone can rectify our declining fertility rate and ensure the existence of a next generation, women keep telling us that it can respond to some of the financial concerns which discourage women from having babies or having only one, or delaying having babies.

Why? Because paid maternity leave means that following the birth of a child there will not be a total loss of income by one, or increasingly the only, income earner in a family. It may mean that a couple may be able to have that second child or bring forward their decision to have a child by even one year. What's one year, you may ask? Considering that physiologically fertility begins declining at 27 and the average age of mothers in Australia is 29.8, this one year may be the difference between having one child [and having] a second child—or [having] none at all.

Third, labour force participation and economic growth. Employers need to hire best people for the job—and they need to keep them there.

This is only going to increase as the market requires increasing numbers of skilled people, and there are fewer from whom to choose. At the moment, without paid maternity leave being provided across the board, women often find themselves in a different line of work following the birth of a child. They may go from leading their field in IT to a part time job in a less skilled area, but one that offers more 'family friendly' hours.

The hospitality and retail industries, for example, characterised by casual hours and shift work, are dominated by students and mothers. This labour force shift—of our highly skilled experts into low skilled casual work—means that Australia loses its most competitive workforce. Something we cannot afford to do in the increasingly competitive global market. It is certainly the British experience, where paid maternity leave, even government-funded, encourages many women to return to work, at least part time. The Swedes also introduced paid maternity leave to encourage workplace retention after the baby is a year old.

Fourth, workplace disadvantage. Women lose their immediate income, often jeopardize career prospects and reduce their lifetime earnings when they leave the workforce to have children. While it cannot make up for the loss of income over a lifetime, paid maternity leave provides some form of income replacement.

With no universal scheme of paid maternity leave in place, the majority of women lose their entire income for at least the first few months following the birth of a child. Paid maternity leave will mean that women can afford to be out of the workforce while recovering from childbirth, establishing a breastfeeding routine and bonding with a child without the stress that they cannot financially afford to be doing this.

Paid maternity leave also provides the cultural recognition within the workforce and within society that women work, and are the bearers of and primary carers, for children. It recognises the non-work related responsibilities of half of the people in the workforce. Recognising paid maternity leave as an industrial entitlement does not mean that employers have to pay but it means employees are entitled to receive it.

These are some of the objectives that a paid maternity leave scheme may meet. Are they important? Well the public thinks so, that's why they're writing in droves. The level of public debate surrounding the issue makes me think that most people agree that we have a problem.

What has caused disagreement in this debate, however, is how should these objectives be met. There are those who think that paid maternity leave is an inappropriate way of solving these problems. They make this clear in their submissions or at our consultations.

First, there seems to be a concern that paid maternity leave reduces a woman's choices because it forces her to return to work. This concern is based on a false assumption that women will only be entitled to paid maternity leave on the condition that they return to work. There is no reason why a government funded scheme would operate in this way.

Returning to work also depends on the cost of child care, government benefits and, for many women, the availability of part-time work. All vital ingredients in the work–life debate.

Second, there seems to be concern that if paid maternity leave is provided as an entitlement for women only in paid work it discriminates against women who are not in paid work. Tied into this is the further concern that as women in paid work generally have more money than women not in paid work, paid maternity leave is not needed.

This concern requires us to acknowledge current welfare arrangements. Government funded maternity benefits currently available to women are primarily targeted at women not in paid work. That is to be applauded and many families are grateful for it. Rather than discriminating against women not in paid employment, paid maternity leave actually addresses a special need faced by working mothers, although at relatively modest costs.

Most women earn between $10,000 and $15,000 a year—a low income. If paid maternity leave was to be available to all women in paid work it would benefit these women. Certainly, some of these women might receive other assistance, but that depends on their partner's income. Those who receive paid maternity leave under current enterprise level provisions are generally those most skilled, better educated women who have the bargaining power to secure this leave.

A government funded scheme for working women will ensure the benefit is equitably spread across the workforce, especially to low income earning women—the opposite of middle-class welfare.

The most major concern in this debate is that employers alone will be forced to pay for maternity leave. A national scheme of paid maternity leave forcing employers to make payments to employees was included in the options paper because it is just this—an option. As stated in the options paper it is not however a desirable option. From my foreword on, that is made clear. I do not support employer funding for a number of reasons.

First, it is the third-world scheme. No OECD countries (including the US which does not provide any form of paid maternity leave) make it mandatory for employers alone to directly fund maternity leave.

Second, the Federal Government and the Democrats have not shown support for an employer funded scheme, while the Opposition talks of a partnership approach, although they have not entirely clarified their position.

Third, employers and employer group spokespersons tell us that women would suffer under this scheme. Employers, especially small business, would stop employing women of child-bearing age to avoid this cost. Indeed some say they have already begun doing so. Any scheme which would result in women being further discriminated against in the workforce is obviously unacceptable and must be avoided.

Amidst the disagreements, myths and concerns, we have an important, significant and shaping public debate taking place. In the end it will bring in the much needed structural changes that will allow women to work and have children. It is heartening to see discussion of the need for policies and programmes that assist women in Australian families to manage their work and family responsibilities—no matter what their circumstances and choices. Paid maternity leave is a necessary part of supporting family choices.

The Government has now embarked on the much more challenging and complicated task of addressing work and family comprehensively. Many of our submissions[,] and many who came to our consultations, stressed how important all the pieces of the jigsaw were—not just paid maternity leave. One thing is clear, we are all talking about the same thing —the happiness and harmony of our future nation!

Abridged.
Source: Pru Goward, Federal Sex Discrimination Commissioner, 'Paid maternity leave: Working for women', made at the 14th Women, Management, Employment Relations Conference, Sheraton on the Park, Sydney, 26 July 2002; Human Rights and Equal Opportunity website: www.humanrights.gov.au

John Howard
The Bali Bombing, 2002

John Winston Howard (1939–) became Liberal Prime Minister in 1996, after a long parliamentary career during which he held senior positions in both government and Opposition. Howard has identified himself with the tradition of his revered Liberal predecessor Robert Menzies, but there are many differences. Menzies spoke for the 'forgotten people'—the middle class—from on high. Howard simply represented himself as a conservative middle-class man, and this is reflected in his use of language and his choice of communicating with his constituency of 'battlers' through regular talk-back radio sessions. Where Menzies was drawn to grand rhetoric, the hallmark of Howard's speech was its ordinariness. Indeed, Howard was careful to avoid the kind of talk that might be perceived in any way to be 'elitist', a charge that he directed against left-leaning intellectuals and those associated with the arts or cultural pluralism. At the same time, Howard laid claim to the Australian legend that promotes an heroic account of British–Australian history, where a fondness for sport and a sense of 'mateship' are portrayed as inherently 'Australian' values. On 12 October 2002, a nightclub on the island of Bali in Indonesia, a very popular holiday destination for young Australians, was bombed and many Australians were killed and wounded. The next day, Howard laid aside his customary emotional restraint when he spoke publicly about the tragedy. His speech to a press conference in Sydney is devoid of a single memorable phrase, yet it touched many Australians—with its emotion, its patriotism and the sense that any regular Australian man would have said and felt the same things.

Ladies and Gentlemen, I know that I speak for all Australians, and I mean all Australians, in expressing a sense of outrage, sadness and horror at what has occurred overnight in Bali. This wicked and cowardly attack, clearly on the evidence available to us an act of terrorism, has no justification and would be widely condemned not only by Australians but by people all around the world.

My very first thoughts, however are with those Australians at present waiting and hoping to hear from loved ones who are so far unaccounted for. Our thoughts will be especially with them at this time of unbelievable stress and anxiety and we can only hope that the prayers and the hopes of as many of them as possible are answered over the coming hours.

The latest information I have is that there are confirmed dead of 169 with hundreds injured. I don't at this stage, nor do the Australian authorities in Jakarta or Denpasar, know the exact extent of Australian casualties. There are many Australians unaccounted for, many. We must therefore prepare ourselves as a nation for the possibility of a significant number of Australian deaths amongst the fatalities.

The indiscriminate, brutal and despicable way in which lives have been taken away on this occasion by an act of barbarity will, I know, deeply shock all Australians and accepting that shock I also express my condolences to the people of Indonesia who I know have lost many of their citizens in this outrage. Many of the Australians in this nightclub were doing something that thousands of young Australians do at this time of the year, they mark the end of a season of sport with some fun in another place. They were carrying on that innocent and understandably exuberant pastime [which] is something that we take for granted as Australians. Sadly and tragically terrorism has touched that innocent pursuit and touched it in a brutal and very barbaric and quite unforgivable fashion.

The view that this is a terrorist attack is not my view alone. It is the current assessment of both the Australian and the Indonesian authorities. A short while ago I spoke on the telephone to President Megawati of Indonesia. I expressed to her my condolences at the loss of life suffered by Indonesia and she conveyed her sorrow and shock at the likely loss of Australian lives.

Both of us agreed that this incident was a brutal reminder that the world has in fact to face the challenge of terrorism. The warnings of the last year or more that terrorism can touch anybody, anywhere, at any time have been borne out by this terrible event. And I can only say again that the war against terrorism must go on with unrelenting vigour and with an unconditional commitment because terrorism strikes indiscriminantly [sic], it strikes at civilian targets, it strikes without justification, it strikes without pity and it strikes in a way that I know outrages the civilised world.

I want to immediately record my thanks to the Department of Foreign Affairs and Trade, the Department of Defence and the Australian Defence

Force for the speedy way in which the crisis response went into action this morning.

A C130 [aeroplane] with a medical team of seven doctors, including experienced surgeons and nurses is already on its way and will be in Denpasar at 8.00 pm this evening. It has a capacity to bring back to Australia litter patients of some thirty and if necessary further aircraft will be despatched to bring people back to Australia for treatment and I've indicated to the Department of Foreign Affairs that all of the resources of the Air Force will be available for this task. We are determined to provide the best possible medical assistance for Australians, we'll bring them back, we'll offer medical treatment for others who have been injured in this outrage. I offer that medical assistance and I also offered police assistance to President Megawati when I spoke to her this afternoon. But we had, in admittably [*sic*] very sad circumstances, a very constructive and positive discussion about the need to work together as closely as possible in the wake of this attack.

I also want to thank Qantas [Airways] for immediately despatching additional aircraft. I've spoken to the Chairman of Qantas, Margaret Jackson, a short time ago and she indicated that the airline stood ready to provide all additional assistance that may be needed.

I want to issue a very strong piece of advice to Australians not to travel to Bali until further notice. In the wake of what has occurred it is clearly not a safe place and I would counsel people in unmistakably clear terms not to take the risk. We have issued a number of travel warnings about Bali and about Indonesia generally in recent times but in the wake of this terrible event they certainly have an added point.

I've spoken to the Leader of the Opposition and offered him briefings from the Department of Foreign Affairs and other agencies as appropriate and [acquainted] him with any additional knowledge I have of the circumstances. We both agree this is a huge national tragedy for Australia and for Australians and it is something that the Australian community should as far as possible confront and respond to together.

I have also had two conversations with the Premier of Western Australia Dr Gallop. Quite a number of the people in Bali and apparently the nightclub were from Western Australia and because of the proximity of Perth and the rest of Western Australia there is always a significant number of Australians from that part of our country in Bali.

Ladies and Gentlemen this is a very sad day, it's tragic that young Australians seeking nothing other than innocent enjoyment, Australians generally—not only young—many of all ages over the years have made Bali a holiday destination, they've enjoyed it and have enjoyed the hospitality of the Balinese people. I can only say again that my thoughts are very much with the families waiting to hear. It is an awful time for them and I hope that they may find some comfort from the fact that their fellow Australians are thinking of them, are feeling for them and are trying in our different ways to share their anxiety and to express the hope that their prayers will as far as possible and in as many cases as possible be answered.

This event is a terrible reminder that terrorism can touch anybody anywhere and at any time; and any country or any people, any leader or any nation that imagines that in some way they have secured immunity from terrorism because of this or that attitude or this or that part or position in the world, or this or that accident of geography is deluding themselves. That is not the case, and this event sadly has brought that home.

Reproduced in full.

Source: Transcript of the Prime Minister the Hon. John Howard MP. Press Conference in response to terror attack in Bali; Sydney, 13 October 2002; www.pm.gov.au/news/interviews/2002/interviews1895.htm

LIST OF ILLUSTRATIONS

Page 12:
The Ministerial Bench: a Sketch in the Assembly.
Wood engraving from the *Australasian Sketcher*. 11 April 1883. State Library of Victoria, Accession No. A/S11/04/83/53.

Page 111:
John Curtin speaking at a rally at the City Hall in Sydney on 12 October 1942.
Sydney Morning Herald Leon/Fairfaxphotos.

Page 221:
Germaine Greer at an Australian Press Conference, 24 January 1972.
Newpix/News Ltd, (replica of the original print).

NOTES

Introduction

1. We borrow this term from, and are indebted to the ideas of, Ken Inglis, expressed in his lecture 'Men and Women of Australia: Speech Making as History'.
2. Goodman, 'Public Meetings and Public Speaking', p. 112.
3. Evatt, p. 185.
4. *Daily Telegraph* (Sydney), 28 October 1898; quoted in H. V. Evatt, p. 112.
5. Nadel, p. 126.
6. Nadel, pp. 119–20.
7. Evatt, p. 184. For accounts of the debates see the *Sydney Morning Herald*, 3 April and 4 April 1906.
8. The Reid–Holman debate was printed as a pamphlet. Evatt, p. 189.
9. Evatt, p. 189.
10. The comparison was made at the time. McLeod, p. 110, also makes the comparison.
11. The seven debates were held over two months in the lead-up to the 1858 Senate elections in Illinois. Douglas won the election, but Lincoln was pushed to nation prominence. Quote from Robert W. Johannsen, *The Lincoln–Douglas Debates of 1858*, Oxford University Press, New York, 1965, p. 3.
12. *The Dawn*, July 1889, p. 8.
13. Pearl Gibbs, interview with Heather Goodall, recorded 6–9 March 1981; quoted in Heather Goodall, 'Pearl Gibbs: Some Memories', in *Aboriginal History*, 1983, vol. 7, no. 1, p. 21.
14. Victorian Police Force, Box 807/1158, Public Record Office of Victoria.
15. This system became dormant in 1982.
16. Menzies, 'Politics as an Art', in *Speech is of Time*, p. 187. This essay first appeared in the *New York Times Magazine*, 28 November, 1948.
17. See Watson, *Death Sentence*.
18. Curran, pp. 4–8.

Part One

19. Tench republished as, Tim Flannery (ed.), *Watkin Tench, 1788*, Text, Melbourne, 1996, p. 46. For the sermon by Rev. Johnson and another account of Phillip's speech see C. M. H. Clark, *A History of Australia*, vol. 1, Melbourne University Press, Melbourne, 1962, p. 878.
20. *South Australian Gazette & Colonial Register*, 17 November 1838, p. 4.
21. *Sydney Morning Herald*, 20 October 1838, p. 3.
22. *South Australian Gazette & Colonial Register*, 17 November 1838, p. 4.
23. For historical context see Reynolds, pp. 70–73.
24. pp. 26–38.
25. Martin, pp. 51–6, incorrectly gives the year for this speech as 1854; *Sydney Morning Herald*, p. 5.
26. J. B. Humffray was the leader of the Ballarat Reform League.
27. Carboni, p. 65.
28. Parkes, pp. 3–6. This version is reprinted in Clark, *Select Documents 1851–1900*, pp. 467–70.
29. Chisholm, pp. 58–64.
30. Reid, pp. 12–13.

Part Two

31. *Age*, 31 July 1914, p. 1.
32. Aveling, pp. 60–63.
33. See also Janette Bomford, *That Dangerous and Persuasive Woman: Vida Goldstein*, Melbourne University Press, Melbourne, 1953, p. 183, for an account of the meeting.
34. *Age*, 29 January 1917, p. 7.
35. *The Advocate*, 10 November 1917, pp. 13–15.
36. See Carole Ferrier, *Jean Devanny: Romantic Revolutionary*, Melbourne University Press, Melbourne, 1999, p. 153, for an account of the speech on Spain.
37. This file of transcripts of radical meetings held in 1936 is over a thousand pages long.

38   In Jones, pp. 43–62.
39   It is likely that this was not whale-meat, but Wellfleisch: boiled pork-belly. See Kersten, p. 118.
40   Reproduced in Wolfgang Benz and Barbara Distel, *Dachau and the Nazi Terror 1933–1945*, vol. 2, published for the Comité International de Dachau, Brussels, Dachau, 2002, pp. 118–23.
41   Jack Horner, 'Pearl Gibbs: A Biographical Tribute', in *Aboriginal History*, vol. 7, no. 1, 1983, p. 10.
42   Gilbert, pp. 13–17.
43   *Herald* (Melbourne), 27 December 1941, p. 10.
44   There are four similar drafts of this speech in Franklin's papers; this is the final draft.
45   Published in Stargardt (ed.), pp. 58–65.
46   *Age*, 4 September 1939, p. 11.
47   Starr, pp. 150–51.
48   Reprinted in Menzies, *The Forgotten People*, pp. 1–10.

Part Three

49   Rivett, pp. 158–9.
50   *Smith*, pp. 217–99.
51   The lines come from the love poem 'There is a Lady Sweet and Kind', usually attributed to Thomas Ford (1580?–1648):

There is a lady sweet and kind,
Was never a face so pleased my mind;
I did but see her passing by,
And yet I'll love her till I die.

52   Reprinted in Holmes and Lake, pp. 140–43.
53   Cairns's words at the Melbourne Moratorium are quoted by Simon Crean, *Commonwealth Parliamentary Debates*, 14 October 2003, p. 21292.
54   Tom Uren, Obituary for Cairns, 2003: (http://evatt.labor.net.au/publications/papers/115.html A tribute to Jim Cairns).
55   Whitlam, *The Whitlam Government*, p. 471.
56   Whitlam, *The Truth of the Matter*, pp. 118–19.
57   Immigration Reference Paper, Department of Immigration, Australian Government Publishing Service, Canberra, 1973, pp. 1–15.
58   Clark, *Speaking Out of Turn*, pp. 30–33.
59   Blainey, p. 25.
60   Maniaty (ed.), pp. 113–17.
61   Earlier that year the newly elected Lange Government had decided not to grant US nuclear warships access to New Zealand ports.
62   For an account of the speech and White's views see David Marr, *Patrick White: A Life*, Random House, Sydney, 1991, pp. 547, 612, 618.
63   SRG Australia Pty Ltd, *A Benchmark on the Changing Attitudes of Australian Women*. Prepared for J. Walter Thompson (Aust.) Pty Ltd, April 1984.
64   Donald Horne, 'Arts Funding and Public Culture', Cultural Policy Studies: Occasional Paper No. 1, Institute for Cultural Policy Studies, Griffith University, 1988.
65   Davis et al. (eds), pp. 330–35.
66   Garth Nettheim, 'Mabo', in Blacksheild et al. (eds), p. 448.
67   Butt et al., pp. 24–5; 35–6; 38–40; 47–8; 58–9; 60–61.
68   For a full text of the Mabo and Others v State of Queensland, see Australian Law Reports, vol. 107; for full text and commentary see Richard H. Bartlett, *The Mabo Decision*, Butterworths, Sydney, 1993.

SELECT BIBLIOGRAPHY

This bibliography lists collections of Australian speeches, as well as some biographical and historical references, that are particularly relevant to the themes pursued in this collection. A considerable biographical literature (not listed here) is available on a number of prominent figures whose speeches feature in this collection.

Australian Dictionary of Biography, Melbourne University Press, Melbourne, various volumes.

Arnold, John, and Deidre Morris (eds), *The Monash Biographical Dictionary of 20th Century Australia*, Reed Reference Publishing, Port Melbourne, 1994.

Aveling, Marian, (ed.), *Westralian Voices: Documents in Western Australian History*, University of Western Australia Press, Nedlands, 1979.

Black, David, *In His Own Words—John Curtin's Speeches and Writings*, Curtin University of Technology, Perth, 1995.

Blackshield, A. R., Michael Coper and George Williams (eds), *The Oxford Companion to the High Court*, Oxford University Press, Melbourne, 2001.

Blainey, Geoffrey, *All for Australia*, Methuen Haynes, North Ryde, 1984.

Brett, Judith, *Robert Menzies' Forgotten People*, Pan Macmillan, Sydney, 1992.

——, *Australian Liberals and the Moral Middle Class—From Alfred Deakin to John Howard*, Cambridge University Press, Melbourne, 2003.

Butt, Peter, Robert Eagleson and Patricia Lane, *Mabo, Wik & Native Title*, The Federation Press, Sydney, 4th edn, 2001.

Caine, Barbara, et al., *Australian Feminism: A Companion*, Oxford University Press, Melbourne, 1998.

Carboni, Rafaello, *The Eureka Stockade*, first published 1855; Melbourne University Press, Melbourne, 1993.

Chisholm, J. K., *Speeches and Reminiscences*, Angus & Robertson, Sydney, 1907.

Clark, Manning, *Select Documents in Australian History 1788–1950*, Angus & Robertson, Sydney, 1950.

——, *Select Documents in Australian History 1851–1900*, Angus & Robertson, Sydney, 1955.

——, *Occasional Writings and Speeches*, Fontana/Collins, Sydney, 1980.

——, *Speaking Out of Turn: lectures and speeches 1940–1991*, Melbourne University Press, Melbourne, 1997.

Curran, James, *The Power of Speech*, Melbourne University Press, Melbourne, 2004.

Davis, Jack, Stephen Muecke, Mudrooroo Narogin and Adam Shoemaker (eds), *Paperbark: a Collection of Black Australian Writings*, University of Queensland Press, St Lucia, Queensland, 1990.

Davison, G., J. Hirst and S. Macintyre (eds), *The Oxford Companion to Australian History*, Oxford University Press, Melbourne, 2001.

Day, David, *John Curtin—A Life*, Harper Collins, Sydney, 1999.

Evatt, H. V., *Australian Labour Leader: the story of W A Holman and the labour movement*, Angus & Robertson, Sydney, 1940.

Flannery, Tim (ed.), *Watkin Tench, 1788*, Text, Melbourne, 1996.

Fraser, Malcolm, *Common Ground: Issues that should bind and not divide us*, Penguin, Camberwell, 2003.

Freudenberg, Graham, *A Certain Grandeur—Gough Whitlam in Politics*, Penguin, Melbourne, 1977.

Gilbert, Kevin, *Because a White Man'll Never Do It*, Angus & Robertson, Sydney, 1973.

Grattan, Michelle (ed.), *Australian Prime Ministers*, New Holland Press, Sydney, 2000.

Goodman, David, 'Desiring Land in Gold-Rush Victoria', in *Dangerous Liaisons: Essays in Honour of Greg Dening*, History Department, University of Melbourne, 1994.

Goodman, David, 'Public Meetings and Public Speaking in Colonial Australia', *Australian Cultural History*, no. 16, 1997/8.

Holmes, Katie, and Marilyn Lake (eds), *Freedom Bound II: Documents on Women in Modern Australia*, Allen & Unwin, Sydney, 1995.

Inglis, Ken, 'Parliamentary Speech', *Papers on Parliament*, Department of the Senate, Canberra, 1996.

——, 'Men and Women of Australia: Speech Making as History', Barry Andrews Memorial Lecture, 7 October 1993, University College, The University of New South Wales, Australian Defence Force Academy, Canberra, 1993.

Irving, Helen, *To Constitute a Nation—A Cultural History of Australia's Constitution*, Cambridge University Press, Cambridge, 1999.

Jones, Frederic Wood, *Life and Living*, Kegan Paul, Trench, Trubner & Co., London, 1939.

Keating, P. J., *Paul Keating Prime Minister—Major Speeches of the First Year*, Australian Labor Party, Canberra, 1992.

Kersten, Lee, 'W Macmahon Ball's report on the Sachsenhausen concentration camp', in Wolfgang Benz and Barbara Distel, *Dachau and the Nazi Terror 1933–1945*, vol. 2, published for the Comité International de Dachau, Brussels, Dachau, 2002.

Maniaty, Tony (ed.), *The Power of Speech: 25 Years of the National Press Club*, Bantam, Moorebank, New South Wales, 1989.

Martin, E. A., (ed.), *The Life and Speeches of Daniel Henry Deniehy*, Geo. Robertson, Sydney, 1884.

McKenna, Mark, and Wayne Hudson, *Australian Republicanism: A Reader*, Melbourne University Publishing, Melbourne, 2003.

McLeod, A. L. (ed.), *Australia Speaks: An Anthology of Australian Speeches*, Wentworth Books, Sydney, 1969.

Menzies, Robert G., *Speech is of Time—Selected Speeches and Writings*, Cassell, London, 1958.

——, *The Forgotten People and Other Studies in Democracy*, Angus & Robertson, Sydney, 1943.

——, *To the People of Britain at War from the Prime Minister of Australia*, Longmans, London, 1941.

Mills, Stephen, 'The Making of a Prime Minister's Speeches', in J. Disney and J. Nethercote (eds), *The House on Capital Hill—Parliament, Politics and Power in the National Capital*, ANU Press, Canberra, 1996.

Murray-Smith, Stephen, *The Dictionary of Australian Quotations*, Heinemann, Richmond, 1984.

Nadel, George, *Australia's Colonial Culture: Ideas, Men and Institutions in Mid-Century Eastern Australia*, F. W. Cheshire, Melbourne, 1957.

Parkes, H., *The Federal Government of Australasia. Speeches delivered on various occasions, November 1889–May 1890*, Turner and Henderson, Sydney, 1890.

Reid, George Houstoun, *My Reminiscences*, Cassell and Co., London, 1917.

Reynolds, Henry, *The Law of the Land*, Penguin, Ringwood, 1987.

Rivett, Kenneth (ed.), *Immigration Control or Colour Bar?*, Immigration Reform Group, Melbourne University Press, Melbourne, 1962.

Ryan, Mark, (ed.), *Advancing Australia—The Speeches of Paul Keating, Prime Minister*, Big Picture Publications, Sydney, 1995.

Silvester. E. K., (ed.), *Speeches in the Legislative Council of New South Wales on the Second Reading of the Bill for Framing a New Constitution for the Colony*, Sydney, 1853.

Smith, Bernard, *The Death of the Artist as Hero: Essays in History and Culture*, Oxford University Press, Melbourne, 1988.

Stargardt, A. W., (ed.), *Things Worth Fighting For—Speeches by J B Chifley*, Melbourne University Press, Melbourne, 1952.

Starr, Graeme, *The Liberal Party of Australia: A Documentary History*, Drummond/Heinemann, Richmond, 1980.

Turner, Ian, *The Australian Dream: a Collections of anticipations about Australia from Captain Cook until the Present day*, Sun Books, Melbourne, 1968.

Uhr, John, 'Political Leadership and Rhetoric', in G. Brennan and F. Castles (eds), *Australia Reshaped—200 Years of Institutional Transformation*, Cambridge University Press, Melbourne, 2002, pp. 261–95.

Watson, Don, *Recollections of a Bleeding Heart—A portrait of Paul Keating PM*, Random House, Sydney, 2002.

——, *Death Sentence: The Decay of Public Language*, Knopf, Sydney, 2003.

Whitlam, Gough, *The Truth of the Matter*, Penguin, Ringwood, Australia 1979.

——, *The Whitlam Government 1972–1975*, Penguin, Ringwood, 1985.

INDEX